The Unforget... Army

The Unforgettable Army

Slim's XIVth Army in Burma

•

MICHAEL HICKEY

SPELLMOUNT
Staplehurst

British Library Cataloguing in Publication Data:
A catalogue record for this book is available
from the British Library

Copyright © Michael Hickey 1992, 1998

ISBN 1-86227-050-3

First published in the UK in 1992 by Spellmount Limited

This edition published in the UK in 1998 by
SPELLMOUNT LTD
The Old Rectory
Staplehurst
Kent TN12 0AZ

1 3 5 7 9 8 6 4 2

The right of Michael Hickey to be identified
as the author of this work has been asserted by him
in accordance with the Copyright, Designs
and Patents Act 1988

Printed and bound in Great Britain by
Biddles Limited, Guildford and King's Lynn

dedicated to all
who earned the
Burma Star

THE BURMA STAR was awarded for service in the Burma Campaign between 11 December 1941 and 2 September 1945, both dates inclusive. For the Army, service in any part of Burma qualified, as did service in Bengal and Assam between the same dates and service in China and Malaya between 10 February 1942 and 2 September 1945. For the Navy, six months operational service in the Bay of Bengal, as defined, including the Straits of Malacca, qualified. For shore-based Naval personnel and for RAF ground crew, the requirements were the same as for army personnel. For RAF aircrew, the qualification was one operational sortie.

Contents

Maps (by Graham Payne)

Illustrations

We have an Empire, which extends right around the world, and our service may be, and often is, in many queer and uncivilised countries . . .

> – 'Service in Hot Climates: A Pamphlet for Officers'
> War Office, 1943.

Sons of the sheltered city, unmade, unhandled, unmeet –
Ye pushed them raw to the battle as ye picked them raw from the street

> – Kipling

Their being repeatedly in the field during tropical rain, their daily marching through inundated fields, and their bivouacking unsheltered amidst mud and water, were trials to which no European constitution could be subjected with impunity.

> – Professor H. H. Wilson, FRS: Official History of
> the First Burmese War, 1824–26

Foreword

by The Rt. Hon. Viscount Slim, OBE, DL

L OOK BACK fifty years. It is a long time ago. At the start of the Asia-Pacific War the Japanese moved fast, seeing off our American Allies in the Pacific and occupying almost all of South-East Asia.

The British Empire, with its Indian and Australian comrades, lost Hong Kong, Malaya and Singapore. This was the greatest defeat in the history of our Empire. A disgrace and a humiliation. It left the British in Burma facing a growing threat to India and Ceylon. Further disaster lay ahead. The enemy advance could not be halted. From the borders of China, Thailand and Malaya to the Indian frontier must surely rank as the longest overland retreat in our nation's history. A courageous backward slog – a fighting retreat – but we were beaten. Together with thousands of refugees, the remnants of our battle-weary troops eventually arrived, unwanted and to no great welcome, at the Indian frontier. Those soldiers, mostly British, Indian and Gurkha, were forced to stare at the stark and harsh realities of defeat. Then came the hard soul-searching for everyone involved, from generals to the lowest ranks. No excuses. New ideas, new tactics, new techniques, new training and morale-building were evolved by the officers and men who forged the new Fourteenth Army. Reinforced by many thousands of multi-racial comrades-in-arms, they faced about and magnificently fought their way back into Burma, giving the Japanese Empire its first major defeat on land, heralding the Allied re-conquest of lost territories in Asia – and turning Defeat into Victory.

Never has an army had to fight and win a war against such a tough, tenacious, vicious and courageous foe as the Japanese. The fighting was mainly in tortuous, steep and rugged mountainous jungle terrain, bedevilled by some of the world's longest and widest rivers flowing across the axis of advance. The campaign demanded more than average hand-to-hand fighting.

For a moment forget the human enemy. The picture is not complete without recalling the devastating effects of climate, allied to the then-prevalent killer diseases of malaria, dysentery and scrub typhus. Challenging enough, but add to these the appalling, lengthy and tenuous lines of communication that had to be rapidly built and serviced in order to ensure the survival of the Fourteenth Army with all its Corps, Divisions, Brigades and Companies, fighting on one of the longest land fronts of World War II, and then the overall daunting nature of their task emerges. Burma was, quite justifiably, at the bottom of the national war priorities. The Fourteenth Army had to help itself and it did so with a vengeance. Improvisation became the norm at every level; initiative, self-help, local invention, plus the ability to do without, were practiced everywhere, from the front line to the rear echelons. There was much to overcome and achieve in order to bring victory in Burma.

Michael Hickey, a soldier and a historian in his own right, has been to war and knows what it means. With his sure touch he describes the essential overall picture, while at the same time he deftly targets the significant battles and incidents, bringing the reader close to events as they happened from day to day. His informative book is welcome for the way it highlights the feel and the tensions of battle in jungle and scrub plain, together with the personalities of the people involved

To survive and win in Burma, a sense of humour was mandatory and luckily, from generals to privates and jawans, it was there in abundance. A key factor in high morale, their sense of humour helped not only to cement the unique bond and very special relationship amongst officers and men but also to develop a tremendous spirit of comradeship that cut across, and gathered in, all the races and religions which represented that great Army. The Fourteenth Army was a truly united multi-racial force with soldiers, sailors and airmen from Britain, India, Nepal, Africa, Burma, America, China and many other countries. It gave an exceptional example, much needed in our world today, of how different nations can work, respect, mix, share, suffer, worship, support, communicate and live in friendship, and overcome and conquer together. The British soldier is always first to pay his tribute to that superb old Indian Army, without which it is doubtful if victory could have been achieved.

This unique spirit and bond of fellowship lives on today through the Burma Star Association in its dedication, its work and its caring. The loyalty of its thousands of members throughout the world is to their continuing comradeship and to all who fought in Burma.

SLIM
House of Lords
August, 1992

Introduction

THE YEAR 1992 has already seen the 50th anniversary of the painful retreat from Burma, and 1993 will see that of the 14th Army itself. There have been many books about this unique formation and its remarkable commander, but it is perhaps time to remind people of the great feats performed in that long and remorseless campaign by ordinary men from many nations, who sustained one resounding defeat and several major reverses before decisively beating one of the most formidable opponents ever encountered by British arms. It is not too much to say that 14th Army took on and defeated the Japanese 'First Eleven'. It was the only occasion in World War II when a Japanese field army was beaten, and this was achieved despite the early calamities, an appallingly unhealthy climate, and a multitude of administrative problems aggravated by the different languages, feeding requirements and religions of what was the last great multi-racial army to fight under the British flag. On top of that, the Burma theatre was at the very back of the queue for equipment of every sort, whether landing ships, transport aircraft or munitions. The war in Burma was 'unfashionable', regarded in London and Washington as the wrong campaign, in the wrong place, at the wrong time. This did not alter the fact that here also was the main Japanese land army, and it had to be destroyed because, like Everest, 'it was there'.

It is important to note that the Japanese army in Burma did not just have to be outmanoeuvred and forced to yield. It had to be *destroyed*. Its extreme martial code demanded that soldiers fought to the death. This, and the fact that by Western standards, the Japanese army behaved abominably to those it conquered, ensured that Slim's command actually loathed their enemy. At first they feared him as well, for he appeared to be endowed with near-superhuman qualities which ensured victory in the jungle. It was because of this that the enemy was deliberately de-humanised, to be regarded as 'the world's finest fighting insect', a case for unconditional extermination. As time passed, the fanatical courage of the Japanese infantry earned them the grudging respect of the men of 14th Army. At the time, few paused to consider what actually caused the enemy to fight to the death; the reasons have their origin far back in the history of Japan, and I have devoted some space in this book to an examination of the process which produced this remarkably dangerous army. The fact that it was eventually overcome by ordinary free men of many races makes the achievement all the more impressive.

The survivors of Slim's Army are now grown old but their children and grandchildren deserve a memorial in the form of a book which will, I hope, be read with appreciation and a touch of the awe in which I have always held these men – and women. There should be great pride in having a relation, alive or dead, who served in that campaign and earned the right to wear the Burma Star. They were part of what their great commander, 'Uncle Bill' Slim, saw as one team: Britons, Africans, Indians, Burmese, Gurkhas. The like of it will never be seen again. War may be an evil thing, but it is well to pause and think how men from the far corners of the earth came together to do an unnatural but totally necessary job.

This is not an 'academic' work, nor does it seek to compete with the many exceptional books written by those who actually took part in the Burma War. Foremost among these is Slim's own *Defeat into Victory*, which will be read appreciatively in a hundred years' time. It is the definitive work on the actual experience of high command in war as well as a wonderfully unself-conscious portrait of a great soldier and human being. Other books are listed in the Bibliography at the end of this volume.

My aim has been to celebrate an army in which I did not serve. I have therefore tried to paint on as wide a canvas as possible, to portray it from the early days of disaster to the final rout of the Japanese Burma Area Army. I have tried to show as many different facets of 14th Army as possible, in a manner which I hope will be acceptable to its veterans.

There is a school of military history (all too frequently found in regimental histories) which asserts that nothing ever goes wrong, that the old Blankshires never faltered and that the leaders never failed. Anyone with campaigning experience knows that this is not so. There were many failures in Burma by formations, units and individuals, and I have described some of them here. Space compels me to be selective and it may seem to some readers that certain battalions or their personnel have been unfairly treated. In every case quoted, the units concerned later performed with distinction. Their temporary shortcomings can be ascribed to fatigue, lack of proper equipment, inadequate training, or human failures, notably in the field of leadership. When these faults had been remedied, often by drastic action on the part of senior commanders (and even senior commanders were not immune from failure, as will be seen) the situation was restored. All the same, I must be prepared to face the criticism of those who feel themselves, or their unit, to have been unfairly singled out. As Thomas Hardy wrote:

> *Still rule those minds on earth*
> *At whom sage Milton's wormwood words were hurled,*
> *"Truth like a bastard comes into the world*
> *Never without ill-fame to him who gives her birth."*

One great quality shines out from this campaign, and that is the enormous extent of the admiration, affection and shared sense of humour, the pride of comradeship and sense of 'belonging' which united British, Indian, Gurkha, Burman and African. They were indeed the great team of which Slim their leader speaks so warmly.

●

I am deeply indebted to many people for their patient help during the writing of this book. Colonel The Viscount Slim OBE kindly read the entire script and made many useful comments, all of which I have embodied. He also allowed me unrestricted access to the Slim papers at Churchill College, Cambridge, and to unpublished correspondence between his father and Brigadier Bernard Fergusson (later Lord Ballantrae) in the mid 1950s. His sister, The Hon. Mrs Una Rowcliffe, told me about HMS *Una*, the armed river craft named after her. General Sir Philip Christison Bt, GBE, DSO, MC, allowed me to interview him about his experiences as commander of 15 Corps in the Arakan. Major Pat Rome MC, told me what it was like to fight at Kohima with the Durham Light Infantry. Brigadier Ken Trevor CBE, DSO, who commanded No 1 Commando at Kangaw, read my draft chapter on the operation and gave his own account of that frenzied battle. Brigadier Shelford Bidwell OBE, who as the author of an authoritative work on the subject gave me much information, has a graver responsibility to bear, having done much to prod me into writing military history when he was editor of the RUSI Journal twenty years ago. Major General David Tyacke CB, CBE, former Chindit and a neighbour, saw the draft Chindit chapters as well, and I am most grateful for his insights into the complex character of the remarkable Orde Wingate. A number of libraries and archives have been most helpful: at Cambridge, Mr Corelli Barnett and his staff at the Churchill Archives, which house the Slim and Roberts papers, enabled me to use my limited time to advantage; similarly, at the Imperial War Museum and National Army Museum, where I quarried in their collections of unpublished material. The Prince Consort Library at Aldershot patiently dealt with my wants and guided me amidst their great collection of regimental histories.

Much time was spent in selected regimental and corps museums; at Durham, I was allowed access to the Durham Light Infantry war diaries and unpublished newsletters; the Gurkha Museum at Winchester made me welcome to dig amongst their matchless archives, as did the Museum of the Regiments of Gloucester, where I came across Lt Colonel Bagot's fascinating memoir. At Salisbury I was able to study the war diaries of the

Royal Berkshire and Wiltshire regiments in the Museum of the Duke of Edinburgh's Royal Regiment; at Aldershot once more, I was welcomed by the staff of the Queen Alexandra's Royal Army Nursing Corps Museum who allowed me access to unpublished memoirs of nursing sisters in India and Burma. The Museum of the Royal Corps of Transport were able to furnish details of the Supply and Transport of 14th Army; and the Museum of Army Flying's archives yielded much information on Air OP flying in Burma. Finally, I would like to say how grateful I am for the endless courtesy and patience of my publisher, Ian Morley-Clarke of Spellmount, and my editor, John Walton, himself an experienced writer of military history, whose advice has been of immeasurable value during the gestation of this book.

To the staffs of all these museums and archives, and to all the individuals who have encouraged, corrected and advised me, I am most grateful. The opinions expressed in this book, however, are mine.

Kings Worthy
Winchester
August 1992

Prelude

"like scarecrows, but . . . like soldiers, too"

O N A HOT clammy day, when the clouds of the gathering monsoon lie
heavy on the jungle-clad hills, a British general stands by the side of the
road which leads from the Burma-India border, near the small town of
Tamu. Past him march the remnants of a beaten army – more precisely a
defeated corps, which has reached the end of the longest retreat in Britsh
military history. For two and a half months, Burma Corps has been steadily
pushed back by an energetic and ruthless opponent. Already, many of its
non-combatant elements have straggled back in disorder up the same road,
mostly without their weapons and with the last vestige of military discipline
gone. On the road, the soldiers have had to contend with thousands of
civilian refugees, panic-stricken, sick, dying in hundreds as they struggle up
the disease-ridden Kabaw valley from the banks of the Chindwin River, the
last natural barrier to be crossed.

The officer by the side of the road stands quietly, returning (not merely
acknowledging, for that is not his way) the salutes of those who recognise
him in their exhaustion. Years later he will recall that morning in a
memorable book. For this is Lt General W. J. Slim, the commander of
Burma Corps, recalling what must have been one of the darkest moments in
his career:

> On the last day of that nine-hundred-mile retreat I stood on a bank beside the
> road and watched the rearguard march into India. All of them, British, Indian
> and Gurkha, were gaunt and ragged as scarecrows. Yet, as they trudged behind
> their surviving officers in groups pitifully small, they still carried their arms and
> kept their ranks, they were still recognisable as fighting units. They might look
> like scarecrows, but they looked like soldiers too.

The Commander

What manner of man was this? Slim was to soldier on in Burma and on the
frontiers of India for another three years before he broke the best field army
put into battle by the Japanese in World War II. Many of the men under his
command were fated to endure further reverses in the next 12 months before
gaining the self-confidence and martial skills which alone could ensure
victory over so formidable an opponent. His presence throughout the

months of trial and the quality of his example and leadership would, in the end, grant them a resounding and well-earned victory.

There is a persistent myth about Slim which needs to be nailed: that he went all the way from Private soldier to Field Marshal, as the celebrated 'Wullie' Robertson had done at the end of the Victorian era to become Commandant of the Staff College, then Chief of the Imperial General Staff at the height of World War I. William Joseph Slim was born in 1891, the son of an unsuccessful hardware dealer and ironmonger in Birmingham. He won a grammar school scholarship and seemed destined for an inconspicuous life as a school teacher in the Black Country, that teeming (and then thriving) grimy centre of British heavy industry. As a schoolboy he was fired by tales of Britain's military prowess in the Victorian age, reading all the military history he could get his hands on. The family's financial situation, following the failure of his father's business, dictated that he went to work as soon as possible, as a trainee teacher at a primary school in a particularly under-privileged and desperately poor area.

Here he came face to face with the raw material of the regiment in which he would shortly serve, for the Royal Warwickshires recruited widely in the Black Country in competition with another fine fighting regiment, the South Staffordshires. Young Slim, still in his teens, quickly got to know his pupils and the low quality of their lives; this was to give him an insight into the British soldier enjoyed by very few other officers in high command in either world war. These boys came from appalling homes, where drunkenness and violence were commonplace; many had what today's psychologists would describe as severe behavioural problems, and discipline, unknown at home save through savage beatings, was hard to impose in the classroom, though Slim found that firmness and kindness worked wonders. He considered nevertheless that if he could reach the end of a day in class without a major catastrophe, a small victory had been won.

The year 1914 found Slim working as a humble clerk in a factory, where the pay was better but job satisfaction minimal. As it seemed that war was imminent he wangled his way, though not a student there, into the Birmingham University Officers' Training Corps, which is as near as he ever got to serving in the ranks. He certainly never enlisted as a Private. When war broke out in August of that year it was seen as a chance of liberation by thousands of young men like him, whose talents would otherwise have been denied. They volunteered gladly in response to Kitchener's appeal for men: Kipling had them in mind when he penned this moving epitaph, 'For an Ex-Clerk':

> *Pity not! The Army gave*
> *Freedom to a timid slave:*
> *In which Freedom did he find*
> *Strength of body, will, and mind:*

By which strength he came to prove
Mirth, Companionship and Love:
For which Love to Death he went:
In which Death he lies content.

By no stretch of the imagination could Slim be described as a 'timid slave, but he had not long been a Second-Lieutenant in the Warwicks before he found that he was that rarity – a natural soldier. Few of the friends who joined with him in the first fine patriotic flush of August 1914 ever returned, and those who did had been so sickened by their experience on the Western front that they gladly cast off their uniforms with their memories, returning to urban anonymity as quickly as possible.

Slim, however, did not serve on the Western front. He went first to Gallipoli where he was severely wounded, to be fatuously boarded as 'Disabled – fit for further active service'. The wound would have crippled many for life, but such was his determination to continue soldiering that he found his way to another battalion of the Warwicks, this time in Mesopotamia. Meanwhile, several things had happened which were to change the direction of his life. At Gallipoli the Warwicks had gone into action alongside the 1st Battalion of the 6th Gurkha Rifles.

Slim had never set eyes on soldiers like this before. Recruited from the peasant farming class in their native Nepal, (where there was a martial class, but the British government did not recruit from it), Gurkhas were of the Indian Army but something apart, soldiering under the terms of a treaty with the King of Nepal, not being citizens of the British Empire. Slim was immediately taken with their bravery, humour, professional pride and evident love of soldiering, and privately determined to spend the rest of his life with them if possible. The first step was to obtain a regular commission so as to continue in the Army after the war. This he managed in 1916 by joining the West India Regiment, reputedly the only one in the British service where an officer could live on his pay without recourse to private means, which he certainly lacked.

Armed with his regular commission in a regiment he was destined never to see, Slim went to Mesopotamia, where General Maude was in the process of rebuilding and invigorating an army which had been roundly defeated in 1915 by the Turks, who had bottled up a large proportion of it in a loop of the Tigris at Kut-al-Amara and forced it to surrender. The battalion of the Warwicks in which Slim found himself was engaged in a form of warfare unknown on the Western front; mobility and manoeuvre were the main requirements. He soon showed that he was a natural leader and instinctive tactician. gaining an MC and another wound during the fighting. In 1919 he transferred to the Indian Army, and in 1920 to the 1/6th Gurkhas where he made his happy home. Between the wars his career advanced, but only slowly, for promotion was often blocked even to officers of proven ability.

As late as the mid-1930s a battalion would contain subalterns of nearly 20 years' seniority who had fought and been decorated in the First War. Slim did all the right things: he went to Staff College at Quetta, taught at the Staff College, Camberley as the Indian Army's representative on the directing staff, and went on to the Imperial Defence College, traditionally a sign that he had been earmarked for higher command. He was 47, however, by the time he was promoted to the substantive rank of lieutenant-colonel. To make ends meet and help educate his children, he took up writing under a pen-name, and for many years enjoyed a steady if not spectacular addition to his income. His writings, mainly short stories, reveal a keen insight to human nature and an attractively dry sense of humour.

As war approached in 1939, Slim was Commandant of the Indian Army's senior officers' school. In 1940 he commanded a brigade in the Sudan and Ethiopia where he was wounded yet again. This time he was the victim of an air attack. The surgeon who removed a large bullet from him also extracted several pieces of Turkish ammunition which he had carried around in his body since his Mesopotamian days. He was less than satisfied with his performance there and felt that he had been extremely lucky, on the sudden sickness of its commander, to be given 10 Indian Division to command in Iraq in 1941. Here he made no mistakes; he seldom if ever failed to learn from those of the past, especially his own; and he was always ready to admit to these. In a short campaign, 10 Division defeated a Vichy French force in Syria after a revolt in Iraq had been successfully put down. His division was sent into Persia to stop the Russians – who had their eyes on the oil of the Persian Gulf – from pushing south from the Caspian shore. While there he became the first British general in World War II to meet Russian generals face to face. His experiences on this occasion are perceptively and amusingly described in his book *Unofficial History*. Slim was now a man to be watched, certainly in the Indian Army. Early in 1942, when the war against Japan was clearly going very wrong, he was ordered to go to Burma and take command of the newly-formed Burma Corps. Like General Maude in Mesopotamia nearly 30 years before, he was to revive the fortunes of a badly defeated army and, in good time, to bring about a famous victory.

The Country

Burma is a very large country, a fact not readily appreciated from a glance at an atlas. When superimposed on a map of Europe to the same scale, its true size is apparent. Burma covers the area of France and the Low Countries, and extends east well into central Germany. To the north it reaches out into the North Sea, abreast of the Northumbrian coast. A long 'panhandle', known as Tenasserim, extends many hundreds of miles to the south from the area of Rangoon. Never more than 40 miles wide, this strip terminates at what was known in 1941 as Victoria Point – which on the same map would lie

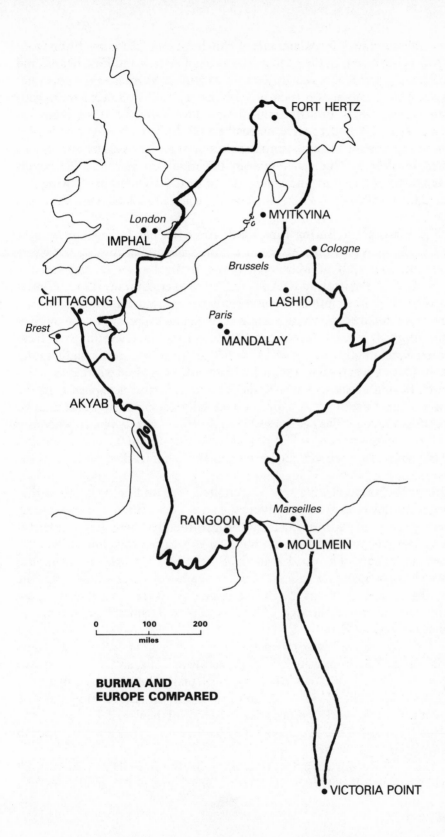

FORT HERTZ

London IMPHAL

MYITKYINA

Cologne

Brussels

CHITTAGONG

LASHIO

Brest

Paris MANDALAY

AKYAB

0   100   200
miles

**BURMA AND
EUROPE COMPARED**

Marseilles

RANGOON

MOULMEIN

VICTORIA POINT

somewhere in the Atlas Mountains of North Africa. To the north and west, Burma is bordered by the Indian provinces of Assam and East Bengal and the Princely State (as it was in 1941) of Manipur. Further to the north lies China, which embraces it round to the east as well. Following southward from China comes French Indo-China (now Vietnam), then Siam, or Thailand. In 1941 there were no road or rail links with India, which lay behind a succession of almost impassable mountains, crossed by a few tracks which quickly became quagmires in the monsoon season. This begins towards the end of May and continues for nearly six months. During this period up to 200 inches of rain fall along the coast and inland onto the Assam hills.

The coastline of Burma runs south from the old Indian border near Chittagong for 1,200 miles to Victoria Point. Several of Asia's great rivers drain into the Gulf of Martaban, between the Bay of Bengal and the Andaman Sea: the Irrawaddy, navigable by river craft for nearly 1,000 miles upstream from its mouth; its main tributary the Chindwin; the Sittang; and the torrential Salween, whose currents and cataracts prevent its use by river craft. All these rivers rise in the great mass of mountains spilling out from the main range of the Himalayas, which more or less reach right round Burma to form a natural frontier which can only be crossed with ease at a few points. Burma's coastal province, the Arakan, is further separated from the main part of the country by a lower but equally impenetrable range of hills, the Arakan Yomas. The central section of Burma is mostly plains, where are grown the staple rice crops. These plains become arid in the dry season and the earth bakes hard in the sun, permitting the use of tracked vehicles off the roads.

Internal communication was by a limited road and rail network within Burma, and by river steamers plying the Irrawaddy, Chindwin and Sittang rivers. Because of expense and engineering difficulty, there were no plans at the outbreak of war with Japan to build an all-weather road link either with Assam or Bengal. The good roads in Burma all lay north-south, up and down the principal river valleys, as did the railways. In 1941, however, the most significant route was the Burma Road, which ran from Rangoon, the main port of entry, through Mandalay, on to Lashio, then across the Chinese border to Kunming.

Burma in the 1930s was prosperous by Asian standards. Large amounts of the annual rice crops were exported, mainly to India, and the country was the world's chief source of hardwoods, particularly teak. Strategic materials such as oil and wolfram existed in large quantities; the latter comprised some ten per cent of the world's production (and 35% of the British Empire's); the oil was produced in the Yenangyaung oilfields, from where it was pumped to refineries outside Rangoon.

Until 1937 Burma was governed from India, but from then on there was a move towards self-government, a trend which was not seen as going fast

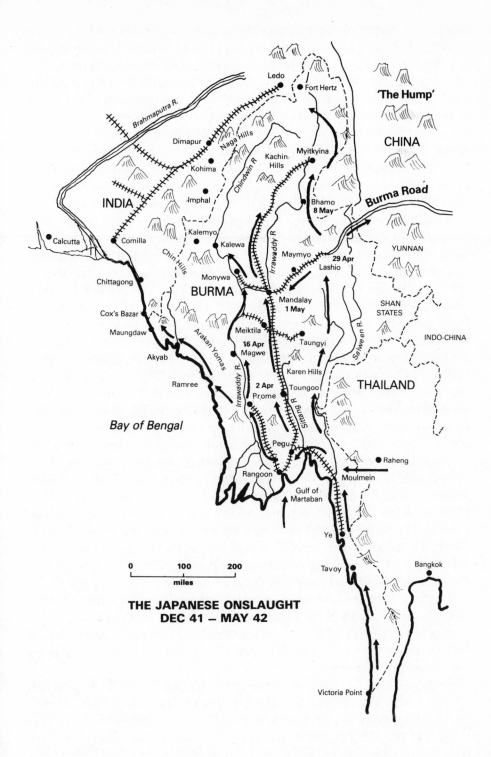

**THE JAPANESE ONSLAUGHT
DEC 41 – MAY 42**

enough by a number of nationalistic Burmese politicians. In 1941 the prime minister, U Saw, was invited to travel to London to discuss his proposals, but these were turned down flat and in high dudgeon he started off for his return to Burma. On his way, in Lisbon, he had talks with the Japanese Ambassador. By this time, Pearl Harbour had been attacked and Britain was at war with Japan. Consequently, when U Saw's Japanese contact was discovered by British Intelligence he was detained in East Africa for the rest of the war. The handling of this delicate situation by the Governor, Sir Reginald Dorman-Smith, was well-intentioned but ill-advised under the circumstances, serving merely to fan the flames of Burmese nationalism and store up trouble for the British once the war started in earnest.

As will be seen, the Japanese had plans for Burma, a fact appreciated belatedly in Delhi and London; measures for reinforcement as the Japanese threat developed were seriously inadequate. The British Army, however, was no stranger to Burma, having fought three wars there in the previous century. The first of these, in lower Burma, took place in 1824 as the result of a deterioration in relations with the Burmese kingdom of Ava, which laid claim to territories already in British hands. The expeditionary force sent from India eventually succeeded in defeating the Burmese but at terrible cost, for it was so incompetently administered that thousands of men died of sickness. The fruits of victory were the transfer to British rule of Manipur and Assam and most of the coastal regions except for an area around Rangoon. Another war was fought in 1852–53 in which it was clear that many lessons had been taken to heart after the earlier calamities. On the medical side, field surgery under general anaesthetic was carried out successfully for the first time when Surgeon Alexander Christison of the Honourable East India Company's army operated on Ensign Garnet Wolseley under the walls of Rangoon. Wolseley went on to be a Field Marshal, a Peer of the Realm and one of Queen Victoria's most famous soldiers. Christison subsequently became Surgeon-General of the Bombay Army. Widowed, he remarried in middle age and had another family, whose eldest child, Alexander Frank Philip, was born in 1893 in Edinburgh. He, too, was fated to play a major part in yet another Burmese campaign.

The final Burmese War, resulting in the annexation of the entire country, took place in 1885–86. King Theebaw and his Queen Supayalatt (inevitably known to the British soldiery as 'Soup-plate') were deposed and exiled. It was nearly four years, however, before the last remnants of military resistance were overcome.

Burma's mixed population has always tended to produce political, religious and social discord, and the British administration which followed the third Burmese War found it impossible to reconcile the claims and interest of the different ethnic groups. The Burmese (in other words the Burmese-speaking majority) live in the great river valleys. The hill tribes –

Karens, Chins, Shans, Mons, and Kachins – tend, unlike the predominantly Buddhist Burmese, to be Christians of various denominations or pagan animists. Historically and instinctively they have always hated the Burmese and in 1941, with few exceptions, they declared their loyalty for the British. Throughout the subsequent campaign, as will be seen, they remained steadfast, little realising that their fidelity would be forgotten by successive generations of British politicians in the post-war years. A similar fate lay in store for the Naga hillmen of Assam, who were destined to play so great a part in the battles for Imphal and Kohima.

The Enemy

"Do not be taken prisoner alive."

O NLY 100 YEARS before Pearl Harbour and the defeat of the British in Hong Kong, Malaya and Singapore, Japan was still a hermit kingdom. After the expulsion of the Christian missionaries in 1638 the country remained unseen by all but a few intrepid European and American travellers and merchants.

Early in the 17th century the power of the Emperor had been usurped by the generalissimo warlord or Shogun, establishing a form of rule based on the Daimyo, local barons whose private armies of mercenary warriors, the Samurai, were the backbone of the state. The Samurai practised a code of behaviour known as Bushido, at its best a form of chivalry not unlike that described in the legends of King Arthur. Every Samurai was bound to his Daimyo by an oath requiring loyalty unto death. Generations of Japanese schoolchildren have been brought up to revere this ideal, exemplified by the '37 Samurai' whose master, whilst undergoing a course of etiquette at court, was insulted by a courtier, whom he wounded in a fight. The Daimyo was applauded for his conduct but Bushido demanded Seppuku or ritual suicide. His followers vowed to avenge him and some months later killed the courtier in an ambush, well knowing that their action also demanded Seppuku, which they duly performed en masse.

For two centuries Japan resisted all foreign contacts but in 1858 the United States forced a trading treaty on the Shogun. The brutish Daimyo and their arrogant Samurai now began to get out of hand, forming outlaw groups (the 'Ronin' or 'masterless men') and indulging in brigandage. After a number of Europeans had been murdered there came a chance for the hereditary Emperor to re-assert his rule in what is known as the Meiji Restoration. In 1866 the old Emperor died and was succeeded by his 15-year-old heir Matsuhito, during whose long reign, lasting until 1912, an amazing change came over the country, which embarked on a programme of modernisation without parallel in recent history. In 1870 the first daily newspaper was printed and the tracks for the first railway laid, linking Tokyo with Yokohama. In the following year feudalism was abolished and two million Samurai were pensioned off. They did not have to look around long for an outlet for their martial skills and energy; in 1873 the Imperial Navy and Army were created on modern lines. The Navy developed under

British influence whilst the Army adopted German and French customs and doctrines. Universal military service was instituted and before long the ranks of the long-service regular cadres were filled with former Samurai, eager to revive and hand on the Bushido tradition.

The person of the Meiji Emperor became the national focus of patriotism and indeed of Shinto worship, as the Son of Heaven. It was now relatively easy to mould the Japanese state and people into a formidable war machine. The government imposed tight control over freedom of expression. Laws were passed in the Diet, or Parliament, confining such freedom . . . 'within the limits of the law'. Any attempt by opposition parties to draft liberal constitutions was rigorously suppressed, as was the short-lived Peoples' Rights Movement. The Constitution of 1889 made no concessions to civil liberties and was passed off to the people as 'the Emperor's Gift' for which they were required to be duly thankful. Over the next 20 years a succession of increasingly repressive laws muzzled the press, suppressed intellectual freedom and forbade all rights of assembly and free speech. Individual thought was brought under control and monitored by 'Thought Police'. Other laws proclaimed the sanctity of the public order system, public morality, and the Imperial Family.

To fill the intellectual vacuum produced by this system of repression, a national doctrine of patriotic militarism was taught in every school and university. In 1887 a Prussian-style cadet system and a professional officer corps were created. Already, the Imperial Army was acquiring the characteristics which were to make it so formidable in Burma, together with the doctrinal rigidity which contributed to its downfall. The 1908 Army Criminal Code, the equivalent of the British Army's Queen's Regulations, lays down that:

A commander who allows his unit to surrender without fighting to the last man or yields vital ground to the enemy shall be punishable by death . . .

A simplified commentary on the Code, the 'Senjin Jutsugi', quotes the example of Major Yuga, who was wounded and captured whilst unconscious at Shanghai, and was then released by the Chinese. He committed suicide to atone for his disgrace . . . 'this act typifies the glorious spirit of the Imperial Army.'

Japan's population now rose steadily, from 32 million in 1868 to 45 million in 1903. As industrial development got under way, hundreds of new factories in all the major cities recruited their labour from the countryside, giving rise to teeming urban slums, much as had been the case a century earlier in England. Japan depended on imports for most of its essential raw materials: wool from Australia, fertilisers from South America, tin and rubber from Malaya, wood pulp from distant Scandinavia, and coal from Manchuria. Engineering expertise was sought worldwide, much of it from Great Britain; in the early years most of Japan's ships, for merchant marine and navy alike, came from British shipyards. British engineers surveyed and built the metre-gauge railway system which served Japan so well for the next 75 years. All the while, the process now known as 'technology transfer' was taking place; the Japanese proved apt pupils, especially in copying, adapting and improving other people's designs. By 1900 Japan was a well-equipped military, naval and industrial power, with an urgent agenda to fulfil.

Remorseless population increase, shortage of strategic materials, limited agricultural resources and deep-seated suspicion of neighbours, particularly Imperial Russia, made it inevitable that the young and vigorous state would soon need to extend its boundaries at the expense of those neighbours. Russia had long been seen as a threat because of the eastward expansion of the Muscovite Empire. Viewed from Tokyo, the peninsular kingdom of Korea was clearly the springboard from which an invasion of Japan could be launched by whichever power held the adjoining parts of the Asian land mass. China, enfeebled by years of weak and chaotic government, had designs on Korea but was forestalled when Japan forced the Koreans to open their ports to its trade. When law and order collapsed in Korea in 1894 the Chinese tried to send in troops, but Japanese agents murdered the influential Korean Queen and the Imperial Army easily defeated the Chinese in open battle. Korea, renamed Chosen, was formally annexed by the Japanese in 1910, but by then the whole balance of power in the Far East had been overturned. In 1900 there had been a rebellion in China (the so-called 'Boxer Rising') against the European powers which had long exploited the opium trade. The international legations at Peking were besieged, and a scratch relief force recruited from all interested parties went to the rescue. The Japanese response was enthusiastic and their troops performed with distinction, prompting the British Government to sign a prudent Anglo-Japanese defensive treaty in 1902.

While embroiled at Peking, the Japanese contingent had carefully noted the mediocre performance of the Russian detachments. Thus encouraged, Tokyo picked a quarrel with Tsarist Russia, leading to the Russo-Japanese War of 1904-05. This was one of the 20th century's decisive conflicts, setting Japan on a road of aggression which ended only with the dropping of nuclear bombs on Hiroshima and Nagasaki in 1945. In 1904, the Japanese were heavily outnumbered by land and sea but had the advantage of a short line of communication to their home base as they laid siege to Port Arthur, Russia's main arsenal and naval base in the Far East. The Japanese soldiers and sailors were well motivated and trained, unlike the Russians who, far from home and with inferior leadership, weapons and tactics, began to disintegrate. This was the first war in which quick-firing field artillery, machine guns, wireless telegraphy, capital ships and torpedo boats were widely deployed. A newly-emergent Asiatic nation thrashed a great European power by sea and land, and the message was not lost elsewhere in Asia where numerous nationalistic movements were being born. In the first decade of the century hundreds of young Indian students went to Japan, returning with ardour to foment trouble for the British Raj. The dragon's teeth had been sown, and the stage was being set for the collapse of European power in the Far East.

From 1908, there were frequent revisions of Japanese military codes to keep pace with the accelerating speed of technology and the vastly increased deadliness of modern armaments. It is interesting to note that in 1904, at the siege of Port Arthur, some Japanese infantry units were commanded by officers who as young men had fought in Samurai chain mail and armour, wielding swords and battle axes. Forty years later, their sons and grandsons would be commanding formations and units in Burma. The 1914 Imperial Army Field Regulations continued to stress the offensive spirit, loyalty to the Emperor, love of country and 'sacrifice of life to the nation by absolute obedience to superiors'. These doctrines persisted in the new Field Service Code of 1941, bearing the signature of General Tojo Hideiki and the ominous warning: 'Do not be taken prisoner alive.'

The Japanese national educational system was geared to the mass-production of recruits amenable to the harsh disciplines of conscript training units. From their earliest schooldays, Japanese children were subjected to a barrage of crudely nationalistic propaganda. The Government controlled the contents of all textbooks. Each new school year started with elaborate ritual worship of the Emperor as Son of Heaven and solemn readings from the Education Act, such as:

Should emergency arise, guard and maintain the prosperity of the Imperial Throne . . . always respect the Constitution and observe the laws.

There was profound contempt for foreigners and much emphasis on the purity of the Japanese race. Koreans and Chinese were particular objects of hatred and ridicule. Arithmetical problems, even in junior classes, were based on naval and military examples. Physical education featured Judo, Karate, Kendo, and fencing with staves. Music in schools emphasised military songs and marches.

The textbooks prepared for children in Japanese elementary schools during the early 1900s indicate the degree of indoctrination. An example from 1903 goes as follows:

Lesson 23. The Emperor attends the annual manoeuvres and watches the sailors and soldiers perform their duties. We must appreciate the Emperor's royal benevolence.
Lesson 24. Kiguchi Kohei was not the least bit afraid before the enemy. He boldly sounded the call to advance on his bugle three times. Inspired by his brave example our troops advanced and defeated the enemy but Kiguchi was hit and fell to the ground mortally wounded. Later they found his body with the bugle still at his lips.

In a reading primer of 1904 a father bids farewell to his soldier son, about to embark for service in the Russo-Japanese war: 'Don't be afraid to die. Don't worry about us here. You must always be faithful to the Imperial Precepts to soldiers and sailors.'

By 1930 several generations of heavily-indoctrinated Japanese youths had passed through the State education system and undergone the rigours of naval or military service before taking their place in the Reserves. A whole nation was ready to take up arms.

The Rising Sun

"Why then do the waves seethe and the winds rage?"

DURING WORLD WAR I the Japanese army and navy played a useful role on the side of the Allies. The German China Coast trading enclave at Tsingtao, home of the Kaiser's Pacific naval squadron, was besieged and taken by Japanese troops. Japanese warships spent the war years on escort and patrolling duties in the Indian Ocean and Western Pacific, and a number of former German colonial possessions passed into Japanese hands as the result of the Peace Treaty signed at Versailles in 1919. These included the Caroline Islands in the Western Pacific, destined to be the scene of bitter fighting in World War II.

The Japanese delegation at Versailles had hoped for more than just their share of the loot. Believing that their nation was about to gain international recognition for its great leap into the world arena, they were mortified when President Wilson of the United States vetoed their proposal for racial equality between members of the new League of Nations. Further humiliation was to come when the USA banned Japanese immigrants, whilst accepting other ethnic groups. The resultant loss of face soon led to a build-up of resentment against the European power bloc, and especially against the United States, now seen as a principal rival in the Western Pacific as well as on mainland Asia, where American influence in all fields was rapidly increasing, notably in China. Resentment fuelled the ultra-patriotic groups who now gained power in top Japanese spheres.

The growth of Japanese naval and military power was giving cause for concern in London and Washington, where in 1921 an international conference was called with the aim of limiting naval armament and adjusting the balance of power in the Far East. It was attended by the United States, Britain and her Dominions and other interested European powers, as well as by China and Japan. The unwritten agenda was the desire of the United States Government to obtain an 'Open Door' into the potentially lucrative China trade, and to ensure American naval domination in the Pacific. It was agreed at Washington that the fleets of the principal world naval powers were to be regulated by setting proportional strengths for capital ships, the laid-down ratio being: United States, 5; Britain, 5; Japan, 3; France, 1.75; Italy, 1.75. The existing Anglo-Japanese Treaty was scrapped and replaced by one in which the USA, Britain, France and Japan agreed to consult each other in the event of any aggression in the Far East.

In Japan the Navy and the Army had developed differently, the Navy following British lines while the Army adopted mainly Prussian practices, and this led to a widening gap between the two services. Japanese naval officers tended to be well-travelled, sophisticated, conversant with Western ways and broader-minded than their opposite numbers in the Army, whose careers were confined to service on the home islands, Korea, and China, and whose narrowly chauvinistic attitudes were continually hardening.

Contempt for all races other than their own, together with an aggressive and headstrong mentality, were characteristic of the Japanese army officer class in the years between the wars, but they were not to be found in the navy, where senior officers continued to adopt cautious attitudes towards war right up to the attack on Pearl Harbour. Their most brilliant admiral, Yamamoto Isoruku, planner of the surprise attack on the American Pacific fleet there, knew that there were two wars to be fought: one in the Pacific and the other in South-East Asia. The latter he recognised as the easier option, for it was clear by mid-1941 that the principal European colonial powers – Britain, the Netherlands and France – were in no position to defend their Asian possessions against a determined attack. France and Holland had already been under German occupation for 12 months, and Britain was still fighting alone against the German-Italian Axis. Yamamoto realised that the destruction of the United States Pacific fleet, especially its aircraft carriers, was essential if Japanese war aims were to succeed in the longer term. He saw that American submarines posed a grave threat to the Japanese merchant marine upon which so much would depend if a newly-won empire was to be sustained. He also knew that to embark on a full-scale naval war without a huge anti-submarine fleet would be to court disaster.

Throughout the run-up to war, Yamamoto repeatedly called for a more cautious approach, but was over-ruled by the clamorous Army lobby. When congratulated on the apparent success of Pearl Harbour, he commented that '. . . we have wakened a sleeping giant, and his reactions will be terrible.' Before his death in an aerial ambush in 1943 his prediction had been fulfilled. By April 1942 Japanese expansionism had reached high water; a month later, the tide had turned at the battle of Midway, and when Yamamoto was killed over 75% of the Japanese merchant fleet had already been sent to the bottom. By 1944 it was proving impossible to resupply the far-flung outposts of the Greater East Asia Co-Prosperity Sphere, and Japan was facing slow defeat by blockade.

All this lay ahead as the Japanese war machine got under way in the early 1930s. It was directed from above by a curious hierarchy. Everything officially stemmed from the Emperor, whose word was final. As he could not be seen to be involved in high level arguments, the politicians and heads of the armed forces had to be in full agreement before anything was referred to the Son of Heaven for endorsement. Because every ministry contained one admiral and one general, either of whom could bring down the government by resigning if he did not get his own way, power lay effectively in the hands of the service chiefs who made all naval and military decisions. At Imperial Councils the assembled ministers, admirals and generals stood before the throne and delivered prepared statements in turn. The Emperor then nodded his agreement to proposals which had already been settled outside the throne-room.

Emperor Hirohito was not in any sense the bellicose monster portrayed by Allied propaganda throughout the war. A scholarly, retiring person (he was a leading authority on marine biology, and had published learned papers on the sea slug) the idea of war appalled him. On the occasion of the Imperial Conference held on 6 September 1941 he went as far as to break his customary silence and, instead of nodding his approval, produced a scrap of paper on which was written, in his own hand, a Haiku – one of those terse poems in which Japanese have for centuries encapsulated their deepest emotions. Composed by his revered grandfather, the Meiji emperor who had led the nation through its astonishing transition from feudalism and into the 20th century, it read:

The four seas are brothers to each other. Why then do the waves seethe and the winds rage?

With hindsight it is clear that this was noting less than an agonised plea for moderation, but it went unheard (and unseen, for it was erased on Tojo's orders from the official record of the conference).

Until 1937 the Navy and Army ministries went their own way, but in that year a 'liaison committee' was set up; even so, land and sea found it hard to agree. The Army wanted to fight a land war against Soviet Russia after first defeating Nationalist China. The Navy thought in terms of a maritime war against the United States and Britain, seen as the only serious contenders for naval domination of the Pacific and Indian oceans. Japan's civilian politicians shrank from the idea of any sort of war but were greedy for its spoils; all were painfully aware that a fanatically patriotic movement, almost entirely consisting of army officers, stalked the corridors of power, ruthlessly eliminating any minister, admiral or general who was not seen by them to be advancing the national cause. Two Prime Ministers and a number of service chiefs fell victim to assassins in the 1930s. The survivors felt that it was wiser to follow the course prescribed by the hotheads.

There was some reason for adopting an aggressive stance. Although the Japanese had worked desperately hard to join the 'club' of major world industrial powers, their exclusion did not protect them from the effects of the Great Depression, which severely penalised them. The United States put up tariff barriers to prevent the entry of cheap Japanese goods, as did the British Empire. There were few outlets for Japan's products in what it had fondly hoped would be a world of free trade eager to 'buy Japanese'. In order to acquire readily-accessible supplies of coal and other minerals the Japanese stage-managed Manchuria's 'independence' from China in 1931. As the Japanese increased their grip on the Asian mainland, the United States – which aimed to seize markets there whilst prohibiting Japan's exports to the USA – became increasingly uneasy. In March 1933 Japan withdrew from the League of Nations, and in the following year gave two years' notice, as was required, to quit the Washington and London naval agreements, which had limited not only the number of battleships but also of aircraft carriers which the Japanese could build.

Exploitation of China meanwhile continued, and tension rose to breaking point. On 7 July 1937 fighting broke out between Japanese and Chinese troops. Chinese aircraft attempted to bomb Japanese naval vessels at Shanghai but missed and hit the city instead. This was the excuse for all-out war, and Japanese troops plunged into the depths of China. They captured Peking and Tientsin by the end of October and were in control of Shanghai by late November. On 13 December the Japanese marched into Nanking, Chiang's capital. Here they exacted a terrible revenge for atrocities allegedly committed by Chinese soldiers against Japanese civilians at Tungchow earlier in the year. The 'Rape of Nanking' went on for some weeks and no accurate estimate of those killed is available. Japanese witnesses included the correspondent of the respected 'Tokyo Asahi', Inai Masatuke, who reported that . . . 'the area was filled with crumpled, twisted corpses piled up on top of each other in bloody mounds'. Masatuke was told by an army officer that there were . . .' about 20,000 dead Chinese by the Hsiakuachi Bridge', where thousands were seen to be lined up and machine-gunned. Foreign observers of the International Committee for the Nanking Safety Zone noted that tens of thousands of Chinese – prisoners of war, refugees, stragglers from the Kuomintang forces – were massacred out of hand. The killing was accompanied by an orgy of looting, rapine and burning of property by soldiers wild with drink. The world had been given a grisly preview of what to expect from a victorious Japanese army.

It was hardly surprising that in their arrogant self-confidence the Japanese war party, seeing other rich pickings, turned towards territories ruled by European powers where oil, strategic raw materials, rice, and rubber were available in vast quantities. Hong Kong, Malaya, Singapore, the Philippines, the Dutch East Indies and Burma were now firmly in their sights. In 1941 President Roosevelt, whose strategic vision was blinkered, to say the least, and who wanted nothing more than to secure an American monopoly over the China trade, imposed an oil embargo on Japan, where war reserves amounted to no more than a few months. Roosevelt assumed that the embargo would make Japan realise that it was futile to challenge America and that it must abandon all ambitions to be a major Asian power. He also believed that the USA would now be able to cash in on the China trade while excluding Japan. He had totally misjudged the mood and intentions of the Japanese Imperial General Staff. War was now inevitable. The only question was: when?

The Defenders

". . a calmness born of supreme ignorance of what war entailed."

IN THE YEARS between the wars Britain gave an extremely low priority to the defence of Burma. Two British battalions were stationed there, one as the Rangoon garrison, another at Maymyo for internal security duties in Upper Burma. Although the latter was an agreeable Indian-type hill-station, neither provided social and sporting facilities on the scale to which units were accustomed in India. The outbreak of war in Europe in September 1939 passed almost unnoticed in Burma and there was no move to place the British garrison on a war footing.

In 1939 the Rangoon garrison unit was the 1st Battalion The Gloucestershire Regiment, which had arrived there from India in 1938, complete with families and all the impedimenta of peacetime soldiering. This included the Colours, the regimental silver and the extensive documentation comprising the battalion's record office. The 2nd Battalion King's Own Yorkshire Light Infantry (KOYLI) had been stationed at Maymyo since 1935.

The Glosters, as they were generally known in the Army (although the 1st Battalion always referred to themselves aş 'The 28th', their pre-1881 regimental number) had left India with mixed feelings. They had been there for some years, as was customary in peacetime, when every infantry regiment had one battalion overseas and the other in the home regimental depot, acting as a training cadre charged with providing drafts to top up the overseas unit. This system had been adopted after the sweeping Army reforms of the 1880s, and in peacetime it served its purpose well, when no greater demands were laid on the Army than those of policing the Empire.

On arrival at Rangoon the Glosters moved into barracks astride the Burma Road at Mingaladon, some ten miles north of Rangoon city, where the families settled into their quarters. One company in turn was based in Rangoon itself for 'Aid to the Civil Power', as there was continual unrest in the city. The Burmese were impatient of British rule, and an active Independence movement made trouble whenever it could, despite strides already made to 'Burmanise' the civil service in preparation for eventual self-government. In addition, numerous ethnic and political groups constantly fought each other; on top of all this was the long-standing tradition of brigandage or dacoity, whose existence predated the three Burmese wars of the previous century. Thus it was that the Glosters spent much of their first Rangoon Christmas quelling outbursts of civil unrest and inter-communal rioting.

The years 1939 and 1940 passed without much sign of urgency on the part of Headquarters Burma Command, even though the threat from Japan was becoming apparent. The Glosters' commanding officer, Lt Colonel C. E. K. Bagot, however, was aware of the impending danger and determined to prepare for it. His attempts to initiate a realistic programme of training for war were hamstrung by the inertia of an army headquarters which was understaffed and under control of the distant Army HQ in Delhi, which had other priorities to attend to. Bagot and his officers had noted the increasing numbers of Japanese 'tourists' in Rangoon and around the countryside, clearly gathering information on British dispositions. The response from on high was to refuse any increases in the supply of training ammuniton. At the same time, the battalion was being steadily stripped of its personnel for service in Burma Army HQ and as instructors for new Burmese forces now being raised.

Up at Maymyo the KOYLI were in a similar position. They lacked steel helmets, entrenching tools, and 2-inch mortars. The battalion held 96 shovels and 46 pickaxes. There were no sniper rifles, and only 20 prismatic compasses for the entire unit. Seven motor vehicles were held against an establishment of 52. Neither battalion was in possession of any hard information on the Japanese army, its organisation, equipment or tactics, other than the pious belief that because of their bad eyesight, Japanese infantry could not operate by night.

Denied barbed wire with which to practise setting out defensive positions, Bagot ordered masses of string and trained his men with that. For transport the battalion had 40 mules, but no pack saddles. There were no Bren Gun carriers for the Carrier Platoon. Formal mobilisation, declared on 7 December 1941 as the storm broke, made no difference. Because of the threat of serious civil unrest all military training had to be done within 40 miles of Rangoon and, in any case, higher authority ruled that the risks of contracting dysentery, malaria and heatstroke made it impracticable to attempt extended jungle training.

So, in the words of their commanding officer, the old 28th prepared for war:

> With characteristic calmness, a superabundance of hope, and a confidence born of supreme ignorance of what war entailed, everyone in Burma, not least the 28th, was about to embark on a campaign with an enemy who had already been War Trained for three years in swamps and jungles, heat and disease and had very naturally learned how to overcome these difficulties.

In the last two months of peace Bagot repeatedly sought clearance from HQ Burma Army to get the families to safety in India and for the regimental records and property, including the colours and silver, to go with them. His requests were turned down, although the families were eventually sent up to Maymyo on 18 December, from where they were evacuated with great difficulty to India early in 1942. The colours were spirited out by air before the fall of Rangoon, but the silver, of which the regiment was justly proud, was almost entirely lost in the great retreat. Carried from place to place, it was finally buried, all five hundredweight of it, near the River Chindwin in the hope of recovery at a later date. In 1945 it was found to have been dug up and looted by Burmese villagers. Only a few fragments were ever recovered; one candlestick actually turned up years later in a Singapore bazaar, from which it was recovered and restored to the regiment. The KOYLI also buried their silver and were luckier; just over a hundred pieces were recovered, but they lost their magnificent set of silver bugles. Their King's and Regimental colours were saved by a company sergeant major who carried them in his pack to India, where they were entrusted to General Auchinleck for safe keeping for the rest of the war.

Even with the families gone, the Glosters at Mingaladon were unfit to take the field. Successive 'milking' of their ranks by Burma HQ had left them, at one point, 14 officers and 340 soldiers short of War Establishment. At least half the battalion were 'time-expired' and due for return to Home Establishment. The fact that they were now marooned was hardly conducive to high morale. Fifty soldiers were unfit for combat duty, as the result of prolonged service in the tropics (many had been overseas for up to eight years). The Quartermaster held a total of 90 rounds of ammunition for all the unit's Thompson sub-machine guns, and the peacetime training scale of hand grenades for the entire battalion had been 12 a year, raised on mobilisation to 96. Bagot drily reported that in three years, 36 men of the Glosters had been allowed to throw one live grenade apiece. In the week of Pearl Harbour, 400 mortar bombs were grudgingly released by the Rangoon ammunition depot. Only by low cunning and initiative would the Glosters be able to equip for battle.

In September 1939, apart from the British battalion, Burma was garrisoned by four battalions of the Burma Rifles (the 'Burifs'), six battalions of the Burma Field Force – a sort of armed police or gendarmerie – and some locally-raised auxiliary units. The four regular Burif battalions were recruited mainly from the robust hill tribes – Kachins, Chins, Kumaons, and Karens, and from Gurkhas domiciled in the country (grants of land had been made to their forbears in recognition of good service in earlier Burma wars). Political pressures compelled the Governor, Sir Reginald Dorman-Smith, to open recruitment to all Burmans, and two entirely Burmese Territorial battalions were formed in 1941. Further pressure resulted in the inclusion of Burmese rifle companies into the regular battalions as well, with markedly adverse effects on their subsequent performance in action. Many of these Burmese soldiers would later appear in the ranks of the Burma National Army, fighting on the Japanese side.

None of these units was organised into brigades, let alone divisions, and there were virtually no supporting arms or services to sustain them in the field. A mountain artillery battery and some field engineers had been 'borrowed' from the Indian Army, but there were no anti-aircraft or anti-tank guns until the eve of the Japanese invasion. Reserves of vehicles, weapons and ammunition of all kinds were totally inadequate. For communication in the field there were practically no radios, and what few there were had to be carried on trucks. Signalling was by telephone (often on the civilian system, prone to tapping and sabotage), heliograph, lamp, and semaphore flag. There was no Intelligence staff, nor were there any trained interpreters capable of interrogating Japanese prisoners (of whom it was fondly thought that there might be a supply) or of deciphering captured documents. Much of the country was unsurveyed and there was a dearth of maps, resort being made frequently to school atlases and commercial road and railway maps.

Between 1939 and 1941 some expansion of Burma's defences took place. Europeans of military age became liable for service in the Burma Auxiliary Force (BAF) and part-time field engineer units were raised, together with the doubling of the Burma Rifles to a strength of eight regular battalions, albeit watered down by the inclusion of the statutory Burmese companies. The 8th battalion was in fact recruited almost exclusively from locally-enlisted Sikhs and Punjabi Mussulmen. A further two Territorial battalions were also formed, although few of these units proved of any use once war broke out. The most useful of these new creations were probably the Special Units of the Burma Field Force, raised during 1941 to provide stay-behind and surveillance units in the event of invasion. Their locally-recruited British, Anglo-Burmese and Burmese officers' intimate local knowledge of terrain and language made them invaluable during the later stages of the campaign and, as 'V' Force, one of the 14th Army's best sources of intelligence.

The huge training requirement thrown up by the raising of all these new units placed a heavy load on the resident British battalions, making inroads on their key personnel, especially senior NCOs. This came on top of earlier 'milking' to produce headquarters staff. Their commanding officers watched in alarm as the Glosters and the KOYLI began to melt away.

Bagot had already made his own appreciation of the likely situation on the outbreak of war after travelling widely by private car around Burma. He considered that much of the Burma Army was virtually useless and probably disloyal, with the exception of the tribally-enlisted troops. Senior British officials of the Burma Civil Service were, in the main, middle-aged, in sight of comfortable retirement and an automatic award such as the CIE. They continued to plod away at their routine work, but most were to prove hopelessly inadequate when faced with the chaos of war.

Although Japanese troops were on Burmese soil within days of the outbreak of war in December 1941, they confined their immediate activities to occupying the undefended airfield at Victoria Point, hundreds of miles to the south. Despite air raids on Rangoon, starting in the week before Christmas and stampeding the civilian population, the Glosters got down to really intensive training. Ignoring Burma Army headquarters, Bagot subjected what was left of his battalion to a succession of gruelling tests, emphasising physical fitness, endurance, jungle tactics and living off the land; he knew that survival would hang on these once the Japanese attack materialised. By the end of February 1942, he had achieved the aims of his programme, and the Glosters – albeit at a strength of barely two rifle companies – carried out one final exercise which satisfied their stern taskmaster and ensured that his unit would rise splendidly to the ordeal ahead.

There was no pre-war RAF presence in Burma, other than small servicing detachments at Rangoon and on the airfields spaced down the Tenasserim strip. These were strategically important, linking India with Malaya and Singapore and as transit stations for RAF units sent to reinforce Britain's key base in South-East Asia. The only naval presence was provided by intermittent visits by HM ships, designed to 'show the flag' rather than fulfil any significant strategic function. The tiny Burma Royal Naval Volunteer Reserve manned a handful of river launches and coastal patrol boats, lightly armed and incapable of offensive action.

The reinforcement of Burma suddenly became very important when it was realised that things were going badly in Malaya, where the Japanese landed at Kota Bharu in the far north-east of the country on 8 December 1941. From then until the surrender of Singapore on 15 February 1942 – the greatest defeat ever inflicted on British arms – numerically inferior Japanese forces seized and maintained the initiative over a progressively demoralised and dispirited defence. The loss of the two capital ships *Prince of Wales* and *Repulse* to aerial attack off Malaya in the opening days of the campaign ensured that regional naval superiority, essential to Japanese war aims, was theirs for the time being and gave them the confidence to proceed with the remainder of their plans for the occupation of South-East Asia. Burma, where no provision had ever been made to meet the threat of invasion by a major power, now lay virtually defenceless.

If the two British battalions had been struggling ot get on a war footing, even greater problems beset the source from which virtually all immediate reinforcements of Burma now had to come. In the 1930s the Indian Army was a regular force of long-serving volunteers, the largest of its type in the world, organised and trained on British lines with two main roles: the security of the North-West Frontier, and 'Aid to the Civil Power'. Its officers were still predominantly British – above the rank of Major exclusively so. In every Indian Army battalion there were usually twelve of them. From the early 1930s, a limited number of young Indians had been sent each year to The Royal Military College at Sandhurst or the Royal Military Academy, Woolwich, from where they were granted King's commissions for service with the Indian Army. The majority attended the Indian Military Academy, or IMA, at Dehra Dun. There were also Viceroy's Commissioned officers, or VCOs, Indians and Gurkhas who had risen through the ranks to constitute the backbone of every unit. They were the repositories of all knowledge, the links with the recruiting areas, and custodians of the regiment's particular esprit de corps. With them lay the responsibility for family and village affairs and the maintenance of harmony where, as was often the case, companies and squadrons of a regiment were recruited from differing religious groups or castes. There was a vague idea that one day the Indian Army would be entirely officered by Indians, but this, it was felt, would not be much before the mid-1960s.

The Indian Army still bore the marks of the great 1857 Mutiny. Most of its brigades included one British infantry battalion, and until the mid-1930s, apart from the élite mountain batteries, the artillery was exclusively in British hands. The old cavalry regiments had begun to mechanise but in 1941 no tanks had been issued. Some horsed Indian cavalry actually served as such in the Burma campaign, where they turned out to be of some use in the reconnaissance role, but no match for Japanese tanks.

It was never intended to use the Indian Army as part of an expeditionary force; but the precedent had been set in 1914 and again in 1939. Indian formations had already performed well in North Africa and the Middle East, and were already serving in Malaya; here, things had gone wrong because, as in Burma, units which had been skimmed of their best men were hurriedly sent into battle with a mass of newly-drafted recruits against a first-class enemy.

An Indian Army regiment was curiously like a miniature feudal state. Reforms in the 1920s had grouped battalions into 18 infantry regiments, each with its own training depot. Gurkhas were different, being Nepalese citizens serving under the terms of an Anglo-Nepalese treaty. This limited the ten regiments of Gurkha Rifles to two battalions in peacetime, each with a maximum of 100 reservists, an arrangement satisfactory for frontier operations but manifestly impractical for general war. Service in the ranks, for Gurkhas and Indians alike, was largely hereditary, son following father in full consciousness that the family's honour rested in his hands. There was a fierce loyalty to the regiment and its British officers which far exceeded any fealty to the King-Emperor, however much this was paraded back in England. By 1940, India was in political ferment, with an unstoppable movement towards independence and the end of the Raj. Once inside the army, the sepoy was hermetically sealed against political infection, a fact most unpalatable to the leaders of major Indian political parties. The army was apolitical to the hilt, and had remained so for generations. The fact that it kept its discipline and standards despite the pressures exerted by inter-communal strife, different religions and the throttling effects of the caste system speaks volumes for all who served in it. It remains as probably the outstanding achievement of the Raj, a closed, well-ordered society in which the differences of religion and race that were finally to tear the sub-continent apart were kept firmly under control.

The Japanese were fascinated by the Indian Army, for which they soon acquired considerable respect. In a highly classified document captured at Imphal in June 1944, they assessed the qualities of the different categories of Indian soldier:

> The most important among the Indian troops are the Gurkhas. Strong Points: Extremely brave, with high fighting morale. Absolute obedience to orders, can endure coarse food and clothing. Rice and salt are sufficient. Weak Points: Fond of drinking. Being of a fighting nature, do not hesitate to draw their knives and kill even in quarrels among themselves. They like football. Favourite food is mutton curry.
>
> Punjabi troops: Strong Points: Bodily strong, and stout. Being so strong, are excellent fighting men. Do not drink. Weak Points: Ardently religious, shun other religions, have strong likings and dislikings about food.
>
> Sikhs: Courteous; do not smoke. Essential not to interfere with their religion. Have at times defied their officers and retired from battle without permission.
>
> Pathans: Physically stout, strong; brave, but very cunning, and easily desert.

During the 1920s the Japanese Imperial General Staff flooded South-East Asia with its agents. Increasing numbers of 'shopkeepers', 'barbers', 'mechanics', 'radio fitters' and 'office workers' were infiltrated into Hong Kong, French Indo-China, Malaya, Burma, Singapore, and the Dutch East Indies. Their purpose was to build up comprehensive intelligence dossiers for use in the forthcoming offensive. They were all extremely competent at their 'cover' jobs. Many a British or Indian Army unit posed for its regimental group photographs during these years, little knowing that the little man behind the camera was a Japanese agent. He would be obligingly provided with lists of names for the group photograph and marked-up copies of these were in the hands of Japanese military intelligence well before the first shots were fired. Loose talk – of unit training, new equipment, reinforcements, or just social gossip – were carefully noted by unit barbers and mess servants, who frequently turned out to be officers and NCOs of the Imperial Army. Whitehall took little notice and the India and Colonial offices slept on. It was

British Government policy throughout the 1920s and '30s to plan on the assumption that there would be no European war in the next ten years, and this was extended to include the rest of the world. Despite the publication in Tokyo of many inflammatory books, such as Lt Comd Tota Ishimaru's *Japan Must Fight Britain*, which sold in thousands to the Japanese officer class, there seems to have been little appreciation by the Western powers of the mood in Tokyo, propelling Japan inexorably towards war.

Throughout the 1930s, rival groups of military plotters struggled for a controlling influence in the nation's strategic policy-making. Fighting between rival groups of officers in the streets of the capital in February 1936 resulted in victory for the 'China faction', which aimed to make further deep advances into the Asian mainland before turning its attention to the rest of South-East Asia. The Cabinet now took steps to put Japan on a war footing, joining the anti-Comintern Pact of 1937 with Germany and Italy. In the same year a general actually became Prime Minister, but had to be replaced after a short time by the more politically experienced Prince Konoye. Efforts to bait the Soviet Union were made in 1938-39, but the Japanese were bloodily repulsed by the Russians in a series of major battles on the Manchurian frontier. Although virtually unnoticed in the West, this campaign served notice that the Soviet war machine was in far better shape than had been thought, despite Stalin's bloody purge of its officer corps.

Germany's sweeping victories in 1940 over Holland and France, both of whose Asian colonies were coveted by Japan, encouraged the Imperial Staff to go ahead with plans for the creation of the 'Greater East Asia Co-Prosperity Sphere'. This amounted to nothing less than the occupation of Indo-China, the Philippines, Malaya, Singapore, Hong Kong, the Dutch East Indies, Borneo, and Burma. Prime Minister Konoye, an able and astute diplomat and politician, counselled caution; like Admiral Yamamoto he sensed that members of the war party were over-reaching themselves. He was immediately ousted and replaced by the hawkish war minister, General Tojo Hideiki, who urged a policy of 'now or never' and was backed overwhelmingly by the younger officers. The navy was less enthusiastic; its building programme was still far from complete, especially in aircraft carriers and anti-submarine vessels; fuel stocks were dangerously low, and many capital ships were in urgent need of modernisation. Rash counsels prevailed, however, and Japan moved further towards the brink.

General Tojo was 57 years old in 1941. His promotion owed as much to administrative ability as to his membership of the General Staff clique, which had emerged triumphant from the in-fighting of the mid-30s. He was mistakenly thought by Emperor Hirohito to have a moderating influence, capable of heading Japan away from all-out war. Tojo was aware of the shortage of strategic materials, the deficiencies of the Japanese merchant marine and of the nation's rapidly dwindling fuel resources. Despite this, he now backed the cynical exercise of forming the Greater East Asia Co-prosperity Sphere, which had become the principal public aim of Imperial strategy. The other aim was defined as the '. . . liberation of Asians from American and British Imperialism'; 'Liberation' of this kind did not mean equality and solidarity. Japan's own special needs remained paramount. In March 1941 the Imperial Rule Assistance Association published a booklet setting out the real purposes of the Co-Prosperity Sphere, which makes this point explicitly.

> Although we use the expression 'Asian co-operation' this by no means ignores the fact that Japan was created by the Gods, or that there is to be automatic racial equality . . .

Some Japanese intellectuals were prompted to wonder if other Asian intelligentsia would relate to the concept of Japan as 'hakko ichu' – 'eight corners of the world under one roof' – but were put firmly in their place at a meeting of the 'Japan Literary Patriotic Association' attended by All-Asia delegates when non-Japanese delegates were described as no more than 'members of the Co-Prosperity Sphere assembled under the august aura of the Emperor'. Once war had broken out in March 1942, the chief secretary of the Imperial Cabinet, Hoshino Naoki, made no bones about it:

> There are no restrictions on us. These were enemy possessions. We can take them, do anything we want to . . . there must be a long period of military government, no promises of independence to local peoples, no encouragement of wilful ambitions . . .

Tojo's strategy did not bargain for a long war, which even he could see would over-stretch the economy. He went for a knock-out blow which would discourage the Western powers from trying to struggle back into the ring. Priority targets were the essential oilfields of Borneo, Java and Sumatra, to be taken intact if possible. In order to reach them, the British had to be ejected from Malaya (which would bring additional bonuses of tin, rubber and palm oil) and Singapore, whose great naval base would be of enormous value in future operations. As far back as 1924, in a British Staff College study, the threat to Singapore had been correctly identified as coming overland from the north. In spite of this the major part of the island's defences, laid out in the 1930s, assumed a main threat from the sea; the great guns were accordingly sited to meet this. Although they could be trained to face North and had the range to reach well out across the Straits of Johore, their flat trajectories and armour-piercing ammunition rendered them virtually useless when it came to repelling amphibious landings from that quarter.

The Japanese planners knew that the American Pacific fleet had to be eliminated at the outset by means of a devastating surprise attack on its main base at Pearl Harbour in the Hawaiian islands. The Americans had foreseen such a move in a series of war games held in 1932. As war approached in 1941, Washington was able to crack Japanese coded signals giving details of the forthcoming attack, but these were not passed on to the commanders at Pearl Harbour, with dire results.

In addition to the urgency imposed on the Japanese planners by the American fuel embargo, the impending start of the north-east monsoon in the South China Sea and of the stormy season in the north Pacific (through which the Pearl Harbour attack force had to pass), dictated a starting date between December 1941 and February 1942. At this time of year the weather in Northern Manchuria (held by a Japanese garrison in case of surprise Russian attack) was so severe that military activity was unlikely. Finally, a large part of the Japanese army was tied down in China, where the Kuomintang armies were still offering resistance. There were many calls on Imperial resources.

Forces available in December 1941 for the great Southern thrust were as follows:

11 out of 51 first-line divisions
700 out of 1,500 combat aircraft (Navy and Army)
480 other land-based aircraft.

The planners accepted that in order to achieve the desired superiority of 2:1 at any given point it would be necessary to shift some formations hurriedly from one zone to another for successive operations. Many alternative options and contingencies had to be considered before the Master Plan was finally agreed in Tokyo on 20 October 1941. It was broken into three phases, each consisting of a number of simultaneous actions:

PHASE 1
Attack on Pearl Harbour. Occupation of Siam, as forward base for operations against Malaya and Burma. Destruction of American air power in the Philippines. Attacks on isolated American island garrisons in the Pacific. Invasions of Hong Kong and the Philippines. Seizure of Jolo Island in the Sulu Sea as the springboard for invasion of Dutch East Indies. Invasion of Malaya and overland drive for Singapore.

PHASE 2
Securing the Southern boundaries of the East Asia Co-Prosperity Sphere in the Bismarck archipelago. Occupation of Malaya and Singapore. Capture of strategic airfields in Tenasserim (Southern Burma), thereby cutting the air link between India and Singapore. Continuation of operations against Dutch East Indies, aimed at occupation of Java.

PHASE 3
Occupation of Java and Sumatra. Invasion of Southern Burma. Capture of Rangoon and exploitation into Upper Burma. consolidation of the perimeter by occupation of the Andaman and Nicobar Islands in the Indian Ocean.

The Imperial Staff timetable for the main phases visualised that the Philippines would be conquered in 90 days, Malaya and Singapore in 100, and the Dutch East Indies in 150. All these objectives were achieved well within their target times.

The Japanese Army

". . . it's all in the sacred name of patriotism."

IN DECEMBER 1941 the Japanese Army had reached a strength of 2.4 million men backed by over three million reservists, the fruit of a universal military service system adopted half a century earlier. Most of these troops were hardened by tough campaigns in Manchuria and China. Their officers and senior NCOs were regulars, but the majority of Japanese soldiers were conscripts or reservists recalled to the colours. In peacetime all males in the age bracket 17 to 44 were liable to some form of military service. Providing they met the minimum educational standard of six years' primary schooling and passed the medical examination, they spent two years in the army before release to the reserve. At the medical board, those given the two highest categories were earmarked for active service units, the remainder being assigned to conscript reserve battalions on completion of full-time service. A class 'A' man had to be at least five feet tall and in good physical condition. Exceptionally tall men in this group were assigned to the Imperial Guard, in which could be found men of six feet and more – rare indeed for Japanese. After 17 years and 4 months on First Reserve, men passed into the First National Army, in which they were required to serve until the age of 40. This force was liable for mobilisation for line-of-communication or home defence duties. Young men wanting to join the regular army were accepted providing they were in the top two medical categories. Only convicted criminals and the disabled were excused the call-up. Officers were provided by the military academies via the reserve army, or by commissioning selected Warrant Officers and senior NCOs, who already enjoyed many officers' privileges.

Military training for the whole nation started in schools at the age of eight, with constant political indoctrination, martial games, and massed PT. This continued through middle and high school and on to university where, on average, two hours a week were allocated under the tuition of attached regular officers. There were annual training camps, lasting up to a week. During the 1930s the time allotted to military training was steadily increased.

Conscripts reported to the nearest regional army depot in January each year for their two-year service. Basic training was rigorous and lasted for five months, with a five-day route march and bivouac in February to harden the recruits to winter conditions. June and July were given over to weapon training, range work, platoon and company exercises, bayonet practice and frequent twenty-mile forced marches in sweltering weather. In August the syllabus moved on to battalion exercises, field firing, swimming and longer marches which had to be accomplished in the same time as the twenty-milers. October and November saw Regimental exercises, more field firing, and the Autumn manoeuvres. Throughout their first year the recruits were subjected to humiliating degradations at the hands of the 'second-year' men. Even when on active service, the Japanese soldier's thoughts often returned to his days as a recruit; poems found in dead soldiers' packs during the Burma campaign reveal a wry sense of humour common to conscripts of all nations:

'Any man who joins this bloody army of his own free will is an absolute fool, but it's all in the sacred name of patriotism.'

'You do a night guard, go straight on to duties next day, and then come back to camp to find yourself a night orderly.'

'There's pay parade every ten days, but you get so little that you can't even buy a packet of fags.'

'The biggest noise of all is the Regimental Commander – he rides on an Arab horse and the guard has to line up and give him an."eyes right".'

'Next, the officers. They get a "Present Arms" when they're leaving Camp, and go back to the arms of their wives.'

'The junior NCO, a proper scrounger; the second year men all ape his style, so the poor recruit does the real work.'

Once into the second year, the conscript enjoyed the status of the 'second year man' and the right to harass the new intake of recruits. Training followed the previous year's cycle but at a higher level and with more emphasis on the morale and 'spiritual' subjects, such as the military ethics of loyalty, courtesy, courage, truthfulness, and frugality; all of these drew heavily on ancient writings and the code of the Samurai. Wherever possible, field training of second-year men took place under active service conditions, possibly in China or Korea, where the young soldiers stood a chance of real battle inoculation.

Officer training was thorough but narrowly based, arbitrary and inflexible. Individual initiative was suppressed, and this produced a predictably conditioned officer corps whose failings were soon recognised in Burma; they were manifest in a mulish tendency to repeat tactical patterns, leading to thousands of unnecessary casualties. Letters found on the bodies of Japanese officers and soldiers reveal the way in which military discipline was bound up with family loyalties, respect for ancestors, and unquestioning obedience to superior authority, whether that of the family, a village elder or a soldier's own officers. The individual was schooled to

The leader. Lt Gen Sir William Slim stands by the shield he personally designed for the 14th Army. Red and black are the colours of the British and Indian Armies. The sword points downwards, in defiance of heraldic convention, because Slim knew he would have to reconquer Burma from the north. The hilt forms the 'S', for his own name. On the handle, in Morse code, is the army's title. *(IWM)*

Moulmein was the first major town in Burma to fall to the Japanese, on
31 January 1942. Their infantry, complete with the bicycles which
invariably accompanied them, march through the deserted streets as the
defenders made their escape across the Salween estuary to Martaban.
(Robert Hunt Library)

On 9 February 1942 the Japanese landed troops west of Martaban and headed north to cut off the retreat of its garrison, which was forced to withdraw. Here, Japanese troops are seen coming ashore at a fishing village near the town, to be greeted by some of the local population.
(Robert Hunt Library)

March 1942 – Japanese soldiers mend a puncture on the way into Rangoon.
This method of transport enabled the invader, as in Malaya a few weeks
earlier, to cover surprising distances and gave him far more flexibility
than that enjoyed by the defence, tied as it was at this stage of the
campaign to motor transport and made-up roads. *(Robert Hunt Library)*

March 1942 – Barely six hours after the rapid departure of
General Alexander and his staff, leading elements of the Japanese
Army enter Rangoon, which they find deserted and undefended.
(IWM)

Volunteers from the Royal Marines formed *Force Viper* in February 1942 'for special service of a hazardous nature'. Under the command of Major Duncan Johnson they commandeered motor launches and patrolled rivers to harass advance Japanese forces and to rescue remnants of defending units wherever possible. Here at Kalewa on the Sittang river, Indian troops are being picked up after the battle of Shwegyin, *Force Viper* was the last to leave Rangoon and, after scuttling their launches, they marched across the mountains to reach Calcutta on 25 May. Of the original force of 100 men there were 58 survivors.

'. . . the collapse of two of the mighty spans signalled the end of British rule in Burma . . .' The Ava bridge was blown on 30 April 1942. Within 24 hours the Japanese were ferrying vehicles across. These were probably part of the Lend-Lease stock picked up by the Burmese Army in Rangoon at the start of the long retreat, and abandoned on the south bank of the river. *(Robert Hunt Library)*

The RAF dropped leaflets on Burmese villages in an attempt to arouse national feelings against the invaders. In the weekly newspaper *La Nat Tha* (The Spirit of the Wind) the premier of occupied Burma, Dr Ba Maw, is shown as a Japanese puppet. Such propaganda had very little effect.

Maj Gen Orde Wingate, 'an eccentric
genius and one of the most colourful
of all Second World War commanders',
is seen (*above*) talking to his men
on the Assam-Burma border.
A much later photograph (*left*),
taken in early March 1944, shows him,
with cheerful and typical disregard
for protocol, sprawling comfortably
on board a Dakota rigged for mule
transport, soon after the launch
of 'Operation Thursday'.
Three weeks later Wingate was
killed in a plane crash. His
death deprived Special Force of
much of its direction and drive.
(*IWM*)

subordinate himself to the public good, with an ultimate loyalty to the Emperor, whose status as Son of Heaven was carried over to the divinity of the whole Japanese race. Another factor which encouraged good performance in battle was the shame to a soldier's family if he failed to do his duty. Emphasis was placed on the worship of the honoured dead, especially if they fell in battle; it was customary for the cremated ashes of dead soldiers to be ceremonially returned to their families so that they could be placed on the house shrine. Any soldier who allowed himself to be captured disgraced the family name.

The organisation of the Japanese army differed considerably from the British. An army commander could be a General or Lt General, depending on the size of his command. Under each army were variable numbers of divisions. There was no intermediate, or corps, level of command. An infantry division was commanded by a Lt General. First came the infantry group, commanded by a Major General, and consisting of up to three regiments, each of three battalions and a regimental artillery unit. The standard Japanese infantry battalion comprised three rifle companies (brought up to four on mobilisation when the reservists rejoined), a machine gun company, and a battalion gun unit.

Each division included an artillery regiment, commanded by a colonel. Under him were two field gun battalions and a howitzer battalion. The division's engineer requirements were met by a regiment equipped for fieldwork construction and bridging. In Burma the Japanese sappers, though very short of mechanical plant, used local materials with great ingenuity to mend bridges and repair bomb damage.

The Japanese in Burma relied to a great extent on pack animals, but each division included three battalions of trucks, which operated on surfaced roads well to the rear of the divisional area. In their advance across the Chindwin in 1944 the Japanese left most of these vehicles behind, intending to use captured British transport when needed. There was a tendency to use captured material of all sorts, and on one occasion a battalion of the Border Regiment found themselves locked in battle with a Japanese unit almost entirely dressed in British uniforms and using captured weapons.

In barracks, the Japanese Army fed well. The staple ration consisted of 1.25 lbs of rice and some barley. A ration cash allowance was used for the purchase of extra rice, wheat, canned rice cakes, dumplings, red beans, vitamin-enriched biscuit, sugar, soya bean flour, canned meats and fish. Other items purchased in bulk by unit quartermasters out of the cash allowance were dried meat and fish, canned fruits, vegetables and fish pickled in barrels, and the pungent seasonings essential to Japanese cuisine: soy sauces and pastes, vinegar, curry powder, salt, chillies and ginger. Tea, condensed milk and rice wine (sake) also featured on the ration scale.

On exercises, Japanese troops were issued with a standard 24-hour fresh field ration weighing just over 4 lbs, consisting of rice, barley, fresh meat and fish, fresh vegetables, condiments and seasonings. This gave almost 3,500 calories per day. A higher-calorie special field ration, weighting 3 lbs, consisted of rice with canned and dried items with some pickles. This was the normal combat ration, but for mobile operations two scales of Reserve Emergency ration were issued; Class A contained 2¼ lbs of rice, canned meat and salt, giving 3,140 calories, and Class B weighing 1¾ lbs, contained rice, hard tack biscuit and canned meat. An iron ration was carried for emergency use. Each meal weighed ½ lb and comprised special biscuits and extracts. Extra nutrition rations were issued to troops engaged on particularly arduous duty, and vitamin pills were a standard issue. Units were actively encouraged to purchase foodstuffs on the civilian market and, if semi-static, to 'dig for victory' in unit gardens. These rations, on paper, gave the Japanese soldier a better-balanced diet than, for instance, those carried by the Chindits on their expeditions of 1943 and 1944. But as the campaign went on, Japanese commissariat arrangements began to break down: by the time of the great battles for Imphal they had collapsed altogether.

The weapons of the Japanese army were mostly derived from those developed in the early years of the century and used with such remarkable effect against the Russians in the war of 1904-5. The standard rifle was the bolt-operated Arisaka pattern, Model 38. Of 6.5mm (0.256″) calibre, it used lighter ammunition than the British .303″. Its sight was graduated from 100 to 2,400 metres and despite the lightweight bullet it was accurate at long range, thanks to the length of the barrel. The medium muzzle velocity of 2,400 ft/sec resulted in low recoil and little muzzle flash. An improved version of the Model 38, the Model 99, entered service in 1939, using a 7.7mm bullet with greater hitting power. Snipers were issued with the Model 97 (6.5mm) and Model 99 fitted with telescopic sight and a monoped rest. A shorter carbine-type version was issued to certain units.

The Japanese placed much reliance on rifle grenade launchers. A spigot attachment was placed over the rifle muzzle and locked into position behind the blade foresight and the grenade was fired by a cartridge in its fin. The projectile detonated 7-8 seconds after discharge. A smoke grenade could also be used. Another type of projector was used for firing the Model 99 grenade from any standard rifle. The grenade was placed in a cup after removal of the safety pin and fired by a round of standard ball ammunition to a range of about 100 yards.

Light machine guns were used in large numbers, the basic model being the 'Nambu' of 1922. Firing a 6.5mm round, it was based on the French Hotchkiss. The Model 96 of 1936 was derived from the Bren Gun used in the British Army, and the similar Model 99 fired 7.7mm ammunition. A heavy machine gun, the Model 92, was also derived from the Hotchkiss and fired 7.7mm ammunition. The variety of calibre in Japanese infantry weapons created supply difficulties in battle, overcome in part by using captured British ammunition and weapons whenever possible.

Apart from rifle grenade launchers, light mortars were used for projecting grenades and flares. The model 97 81mm mortar, with a range of up to 3,000 yards, was widely deployed in the jungle. Hand grenades were a primary infantry weapon, and many successful assaults were led by soldiers armed solely with satchels of the Model 97 grenade of 1937. Weighing just over a pound, it was activated by first removing the pin, then striking the head of the fuze sharply on a hard surface and throwing it immediately, for it was prone to erratic fuze burn.

For heavier close-range support the Japanese placed great reliance on infantry guns, of which there were several patterns. The Model 94 of 1934 could fire high explosive and armour piercing ammunition. Despite its small calibre of 37mm its muzzle velocity of 2,300 ft/sec gave it a maximum range of well over 5,000 yards.

The model 94 weighed 714 lbs but the 70mm Model 92, a mini-howitzer, weighed only 468 lbs. Used as an assault gun, it could be manhandled almost anywhere, as in the Arakan. Used at ranges from 110 to 3,000 yards its powerful shell had a 40-yard danger area of burst.

Pack artillery was widely used. The Model 41 of 1904 was a tried and trusted weapon; carried when dismantled in 299 lb loads, it was remarkably consistent; at 3,200 yards 75% of its rounds fell within a rectangle 20 by 30 yards, and at its maximum range of 7,800 yards the pattern measured 100 by 200 yards. By 1941 it was being superseded by the Model 94 pack gun which broke down into eleven units, or six pack horse loads, the heaviest of which weighed 210 lbs. Maximum range for the 75mm shell was over 8,000 yards.

The standard Japanese tank used in Burma was the model 97 of 1937. Modelled on an obsolete Vickers design, as were the various 'tankettes' used from time to time, it was barely capable of taking on the light 'Honey' tanks of the British 7th Armoured Brigade during the fighting of 1942 and no match at all for the Lee-Grants and Shermans with their 75mm guns, which appeared in 1943. The only occasions on which the Japanese met with success in a tank-versus-tank fight was when they happened to be using captured British equipment.

The Japanese soldier's equipment had been carefully thought out to meet the requirements of an infantry largely reliant on pack transport. Wherever possible everything was lightweight and capable of being carried by men or mules. All infantry support weapons in the battalion were designed for pack transport and each rifle company had a two-wheeled horse-drawn cart which could carry up to 400 lbs.

Combat uniform was loose-fitting. Under his outer garments the Japanese soldier wore a breech-clout, and many men had a Senninbari, or 'thousand stitch good fortune belt' usually made by a member of the family.

This was believed to endow the wearer with good luck, courage, even immunity from enemy fire. A loose tunic and breeches worn with puttees, and a soft peaked field cap bearing a red star badge, completed the simple uniform. Footwear could either be the standard issue leather marching boot or the two-toed 'tabi', favoured in the jungle. In his pack the infantryman carried spare shoes, a bivouac tent, extra socks, towel, soap, sewing kit, field dressing, spare breech-clout, and rations for several days. A blanket or greatcoat was rolled on top of the pack. Various bags and sacks were added to the soldier's equipment for the carriage of ammunition, grenades, and special gear. An entrenching tool was carried on a loop of rope, and the soldier was issued with a serviceable water bottle, an ineffective water sterilising kit, and a set of mess tins which slotted into each other.

For its air suport the Japanese army relied on two separate air forces; usually it was the army air force which gave this support, but in many operations, especially near coastlines, the navy air force appeared overhead. Both air forces were essentially for strike purposes, organised for a short and decisive war. Consequently, as the Burma campaign wore on, the army's air support began to suffer from lack of maintenance, shortage of spares, and the cumulative effects of well-directed Allied airstrikes. The quality of Japanese combat aircraft came as an unpleasant surprise to their opponents in the first months of the war and it was not until 1943 that the RAF was equipped with aircraft which outfought and outperformed those of the enemy.

The Japanese army's appalling record in its treatment of prisoners had political as well as historical foundations. The Hague Convention of 1907, ratified by a Japanese government eager to show that it was ready to adopt Western codes of conduct, stipulated that prisoners of war were to be humanely treated, and that non-commissioned personnel could be ordered to work providing such work was not excessively arduous or connected with the war effort. As far as food, accommodation and clothing were concerned, prisoners were to be treated on the same basis as their captors, and they should be subject to the appropriate military orders and regulations of the captor army.

Japan did not sign the 1929 Geneva Convention which amplified the Hague Convention, but issued a vague declaration in 1942 saying that issues of food, clothing and accommodation '. . . would take national and racial customs into account'. In fact, prisoners taken in Malaya and Singapore had to sign an illegal 'no-escape' undertaking, after which they were starved, deprived of proper medical attention, crowded into insanitary camps, and given unnatural and brutal punishments. Furthermore, they were widely used as slave labour on military projects such as the Burma-Siam railway.

The International Red Cross was not recognised by the Japanese in South-East Asia. In fact, they executed the Red Cross delegate in Borneo in

1943, together with his wife. No outside assistance whatever was granted to Allied prisoners held in Burma. Indian prisoners, considered to be members of the Greater East Asia Co-Prosperity Sphere, were taken away from their British officers and ill-treated unless they joined the renegade Indian National Army. Neither in Malaya nor Burma did a single Gurkha yield to these methods of persuasion.

The root of Japan's abominable treatment of all prisoners lay in the remorseless brainwashing to which its people had been subjected for many years. Capture was dishonourable, not only for the captive but also his family. Death in combat, or failing that, suicide, was the only acceptable way to leave the battlefield. Allied prisoners of the Japanese soon realised what this meant for them.

Japan Invades

". . . an air of subdued urgency bordering on panic."

A ROUND THE southern fringe of the Far Eastern theatre the Allies could field some 300,000 troops and 900 aircraft. The quality of both was variable and there were problems of shared command, language and communications. Even so, the resources available to Tojo and his planners were barely adequate for their enormous task. Of Japan's 51 infantry divisions, 25 were fully committed in China, 13 in Manchuria, two in Korea and two in Indo-China (in case the Vichy French government there decided to invite the Japanese to leave).

One of the divisions in China was given the task of seizing Hong Kong, which fell on Christmas Day 1941, after less than three weeks' fighting. Four of 25th Army's divisions were ordered to invade Malaya and take the Singapore base; the job was done by three of them. The 15th Army's two divisions were assigned to Southern Burma: reinforcements were to follow through Rangoon and capture the rest of Burma.

By occupying the British airfield at Victoria Point at the southern tip of Tenasserim on 16 December, the Japanese severed a key strategic artery of the British Far Eastern empire. There was then a lull of over a month while they shifted troops between theatres and prepared to invade Burma from across the Siamese frontier. The formations assigned to this were the 33rd and 55th divisions of Lt General Iida's 15th Army. The 55th, concentrating around Raheng opposite Moulmein, was retrained to operate with pack animals. The 15th Army's 12 battalions used only 600 motor vehicles and less than 1,000 pack horses for their logistic 'tail'. Within days of the declaration of war, Lt General McLeod, commanding Burma Army, was told that reinforcements were on their way. At one point he was half expecting not only the British 18 Division, then rounding the Cape on its way to the Middle East, but also the battle-tried Australian 7th Division, homeward bound after sterling service in the Western Desert. In the event, the immediate reinforcement of Burma came from whatever could be scraped together from India and the Middle East; three 'unallotted' British battalions and some raw Indian Army formations. They were to be followed, if Rangoon could hold out, by an armoured brigade from Egypt.

With the enemy at the gate, Headquarters Burma Army was toiling under a bizarre chain of command. In 1940 operational control in Burma had been by Far East Command in Singapore, but administration nominally remained in the hands of the War Office in London. In practice, it was done by the Burma government, with results already seen as the Glosters attempted to prepare for war. On the outbreak of hostilities with Japan in December 1941, operational and administrative control both passed to GHQ India in Delhi. After four weeks, operational control shifted once more, this time to South-West Pacific Command, a short-lived organisation, and reverted to GHQ India a month later.

Lt General McLeod, commanding in Burma, was faced with running a defensive campaign against a powerful enemy whose point of entry into Burma would be so close to Rangoon that the city, his main base, would be under immediate threat. Hitherto, all priorities had gone to the defence of Malaya and Singapore, and Burma was seen merely as providing useful transit airfields on the air route from India. Now, with Malaya doomed, McLeod saw one of his promised reinforcements, the British 18th Infantry Division, diverted to Singapore, where it landed just in time to march into captivity. The Australians, worried by the Japanese advance to the north, claimed their 7th Division back. There were no stockpiles in Burma, and McLeod's administrative staff officers had to improvise depots for use if, as now seemed likely, the army was forced off its Rangoon base and up the Irrawaddy and Sittang valleys. That this was achieved despite collapsed civilian morale, the flight of most of the labour force, and continual air raids, reflects great credit on all concerned. Movement of stores up-country was accomplished mainly by rail and river transport. Many of the civilian staff had fled from the rail depots, but Anglo-Burmese enginemen and signalmen stayed bravely at their posts, as did most of the senior railway officials. Trains packed with refugees were soon travelling north towards Mandalay, and river boats bore their cargoes of military stores, some of which were destined for delivery to the Chinese at Bhamo, up to 1,000 miles upstream. Hospital ships and trains were hastily improvised, to be staffed by volunteers from all walks of life.

General Sir Archibald Wavell, as Far Eastern C-in-C, visited Burma Army HQ in Rangoon on 21 December 1941 and saw that all was not well. He inspected the Glosters, noting that they were down to an effective fighting strength of two companies and under-equipped for jungle warfare, as were the 2nd KOYLI. He later described the administrative system as 'so inadequate that it might be termed non-existent'. He could hardly blame McLeod, who was trying to meet a disaster situation with an army headquarters little larger than that of a division. The reinforcements promised by London and Delhi had simply failed to appear. McLeod was replaced within a week of Wavell's visit and succeeded by Lt General T. J. Hutton, MC, Wavell's Chief of Staff in India, who brought with him a hastily assembled party of staff officers for the Rangoon headquarters and his own personal reputation as a logistician, although he had never commanded a major formation in battle. He immediately speeded up the establishment of dumps in Central and Upper Burma, seeing a fighting retreat up the centre of the country as the only way of saving his army when the Japanese arrived in strength. Hutton's foresight – the hallmark of good military administration – enabled his successor to withdraw the remnants of Burma Army into India six months later.

While the Japanese prepared for invasion, frantic efforts were being made to get the defences into shape. When part of 17 Indian Division arrived at Rangoon early in January 1942 it immediately began to deploy to meet the threat, while its commander, Maj General 'Jackie' Smyth initially set up his HQ at Moulmein. Two of his brigades had been sent off to Malaya, where they were overwhelmed and captured, and at this time the division consisted only of its HQ and 16th Indian Infantry Brigade. Smyth entertained no illusions as to the gravity of the situation. A tough Indian Army soldier who had won a spectacular VC in France early in World War I, he had already commanded a British infantry brigade in the retreat to Dunkirk before returning to India to raise and command the 19th Division at Secunderabad. From there he was summoned at very short notice to command 17 Division, which he joined on its final exercises prior to sailing for its original destination, the Middle East. It was also the day on which Pearl Harbour was attacked, and 17 Division, less the brigades diverted to Singapore, was ordered to Burma instead.

After one sobering look at his new command, Smyth asked for more time for training, as his shrunken division – trained and equipped for mobile desert warfare – must now be re-trained for jungle operations. The Japanese onslaught, however, made immediate demands on any troops available in India. When Smyth sat down to be briefed by Wavell at HQ Delhi on 28 December, 17 Indian Division still consisted of no more than its HQ and one brigade, untrained for jungle operations and equipped for mechanised warfare.

The saga of 16th Infantry Brigade in 17 Indian Division typifies the lack of readiness for war which characterised the whole of Far East Command at that time. None of the battalions had been with the Brigade for more than six weeks, and no higher training of any sort had been attempted in any of them in the past year. Three months before arriving in Burma one battalion had been in Waziristan on the North-West Frontier, another digging useless coastal defences elsewhere in India. There had been almost no individual training for months. There was no headquarters signals section when the brigade left India; it joined during the journey. All three battalions had been 'milked' of their experienced men. Drafts of raw recruits, some with less than three months' service since leaving their villages and many unable to understand Urdu, the Indian Army's lingua franca, were joining right up to the time of embarkation for Rangoon; one such draft joined three days, another an incredible *three hours*, before the ship sailed. Only a few of the older soldiers had ever seen, let alone thrown, a hand grenade, or handled a light machine gun; less than half of the brigade's officers had ever fired a pistol course. Nobody had any jungle experience or training. These troops were expected by Wavell to meet and throw back crack Japanese formations already hardened by years of service and elated with victory in Malaya and Singapore. It is not surprising to find that after a recent inspection the Director of Army Training in India considered that 17 Division was . . . 'not fit to take the field against a first class enemy'.

Smyth felt that Wavell had grossly under-estimated the Japanese Army and particularly the martial qualities of its soldiers, against whom his unseasoned Indian units were about to be pitched. Years later, he was to recall that interview. Wavell . . . 'never lost his complete contempt for the Japanese soldier, an opinion which was certainly not shared by General Slim and other commanders who had to meet him in the field'.

On the arrival of 16th Brigade in Burma, 17 Division was reorganised. It now consisted of 2nd Burma and 16th Indian Brigades. These were shortly joined by the 46th and 48th Indian Infantry Brigades. The sole British unit in the division was the 2nd Battalion, KOYLI. The Burma brigade was of doubtful value – three battalions of Burma Rifles and one Indian battalion to stiffen them. The division was given a vast area to defend, from the Southern end of Tenasserim to the frontier with Siam opposite the Three Pagodas Pass – some 800 miles of frontage.

On 23 December came the first of many air raids on Rangoon, which was defended by a handful of anti-aircraft guns, one squadron of RAF equipped with American-built Brewster Buffalo fighters, and the American Volunteer Group or AVG. This extraordinary unit of mercenary volunteer pilots was commanded by a former US Army Air Corps officer, Brigadier General Claire Chennault. It had only been made available for the defence of Rangoon by Generalissimo Chiang Kai-shek because virtually all American Lease-Lend supplies destined for Nationalist China had to pass through the port, then up the Burma Road and into China. The AVG was equipped with Curtiss P-40s, much better aircraft than the cumbersome Buffalos. The RAF and AVG squadrons were greatly assisted by an effective, radar-based early warning system, enabling them to get airborne in good time to meet the Japanese bomber formations and punish them severely. Before the Allies were driven from the sky, they had shot down over 200 Japanese aircraft. The first air raid on Rangoon, however, caused much damage and killed 1,500 civilians. Panic spread like wildfire. The dock and public service labour forces evaporated and the large Indian community began to take to the roads, little realising the horrors lying in wait for them as they tried to regain Indian soil.

By the middle of January 1942 the Japanese were ready to move in Tenasserim. The airfields at Tavoy and Mergui were given up without a fight. Smyth wished to fall back immediately to the line of the Sittang river in order to protect Rangoon but General Hutton, under orders from Wavell to hold off the invader as long as possible while reinforcements arrived at Rangoon, insisted that 17 Division defend Moulmein, then fall back only as far as the Salween River. The defence of Moulmein lasted barely 24 hours, and only a surprising lack of activity by the Japanese air force prevented a disaster as the garrison evacuated the port by sea, in broad daylight, on 31 January. With the enemy in close pursuit, 17 Division took up a defensive position on the line of the Salween with an extended frontage of almost 100 miles. Here the 2nd KOYLI became the first British troops to go into action in Burma: not an auspicious occasion as they lost all their 108 mules in the ensuing confusion. The Japanese began to cross the river at many points on 13 February, and the withdrawal was resumed on the following day. By this time Smyth had managed to concentrate most of the division in front of the next water obstacle, the Bilin River, where a resolute stand was made in which the 2nd KOYLI distinguished themselves. The fighting was at close quarters and their 'A' Company was left only a dozen men strong.

After several days of ferocious fighting Smyth had to order a further retreat on 20 February, to a concentration area some 15 miles short of the Sittang Bridge. Unfortunately, a radio message passed to one of his brigades in clear was intercepted by the Japanese, who drew the obvious conclusion that the defenders were about to break contact and dash for the Sittang. They sent columns round the landward flank and a race for the bridge began.

The depleted KOYLI battalion was joined at this point by the newly-arrived 2nd Battalion, Duke of Wellington's Regiment. The two Yorkshire units were old rivals and the 'Dukes' laughed to see the light Infantrymen hard at work, digging slit trenches with their bayonets, there being no proper tools available. After a heavy air attack which inflicted casualties on the 'Dukes', they got the message and dug in with whatever tools they could find. Hard experience was already bringing its lessons home.

The Japanese 33rd Division had a clear mission – to 'bounce' the Sittang position, capture the bridge intact, and mop up any elements of 17 Division left on the wrong side. On 21 February, the defenders, hampered by masses of useless vehicles, were jamming the road leading towards the bridge and under heavy air attack from both sides. Not only were Japanese fighter-bombers continually strafing the packed columns of transport, but the RAF and AVG had been told by HQ Burma Army to treat any movement on the far side of the bridge as hostile, and did so.

Early on 22 February the first elements of 17 Division – its HQ and one brigade – began to cross the bridge. This carried a single railway track but had been planked to permit the passage of motor transport. An inexperienced driver lost his nerve and went off the trackway, blocking the bridge for over two hours, and chaos was never far away. Panic broke out at 0830 hrs when the leading Japanese units burst out of the jungle and launched an attack on the bridge garrison, which was provided by 48th Brigade. By nightfall only a small part of 17 Division was safely across and the improvised ferry had been put out of action. Smyth, however, appears to have thought that most of his division was safely across.

Throughout the night a fierce battle raged as the Japanese tried to force their way onto the bridge, but early on the morning of 23 February, following a confused telephone conversation between 48th Brigade and Divisional HQ, Smyth authorised Brigadier Hugh-Jones to blow at his discretion. Hugh-Jones gave the order at 0530 hrs; as the echoes of the explosion died away an unnatural quietness descended on the battlefield. Most of 17 Division was still on the far bank and in the next few hours, as the Japanese closed for the kill, groups of British, Indian, Gurkha and Burmese soldiers made their way to the river bank in efforts to escape. Amongst these were the KOYLI, or what remained of them. In the words of their regimental history '. . . as dawn broke on 23 February 1942 morale in the battalion was not high. Panic was very near.' The commanding officer, Lt Colonel Keegan, set a fine example of calmness, encouraging the survivors to cross by swimming or rafting, as all the country boats had been destroyed by 17 Division's engineers and the powered ferries sunk by Japanese bombing. The regimental history record continues:

> The river presented an extraordinary spectacle. An air of subdued urgency bordering on panic hung over everything. Hundreds of British, Indian and Gurkha troops were constructing rafts from anything which might conceivably float . . . low-flying Jap aircraft cruised up and down the river machine-gunning swimmers.

Fires blazed and ammunition exploded. Colonel Keegan was wounded and by 1700 hrs only two companies of the KOYLI, with some Burifs, were still at their defence positions in the rapidly shrinking bridgehead. After dark, the wounded were rafted over; it took three hours in the strong currents and tides of the Sittang. Amongst the last to cross were Keegan and the CO of a Gurkha battalion. Large quantities of weapons and equipment, including virtually all the transport of two brigades and the divisional artillery, were abandoned.

From this disaster only 149 officers and 3,350 men of 17 Division were saved; with them came 1,420 rifles. Most of the troops had discarded their equipment and the majority had thrown away their boots in order to swim the 500-yard river. The shattered 17 Division was taken out of the line for refitting. Smyth was relieved of his command, reverting to the substantive rank of Brigadier. It was his misfortune to be on the spot when very little could have been done to avert a ruinous defeat. He had taken to the field when medically unfit to be there; he was under treatment for an anal fistula, a debilitating and acutely uncomfortable condition requiring drastic medication. In great pain, dog-tired, and faced with implementing a tactical policy with which he profoundly disagreed, Smyth had done his best.

There was now a further change in the Far East command structure, for as the result of an Anglo-American summit conference in Washington in January 1942, an Allied Joint HQ had been set up in the Dutch East Indies. Known as ABDACom (American-British-Dutch-Australian Command), its operational area was vast, stretching from Burma to Australia. Between these lay the entire area now threatened by the Japanese strategic offensive. The Americans insisted that Wavell be appointed to head this almost toothless organisation. He set up his HQ in Java, where he was seriously out of touch with events as they developed in Burma, which he visited only twice before the fall of Rangoon. Hutton, the new Burma Army commander, was clearly in awe of his former chief and accepted Wavell's views on the basic inferiority of the Japanese fighting man. These were passed on to Smyth despite the latter's efforts to convince his superiors that Burma was about to be conquered by a first-class enemy. Wavell's persistence in his beliefs exercised an adverse effect on British military fortunes in Burma for months to come.

The Loss of Burma

". . . it is as humiliating as hell."

A S THE Sittang disaster moved to its climax, further reinforcements were arriving at Rangoon in the shape of Brigadier J. H. Anstice's 7th Armoured Brigade, consisting of a brigade headquarters, the 7th Hussars and the 2nd Royal Tanks. Its infantry element was provided in turn over the next three months by British battalions which had arrived in Rangoon from India; these were the 1st West Yorkshires, the 2nd Duke of Wellington's (who had already sustained heavy casualties on the far side of the Sittang), and the 1st Cameronians. After the fall of Rangoon, the 1st Royal Inniskilling Fusiliers were flown into Burma as the last British or Indian reinforcements for Burma Army. The 7th Armoured Brigade's artillery comprised a battery apiece of field and anti-tank guns. Its logistic support consisted of 65 Company, Royal Army Service Corps, whose soldiers quickly displayed that versatility in the fields of supply and transport for which their corps was renowned. This brigade's arrival was providential, as it had been fighting hard for many months in North Africa and was battle-hardened, albeit under very different conditions from those it now had to face.

All the armoured brigade's equipment and vehicles had to be unloaded at Rangoon docks by soldiers, as the civilian dock labour force had fled. While four of 65 Company's sergeants operated cranes, its drivers unloaded 1,500 vehicles in the next few days. Around them, civil disorder was widespread. Looting and arson were rife, and the situation was made worse by the release onto the streets of the inmates of the jails and lunatic asylums, who roamed wildly around the near-deserted city, further demoralising those citizens who remained. A bizarre note was struck by the freeing of animals from Rangoon's zoo; the Glosters' padre, pausing for a rest on what he took to be log, found that he was sitting on a sleeping crocodile.

Amidst these alarming scenes 7th Armoured Brigade prepared for battle. Their tanks were American-built General Stuarts, known as 'Honeys', armed with a 37mm cannon and a machine gun. The 37mm gun was similar in calibre to the 2-pounder used in the British Army but had a higher muzzle velocity and thus greater killing power against enemy tanks. However, there was no 37mm high explosive ammunition in Burma, and solid shot had to be used exclusively for the rest of the campaign.

Hutton was now under criticism in London and Delhi for his conduct of operations. Lord Linlithgow, Viceroy of India (who had ventured nowhere near the front in Burma) cabled Whitehall expressing his view that the reverses of the past few weeks were due to poor leadership. He also spoke to Wavell when the C-in-C flew to Delhi from Java on 28 February. Wavell flew at once to Magwe where he publicly berated Hutton on alighting from his aircraft. He then picked up the luckless Smyth and took him back to India, icily ignoring him en route and walking away without a word on arrival back at Calcutta.

Rangoon's fall was now inevitable, and the only hope of averting total disaster was to retreat up the valleys of the Sittang and Irrawaddy to Upper Burma, then across the hills to Assam or China if the Japanese could not be halted. Preparations for the demolition of key installations in the Rangoon area had been under way for some time. At this point Lt General the Hon Sir Harold Alexander took over as Army Commander, but Hutton remained as Chief of Staff.

Alexander had distinguished himself during the retreat to Dunkirk, where his calmness amidst chaos and defeat had greatly impressed Churchill, who nominated him for the Burma command. The Prime Minister invited him to dinner at 10 Downing Street on the eve of his departure for the hazardous flight to Rangoon, recalling the occasion in his memoirs:

> Never have I taken the responsibility for sending a general on a more forlorn hope. Alexander was, as usual, calm and good-humoured. He said he was delighted to go . . . Nothing ever disturbed or rattled him, and duty was a full satisfaction in itself, especially if it seemed perilous and hard . . . the pleasures and honour of his friendship were prized by all those who enjoyed it, among whom I could count myself. For this reason alone I must admit that at our dinner I found it difficult to emulate his composure . . .

The new commander arrived in Rangoon as the demolitions were getting under way, taking command on 5 March. His orders were to hold onto the city, and at first he was confident that he could do so, countermanding Hutton's orders for evacuation. Within 48 hours he had changed his mind, ordering a withdrawal north towards Prome on 7 March. Until the last minute British troops, including the Glosters, had been running essential services, slaughtering cattle, baking bread, repairing bomb damage on airfields, shooting looters and driving trains, whilst 7th Armoured Brigade ran the docks. Now, the last ships had left for India with their loads of sick, wounded and refugees. Before leaving Rangoon, the Glosters paid a visit to the Burma Army ordnance depot where, in what must have been the fulfilment of a quartermaster's dream, they systematically pillaged it to re-equip the battalion with uniforms, weapons, and ammunition. They also appropriated a number of American scout cars destined for Chiang Kai-shek under Lease-Lend, before destroying anything that could not be moved.

The last British troops pulled out of Rangoon in sombre mood, realising that having lost their base they now faced almost certain military disaster. The only way out was via Upper Burma and over the almost trackless hills to Imphal, which had to be reached before the onset of the monsoon in May, when all routes off surfaced roads would become impassable. Alexander's headquarters staff left the city to the sound of exploding demolition charges, to find that the Japanese had already flung a road-block across their route to the north at Taukkyan on the Prome road. Despite fierce attacks by 7th Armoured Brigade, the enemy could not be dislodged and at one point it seemed that the bulk of Burma Army and its commander were about to be captured. Suddenly the road was clear. The Japanese commander at Taukkyan had been told to keep the block in position until the main force for the capture of Rangoon, which had been ordered to carry out a wide sweep to the north and then attack from the west, had passed through. Having fulfilled his orders to the letter he followed on, leaving the scene just when he could have taken Alexander. This was characteristic of the rigid Japanese tactic that contributed significantly to their final downfall.

A new problem facing the retreating army was widespread activity by the newly-formed Burmese Independence Army, or BIA, in support of the Japanese. Some years before the war a number of Burmese student leaders, all known to be strongly anti-British, had been approached by Japanese military intelligence agents. Prominent amongst them was Aung San; 25 years old in 1942, he came from a prosperous family and had been educated at Rangoon university where he was president of the radical students' union, after which he formed the Thakin ('Masters') Party, ultra-nationalistic, communist and idealist. In 1939 it was forced underground and its leaders arrested. Aung San and some of his colleagues escaped in 1941 and were on their way to China when Japanese agents picked them up and took them to Tokyo for special training. Returning secretly to Burma Aung San was ready to take the field in support of his Japanese allies when they arrived in 1942.

As intelligence gatherers and interpreters the BIA were useful to the Japanese but proved a liability on the battlefield, having been assured of their invulnerability to bullets. In July 1942 they were disbanded by the Japanese who then allowed Aung San to form the Burma National Army, or BNA, a more conventional force of some nine battalions which was used for internal security duties in occupied Burma.

Alexander's arrival was followed by a reorganisation of British forces in Burma. The 1 Burma and 17 Indian Divisions were formed into Burma Corps or Burcorps, commanded by Lt General W. J. Slim, DSO, MC, who established his headquarters at Prome, 180 miles up river from Rangoon, and took stock of the situation. A few weeks earlier he had been commanding 10 Indian Division in Persia, from where he was ordered to Burma.

While Alexander, as Army Commander, gave general directives on the conduct of the campaign and dealt with the problems of collaborating with what was left of the civil government and the Chinese-American forces in the north, Slim was free to concentrate on fighting the battle. The first priority was to weld his two divisions into a credible fighting force. He found 17 Division, still more or less in shock, recovering from its defeat at the Sittang bridge and 1 Burma Division, mainly composed of shaky Burif units stiffened with a handful of Indian and British battalions, was as yet unproven with no traditions to live up to. By happy chance, however, the two divisional commanders, Maj Generals 'Punch' Cowan of 17 Indian and Bruce Scott of 1 Burma, had served with Slim in the 1/6th Gurkha Rifles. He knew them both very well. In his own words,

> . . . we had served and lived together for twenty-odd years; we – and our wives – were the closest friends; our children had been brought up together in the happiest of regiments. I could not have found two men in whom I had more confidence or with whom I would rather have served.

His trust was reciprocated; Slim later found that his appointment to Burma Corps owed much to the backstairs lobbying of his divisional commanders. Cowan, as Smyth's successor at 17 Division, found it ironic that he, who a few months before, as Brigadier General Staff (Training) at GHQ India, had declared the division unfit for war, should now be its commander as it prepared to rejoin the battle.

The divisional and corps staffs, hurriedly assembled, began to shake down. In HQ 1 Burma Division the principal administrative staff officer was Lt Colonel Amies, who had joined HQ Burma Army a year earlier on a routine peacetime posting, complete with family. In July 1941 a paper exercise was held which gave a gloomy forecast of what to expect if the Japanese invaded Burma. Reality proved infinitely worse. On arrival at HQ Burma Division Amies found that it was one in name only:

> Signals, Ordnance, Workshop, Provost – to quote a few – barely existed. Vehicles and equipment for operations were hopelessly inadequate. Communication with brigades was by civil post and telegraph. Telephones were rare, primitive and inefficient . . .

Officers' wives were pressed into service as cipher sergeants in the headquarters, recruited into the Womens' Auxiliary Service (Burma), or 'Wasbies', an organisation which turned itself to a variety of duties, providing transport drivers, nurses and canteen workers. 'Wasbies' had para-military status and were subject to military law. They were supplied with all the items of camp kit issued to army officers, but were required to provide their own uniform. They gave valuable service throughout the remainder of the war.

Slim's first step was to concentrate his two divisions, at that time dangerously dispersed. He was enabled to do this by the arrival of Chinese troops from the north. Marching down the Salween valley, they took position on Burcorps' left flank. Although designated the 5th Army, these Chinese were a mixed bag. One of their divisional commanders, Maj General Sun Li Jen (known as 'Sun'), would have done credit to any army. A graduate of the Virginian Military Academy, he spoke perfect English, was eager to cooperate and professionally competent. Other Chinese generals were less useful. Few spoke English and their staffs, if they could be described as such had no training. Their units had virtually no transport or administrative 'tail' and relied on living off the land for their food. Chinese commanders' promises of action had to be viewed with suspicion, for they seldom appeared at the appointed place at the right time. Some even insisted on being bribed with US dollars before committing their formations to an attack. Their soldiers, however, were tough and experienced at fighting the Japanese. A Chinese Army was equivalent in numbers to a British division and a Chinese division to a British brigade. Furthermore, only two-thirds of the men actually carried rifles; the rest constituted a portering force which humped the division's support weapons and reserves of ammunition.

At once, Slim initiated small-scale offensive actions against the Japanese, now consolidating in the lower Irrawaddy and Sittang valleys as their reinforcements began to pass through the reopened port of Rangoon. The Glosters, with their exotic collection of looted guns and scout cars, excelled in the role of divisional reconnaissance regiment. One of their early successes took place on 19 March at Letpadan, where the local Burmese were in the act of holding a full-blown parade and civic welcome for the victorious Japanese. The Glosters interrupted the festivities at their height, inflicting heavy casualties before disengaging. It was the first serious reverse inflicted on the invader and did much to restore morale in 17 Division.

There was now very little air suport for the defenders. When the RAF and American Volunteer Group were driven out of Rangoon they moved to Magwe, but they had now lost their solitary early-warning radar, so valuable in the earlier stages, and also the services of the Burma Observer Corps, which had passed warnings of incoming Japanese bombing attacks via the civil telephone system. Very soon a heavy Japanese air raid on Magwe airfield caught the defenders on the ground, and most of the surviving RAF fighters, together with many of the AVG's precious P-40s, were lost. the AVG was withdrawn to China on Chiang's orders, and the few remaining RAF fighter aircraft were redeployed to safe airfields in India. From now on, the Japanese had command of the air. Despite this, the RAF continued to use its few transport aircraft to fly supplies in and evacuate wounded and sick, as well as many civilians. A handful of dedicated pilots of the Indian Air Force flying Westland Lysander Army Co-operation aircraft, gave what support they could to the beleaguered troops on the ground.

Apart from the activities of the Burma Independence Army, Burcorps now had trouble with bands of pro-Japanese Burmese guerillas and dacoits, who picked off stragglers, putting them to death in the most barbarous fashion. It quickly became standard practice never to leave sick and wounded in the care of the local population. There were many cases of atrocity and treachery. A patrol of the 7th Hussars was greeted in a village by civilians bearing food, then hacked to death. A river launch of 'Viper Force', manned by Royal Marines and operating on the Irrawaddy, was welcomed at a riverside village and the crew feted at an evening feast. During the night the Japanese, summoned by the village headman, surrounded the huts in which the marines were sleeping. After a short fight the survivors were used as live targets for bayonet practice, watched by appreciative villagers. Not all Burmese behaved in this way, and in fact it is doubtful if more than five per cent of the whole population were politically motivated enough to play an active role in the pro-Japanese movement. Most of the hill tribes, traditional enemies of the Burmese, remained loyal to the Crown, providing recruits for the special and irregular forces which were to give the Japanese so much trouble later on, and as intelligence gatherers in the hills.

It is hardly surprising that in an army which was steadily retreating, any signs of civilian sabotage were dealt with summarily. Colonel Amies recorded one such incident.

> At one of our night halts the Defence Platoon (from the Cameronians) brought before the General a Burmese villager and young lad they had caught with bits of telephone wire and whom they suspected of spying for the enemy. The General heard such evidence as there was, gave a nod, the Scots riflemen grinned, and shortly after, I heard shots from a field over the hedge . . .

To the rear of the retreating army lay Mandalay, a key rail, road and river junction. It was bombed on 3 April with heavy civilian casualties and much damage. This was the final straw as far as civilian morale was concerned. Law and order collapsed and the army had to run the city's essential services. The Japanese advanced steadily up the Irrawaddy despite the spirited resistance of 'Viper' Force, and the Yenangyaung oilfields, of major strategic value, were now threatened. Preparations for their demolition were made by the devoted senior officials of the Burmah Oil Company, who had kept them going to provide Burma Army with fuel. As dense clouds of smoke began to rise over the oilfields, the Japanese mounted a determined flanking attack with the aim of surrounding 1st Burma Division, which only narrowly escaped, losing much of its equipment and transport in the process.

The Royal Inniskilling Fusiliers were in the thick of the fighting at Yenanyaung. Their commanding officer was killed, and disaster overtook 'D' Company when it mistook a large body of Japanese for the Chinese unit with whom they were trying to make contact. The Company fought desperately when the mistake was realised, but it was too late; they were all killed or captured, only a handful managing to escape later and return to the battalion. An American press correspondent with the Inniskillings had never seen the British Army in action and was impressed by the demeanour of this unit in the face of disaster:

> An Inniskilling Major, with two other officers and myself, walked forward to inspect the outposts. We passed groups of men resting beside the road, from which a voice quietly said, '"A" Company, Sir . . . "B" Company, Sir' . . . we stopped beside an oil derrick, where the Major struck a match; for a fleeting moment it flickered over the bodies of two Inniskilling officers. 'These men must be buried, according to regimental custom, tonight . . .' Within 24 hours the major, too, was dead.

Far to the north-east, a Japanese column routed a Chinese division and entered Lashio, cutting the Burma Road. The end was near for Burcorps, and Slim knew that he had to extricate his troops with as much of their equipment as possible, back across the Chindwin River and over the hills to Assam. The battered Chinese prepared to retreat into Yunnan, but such was the vigour of the Japanese offensive that two Chinese divisions, led by the indomitable Lt General Stilwell, had marched into India. Burcorps fought a fierce rearguard action at Kyaukse, south of Mandalay, in order to buy time for 7th Armoured Brigade to get its tanks back across the Irrawaddy over the great Ava bridge, reputedly the largest in Asia and a standing tribute to the prowess of its British builders. This, too, was blown early on 30 April and the collapse of two of the mighty spans signalled the end of British rule in Burma.

With the Ava bridge down and Burcorps across the Irrawaddy, there was a grim race to the banks of the Chindwin, the last river barrier to be crossed on the march to safety. For once, the Japanese were outmarched. There were no bridges over the Chindwin, and the ferries were hopelessly inadequate for the tanks, guns and heavy equipment of Burcorps. These were now destroyed by their devoted crews, who formed up as infantry on the west bank and steeled themselves for the long march ahead. Colonel Amies watched the melancholy scene at Shwegyin:

> Hereabouts army, corps, fighting troops and services of both divisions were discarding and destroying vehicles, weapons, equipment and baggage which either could not be ferried across the river nor transported from the opposite bank up the dirt road under construction through the mountains to Assam. Abandoned cars, trucks, and impedimenta of thousands of refugees, European and Asiatic, Eurasian and Anglo-Burman, were mingled amongst the heaps of junk . . .

A single 'Honey' tank bearing the name 'Curse of Scotland' was actually ferried across further upstream, to be taken on strength by an Indian cavalry regiment, with which it served for the rest of the campaign. It is pleasing to record that it was driven triumphantly back into Rangoon in 1945.

From the ferry point at Shwegyin to Imphal is about 100 miles as the crow flies. But the route for this last stage of the retreat passed through hills and valleys harbouring lethal diseases. Unit records list cerebral malaria, tick typhus, cholera, dysentery, even plague. Although strenuous efforts had been made from the Imphal end to improve the track, it was barely suitable for jeeps. Lorries sent forward to assist the marching troops were driven by inexperienced men of the Royal Indian Army Service Corps, who did their best but had to be replaced by trained drivers from 7th Armoured Brigade. They worked a shuttle service, taking men from the tail to the head of the columns and returning for more. In this way did Burcorps regain safety.

Although many non-combatant personnel of Burma Army had melted away and were to be seen later entering Assam in bad order, the fighting troops maintained their discipline. In this they took example from their leaders. Alexander had gained the respect of the prickly Stilwell after an awkward first meeting in March, when the American had trouble in understanding his superior officer's accent. As he records, when he told Alexander that he was in command of Chinese forces as well as being the President of the United States' representative in the Burma-China theatre, the response was 'How Extraoooordinary!' The two generals soon established a satisfactory relationship. Stilwell also got on well with Slim after their first meeting, when he noted the British general's economic use of words. Later, he recalled, standing on a hilltop with Slim as they watched . . . 'a scene of considerable military confusion', he pointed out to Slim that whilst the British and Americans differed in their ways, they certainly seemed to share a common ancestor. When Slim asked who this might be, Stilwell told him: Ethelred the Unready. Both laughed, and the seeds of their good working relationship were sown. Although approaching 60, Stilwell led his two Chinese divisions out to India on foot.

As the first troops of Burcorps entered the Plain of Imphal it became clear that they were not going to receive a friendly welcome. None of them expected to be greeted as victors, but as they were directed to bivouac areas high up on exposed hillsides, just as the monsoon began to break, morale sank. Slim went to see the Commander of 4 Corps, Lt General Noel Irwin, to complain about the inadequate administrative arrangements. Irwin dismissed him brusquely, and when Slim objected to the rudeness of the interview he was cut short by Irwin with 'I can't be rude to you – I'm senior!' After this, Slim's relations with Irwin remained bad, and with good reason. At the Battle of Gallabat in 1940, when Slim commanded an Indian infantry brigade during the Abyssinian campaign, a battalion of Irwin's old regiment temporarily broke and ran following a heavy air attack by the Italians. Slim sacked the commanding officer, an old friend of Irwin's, and took the battalion out of the line. The incident is described in Slim's *Unofficial History*, and although he points out that the battalion (the 1st Essex) subsequently performed outstandingly well, the incident rankled with Irwin.

Elsewhere in the retreat the army's leadership had held up well. The case of Colonel Bagot and his splendid Glosters has been cited as an example of what regimental spirit could achieve in otherwise hopeless circumstances. General Bruce Scott had shown outstanding leadership amidst the blazing ruins of the Yenanyaung oilfields, personally guiding parties of men through the smoke and flame. It was noticed that Alexander's jeep crossing the Indian border carried an aged Indian civilian, one of thousands of refugees trying to regain their homeland.

As Slim stood by the side of the road watching his men pass, he was in a self-critical mood, particularly with regard to his own generalship. None who had served with him would have agreed, for his leadership from the start had been outstanding. He clearly had that dreadful retreat in mind seven years later when he addressed a Sovereign's Parade at Sandhurst as a Field Marshal and Chief of the Imperial General Staff:

> If you have these qualities of courage, initiative, will-power and knowledge you will be a leader, but you won't necessarily be a good leader or a leader for good. And you won't have that grip you must have on your men when things go wrong. When a man's heart sinks into his empty belly with fear; when the ammunition doesn't come through; when there are no rations; and your air force is being shot out of the skies; when the enemy is beating the living daylights out of you – then you will want one other quality, and unless you have got it you will not be a leader. That quality is self-sacrifice and as far as you are concerned it means simply this: that you will put first the honour and interest of your King and Country, that next you will put the safety, the well-being and the security of the men under your command, and that last, and last all the time, you will put your own interest, your own safety, and your own comfort. Then you will be a good officer.

It is fair to say that the main burden of the fighting in the first three months of the Burma war fell on the British battalions forming the peacetime garrison and on those shipped and flown in as last-minute reinforcements. The steadiness of these much-depleted regular units stiffened the resolve of the young Indian and Gurkha soldiers, whose performance is all the more remarkable when their lack of experience even of peacetime soldiering is taken into account. Later, as will be seen, they too would perform magnificently. The fortunes of a draft of young officers sent to the Glosters, shortly before the fall of Rangoon, illustrate the typical level of attrition. Of 14 in the party, none survived unscathed six months later. Four were killed in action, five wounded, one was posted missing and never seen again, and four were evacuated sick. By mid-April, after six weeks of combat, the Glosters were down to nine officers and 160 soldiers. Their second-in-command and adjutant had been killed in action and the CO wounded (he returned, however, and continued to fight). In the early stages of the campaign this battalion was still going into action clad in khaki drill uniform and wearing solar topees or pith helmets. Only in the latter stages were these replaced by the more practical Australian bush hat. Pre-war standards were maintained, deliberately, in order to sustain regimental pride and morale. All ranks shaved daily, even after publication of a General Order permitting the growing of beards. When General Stilwell visited the Glosters he was entertained in a well-camouflaged officers' mess where, after drinking a large part of the Mess Sergeant's lovingly-hoarded reserve of Scotch, he feasted on local produce including roast sucking pig. He repaid this courtesy by complaining to General Cowan that the British Army was treating itself to unnecessary luxuries in the field. When Cowan mentioned this to Colonel Bagot he replied crisply that '. . . we fight the better for it, and no-one so far has complained of our performance'.

Morale was a major consideration during the retreat, for most units had received no mail for four months and there was a general dearth of the small luxuries which make life endurable in adverse conditions, such as stationery, toilet requisites, tobacco, beer and confectionery. There was no NAAFI organisation. Burma Army ran on Indian lines using independent unit contractors, most of whom made for India and safety as soon as hostilities broke out. Rations were often short and the Japanese air forces were always ready to punish any unit that failed to conceal itself when at rest, or whose march discipline was bad.

The casualty lists speak for themselves. British and Indian killed and wounded amounted to 3,670, with over 5,000 missing. Of the Burmese troops 350 were killed or wounded in action and over 3,000 went missing; most of these returned to their villages or went over to the BIA. The Japanese admitted to 4,500 killed and wounded. The last word can be left with Stilwell, who wrote afterwards:

> I claim we got a hell of a beating. We got run out of Burma and it is humiliating as hell. I think we should find out what caused it and go back and retake it.

The Road to Recovery: I

". . . a task beyond their training and capabilities."

A S THE exhausted survivors of Burcorps reached their inhospitable bivouac areas at Imphal, the monsoon broke in earnest, adding to their tribulations. They had not expected to be greeted as heroes and were painfully aware that they had been driven out of Burma by a stronger and more aggressive enemy. The derision in which General Irwin obviously held them was, however, resented, and it was only through the efforts of their own commanders and Maj General Savory, commanding 23 Indian Division at Imphal, that a general collapse of morale did not take place. To assist in its defence, 17 Division was retained at Imphal while 1 Burma Division was broken up. During the latter stages of the retreat, many of its tribally-recruited hillmen were given their rifles, 50 rounds of ammunition and three months' pay and told to return to their villages to await the return of the British. Nearly all kept faith and were to play a useful role later in the campaign.

Slim calculated that of the fighting element of his corps which arrived at Imphal, eight per cent were too ill for further soldiering. The Japanese were, if anything, in worse condition, having far outrun their rickety administrative services. A Chinese general had told Slim some months earlier that in his experience the Japanese were prone to open an offensive with inadequate logistic backup, hoping for a decision within nine days, after which their immediate reserves were in danger of being exhausted. The future commander of 14th Army remembered this; it was to be in his mind two years later during the great Japanese drive on India.

The Japanese, who had relaxed their pursuit once they reached the Chindwin, now had thousands of sick men on their hands. They had little transport for their evacuation, and in any case the monsoon had washed out most of the tracks on which their ambulances tried to operate. Their doctors did their best, but disease began to spread: malaria, typhus, dysentery and typhoid began to take their toll. The monsoon of 1942 was a time of recuperation for both sides, as the British stood guard on the borders of India and the Japanese confined themselves to patrol activity. At sea, the Imperial Japanese navy enjoyed the superiority gained by the sinking of the *Prince of Wales* and *Repulse* and the subsequent defeat of the Allied fleet in the Dutch East Indies. A Japanese naval raid into the Bay of Bengal with the aim of finishing off the British Fleet based at Trincomalee in Ceylon, was able to sink several elderly heavy cruisers and the small aircraft carrier *Hermes*. The outlook for the defenders was gloomy; in the space of little more than six months, the world's greatest colonial power had been thrashed by an emergent Asian nation. Throughout the Far East, liberation movements gained strength and momentum as they saw the chance of early independence from their European masters.

Encouraged by their string of easy victories, the Japanese now gave in to a fatal temptation. The Imperial General Staff decided to extend the original bounds of expansion and, ignoring warnings from the Naval Staff who had already diagnosed a bad case of 'Victory Disease' in the General Staff's plans, task forces were despatched to Port Moresby in Papua and Tulagi in the Solomons. The seizure of these would provide bases from which land-based aircraft could dominate the Coral Sea, into which it was intended to lure the American Pacific Fleet to destruction. Following this would come the invasion of Samoa, Fiji and New Caledonia. Australia would then be cut off from the American support on which it had relied since the collapse of British power in South-East Asia.

Unknown to the Japanese naval staffs, their ciphers had been broken by American naval intelligence; the plans for breaking into the Coral Sea were already known to Admiral Nimitz, US naval commander in the Pacific. The American aircraft carriers which had providentially escaped destruction at Pearl Harbour now made their decisive contribution to the world's first naval battle where the opposing fleets never saw each other and in which naval air power was the deciding factor. Both sides lost valuable carriers in the Battle of the Coral Sea but the lasting advantage had passed in a single throw to the Americans. The Japanese plan to take Port Moresby had to be called off in the face of vigorous Australian resistance; the tide had at last been stemmed.

As ever, the Americans learned quickly from early mistakes and those of their enemy. On 4 June 1942, as the remnants of Burma Army were sorting themselves out on the sodden Plain of Imphal, Japanese carrier-borne aircraft were launched at the American bases on Midway Island, to trigger off one of the decisive battles of world history. When it ended, seven Japanese aircraft carriers – four fleet and three light – their entire carrier force in the western Pacific – had been sunk and the initiative at sea passed irreversibly to the Americans. There now began a series of bloody amphibious battles as the Americans 'island-hopped' towards Japan itself, steadily eating away at the outer markers of the Greater East Asia Co-prosperity Sphere. Admiral Yamamoto, who had advised against a headlong rush into war, now foresaw certain defeat; but it was to be many months before the tide began to turn in Burma.

With the dispersal of Burma Army, Alexander returned to England to receive Churchill's thanks for saving at least some of the wreckage in Burma. Slim was sent to Ranchi as commander of 15 Corps. In Assam there was fevered activity as a huge base and administrative infrastructure was set up. On the Plain of Imphal thousands of British and Indian troops began a programme of re-equipment and retraining. Further to the north west, in the Brahmaputra valley, a great army base complex was started at Dimapur. Thousands of coolies, supervised by American and British engineers, embarked on a vast programme of airfield, railway and road building. Some indication of the scale of this is that by 1944 some 200 new airstrips and all-weather airfields had been completed. Work began on a new overland route to China to replace the Burma Road. General Stilwell's aim was to regain enough territory in northern Burma for the new road to be extended from Ledo into Yunnan. Meanwhile, an air supply system was created to carry war supplies to Chiang Kai-shek. From April 1942 a steadily-increasing force of American transport aircraft flew men and material across the 'Hump', that forbidding extension of the Himalayas which separates India from southern China. Over 300 aircraft eventually plied this hazardous route in all weathers, returning from Yunnan laden with Chinese troops for training in India.

The industrialised north-east of India was rapidly becoming an arsenal, working for the Allied war effort, but there were major political problems. Although some two million Indian citizens volunteered for war service following the Viceroy's unilateral declaration of a state of war with Japan, the influential Congress Party continued its strident 'Quit India' campaign. Congress held power in eight provincial governments, and its Hindu leaders resigned en masse in 1942, more interested in ejecting the Raj than facing up to the threat of Japanese aggression. Mahatma Gandhi went so far as to call on the British people to 'submit peacefully' to the Axis powers. Nehru commented that the Japanese were no worse than the British. Churchill decided to send a mission to India for negotiations with the Congress leaders. It was headed by Sir Stafford Cripps, a Labour member of the wartime coalition government, who was authorised to give a promise of Independence and Dominion status for India at the end of the war, providing Congress abandoned its campaign and supported the war effort for the duration. Whilst Nehru was inclined to accept, Gandhi was not. For many years he had been the guru of the independence movement, preaching non-violent opposition to the Raj. He now likened the acceptance of Cripps's offer as 'signing a worthless cheque drawn on a failing bank'. The 'Quit India' campaign went ahead and Cripps returned empty-handed to London. He was possibly the worst emissary Churchill could have sent. A dogmatic Socialist, Cripps was described by his biographer as . . . 'possessing saintly qualities', but even this was qualified by the admission that they were accompanied by the rigidity and arrogance which so often go with them.

The non-co-operation campaign now spread throughout India; strikes, industrial sabotage, arson, civil disturbances and violent clashes between Hindus and Muslims soon made it necessary to send troops in to maintain order. At the peak of the troubles in September 1942, 57 British and Indian battalions were diverted from operational duty to internal security. There was considerable disruption of the railway and telegraph systems, and in some places there were murderous attacks on European citizens. Despite these diversions, work went ahead on the logistic system in support of the field army on the remote Burma front.

General Wavell, now Commander-in-Chief India, was determined that in spite of all difficulties battle should be offered again as soon as possible. He was under heavy pressure from London, receiving strings of agitated signals from Churchill demanding rapid offensive action. Wavell was in sympathy with this aim, realising that unless something was done, however modest its scale, the morale of his Indian and British troops would sink to the extent that by 1943 they would be incapable of mounting any form of operation. He was wise enough to know that the British reinforcements now arriving in the theatre were wartime conscripts whose only wish, understandably, was to get home in one piece and to do as little fighting as possible. He also knew that the ferment of independence now at work across the sub-continent would sooner or later get hold of the Indian Army. The only way to motivate such a mixed force was to try and beat the Japanese in an area where there was a reasonably good chance of success. His original plan was for an amphibious operation down the Arakan coast, with the aim of capturing the important airfields on Akyab Island, but this was frustrated due to the lack of landing craft, the campaign in Madagascar having used up all assault shipping in the theatre. A more modest plan was therefore adopted: an overland advance down the Arakan, followed by a scaled-down landing from the sea by units of the British 2 Division training in India for amphibious operations.

On 17 September 1942 Wavell issued an operational directive to Lt General Irwin, now commanding Eastern Army, as the old Indian Eastern Command had been renamed. He was to re-open operations in Upper Burma during the dry season of 1942-43. These were to start with an improvement of communications with the aim of retaking Burma and re-opening the Burma Road as soon as possible, and to bring the Japanese to battle in order to erode their strength on land and in the air. The immediate objectives in the autumn of 1942 were the capture of Akyab and the re-occupation of the upper Arakan; to strengthen Eastern Army's position in the Chin Hills; to occupy Kalewa and Sittaung on the Chindwin, from where raids could be launched against the Japanese lines of communications; and to make administrative arrangements for a rapid advance into Upper or Lower Burma if the chance presented itself during the 1942-43 campaigning season.

The implementation of this tall order required the construction of an all-weather road south from Chittagong to Cox's Bazar, followed by steady infiltration down the Arakan once maintenance of the forward formations was possible. In Assam, Irwin was required to establish his forward troops in the Tiddim area and around Tamu as a prelude to the capture of Kalewa and Sittaung. This would deprive the enemy of the use of the Chindwin and seriously affect his lines of communication. An entirely novel concept, introduced by Wavell, was a long-range penetration operation, to be carried out by a newly-created force raised from 77 Indian Infantry Brigade, nearing the end of an arduous training programme in Central India. Wavell had always favoured the unconventional and, as will be seen, this force and its leader were unusual to the point of eccentricity. Wavell's final directive dealt with roads; the road from Dimapur to Palel was to be improved to two-way all-weather standard, and the roads from Imphal to Tiddim, and Palel to Tamu, to single-track all-weather standard, before the 1943 monsoon.

The formation selected for the advance in the Arakan was the newly-formed and inexperienced 14 Indian Division, commanded by Maj General W. L. Lloyd. In September 1942 it began to advance cautiously from its concentration area behind Chittagong. When this force reached Cox's Bazar a halt was called in order to build up resources and establish supply depots. It was not until December that Lloyd decided that he could resume the advance, and a probe was made down the Mayu Peninsula. This runs south-east towards Akyab, coming to an end at Foul Point where a narrow stretch of water, less than ten miles wide, has to be crossed in order to reach Akyab Island. Running down the peninsula like a spine is the Mayu Range of steep, jungle-covered, but not particularly high hills flanked by lower foothills. Between the hills and the sea is a narrow strip of flat land laced with dozens of swamps and tidal creeks or chaungs. The land route down this coastal strip consisted of unsurfaced tracks interrupted by many ferry points. At low tide it was possible to drive for miles down the firm beaches, but at other times country boats had to be used on the chaungs. Movement was consequently a slow business, and although 14 Division's sappers built bridges over many of the chaungs these were to prove highly vulnerable to enemy air attack.

On the landward side of the Mayu Range was the Kalapanzin or Upper Mayu valley whose only motorable overland access to the coast was by a disused railway track, built in the 1890s to carry goods from Buthidaung in the interior to the little port of Maungdaw. Two tunnels on this road piercing the Mayu range featured prominently in operations during the next 18 months. Some miles north and parallel to the old railway, a packhorse track crossed the hills. Starting at the coastal village of Wabyin it traversed the Ngakyedauk Pass (anglicised early in the campaign to 'Okeydoke'), and this was also to play an important role in both Arakan campaigns.

The success of Wavell's plan depended on speed of execution, for in the autumn of 1942 Akyab was still only lightly held by the Japanese, most of whose efforts had been directed at the ejection of Burma Army; their redeployment to the Arakan had not got under way in September, but the glacial speed of 14 Division's advance gave them plenty of time to prepare defences covering the approach to Foul Point. At the end of December a patrol of the Inniskillings had actually reached the Point, but the Japanese were already strongly entrenched in deep bunkers around Donbaik, a few miles further north.

Across the Mayu range, units of 14 Division had entered the outskirts of Rathedaung, an important market town on the Mayu estuary. Here the advance ground to a halt again, having outrun its administrative tail. This was a tedious business, for the division was at the end of a tenuous line of communication over a hundred miles long. Large stockpiles of ammunition, food, fuel and engineer stores had to be brought forward, using a makeshift fleet of small boats ('Wavell's Navy') to augment the inadequate roads. By the time the advance was resumed on 6 January 1943 the Japanese had completed their defences, which proved to be extremely strong.

Rathedaung was now a bristling fortress of bunkers, cleverly sited for mutual protection and heavily wired in. On the coastal strip Donbaik was similarly defended. The Japanese were masters of fieldwork construction, using layers of tree trunks for overhead protection and positioning each bunker so that it could bring fire to bear on its neighbours. Each position was manned by up to a platoon of determined infantry with machine guns, light artillery and grenade launchers. Apart from barbed wire, protection was given by cunningly-concealed beds of panjis, sharpened bamboo stakes on which attackers could impale themselves. A bunker could easily withstand direct hits from field artillery shells and even 250-pounder bombs. A series of costly frontal attacks in succession by 14 Division's brigades failed to move the Japanese. After a particularly bloody repulse on 18 February, Wavell went forward to confer with Irwin, and as a result the 6th British Infantry Brigade was sent to join the attack.

This formation had been specially trained for amphibious operations with the rest of 2 Division; it was now thrown against untouched wire and well-concealed Japanese positions, with predictable results. Augmented to twice its normal size by the addition of an Indian infantry brigade, it assaulted with great panache and courage and its troops got in amongst the defences. But the bunkers were now blasted clear of natural cover by high explosives, and the attackers, unable to gain entry into the strong-points, were shot down and thrown back to their start lines. This had been a bloody introduction to battle for the units concerned.

Brigadier Cavendish, commanding 6th Brigade, had the use of no less than six battalions: 1st Royal Scots, 1st Royal Welch Fusiliers, 1st Royal Berkshires, 2nd Durham Light Infantry, 1st Lincolns, and 5/8th Punjab, with two field regiments of artillery in direct support. Even this force of good regular battalions, well backed up by their gunners, could not succeed. Irwin, however, persisted in continuing the frontal attack. Even the bravest units eventually run out of courage, and after a week of these bovine attacks the morale of 6th Brigade began to show the danger signs. The incidence of self-inflicted injuries rose, and lightly wounded men could be seen making their way back to the regimental aid posts not by themselves, but enthusiastically helped by several comrades. At times, some coercion had to be applied to get an attack going.

It was time for the Japanese counter-stroke, and a redoubtable opponent now entered the field. Colonel Tanahashi, commanding the Japanese 112th Regiment, launched a surprise attack far inland in the Kaladan Valley, which drove in the British outposts; he followed this at once with an attack on Rathedaung, almost succeeding in surrounding one of Lloyd's brigades. His aggressive approach to battle was in sharp contrast to that of his enemies and, as will be seen, produced results out of all proportion to the numbers of men at his disposal.

At this point, with the Japanese poised to bring off a resounding victory in the Arakan, it is necessary to look at the peculiar chain of command under which Lloyd was having to work. In overall command was General Wavell, as C-in-C India. Under him were the former Indian Army Commands, now renamed 'Armies'. Of these, Eastern Army, under Irwin, was directly concerned with operations in the Arakan and Assam. Irwin's headquarters were at Barrackpore, near Calcutta, while Slim's 15 Corps headquarters were at Ranchi, some 500 miles to the west, but capable of immediate movement to the front. This HQ was now fully operational, well-trained, and the logical link between Eastern Army and Lloyd's 14 Division. Irwin declined to use it to help with increasing command and control problems as more formations were pitched into the Arakan, until 14 Division was swollen to a strength of nine brigades – the equivalent of a corps.

The work load was well beyond any divisional headquarters staff, and Irwin should have recognised this. Moreover, none of the extra brigades thrown into the fighting had been able to carry out any form of collective training under HQ 14 Division, nor were they given time to familiarise themselves with the extremely difficult terrain of the Arakan. Standards of individual training varied widely between, and even within, units. The British battalions of 6th Brigade still contained officers and men who, after long tours of garrison duty in India, were unfit for the front line on grounds of age or medical condition. Most of the Indian battalions had a high recruit

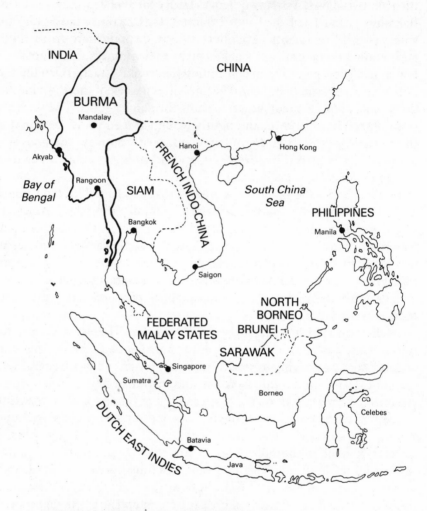

BURMA AND SOUTH-EAST ASIA
on the eve of Pearl Harbour [7 December 1941]

content and very few long-service Indian NCOs and British officers.

The first British Arakan offensive, which has been described as perhaps the worst-managed British military effort of the war, was doomed to failure by more than confused command structures. It was in fact a heavily watered-down version of a grandiose scheme thought up by Churchill in his Whitehall map room. He visualised an early reconquest of Burma with a series of dashing amphibious landings along the Arakan coast, culminating with the recapture of Rangoon from the sea. Code-named 'Anakim', the great design took no account of the almost total lack of landing craft in the Bay of Bengal, or the fact that command of sea and air was at that time firmly in Japanese hands.

Wavell still persisted in his belief that there was an unwillingness on the part of British and Indian troops to get to grips with the Japanese, an enemy he considered inferior in every respect – in physique, weaponry, in equipment of all sorts, and in all-round soldierly qualities. His assessment was flawed; Wavell had not personally fought the Japanese. Slim and his colleagues could have told him otherwise, but their opinions were not sought. It is hard to visualise at this distance the load carried by Wavell. He had borne the entire responsibility for trying to save the Empire's bacon in the Far East, and it is hardly surprising that this wise, brave and cultured soldier was now prone to venting his frustrations on subordinates.

Irwin, by this stage, was apparently impervious to expert advice. Earlier in February he had called for armour from Slim's corps tank brigade to support the attacks at Donbaik, but asked for only a troop of Valentines, infantry support tanks mounting a 2-pounder gun of little or no use against bunkers. Both Slim and the commander of the tank brigade advised the use of tanks in mass, but Irwin would not listen. The Valentines, used in penny packets in direct contravention of all armoured warfare principles, were frittered uselessly away.

By March 1943 Wavell was aware that the offensive had stalled but received scant sympathy from Churchill when he recommended that the objective of capturing Rangoon in 1943 was no longer realistic. Meanwhile, Japanese reinforcements were poured into the Arakan. When 14 Division set forth so hopefully in the previous September there had been only two weak battalions in its path. It was now faced by General Koga's formidable 55 Division. As the last fruitless attacks on Donbaik petered out, the Japanese counter-stroke burst upon Lloyd's baffled and dispirited troops.

At this point, Slim was belatedly called forward by Irwin and invited to report on the state of play. This was embarrassing, as he had no executive power and could be seen, he felt, as a spy sent to observe Lloyd's performance. He quickly concluded that Lloyd had been given too many brigades to command and feed. He also noted all the signs of collapsing morale with which he had become familiar in the previous year. In his report, mincing no words, he commented adversely on the futility of repeated frontal attacks on prepared positions. His report, forecasting imminent disaster in the Arakan, was disregarded by Irwin, and Slim went off on leave, to be recalled at very short notice early in April. He was then directed to take his corps headquarters forward to Chittagong and assume operational (but not administrative) command of the situation. Things had gone very wrong indeed.

The Japanese offensive was launched on 25 March. By now, Irwin had decided to remove Lloyd from command and, until his successor arrived, to take personal control at 14 Division. He arrived in the forward area on 29 March and Lloyd took his departure. On 1 April the situation became critical. Irwin had issued a 'no withdrawal' order the previous day, clearly not realising the gravity of the crisis. To the east of the hills, 47th Brigade was thin on the ground and infiltrated by the Japanese, who were moving fast towards the coast with the aim of cutting 14 Division's line of retreat. On 3 April, Maj General Lomax, with part of his 26 Indian Divisional HQ, took over from Irwin as the situation went out of hand by the hour. By nightfall, the Japanese had established their familiar roadblocks, cutting off the Royal Berkshires and two brigades, the 6th and 47th. Lomax had to ignore Irwin's orders to conduct a deliberate withdrawal, and ordered his units to fight their way independently back to the coast. The Inniskillings, who had suffered very heavy casualties at Donbaik, were in the hills when the order was given to form small parties and make for a rendezvous up the coast road. About half the battalion survived to rally there. It was a nightmare march; Fusilier Dunn, weakened by sickness and resolved not to hold back his friends, lay down by the side of the track with the words 'I can take it'. He was never seen again.

In his earlier report, Slim had commented on the low state of morale in the Arakan, writing privately to Irwin that '. . . we are fighting an enemy army in which the best men go into the infantry, and we shan't make much progress until we follow suit'. It has to be said that at this stage of the fighting there are well-documented reports of British battalions disintegrating; in many Indian units, ill-trained and under unfamiliar officers recently joined from England, most of the soldiers were as terrified of the jungle as they were of the Japanese.

On the night of 5/6 April the Japanese, led by Col Tanahashi, broke into the forward area of 14 Division and overran the HQ of 6th Brigade, whose commander, Brigadier Cavendish, was killed (probably by friendly artillery fire). All the brigade's maps, code-books and ciphers were lost, together with much other equipment. Japanese, British and Indian troops were totally intermixed in a confused battle, from which Slim now had to extract what he could and get the demoralised wreckage of 14 Division to safety. He soon established a good relationship with Lomax, who greatly impressed him by his calmness and professionalism. On 14 April Irwin finally passed all operational control of the battle over to Slim.

One more attempt was made to regain the initiative, by setting a trap for the Japanese. On paper it was a sound plan; the enemy would be lured forward into a 'box' whose lid, represented by a brigade held in readiness, would be slammed shut. It was actually a tactical idea lifted from Japanese textbooks, an attempt to replace the bone-headed frontal assaults which had destroyed 14 Division. It would have been a triumph if the troops had been up to it, but they were not. Slim now realised that the only course open was to withdraw in good order, despite Irwin's instructions to the contrary, to the start line from which 14 Division had set out four months earlier.

By retiring to the area of Cox's Bazar Slim would compel the Japanese to stretch their supply lines once more, and this would be difficult given the extent of the demolitions which 14 Division's engineers were able to carry out on the many bridges – so painstakingly built by them a few weeks earlier – as they retired north. Large quantities of equipment had been lost and 55th Brigade and the Lincolns had to destroy all their transport. The flight of the civilian labour force from the divisional maintenance area left large stockpiles intact on the ground. The RAF did their best to destroy these, but much was captured.

Irwin's final shot was to signal Slim at the end of May, criticising his handling of the battle and hinting that he would recommend that he be removed from command of 15 Corps. There is a delightful (and true) story of Slim's reaction. On reading the signal he remarked to his ADC, 'I suppose this means I've got the sack. I'll join the Home Guard in England. I wonder if I'll find Irwin there!' On the same day, however, Slim heard that Irwin had been replaced as GOC Eastern Army by General Sir George Giffard. On receiving news of his own dismissal, Irwin was man enough to send Slim a splendid signal: 'You're not sacked. I am.'

Giffard was determined from the start that the Army in Burma would be soundly organised and given the logistic support so lacking to date. Slim briefed him on the conduct of operations on the Arakan, stressing the need for rigorous training if the Japanese were to be beaten in the jungle. Giffard saw to it that these things came to pass. In the months to come, 14th Army would owe him a great debt.

Japanese confidence was now at a peak. Koga's division had played a leading part in the 1942 campaign; once more it had routed a numerically superior force. On the other hand, British/Indian morale was at its lowest ebb. The Arakan campaign had virtually overwhelmed the medical services with battle casualties and sickness, and at the time little attention could be spared for the alarming number of psychiatric cases. In his report on these operations the Command psychiatrist of Eastern Army suggested that no useful purpose would be served by trying to draw up statistical returns as

'. . . the whole of 14th Indian Division was for practical purposes a psychiatric casualty'. The formation was never returned to front line duty and spent the rest of the war as a training division in India.

Characteristically, Wavell shouldered the blame for the whole sorry business, writing later that '. . . I set a small part of the army a task beyond their training and capabilities.'

The Road to Recovery: II

"Dese Japan soldier no savvy war bush proper."

S LIM'S CORPS headquarters stayed behind for some weeks to help
Lomax sort out the aftermath of the Arakan campaign and get 26
Division installed in secure positions protecting Cox's Bazar, where they
would sit out the monsoon. A forward outpost was left at Bawli Bazar, 40
miles to the south-east, to keep the Japanese under observation. They too
had settled in for the rainy season, 30 miles south of Bawli, on a line running
from the coast at Maungdaw, along the old railway and on to Buthidaung.
All was now quiet, apart from patrolling by both sides.

It was time to take stock. Slim knew that the first battle to be won was that
for the minds of his soldiers. He had noted the steady collapse of morale and
fighting spirit in 14 Division as it progressively lost out to the Japanese.
Confidence had to be restored as a prerequisite for victory, and it could only
stem from sound training. General Sir George Giffard was an officer much to
Slim's liking. His distinguished appearance, acute mind, and willingness to
back his subordinates, once he was satisfied with their professional ability,
stamped him as an ideal commander for the recovery of Eastern Army. He
listened carefully to Slim's debrief on the recent campaign, then went
forward to see for himself and meet the troops. Giffard was no soap-box
orator; in fact, as Slim quickly discovered, he really hated any form of
publicity. In consequence, his great achievement in reforging a broken
weapon into a battle-winner has gone unchronicled. He knew, like Slim,
that training was the secret, and that an army must first establish its
administrative services on sound lines before taking to the field. Within
weeks, Slim and Giffard were planning an offensive in the Arakan for the
next campaigning season. To 15 Corps were allocated two Indian infantry
divisions, the 5th and 7th, which were deployed around Cox's Bazar while
Lomax and his 26 Division held the line. Many lessons, painfully acquired,
were incorporated in the intensive training programmes to which Slim
subjected all formations in his corps. A newly arrived formation, the 81
West African Division, was assigned to the Kaladan Valley to protect 15
Corps' left flank. It was chosen as the 'guinea pig' for trials in air supply, the
first division in the command to go entirely over to this method of support,
where results depend on simple, well-practised and foolproof procedures
and the economical use of resources.

The arrival of the West Africans introduced an exotic element into the campaign. The Royal West African Frontier Force, whose battalions were recruited in Nigeria, the Gold Coast, the Gambia and Sierra Leone, had been raised for use in the Internal Security role. Its lightly-equipped battalions were trained for bush warfare but not for operations against an enemy of the calibre they were about to meet. Each battalion had a very high content (up to 80 in some cases) of European officers and NCOs – too many, Slim thought, noting that British corporals were serving in the RWAFF as second-in-command of rifle sections. This, he considered, absolved the African NCOs from making decisions and could raise problems if the British personnel became casualties. The British who served in the RWAFF had always been of high calibre, men who wanted to serve with native troops. Unfortunately, due to wartime expansion many officers and NCOs posted to 81 Division lacked the sympathetic approach found in older 'Coasters', who genuinely loved their soldiers.

Major Charles Carfrae, who found himself posted to West Africa in 1941 as a junior officer, was thoroughly taken by the Africans under his command. Their training, he noted, was often on a different plane from that of the British army. At Kaduna, depot of the Nigeria Regiment, he watched, fascinated, as new recruits from the bush were given instruction in basic military English by an African NCO who evidently had little more grasp of his subject than his pupils. In chorus, and with appropriate gestures, the men chanted after him: 'Thees my feet', 'thees my hand', 'thees my arse', 'thees my eyes', 'thees my belly' . . . and so on. Carfrae began to wonder what he was in for. He soon learned to identify with the soldiers in his platoon, recognising their spontaneity, lack of repression, love of laughter, and respect for their superiors. They were eager to please and sang happily on the line of march; but they were also prone to superstition at times of stress, fingering charms which they kept in little leather pouches. Few had any idea of the quarrel that had brought them to Burma, and they had little time for Indians or Burmese. But this was their contract as soldiers, and they came obediently to the battle.

Another British officer, Captain Cookson of the Gambia Regiment, went with his battalion to Burma in 1943. The unit's strength was around 1,000 men, of whom many were non-combatant 'carriers' or porters, serving in lieu of motor transport, balancing heavy loads on their heads as they marched through the jungle. The presence of this mass of unarmed men worried Slim when he first saw them in Burma. In a later action, Cookson also found that they could be an embarrassment, when his company was cut off and he found himself with 50 men, most of whom were porters.

Before long . . . we dumped all unnecessary loads into the jungle so that the carriers should have a chance to use their machetes in self-defence if it became imperative for them to do so. Among the dumped loads was the Company safe, a steel box weighing 50 pounds, which was full of the Army Forms deemed indispensable even on a campaign, as well as the balance of the Company accounts, amounting to 74 rupees. If I had the vaguest inkling of the endless correspondence that was to ensue between the paymaster and myself concerning the conditions under which the money was to be written off, I would have carried away the safe single-handed. Cookson's company had 40 carriers, and every European NCO had an African understudy . . . except the Colour Sergeant, who had Moses, the Corporal Clerk, a Nigerian from a mission school who sat copying payrolls or earnestly improving himself on the works of Thomas Carlyle.

The idea of air supply greatly appealed to the West African soldiers who, as Cookson reports,

> . . . took full advantage of this opportunity to replenish their wardrobes, and with their ingrained love for brilliant colour stitched themselves some startling pieces of underwear from scraps of parachute silk . . . they were so proud of these distinctive garments that disciplinary measures had to be taken to make them keep their trousers on and prevent them from revealing our positions by vivid flashes of lingerie . . .

British officers quickly learned the pidgin which was the RWAFF's lingua franca – as was Urdu to the Indian Army – and to respect the bushcraft which came so naturally to them. One platoon commander leading his men along a jungle path heard a metallic click immediately ahead, which sounded to him like a gun being cocked. 'I was convinced we were approaching an enemy position and wondered why it had been sited in such a remote spot. "Sah", whispered the platoon sergeant. "I savvy dis palaver. One small bushbird make dis talk, it never be mortal man." Roars of laughter from soldiers . . . ' Another African NCO, as a heavy Japanese artillery 'stonk' hit the centre of the company's position, which happened to be empty, commented 'Dese Japan soldier no savvy war-bush proper. Look! Dey carry ammunition till dey tire, den go throw it yonder where it humbug no man'.

Enter Wingate

The directive from Wavell which had launched the Arakan offensive also mentioned a long-range penetration operation whose aim would be to cause chaos on the Japanese lines of communication in central Burma. During the latter half of 1942, far away in India, the force selected for this enterprise was training for its new and exciting role. Even as Burma Army retreated up the Irrawaddy valley in 1942, Wavell was thinking ahead. He had always been interested in unconventional warfare and the unusual personalities who seemed to excel at it, and he had asked for the services of an officer with whom he had had dealings in the past.

Orde Wingate was serving as a Captain in the Royal Artillery in Palestine in 1938 when Wavell was General Officer Commanding. Wingate identified closely with the Zionists, whose object was to set up a Jewish national home in what they considered their historic and God-given land. The Palestinian Arabs strongly opposed Zionist aims and a dangerous internal security situation arose, policed somewhat unenthusiastically by the British who exercised the League of Nations' mandate to govern the country. With Wavell's connivance and Captain Wingate's help, Jewish 'night squads' were trained in the techniques of irregular and undercover operations.

On leaving Palestine, which was getting too hot to hold him, Wingate returned to England, but in 1940 Wavell, now C-in-C Middle East, appointed him to train and lead Abyssinian irregulars fighting the Italians. After eight months of intensive soldiering, culminating with the triumphal return of Emperor Haile Selassie to his throne and people, Wingate suffered a nervous breakdown and attempted to take his own life. Sent back to England to recuperate, he was gloomily resigned to the apparent failure of his career, but Wavell called for him to train and form the Long-Range Penetration force in Burma. He arrived at HQ India early in 1942 and at once went off to the front, accompanied by Major Michael Calvert, a robust Sapper who commanded the Bush Warfare School. Burma Corps was already in full retreat following the fall of Rangoon, but Wingate saw enough of the country to make his own plans. On his return to Delhi he got down to detail. In his report to Wavell he recommended the formation of groups capable of operating on the same basis as the Japanese; mobile, fit, skilled in sabotage, and able to cover great distances on foot, using mules to carry support weapons such as mortars and medium machine guns. There would be no cumbersome 'tail'. The columns, as Wingate termed them, would be supplied by air.

There was no question of Wingate being allotted an élite formation. At this time, most spare battalions in India were fully committed to internal security and he had to accept 77th Indian Infantry Brigade. This was something of a mixed bag: the 13th King's (Liverpool), 3/2nd Gurkha Rifles, 2nd Burma Rifles, and 143rd Commando Company consisting of volunteers from about forty regiments and corps, all still wearing their parent regimental cap badges. In addition, there were eight RAF sections, equipped with radios for contacting supply drop and fighter-bomber support, and a Brigade mule transport company of the Royal Indian Army Service Corps.

The King's battalion had been used for garrison and line-of-communication duties. Many of its men were in their thirties or even older, married with families, and of low medical categories. Wingate weeded the unit ruthlessly and nearly half its personnel went, including the commanding officer. The rest, reinforced by younger men from other regiments, went off to Central India to train for their new role. The 3/2nd Gurkhas were an untried unit of young soldiers, with few long-serving

British officers, and the 2nd Burma Rifles were the only Burif unit which had stayed together in the retreat. They owed their continuing existence to the sturdy refusal of their CO to disband them when they arrived at Imphal. Loyal, and intimately familiar with their country and its peoples, they were to be of immense value in the months ahead.

Wingate was now gathering around him a cadre of officers amenable to his curious personal style. He remains one of the most enigmatic characters in British military history, and it is certain that the debate on his life and works will continue for years to come. Born in 1903 into a military family (his cousin, Sir Reginald Wingate, was Commander-in-Chief, or Sirdar, of the Egyptian army), he grew up with a strong leaning towards unconventional forms of soldiering. He was not a popular gentleman cadet at the Royal Military Academy, where he stood away from the herd, faced down any attempts to bully him into conformity, and went his own way. He became a fluent Arabic speaker and served in the Sudan Frontier force, that nursery of outstanding officers. Although he passed the Staff College examination, he was not accepted as a student – possibly because of his intractable nature and 'unclubbability'. Instead, he went to Palestine, where Wavell marked him for future reference.

Unlike Montgomery, who with his black beret and multiplicity of cap badges was merely playing the part, Wingate was a true eccentric, careless of others' opinions and totally unaware of his strangeness. His pith helmet, beard, the alarm clock he carried around as a reminder to all that time mattered, the raw onions he munched in public – these were not mere attention-getting artifices. His character certainly owed much to his strict religious upbringing at the hands of parents who were Plymouth Brethren.

His manner often alarmed strangers. One officer recalled a three-day train journey from Delhi to Calcutta in a compartment shared with Wingate.

I secured a compartment to myself, or so I thought, until at the last moment, something wearing a uniform vaguely reminiscent of a British Colonel's shot into the compartment and then began to load up all available space with untidy parcels hazardously secured with odd bits of string. The first thing I noticed about my new companion was that he was pig dirty, and the next, that he was as mad as a hatter. [After three unnerving days and nights Wingate's fellow traveller who was Colonel Field, British liaison officer at Stilwell's and Chiang's headquarters concluded that] . . . he regarded himself as a cross between God and Oliver Cromwell and his conversation was copiously larded with quotations from their recorded utterances . . .

Others saw him differently. In a posthumous tribute, Slim wrote:

Wingate had clear vision. He could also impart his belief to others. Above all, he could adapt to his own purpose the ideas, practices and techniques of others, once he was satisfied of their soundness. To see Wingate urging actions on some hesitant commander was to realise how a mediaeval baron felt when Peter the

Hermit got after him to go crusading. Lots of barons found Peter the Hermit an uncomfortable fellow, but they went crusading all the same.

Wingate now devised a badge for his men, who needed something with which to identify, coming as they did from so wide a variety of regiments. He chose the Chinthes, that mythical beast which, carved in stone, stands guard at the entrance to every Burmese temple. Anglicised to 'Chindit' the name stuck, and would gain immortality.

From experience gained while training in India, the Chindits evolved their own clothing, equipment and ration scales. Normal dress was based on standard khaki drill, dyed green. The Australian bush hat was adopted and steel helmets abandoned as useless. Each man carried a mosquito net, a machete or kukri for clearing scrub or chopping firewood, a groundsheet, a blanket, a pair of hockey boots, water sterilising kit, first field dressing, 50 rounds of .303″ ammunition, and six days' rations. One day's ration, as devised by Wingate, was 12 hard tack biscuits, 2oz nuts and raisins, 2oz tinned cheese, 4oz dates, a bar of chocolate or a handful of boiled sweets, 20 cigarettes, matches, Vitamin 'C' tablets, tea, sugar and tinned milk. The basic load was 50 lb a man, far exceeded after a supply drop, when a week's rations had to be carried by all ranks. Wingate insisted that Chindits accustomed themselves to living off half rations or less, and many were forced to do so in the forthcoming expedition. From the start there was general dissatisfaction with the rations, soon recognised as providing less than the vitamins and calorific value required by men engaged on continuous arduous work.

Mule management was a new skill to be acquired by all. The mules of 77 Brigade – 1,000 of them – arrived in November 1942. They were unbroken, untrained and in poor physical condition. Apart from a small team of instructors, the brigade had to learn the hard way, as none of its personnel had any experience of animal management. The unit muleteers, mostly Gurkhas, were raw recruits but physically tough, as they needed to be. The man leading a mule in long-range penetration operations had to be as good or better a fighting soldier than his comrades, for the physical effort was enormous. As Wingate wrote at the time:

Double pay for muleteers is underpayment . . . the great difficulty in our army is to find the indispensable minimum of persons who can tell one end of an animal from the other . . .

In the event, the Chindits surprised themselves by the speed with which they mastered the mule. Considering that the average Liverpudlian soldier had probably never been near a farm animal in his life, there is something very impressive about the ease with which he grasped the principles of animal transport.

The air supply system worked well from the start, thanks to the inclusion of the RAF sections with their powerful radios, in touch with bases in Assam. Supplies for parachuted delivery were packed into used kerosene tins and then into wicker hampers with straw packed round them to absorb shock on landing. Some stores, such as rice, could be free-dropped in hessian sacks. From time to time luxuries such as toothpaste, soap and razor blades would be delivered, together with mail and newspapers. Other, more exotic items airdropped to the Chindits included snuff, false teeth, books, and a spare monocle for Bernard Fergusson, the elegant commander of No 5 Column.

Early in February 1943 Wingate assembled his force at Imphal and prepared to march forward to the Chindwin. His task was first to cut the Mandalay-Myitkyina railway, then the lines of communication of the Japanese forces in northern Burma. Having done this, the Chindits were to harass the enemy in the Shwebo area and finally, if possible, cut the Mandalay-Lashio railway. It had been intended to launch the expedition in conjunction with a Chinese offensive in the north, but this failed to materialise and Wingate's first operation was launched in isolation. In retrospect, this was a mistake, for LRP operations are the modern version of the old 'cavalry raid', invariably undertaken in conjunction with a major operation elsewhere in order to divert the enemy's attention. As it turned out, Wingate and his force drew on themselves the undivided attention of the Japanese in central Burma, and this made life extremely difficult for them.

Before setting out into enemy territory across the Chindwin, Wingate issued an Order of the Day reflecting his personal brand of Christianity as well as the state of exaltation with which he was clearly seized at this point. It concludes:

> . . . Finally, knowing the vanity of man's efforts and the confusion of his purpose, let us pray that God may accept our services and direct our endeavours, so that when we have done all we shall see the fruit of our labours and be satisfied.

It was essential that the Japanese observation posts along the banks of the Chindwin should be hoodwinked as to the true direction of the main Chindit force. A diversionary crossing was accordingly made by two columns, well to the south. The commander of this force took pains to expose himself to the view of any unseen observers, wearing Brigadier's badges of rank and red tabs on his uniform. Once across the river and out of contact with the enemy, the southern columns were to march hard for the Irrawaddy and rejoin the main body in the hills on the far side. From there, part of the group was to make for the Kachin Hills, where Burma Rifles personnel would be detached to organise a revolt amongst the tribes.

Having safely crossed the Chindwin, Wingate and the main body traversed several ranges of hills before receiving their first air drop on 22

February. Within a few days they had made contact with the enemy, who appeared surprised by the sudden arrival of what they initially thought was a much larger force in their midst. Opposition stiffened, and on 4 March No 4 column was scattered, its men returning to India in small parties as they had been taught. A column of the southern group had also run into trouble and had been dispersed a few days previously. Soon, only five columns were left, pressing on even deeper into enemy country. The column commanded by Major Bernard Fergusson of The Black Watch reached their railway targets and carried out a series of demolitions; Calvert's men blew up two major rail bridges and cut the line in 70 places, before mounting a successful ambush without loss to themselves. On reaching the Irrawaddy at Tigyaing, Fergusson marched his column in threes up the main street, a piper at their head, warning the excited population, however, that this was not a permanent re-occupation, merely a temporary diversion.

By 24 March, when Wingate received orders to return to India, the expedition had reached an area 60 miles across the Irrawaddy and stirred up a hornet's nest. The Japanese were determined to cut off the force, and nearly succeeded in doing so. Columns were now operating in open, arid country at the extreme range of the RAF's transport aircraft, which continued to provide a highly effective service despite the constant presence of a strong Japanese air threat. The hunt was up and in the lead was the crack Japanese 18th Division, which had taken part in the capture of Singapore.

Hard pressed, 77 Brigade split into ever-smaller groups as it threaded its way back to the Irrawaddy. Increasing enemy air activity made air supply more difficult, especially to small groups marching to safety across the central plain where cover and water were scarce. Exhaustion, thirst, malnutrition and sickness began to claim their victims. The seriously sick and wounded had to be left to their fate at the hands of Burmese villagers or the Japanese, who were often in such hot pursuit that they were able to interfere with airdrops, driving the Chindits off their precious stores to capture them intact. Wingate aimed to cross the great river at Inywa, where he had gone across on the way in, thinking that this would deceive the enemy; but as No 7 Column tried to cross, it was ambushed on the west bank. It was now virtually a case of every man for himself as the Japanese closed in for the kill. The mules, so carefully trained, and which had served so faithfully, were shot, and anything which could not easily be carried was abandoned. The southern group, having lost their commander in action, made for the Kachin Hills. Other groups marched north-east, ending up in China.

As pressure increased, so did the unpleasantness. One officer was captured by Japanese troops while on patrol. Tied to a tree, he was used for the customary bayonet practice but was still alive next morning when his column commander found him; he asked for a lethal injection of morphine;

as this was being administered, a concealed sniper killed the column commander.

Fergusson had tried to break out with No 5 Column to the east and seek cover in the Kachin Hills. Ambushed by night when his men were split on both sides of a river, he had to make the agonising decision to leave one party to their fate. Later, he wrote:

I made the decision to come away. I have it on my conscience for as long as I live: but I stand by that decision and believe it to have been the correct one. Those who think otherwise may well be right. Some of my officers volunteered to stay but I refused them permission to do so.

This was the way of the Chindits, and all ranks knew what they might have to face under such circumstances. The survivors of Fergusson's column now had to endure a nightmare fifteen days' march, reaching the Chindwin again on 24 April, and Imphal two days later. Out of a starting strength of 300 men, only 95 made it to safety. The irrepressible Calvert continued to use up his explosives all the way home, blowing up anything that came to hand. Wingate himself, with a small group, crossed the Chindwin on the night of 28 April.

The results of this first expedition cannot be assessed in terms of military gains, for these were insignificant. A few Japanese had been killed, but nowhere near as many as the number of Chindits who failed to return. The excellent Japanese railway troops and engineers quickly repaired broken bridges and mended the railway tracks cut by Fergusson and Calvert. The enduring value of Operation 'Longcloth', as it was code-named, lay in its incalculable psychological impact. Skilfully handled by the Ministry of Information, it was presented to readers of Britain's newspapers as a triumphant reversal of the downward trend in the war against Japan. British soldiers – and very ordinary ones – had fought alongside their Gurkha and Burmese allies and beaten the Japanese at their own game. In the Arakan, the men of 15 Corps gained heart, as did those guarding the gate of India on the plain of Imphal. It had also made the Japanese think. Was it a mere raid? A probe to gather intelligence before a major offensive? Or, noting the presence of the Burma Riflemen in each column, was it the prelude to a native uprising? One other aspect baffled the Japanese as they interrogated some of the prisoners from the King's battalion. They could not understand why such elderly soldiers, men in their late thirties with large families on Merseyside, had been ordered to fight in Burma.

Many useful lessons were learned on the British side. The high sickness rate owed much to imperfect preventive measures, as well as to Wingate's personal conviction that the mind could overcome illness, thus reducing the need for medical officers and their orderlies. Attention was also given to the ration scales; the emaciated condition of 'Longcloth's' survivors had shocked all who saw them. Most of them were in fact so ill that they were graded unfit for further active service. The average weight loss per man was around forty pounds.

If the King's battalion had emerged with credit, equal praise was earned by the youthful Gurkhas and the Burma Riflemen. Wingate now knew that it was not necessary, as he had once thought, to recruit a special kind of officer and soldier for LRP operations. He found himself a national hero and for a short time the spotlight shone upon the Burma theatre, where the troops had begun to think of themselves as forgotten men and – more alarmingly – that they would never be able to beat the Japanese.

Churchill saw the expedition as a ray of light in an otherwise dark sky. On 24 July 1943, in one of his famous minutes to General Ismay, he wrote:

> There is no doubt that in the welter of inefficiency and lassitude which has characterised our operations on the Indian Front, this man, his force and his achievements stand out; and no question of seniority must obstruct the advance of real personalities in their proper station in war.

By now, Churchill had lost confidence in Wavell and was searching around for new commanders to replace the team which he considered had failed in Burma. He was actually thinking of replacing Wavell with Maj General Sir Oliver Leese, who had greatly impressed him as commander of the Guards Armoured Division and was earmarked for command of 30 Corps in North Africa. He was also considering Wingate as GOC Eastern Army, with responsibility for re-conquering Burma. Nothing came of this; but it is interesting to speculate on the possible outcome of such a curious pairing.

Clearly branded with the right marks of approval, Wingate immediately started to raise and train the far larger LRP force with which he was to resume operations in the next dry season. This time he would be commanding a whole division of Chindits, and he would command them at the rank of Major General.

Design for Victory

"Intelligent free men can whip them every time."

A S THE Arakan campaign ground miserably to a close and the first Chindit expedition marched across the central plains, a baffled and demoralised army was beginning its transformation into a victorious war machine. Giffard's aim was to restore confidence and his corps commanders were charged with implementing a patrolling programme which, beginning at platoon level, steadily worked up to large-scale raids, always against carefully selected targets chosen with a view to certain success. These 'Tiger patrols' had one aim: to kill the Japanese. There was no expectation of bringing back prisoners, for it was clear to all that the enemy would stand and die rather than surrender. No quarter was therefore given or expected. Before long, isolated Japanese detachments, whether in the Arakan or along the line of the Chindwin, found themselves overwhelmed by brigade-sized attacks. It was now the Japanese soldier's turn to feel that he was being beaten to the ground.

A vast training organisation was functioning in India by the autumn of 1942, where two complete divisions, staffed by instructors with combat experience against the Japanese army, acted as battle schools through which all newly-arrived battalions and regiments passed before moving forward. Here were taught the tactics of jungle warfare, standard procedures for ground-air cooperation on which so much depended as the army grew more reliant on air supply, and the vital disciplines of health and hygiene which were to bring down the sickness rate so dramatically. In the recent Arakan battles there had been 120 cases of sickness for every battle casualty. By 1944 the ratio was down to 20:1. In 1945 it would be as low as 6:1. Soon, all officers were required to teach their men the basics of preventive medicine, using a specially-published War Office pamphlet, *Service in Hot Climates*. It started off resoundingly enough: 'We have an Empire, which extends right around the world, and our service may be, and often is, in many queer and uncivilised places . . .' The reader is soon confronted, however, with the mundane business of health measures which must be observed: 'The hair of the head should be kept short and clean all over . . . to plaster the hair with expensive unguents merely hinders the removal of waste materials'. There were some encouraging things to note about water, especially the assurance that '. . . chlorination . . . has not the slightest effect in making men sterile, as some people think'. Sexual morality was treated coyly: 'Fellows whose thoughts are governed by unclean sexual desire, are soon led to the risk of infection with two serious diseases or, even more, to immoral and unnatural practices which not only undermine the character but involve other persons . . .' The reader is left to ponder on the nature of these practices, for they are not named.

Having cleared that fence, the anonymous author plunges into a lurid catalogue of tropical diseases, vividly describing their more unpleasant symptoms. The pamphlet abounds with information such as the World War I typhoid statistics: all British troops were immunised against it with the familiar TAB injection, and the maximum rate was 31 cases per thousand men in 1915, compared to the French who, it is inferred, were insanitary in the trenches, allowing human excreta to pass via unwashed hands into food, giving a 1915 French Army rate of 2,658 cases of typhoid per 1,000 men. Other afflictions on which officers were required to lecture their men were dysentery, typhus, rabies, plague, snake bite, heat stroke, worms, and the particularly gruesome worm infections brought about by drinking unpurified water.

Every man soldiering in the jungle had to cope with additional personal problems. Leeches abounded; these obscene creatures, looking like animated shiny black match-sticks, seemed able to detect the approach of a human body at several yards' range. They moved rapidly towards their next meal, base-over-apex in a purposeful rush. Having attached themselves to skin or outer garment, they searched at once for an area of soft skin which they could puncture in a single-minded hunt for blood, their staple diet. An anti-coagulant applied by them to the entry point ensured that the victim's blood did not clot. A leech would find its way through the lace-holes of boots and several layers of clothing to reach its feeding place; once there and drinking, it swelled to many times its original size, hanging like some shiny excrescence until forced to let go by the application of a lighted cigarette. Rapid infection resulted if a leech's head was left behind under the host's skin; after its departure the puncture hole bled freely for some time because of the anti-coagulant.

Foot rot was endemic whenever it was impossible to dry the skin between the toes and could quickly cripple a man if left untreated. The more serious trench foot was also widespread despite all efforts to keep it at bay. Dietary deficiencies, especially in the two Chindit expeditions, led to the eruption of painful boils and carbuncles. Insect bites festered into huge jungle sores, painful and debilitating. Copious use of foot powder helped, but in the monsoon, men had to accept sodden clothes and footwear for weeks on end. It is hardly surprising that skin diseases, minor septic conditions and the common cold – with malaria, dysentery and venereal diseases – accounted for 70% of hospital cases in 14th Army in the first year of the campaign. Good preventive medicine and unit health discipline had combined to bring this figure down to 49% by 1945.

Disciplinary action was taken against any man whose malaria was found to be due to failure to take the daily dose of the revolting Mepacrine, which turned men yellow (and, it was rumoured, rendered them impotent and sterile, a story gleefully spread by the Japanese, who still relied on quinine, but made a point of using captured stocks of British medicines whenever they could lay hands on them).

In order to reduce manpower wastage, special fever hospitals were set up behind the forward areas, where all malaria cases were taken for a three-week course of intensive medication. Hitherto, such patients had been put into the normal casualty evacuation chain, which meant losing a man with malaria for weeks on end as he found his way slowly back to his unit from some hospital in India.

From 1943, increasing numbers of British nursing sisters from the Queen Alexandra's Imperial Military Nursing Service, known universally as 'QAs', were working in the forward area, with an immediate effect on morale. At a typical Combined Indian General Hospital in a divisional area could be found British and Indian doctors and nursing sisters, with Anglo-Indian, African, British and Indian nursing orderlies. All problems of language, caste, religion and diet were triumphantly overcome. The British Sisters soon acquired an awesome reputation for efficiency and fine nursing, tempered with the strictest discipline. An outstanding example was Matron Agnes McGearey, a deceptively petite and elegant lady who stood no nonsense, even from the Supreme Commander Mountbatten, as he discovered when he fell into her hands after an accident involving his eyesight. She presided over a hospital receiving casualties from the second Chindit expedition and earned undying praise for her work. Known as 'Sister Saf Karo' (make it clean) she wheedled champagne from unlikely sources and fed it to her patients.

Another QA sister, Captain Jean Bowden, found herself serving in No 44 General Hospital near Chittagong, where the Sisters had to contend with an absurd uniform of white drill cloth fastened with eighteen pearl buttons. After dark, the wearing of mosquito thigh boots was compulsory; as one of the QAs reported:

> . . . the idea of stalking round the wards at night in this peculiar outfit affected newly-arrived QA officers to the point of hysteria; but that was the order and they complied.

The wards were no more than bashas made with palm fronds, so the nursing sisters got their patients to improve them. Earth floors were flattened and swept; beds were repaired and orange boxes used to make partitions. Paint was scrounged, lawns were laid and flower beds planted out. The West Africans were particularly appreciative, clearly regarding their nurses as a cross between magician and kindly relative. Soon, new kit began to arrive; white bedspreads, blankets, bedjackets, sheets. 'The Africans were in seventh heaven' wrote Sister Dyer after an issue of brightly coloured dressing gowns.

A similar hospital, 66th Indian General, was situated on the line of communication near the Dimapur-Imphal road. Some indication of the level of work is given in the QA centennial book:

> . . . this amazing cluster of bamboo huts, interspersed with rough reeds . . . more like a native village in a jungle clearing than a busy hospital. 51,000 passed through this 100-bed hospital in 1944, often 300 in one day. The operating theatre functioned 24 hours a day . . . then back on ambulance trains . . .

Much of the credit for the vast increase in medical facilities must go to Mountbatten, one of whose first priorities on arrival as Supreme Commander was to press for more nursing sisters. But Giffard and Slim must also be given their due for recognising the link between good medical care and health discipline, and seeing that both were accorded the priority they merited. If any further testimony is needed as to the regard in which hospital staffs held their British Nursing Sisters, it is in the letter received by one of them on her departure for England at the end of the campaign:

> With the compliments of the Indian Army Medical Corps Personnel: We all staff feeling sorry for your transfer. As we can say boldly that your treatment with us just like SISTER (not as per designation). Therefore we request to God for your health, happiness and future prosperity.
>
> S. I. Hassan
> QM Havildar, IAMC
> (on behalf of personnel)

The basic theme of training doctrines in 15 Corps, and afterwards throughout the whole of 14th Army, was that from now on, units subjected to the familiar Japanese tactics of flanking hook and road-black should sit tight, adopt all-round defence and trust in air supply. By doing so, it would be the enemy who was surrounded. Another training maxim aimed to teach self-reliance and a positive approach down to the level of the individual soldier in his slit trench. In 1941, addressing the officers of his division in Iraq, Slim had told them what he was now impressing on all members of his corps: '. . . we make the best plans we can, and train our wills to hold steadfastly to them in the face of adversity . . . But in the end, every important battle develops to a point where there is no real control by senior commanders. Each soldier feels himself to be alone . . . the dominant feeling of the battlefield is loneliness . . .' This was nowhere more true than in the jungle.

The New Command

1943 also saw the creation of an entirely new Allied command structure. A Supreme Allied Commander was appointed to oversee South-East Asia. At the Quebec summit conference, where Churchill produced Wingate as an unannounced but highly successful star turn, the Allies agreed the appointment of Vice Admiral Lord Louis Mountbatten to this post. Now aged 43, his dashing if at times dangerously reckless performance as a destroyer captain in the first two years of the war had led to promotion as Chief of Combined Operations in London over the heads of hundreds of others. A natural aristocrat with close Royal connections, he and his personable wife, Edwina, the wealthy Cassels heiress, acquired a reputation as leading socialites in the 1920s and 1930s, moving in elevated circles closed to most serving naval officers. They had many friends in the world of show business, notably Noel Coward, whose film *In Which We Serve* is a thinly-disguised account of Lord Louis' naval exploits. Mountbatten's father, Prince Louis of Battenberg, had been a distinguished naval officer, compelled in 1914 to resign his post as First Sea Lord and professional head of the Royal Navy because of popular anti-German hysteria. His son was profoundly moved by this: it drove his ferocious professional ambition, eventually realised in 1955 when he in turn became First Sea Lord.

Mountbatten brought to his new job an air of confidence and style. He was ready and willing to play to the gallery and thoroughly enjoyed doing so. More importantly, he was able to focus attention at home on the sprawling theatre of war for which he was responsible. Very soon, the entertainments provided for the troops began to improve as well-known artistes toured South-East Asia, braving unknown perils of climate, health and the attentions of the enemy. Prominent amongst these were the comedian George Formby and Vera Lynn, the singer whose appearances to enthralled audiences, often close to the front areas, earned her the title of 'Forces' Sweetheart'. Better leave arrangements, film shows, the provision of good sports kit, even a beer ration, enabled the troops to escape, however fleetingly, from the realities of life in an unpleasant, unhealthy and dangerous war zone. Before long the Command had its own newspaper, *SEAC*. Professionally produced, and edited by Lt Colonel Frank Owen, in peacetime the editor of the *Evening Standard*, it made a great contribution to morale by featuring up-to-date news which could be trusted by the readership. *SEAC* reached the forward troops in many ways, not least by parachute, for it was a standard item on the manifest of every air drop.

Serving under Mountbatten was a carefully chosen Allied staff. Stilwell, wearing several hats, was Deputy Supreme Commander and Chief of Staff to Chiang Kai-shek, Commander of all United States forces in the China/Burma/India theatre, and Commanding General of the Northern Combat Area Command (the American-Chinese forces in northern Burma). Another

American, Lt General Wheeler, was chosen as Principal Administrative Officer in view of the enormous logistical resources now made available to the theatre by the United States government. Wheeler turned out to be an administrator of genius. General Giffard was made commander of British Land Forces, to be known as 11th Army Group. His area of responsibility included Burma, Ceylon and the Indian Ocean garrisons. Slim went to the new 14th Army, with headquarters at Comilla, responsible for actually fighting the battles to liberate Burma. To replace him at 15 Corps came Lt General A. F. P. Christison who, though not an Indian Army officer, was an old friend and colleague of Slim's. Christison was the son of the surgeon who had carried out the pioneering operation on Garnet Wolseley outside Rangoon as long ago as 1852. He had not intended to be a career soldier. Having taken a degree in medicine at Oxford in the fateful summer of 1914, he was commissioned into The Queen's Own Cameron Highlanders. Some months before, when Lord Haldane inspected the Oxford University Officers' Training Corps at its camp, he stopped in front of Cadet Christison to ask him if he intended going into the Army. 'No Sir' was the reply. 'I think you will be, and maybe sooner than you think' was Haldane's enigmatic answer. The young man saw his first action at Loos in 1915 where he gained an MC for rallying a shaky platoon by singing, in Gaelic, the March of the Cameron Men and leading them back into the fight.

Between the wars, Christison attended Staff College but in an army where promotion blocks abounded he was obliged to transfer to the Duke of Wellington's Regiment. He commanded the 'Dukes' in India and took the opportunity to learn Urdu. Later, he returned to India as commander of a Gurkha brigade, a rare distinction for a non-Indian Army officer. During this tour he improved his language qualifications by passing the advanced Urdu test. He had been told by a wise old friend, many years before, that if he took the trouble to learn his soldiers' languages he would hold the key to their hearts. As with his Gaelic, so it was with the Urdu. Wherever he went around his corps area he was able to converse fluently with his 'jawans', something they warmly respected. But Christison came to Burma in some sadness. His son, a Captain in the Duke of Wellington's, had been killed in action at the Taukkyan road block outside Rangoon in March 1942, commanding the battalion's carrier platoon.

The command structure in India was also changing. Wavell, promoted to Field Marshal in January 1943, was appointed Viceroy and took over from Linlithgow in October. He was succeeded as C-in-C India by General Sir Claude Auchinleck, whose vast area of responsibility extended from the front lines on the India-Burma border to the Near East. As C-in-C he was responsible for the huge recruiting, administrative and training organisation which had been set up in India; in his Command was also the teeming and intricate system of roads, railways, airfields and pipelines on which 14th

Army relied. Auchinleck's principal administrative officer, overseeing the whole infra-structure, was Lt General Sir Wilfred Lindsell.

On transferring his headquarters from Delhi to Kandy in Ceylon, Mountbatten immediately announced that in future the war against Japan would be prosecuted throughout the year, without stopping for the monsoon as had been the case until now. To him, this practice smacked too much of 18th century warfare, with armies leaving the field on the approach of cold weather and going into winter quarters. In making this decision, he claimed that adverse weather would be an ally in the war of disease, and he enlisted the help of the world's leading experts in tropical diseases, whilst the Japanese, short of drugs and medicines, faced growing sick lists.

The Supreme Commander now began visiting his far-flung command in order to put his message across and to infuse everyone with a sense of purpose and optimism. He was remarkably successful. An instinctive charismatic showman who did his homework, he learned enough phrases of the many languages of SEAC to use them effectively in his informal but carefully stage-managed talks. His message was simple, repeated almost word for word in hundreds of remote locations. The audiences loved it and would remember what he had said for the rest of their days:

> . . . If the Japs try their old dodge of infiltrating behind you, stay put. We will supply you by air. There will be no more retreats. We are not going to quit fighting when the monsoon comes, like drawing stumps at a cricket match when it rains. If we only fight for six months in the year the war will take twice as long. The Japs don't expect us to fight on; they will be surprised and caught on the wrong foot. We shall fight in places like the Kabaw Valley. We have got anti-malarial devices and we shall have the finest hospitalisation and air evacuation scheme that the Far East has ever seen. The Japs, who have nothing, will have to fight nature as well as us . . . Who started this story about the Jap superman? I have seen the Japs in Japan. Millions of them are unintelligent slum-dwellers, with no factory laws, no trades unions, nothing except an ignorant fanatical idea that their Emperor is God. Intelligent free men can whip them every time.

The effect was electrifying, nowhere more so than amongst the African troops. Mountbatten arrived unannounced one morning as the 11th battalion of the King's African Rifles were moving up to the front and talked to the Askari in their bivouacs. One of their British officers noted that his men '. . . had their tails right up and knew that they could beat the Japanese anywhere'. Mountbatten spoke to them in Swahili, asking them what District they came from, how long they had been in the KAR, what was their tribe, were they married, and if so, how many children they had – all subjects dear to the African soldier. At a 'baraza' or platoon conference around a camp fire that night, the excited Askari confided in their platoon commander: 'You can see he is a great chief and Brother to the King – you only have to compare him with the King's head on our coins to see the likeness. Truly then our lord the King has not forgotten us, and under his brother's command we cannot fail'.

A new sense of confidence began to spread around the Command. Far away in the headwaters of the Kaladan, the West Africans fingered their amulets and charms and felt that the Joss was good.

'Once more unto . . .'

*"You call yourselves a forgotten army. Well, you're wrong.
At home they haven't even heard of you."*

T HE ALLIES had carefully considered the strategy to be adopted in the war against Japan when they met in Quebec for the 'Quadrant' summit conference in August 1943, and this was reflected in the directive issued to Mountbatten as he assumed command in South-East Asia. He was to engage the Japanese closely in order to wear them down and occupy as much of their armed forces as possible so as to divert them from the crucial Pacific theatre. It was essential to keep China in the war for the same reason, and every effort must be made, Mountbatten was told, to broaden contacts with Chiang Kai-shek, to sustain air maintenance over the 'Hump' and, once new roads had been built, overland via Ledo. The directive required Mountbatten to use sea and air power to occupy some point which would compel the Japanese to react, thereby exposing themselves to massive counter-attack. He was accordingly promised a major battle fleet, to be based in Ceylon, and a generous allocation of assault shipping and landing craft, hitherto conspicuous by their absence in his theatre. In the autumn of 1943 Mountbatten's staffs were planning to implement a series of coordinated operations:

1. The recapture of the Andaman Islands; this was intended to be the lure which it was hoped would draw the Japanese fleet out for destruction in the Bay of Bengal.
2. An advance in the Arakan with the aim of capturing the port and airfields on Akyab Island.
3. An advance to the Chindwin, with another drive down the Hukawng valley from Ledo to Myitkyina, thus reopening the overland route to Yunnan.
4. The capture of Indaw by means of a bold airborne operation as a preliminary to a seaborne assault on Rangoon.
5. A major incursion by Wingate's Special Force to divert Japanese attention from the other operations.

Most of these plans had to be scrapped or drastically modified. The promised assault shipping was still needed in the Mediterranean. When Chiang Kai-shek was told that there was to be no immediate seaborne landing at Rangoon, he withdrew his earlier promise of additional troops for northern Burma. In fact, he never had much intention of getting deeply embroiled in the Burma campaign, certainly no more than was required to keep American supplies rolling in. His best troops were now earmarked for campaigns against Mao Tse Tung's Route Armies in their remote fastnesses. Consequently the Japanese had little difficulty in pinning down the residual Chinese forces in north Burma with one weak division.

SEAC now drew up a revised set of plans for the 1943-44 campaign. Lt General Scoones's 4 Corps would advance in strength from Imphal to the Chindwin and, if feasible, exploit across the river. At the same time Stilwell's troops were to advance down the Hukawng valley, helped as much as possible by Wingate's Special Force. Christison's 15 Corps was to advance down the Arakan with a division either side of the Mayu Range and with the 81st West African division moving down the Kaladan valley, fifty miles inland, as a flank guard.

As the monsoon of 1943 died away, patrol activity in the Arakan increased. Newly-arrived battalions in 5 and 7 Indian divisions had been working up their skills for some months and were now confident that they could beat the Japanese. The 1st Queen's Regiment had been blooded soon after their arrival when a patrol base was raided by an enemy party which tried an old trick. A Japanese officer shouted 'Tikhai, it's Johnny Gurkha!', knowing that a Gurkha patrol was also operating in the same area. Momentarily thrown by this, the British were rushed by the enemy, whose leader killed two men and wounded a third with his sword before he was despatched. On another occasion, when a Japanese patrol infiltrated into the Queen's battalion HQ area, it was stalked by an ad hoc group led by the second-in-command, Maj Grimston, and the regimental Quartermaster Sergeant. Grimston, a Sussex and Army cricketer, grabbed a sack of grenades and set about eliminating the intruders. His grenade-throwing style was greatly admired by the spectators, one of whom compared it to '. . . a good return to the wicket from the covers'. The RQMS was badly wounded but Grimston carried on until the Japanese had been dealt with.

If Mountbatten's staff had plans, so did the Japanese. The first Chindit raid had convinced them that the Allies would try to reconquer Burma early in 1944, before the monsoon. They were seriously overstretched maintaining forward positions on the line of the Chindwin over supply lines which were coming increasingly under attack by Anglo-American aircraft. If the British launched two simultaneous attacks, one in the Arakan and one from Imphal, it would be difficult for them to switch forces from one front to the other because of the extremely poor lateral road network behind the Japanese lines. The Japanese plan for 1944 was therefore drawn up. It would start with an advance against the Chinese in northern Burma by two divisions of 33rd Army. With their right flank secured, a major offensive could be launched across the Chindwin with the aim of capturing Imphal and its large stockpiles, and advancing over the Naga Hills to capture 14th Army's base area at Dimapur, which now sprawled for ten miles on both sides of the railway. With this prize in their hands, the Japanese could push on into northern India, to be greeted as liberators by a population seeking to cast off the rule of the Raj.

In order to tie down British forces and prevent reinforcement of Imphal by the transfer of divisions from the Arakan, an offensive was to be started there first. The code-name for the main Japanese thrust was 'U-Go' and that for the Arakan attack, 'Ha-Go', scheduled to start early in February 1944 with 'U-Go' a month later, by which time the Japanese High Command hoped that 15 Corps would have been so badly mauled that it would be unable to help fend off the thrust to Imphal and Dimapur.

Christison began to edge forward in the Arakan in December 1943 against light Japanese opposition. He was still tied to an overland operation, for not only was there still a desperate shortage of landing craft, but the Japanese were still strong at sea and in the air; the battle fleet promised to Mountbatten was not yet on station and unlikely to be so for some months. By the end of the month, 15 Corps had taken the port of Maungdaw, which Christison now used as a base for the semi-private 'navy' he had assembled with the assistance of friendly RNVR officers; it consisted of a collection of armed launches and sampans, invaluable amongst the creeks and chaungs of the coast. The Corps Commander used various means to get around the operational area; his diaries record transport by horse, jeep, the District Commissioner's launch *Stella*, a hollowed-out tree-trunk powered by a Johnson Seahorse engine, several types of light aircraft, a seaplane, an amphibious jeep, armoured car, Bren Gun carrier, and on foot. As the Corps nosed forward, an all-weather road was built in its wake. Hundreds of thousands of mud bricks were used for the road-bed and kilns were set up every few miles to provide them. Timber bridges spanned the numerous creeks and administrative units followed the fighting troops forward. At the end of the year 5 Division was up against the Japanese strongpoints around Razabil, where the previous year's offensive had come to grief. This time, however, there were to be no brave but futile frontal attacks.

Before launching his offensive, Christison had suggested that Wingate might consider launching Special Force into the void between 15 and 4 Corps. There was never a defined 'front line' in Burma and apart from special groups living in the hills, picking up information from the tribesmen, there were no fighting formations in the 300-mile gap. The meeting at which this possibility was discussed is best described by Christison:

> I found Wingate with an RAF photo mosaic spread on the floor. We discussed
> the project and he crawled about on the mosaic on hands and knees, smoking a

cigarette in an absurdly long holder. Presently, the ash dropped; he said 'Tut Tut' and waggled his beard to brush it off. I thought, here's a rum sort of fellow'.

Wingate turned the scheme down flat with the words 'If I have to work under a corps commander, it's not on!' The left flank therefore had to be entrusted to the 81st West African Division, at this stage lacking artillery and reliant for its transport on hordes of porters. It started off down the Kaladan valley, building a road as it went and constructing light aircraft strips, which were to be useful in the weeks to come.

Intelligence reports reaching 15 Corps indicated that the Japanese were preparing for action as well. It was important to obtain firm unit identifications and Christison ordered increased patrolling. A 'V' Force report indicated that two Japanese officers regularly fished a certain pond in the Buthidaung area. Maj General Frank Messervy, commanding 7 Division, called for confirmation, and a party of Gurkhas, all volunteers, set out to ambush the pond. Three days later they arrived at Messervy's headquarters carrying a wicker basket and asked to see the General. In Messervy's presence they emptied the basket on the ground; two Japanese heads and several fish bounced out. On being told to take these away they obliged, but hung around the entrance to the command post. 'Well . . .?' said Messervy. 'Please, sahib, may we have the fish . . .?'

At the beginning of February 15 Corps had advanced to a line running from just south of Maungdaw on the coast to the outskirts of Buthidaung inland. Its 5 and 7 Divisions were tenuously linked by the precarious fair-weather road over the Ngakyedauk Pass and, 12 miles further north, by the even more primitive packhorse track over the Goppe Pass. The all-weather road through the Mayu Range was still firmly in Japanese hands, defended by numerous well-constructed bunkers set on top of hills which dominated the valley floor.

A large Corps maintenance area had been set up at the eastern end of the Ngakyedauk Pass by the end of January, a prudent decision on Christison's part, in preparation for the final push forward towards Foul Point and on to Akyab. The Japanese knew all about this and it was a primary objective of the attack they now launched out of the blue. Operation 'Ha-Go' burst upon 7 Division early on the morning of 4 February. The Japanese 55th Division, its spearhead, was commanded by Lt General Hanaya Tadashi. Hanaya was a notable brute; a hardened veteran of the China campaign, he was greatly feared by his own staff, whom he frequently struck in public if they displeased him, and he had been known to order junior officers to commit hara-kiri after failing on a mission, telling them that they could use his sword if they wished. Overall command of the Japanese attack was in the capable hands of Lt General Sakurai Shozo. The attack on 7 Division was carefully planned and led by Maj General Sakurai Tokutaro. This Sakurai, who was not related to the 28th Army Commander, was one of the Japanese army's 'characters'. Known to all as 'Tokuta' he was renowned for his eccentric behaviour at social functions, where his party trick consisted of stripping naked and smoking cigarettes through his nostrils – and other orifices – as he performed a wild dance. This martial strip-teaser had a reputation for ruthlessness and was to confirm it as commander of 55 Division's Infantry Group. 'Tokuta's' spearhead was the regiment commanded by the formidable Colonel Tanahashi, already distinguished in the previous year's campaign as the man who stormed into 6th Brigade's HQ and captured its commander. He was ordered to make directly for the eastern end of the Ngakyedauk Pass and to block all attempts by 5 Division to come to 7 Division's rescue. After 7 Division had been dealt with, it would be 5 Division's turn. A smaller Japanese detachment was sent to seize the Goppe Pass and attack the rear of 5 Division, and, once Tanahashi had reached the Ngakyedauk Pass, another force under Colonel Kubo would cross over and attack 5 Division's lines of communication while yet another column, under Colonel Doi, pinned down 5 Division's forward brigades.

This bold plan almost succeeded, but it was seriously flawed. Like many other Japanese plans it depended on strict adherence to a rigid timetable. The old Chinese general who advised Slim during the 1942 retreat was wise to this, knowing that unless Japanese commanders could get their hands on their opponents' supplies within nine days, they would be in dire trouble. Everything in 'Ha-Go' hung on speedy capture of Christison's corps maintenance area at Sinzweya at the eastern end of the Ngakyedauk. Foresight had provided it with some defences; Christison had sent last-minute reinforcements over the pass, including some priceless Lee-Grant tanks, on the eve of the Japanese attack, and all personnel in what was known as the Admin Box were ordered to lay mines, wire themselves in, and prepare to fight it out. There were to be no more withdrawals.

In the light of dawn on 4 February Tanahashi Force advanced, moving fast (but not very silently) between two of 7 Division's brigades, who mistook the familiar sounds of pack mules and marching feet for a routine RIASC re-supply detail. With full daylight it was clear that the Japanese had stolen a march. Even before dawn, scattered firing could be heard in the mist as some 6,000 determined enemy troops moved rapidly, in column of march, straight for the approach to the Ngakyedauk Pass and the Admin Box, where the vulnerable stockpiles and ammunition dumps had been fortified as much as possible. Tanahashi's men cut every telephone line they could find and the defenders soon found themselves without reliable communications. By chance, the Japanese column heading for the Goppe Pass collided head-on with an RIASC mule column, moving forward with daily supplies for 7 Division. The subaltern in charge bravely stood his ground and his Pathan muleteers gave such a good account of themselves that the enemy column veered off to the left, abandoned its attempt to reach the Goppe, and recoiled in confusion onto Tanahashi's force. In Christison's opinion this furious little encounter was the actual turning point of the Arakan battle, for if the Japanese had managed to get over the Goppe Pass they would have turned south to attack 5 Division's headquarters and administrative areas as well as threatening 15 Corps HQ, sited near Bawli Bazar and defended by middle-aged Indian Army pensioners.

At the end of the first day Tanahashi could congratulate himself and his troops, who had brought off a successful hook around 7 Division's left flank, overrun Taung Bazar and were now pressing hard for Messervy's divisional HQ and the Admin Box. It was now imperative for Tanahashi that the Box be taken quickly, for his supply column had become separated from the main body and scattered. Without British ammunition and rations, Tanahashi's position would quickly become precarious. During the night of 6/7 February, the Divisional HQ was overrun; Messervy and his staff had to take to their heels, the general losing his hat in the confusion. The night was alive with tracer, explosions, flames from burning signals trucks and the shouts of rampaging Japanese infantry, described by a witness as like the sound of a football crowd at a cup tie. Messervy ordered his HQ staff to make their way over to the Admin Box, a hazardous five-mile journey across ground now swarming with excited Japanese who shot at anything that moved. Messervy, clad only in vest and pyjama trousers, got his group to safety. As he fought his way out, personnel and staff of the headquarters suddenly found themselves in the front line. Listeners to the frantic radio traffic in the last moments of the doomed HQ could only guess at what was going on. Finally they heard a voice over the air saying 'Put an axe through that set'; then silence.

Inside the Admin Box the garrison, described as 'mostly odds and sods', and including the surprised staff of the officers' clothing shop, prepared to sell their lives dearly under the inspiring leadership of Brigadier Evans, the commander of the Brigade from 5 Division which had crossed over the Ngakyedauk Pass only the previous day.

Evans found himself in charge of a very mixed bag of troops. The only combat units in the Box were the 2nd West Yorkshires, the 4/8th Gurkhas (less two companies which had become lost but fought their way in later) and two squadrons of tanks from the 25th Dragoons. He was well off for artillery, having six batteries of mixed calibres; but most of the 8,000 men in the Admin Box were administrative specialists manning stockpiles of ammunition, fuel, rations and other military stores. Clerks, signallers, postmen, muleteers, canteen staff, civilians, sanitary orderlies – all grabbed rifles, dug in, and prepared to fight. The Box was sited in a natural amphitheatre about a mile square, mainly dried padi fields, surrounded by brush and forest providing ample cover for the attackers. In the middle stood an isolated hillock, some 150 feet high, where large stocks of ammunition had been dumped. Known as 'Ammunition Hill', it was overlooked from all points of the compass. The Japanese had dragged numerous infantry guns along with them as well as hundreds of mortars and grenade launchers, and these now commenced a relentless bombardment of the Box.

The position of 7 Division now appeared desperate. Its commander had lost virtually all his HQ signals staff, together with their ciphers, and he could no longer exercise proper control over the battle. Messervy was no stranger to crises of this sort. When commanding 7 Armoured Division in North Africa his HQ had also been overrun by German Panzers and he had been taken prisoner, escaping on that occasion by pretending to be his own elderly soldier-servant. One of the artillery units which found itself in a neighbouring Box, formed by 33rd Indian Infantry Brigade of which it was part, was the 136th (1st West Lancashire) Field Regiment, Royal Artillery. This was a very close-knit unit, not unlike the 'Pals' battalions of World War I. Its officers and men had soldiered together for many months, and after thorough training in India they had been sent forward to 7 Indian Division, which alarmed some of them at first. Soon, however, they realised that they were serving in a first-class division and easily adjusted to the role of supporting Indian units. The first sight of an Indian infantry battalion, the 7/16th Punjabis, during a field firing exercise had been a revelation: 'As far as we could see, the infantry were all six feet tall. Their turnout, bearing and march discipline would have done credit to the Brigade of Guards', noted their historian. They were equally impressed by the short stature and apparent youth of the Gurkhas, their cheerfulness and evident soldierly virtues. Observation Post (OP) parties were supported by mule detachments of the RIASC, with whom they struck up a firm friendship. Soon, the Lancashire gunners were happier existing on a diet of chapatties and curry than the monotonous British rations. Anything was better than bully beef which, in that heat, liquified in the can and could be poured out in a greasy mess known as 'working mule'. They had absolute faith in their divisional commander, who was known to all as 'General Frank'. Before joining 7 Division they had carefully calibrated each 25-pounder gun, knowing that in jungle warfare, men's lives – their own in particular – would depend on extreme accuracy.

The 136th had been addressed by the Supreme Commander before going to the Arakan. He came to speak to a mixed British/Indian artillery camp and was well received, 'unlike certain senior British officers', the regimental chronicler records. Mountbatten, who had the gift of sensing the mood of his audience, concluded his remarks to the gunners with: 'You call yourselves the Forgotten Army. Well, you're wrong. At home they haven't even heard of you'. He was cheered to the echo for it.

To reach their gun area, the 136th had to cross the Ngakyedauk Pass, a hair-raising ascent of 1,000 feet in 1½ miles. A notice at the bottom of the pass read 'Sweat made this road – Carelessness will break it!' The gun-towing 'Quads', grinding up in bottom gear as ordered, just managed to reach the top, negotiating the short steep straights and acute hairpins.

Installed within 33rd Brigade's Box, the 136th had a spectacular baptism of fire. On the first day they were firing over open sights as eight guns worked at top speed for five minutes to stop an infantry attack in its tracks. The batteries were facing in all directions and targets had an alarming habit of materialising out of nowhere at extremely close range. If any hint of their predicament was needed, it came in the form of a signal from higher level: 'Hold out, and you will make history,' followed by 'All units on half rations at once'. Now they knew that things were critical, but the arrival of some of the 25th Dragoons' tanks boosted morale. At 0300 hrs on 9 February a mass of infantry with fixed bayonets was spotted bearing down on the battery positions, and all guns were brought to bear with devastating effect at such close range. Then, as the canister rounds tore into the mass of men in front, it was seen that some were Sikhs, retiring from their trenches and intermixed with the Japanese. In the morning the bodies of 30 of them, with many more Japanese, lay on the ground within yards of the guns.

Airdrops began to take place after four days; Dakotas escorted by Spitfires appears overhead and all ranks who could took cover, much of each drop being free-fall. Coloured streamers marked important commodities and after the drop there was a rush to help the RIASC sort out the loads. All this took place in full view of Japanese OPs and called for considerable bravery on the part of the supplies personnel who bore the brunt of it. During one such drop a horrifying incident took place; a parachute failed and a load of petrol crashed into the mule lines of a neighbouring Indian artillery unit. One of the muleteers was hurt, and one of his comrades rushed to his assistance carrying a naked light. The British gunner watched helplessly as the wretched mules, their voice boxes cut (a standard practice, to avoid noise at night) were engulfed in the fire to die mutely in dreadful agony, as did both muleteers. The surviving mules were quickly put out of their misery, and the enterprising quartermaster issued fresh meat that night. Not many felt able to eat it.

There was no running surface water in the Box, the only source being several hundred yards outside the perimeter and close to Japanese positions. Each Battery's water truck took turns to run the gauntlet, dashing out over open ground, pumping the tank full, and then returning, often under fire. With chlorine and salt added, it was ready to drink in two hours. Because of its foul taste it was issued as very sweet tea, thick with condensed milk. The water in soldiers' bottles looked like barley water. Despite this, all ranks agreed that the regiment's water dutymen were heroes.

Some men of the 136th had been caught up in the Admin Box when the

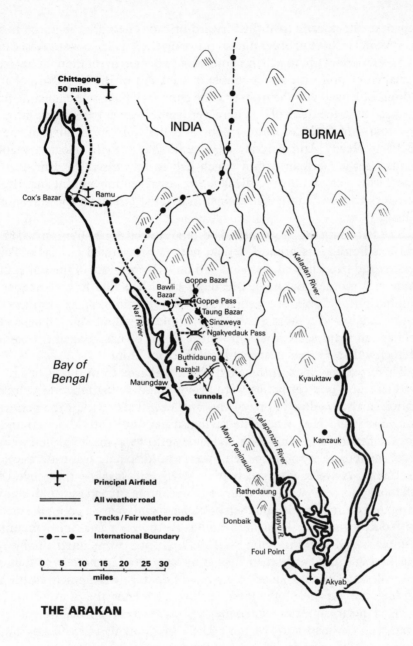

Chittagong
50 miles

INDIA

BURMA

Cox's Bazar
Ramu

Naf River

Kaladan River

Goppe Bazar
Bawli Bazar
Goppe Pass
Taung Bazar
Sinzweya
Ngakyedauk Pass

Bay of Bengal

Buthidaung
Razabil
Kyauktaw

Maungdaw
tunnels

Mayu Peninsula

Kalapanzin River

Kanzauk

Rathedaung

Mayu R.

Donbaik

Foul Point

Akyab

✈ Principal Airfield

═══ All weather road

▪▪▪▪▪ Tracks / Fair weather roads

●━●━ International Boundary

0   5   10   15   20   25   30
miles

THE ARAKAN

107

Japanese attack came. All the forward brigades had been required to send their vehicles there in order not to clutter up the brigade boxes. 'Rest camps' had also been set up, to which soldiers could be sent in rotation for hot baths, a change of uniform, and a couple of days out of the line. Now that the Admin Box itself was the front line the gunners who had been resting found themselves in the thick of it. There were some heavier guns there, including two four-gun 5.5in medium troops and the four 3.7in guns of the 8th (Belfast) Heavy Anti-Aircraft Regiment. These high velocity weapons, similar to the German 88mm which had so impressed the British in the desert war, were doubly useful, shooting down a number of Japanese fighter bombers and proving lethal against individual targets in the surrounding hills.

By 8 February the situation had become clearer, for 7 Division had rallied and was holding its ground. It had not, as proclaimed on Radio Tokyo, broken and run when surrounded. All ranks were aware of the stakes of the game and morale was high. Messervy handed a rifle to his sweeper – a humble 'untouchable' of a menial caste so low that in India its members were not even allowed to bear arms. He was told to go out and kill a Japanese soldier, and did so. Christison sent a signal of encouragement assuring Messervy that 'Help is nearer at hand than you think'.

There was no spot in the Box which was free from direct or indirect Japanese fire, and casualties were heavy, many being taken to a dressing station in the shadow of one of the smaller hillocks within the perimeter, known as MDS Hill, where life-saving surgery was carried out around the clock under incessant fire. Although every effort was made to build splinter-proof shelters, many of the patients were wounded here again after receiving treatment. A week into the battle, MDS Hill became the scene of an infamous act. It was overrun by screaming Japanese soldiery who slaughtered the wounded on their stretchers, and then set about the medical staff, doctors and nursing orderlies alike. As the West Yorkshires mounted a counter-attack the surviving staff and patients were lined up by their attackers and used as human shields by laughing Japanese, who then shot most of them in cold blood. Finally, six doctors were put to death after tending the Japanese wounded. A few days later the West Yorkshires avenged this terrible deed when they ambushed a party of enemy in a nearby river bed. On inspection of the bodies, many items identified as coming from the MDS were found. One of the Japanese was even wearing General Messervy's red-banded cap. A rare prisoner confirmed that this was the soldier who had picked up the cap in the wreckage of 7 Division's command post; he was known by his comrades, in the few days remaining to him, as 'Shogun' or 'Warlord'. The hat was returned to its rightful owner, who wore it for the rest of the campaign.

As the incessant bombardment continued, the inevitable happened; on the night of 9/10 February a Japanese shell detonated the main dump at Ammunition Hill, which blew up spectacularly. The position of the enemy guns had been revealed, however, and brilliant counter-battery fire now destroyed them. A few hours later, after a large group of Japanese had been killed marching across open ground, sets of marked maps and operational orders were recovered. They revealed that 'Ha-Go' had fallen fatally behind schedule. The writing was on the wall but Hanaya persisted in attacking the Admin Box instead of bypassing it and gambling on the capture of stores elsewhere.

Twice, the Japanese and their allies of the Indian National Army got onto the top of Ammunition Hill, defended by gunners who nearly all died, to be driven off each time by the tireless West Yorkshires and the tanks of the 25th Dragoons. The defence of this area was in the hands of the commanding officer of the 24th Light Anti-Aircraft Regiment, whose men, when not firing their guns over open sights, fought as infantry, shoulder to shoulder with an assortment of men from every regiment and corps. After the massacre at the Dressing Station, everyone knew that there would be no mercy for the wounded or prisoner. No Japanese who now entered the area left it alive. Further away from the Box was another Main Dressing Station on the banks of the Ngakyedauk Chaung at its junction with the Kalapanzin River. From here it was possible to evacuate casualties further up the valley in sampans and country boats. The Japanese arrived here unexpectedly on 6 February and the doctors unanimously decided that in view of the track record of the Japanese Army, they could forego their non-combatant status. They enlisted the help of any patients capable of holding a rifle and between them managed to hold the enemy at bay for 24 hours while the seriously sick – mostly cerebral malaria cases – were spirited safely away in boats. Finally, this improbable garrison took the patients' rifles from the unit armoury – 150 of them – together with their ammunition, and got safely away.

The Ngakyedauk Pass was cleared of Japanese, then retaken by them in some of the most ferocious fighting of the war. But help was on its way. From the north came Lomax's 26 Division, followed closely by 36 Division. The Japanese were now tied to an anvil formed by 7 Division, and the two fresh formations were the hammer. By 19 February there were signs that the Japanese were pulling out, after a final desperate attack which brought them to within small arms range of Messervy's new HQ. On 24 February Maj General Briggs of 5 Division crossed the Ngakyedauk Pass in a tank, from whose turret he dismounted to present Messervy with a well-earned bottle of Scotch. The fight was won; more than 5,000 Japanese lay dead on the battlefield and unknown numbers in the surrounding hills. There were virtually no Japanese prisoners.

As this battle raged, a remote struggle was taking place in the depths of the Kaladan Valley, down which 81 West African Division had been advancing for some weeks, steadily pushing their road ahead as they went. General Hanaya had assessed this threat to his right flank and considered it could be met by a solitary battalion which he ordered to withdraw, fighting a series of rearguard actions as it fell back in the path of the Africans.

By 21 February the West Africans had reached the village of Medaung, about 15 miles east of Buthidaung, where they built an airstrip capable of handling Dakotas. By the 25th, they were at Kyauktaw, an important riverside village dominated by Pagoda Hill, rising some 250 feet above river level. The divisional commander, Maj General Woolner, was under instructions from Christison to prevent the Japanese from mounting operations against 7 Division from the Kaladan Valley. He decided to move further down the valley and his troops started out on 29 February. For reasons best known to himself, he did not consider it necessary to place a strong detachment on top of Pagoda Hill, which overlooked the countryside for miles around. Consequently, when a Japanese probing attack was launched it flung the West African Division back in confusion. Matters had not been helped by the absence of its reconnaissance unit, borrowed for use on the far side of the Mayu Hills. All that Woolner had was a shaky unit called the East African Scouts, which he had been mis-employing as divisional headquarters defence unit (probably because he had little faith in its operational ability). Apart from being Swahili-speakers its soldiers were not regular King's African Rifles personnel, but an assortment collected by the Scouts' officers, most of whom were big game hunters and safari guides. In the entire unit there was only a handful of European officers and NCOs, and once these had become casualties the unit melted away into the bush. Christison ordered Woolner to sort out his division and retire back up to the head waters of the Kaladan. Woolner, who had aired some peculiar views on bush fighting, was shortly thereafter removed from his command by Christison, to be replaced by Maj General Loftus-Tottenham, an experienced Gurkha soldier. One of Woolner's theories was that his soldiers should not dig in at any time, but stay upright and fight their enemy like men. The results of this eccentric doctrine were to be seen as soon as a serious Japanese attack was made on his division.

By the end of the first week in March Christison was re-deploying to complete the defeat of the Japanese in the Arakan. Supported by a massive artillery barrage, the heaviest yet seen on this front, 7 Division broke through to Buthidaung. After three days of stubborn resistance the town was captured. A day earlier, 5 Division began to clear the western end of the old railway road so as to secure communication between the two divisions. It was also essential to clear the well-established Japanese strongpoints around Razabil which had given so much trouble a year earlier. It took a great concentration of artillery fire, aerial bombing and infantry assault to do it, but the job was done, the Japanese garrisons fighting to the last, to the grudging admiration of their assailants. The last enemy strongpoint overlooking the tunnels was silently abandoned on the night of 18/19 March.

The 14th Army had won its first battle. The effect on morale was out of all proportion to the scale of the battle. Victory now actually seemed possible.

Operation 'Thursday'

"Turn you to the strongholds, ye prisoners of hope."

A S CHRISTISON rounded off his successful campaign in the Arakan, 15 Corps was already changing as new formations arrived to replace first 5 and then 7 Divisions, who were now redeployed successively to the Assam front, where 4 Corps was dealing with the main Japanese thrust.

Operation 'U-Go' began on 7 March. Two days earlier, the second Chindit expedition, Operation 'Thursday', had been launched. Following his appearance at the 'Quadrant' conference, where he had been produced by Churchill rather like a conjuror's rabbit, Wingate had been promoted to command Special Force, which for purposes of security and deception was given the title of 3 Indian Division. Its units were actually a mixture of British battalions from the disbanded 70 Division, with Gurkhas and West Africans, supported by British gunners, and American Army engineers for rapid construction of airstrips deep in enemy territory on which Dakotas could land. It was to be a very different operation from 'Longcloth'.

This time, the greater part of the force would be lifted into its operational area in gliders and transport aircraft. For this, Wingate enjoyed the services of what amounted to his own independent air force, No 1 Air Commando. Headed by two brilliant young aviators of the United States Army Air Corps, Colonels Cochran and Alison, it comprised squadrons of combat and transport aircraft as well as WACO CG-4A gliders, capable of carrying light vehicles, field guns, engineer tractors, mules and combat troops. Mindful of the need to evacuate casualties by air instead of leaving them behind, the Air Commando also had a number of light aircraft equipped to carry two stretcher cases.

Operation 'Thursday' was to be more than a raid or a reconnaissance. Wingate saw it as nothing less than a full-scale invasion. Its strategic function was twofold: firstly, to divert Japanese attention from Stilwell's advance towards Myitkyina and cut enemy lines of communication to the northern front; secondly, by aggressive operations in the Mogaung-Indaw area, to interfere with the first Japanese build-up for 'U-Go'. Once the Chindit brigades had been inserted, they were to construct heavily defended bases, or 'Strongholds' – a term derived from the Old Testament in which Wingate was well versed. He had in mind the words of the prophet

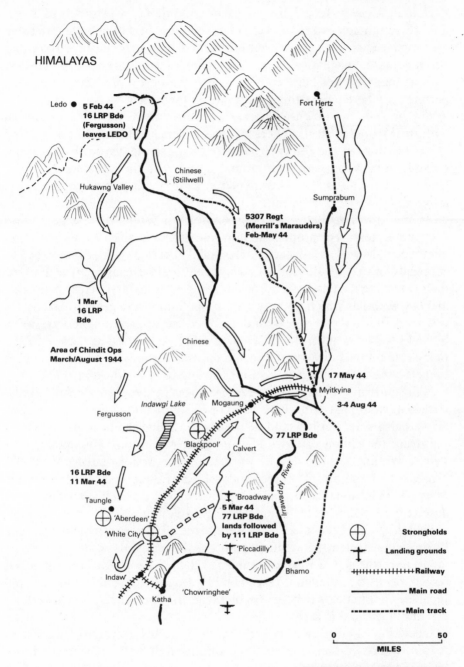

HIMALAYAS

Ledo •

**5 Feb 44
16 LRP Bde
(Fergusson)
leaves LEDO**

Fort Hertz •

Hukawng Valley

Chinese
(Stillwell)

Sumprabum •

**5307 Regt
(Merrill's Marauders)
Feb-May 44**

**1 Mar
16 LRP
Bde**

Chinese

**Area of Chindit Ops
March/August 1944**

17 May 44

Fergusson

Indawgi Lake

Mogaung •

Myitkyina •

3-4 Aug 44

'Blackpool'

Calvert

77 LRP Bde

**16 LRP Bde
11 Mar 44**

Taungle •

'Aberdeen'

'White City'

✠ 'Broadway'

**5 Mar 44
77 LRP Bde
lands followed
by 111 LRP Bde**

✠ 'Piccadilly'

Irrawaddy River

Indaw •

Bhamo •

Katha •

'Chowringhee'

✠

⊕ **Strongholds**

✠ **Landing grounds**

+++++++++++++++ **Railway**

───────── **Main road**

------------ **Main track**

0   50

MILES

OPERATION 'THURSDAY'

Zechariah (Ch.9, v.12); 'Turn you to the stronghold, ye prisoners of hope.' The 'Strongholds' were to act as pivots for highly mobile offensive operations against Japanese communications centres, headquarters and administrative installations. Each was to be made inaccessible to vehicles, with an airstrip built close enough to be covered by fire from within the perimeter, where field artillery, mortars and light anti-aircraft guns would be dug in. A mobile defence force was to prowl outside the defences, to deal with any Japanese patrols. There was one weakness: although air power had given the Chindits the ability to outflank their enemies vertically, it was not possible to provide them with ground mobility to the same degree. Once landed, the Chindits of 1944 were no more mobile than their predecessors, moving at the pace of their mules.

Animal transport had been indispensable on Wingate's first expedition and mules featured prominently in the load manifests for Operation 'Thursday', as well as 547 pack horses and 250 bullocks. All the mules were surgically muted by the Indian Army Veterinary Department to prevent their betraying the position of columns at night, as had frequently happened in 1943. Animals which underwent this operation were generally ready for full work within two weeks and suffered no apparent ill effects. The bullocks were 'meat on the hoof' but could also be used as pack animals. Being ruminants, however, they could only be worked for about six hours in every 24; the rest of the day was for sleep and chewing the cud.

Wingate firmly believed that his presence 'in the enemy's guts', as he termed it, would have a decisive effect on the impending Japanese offensive. He was also sure that it would help Stilwell, facing the formidable task of capturing the clutch of airfields centred on Myitkyina. His opinion was shared by Slim, Giffard and Mountbatten. The first essential was to gain command of the air. The 3rd Tactical Air Force, commanded by Air Marshal Sir John Baldwin, was ordered to achieve this. The first aim was to deceive the Japanese as to 'Thursday's' operational area. Airstrikes, dummy supply drops, and faked landings were made all over central and northern Burma while a relentless air offensive drove the remnants of the Japanese air forces from the sky. Strategic bombers of the US Army Air Force attacked targets deep in the enemy rear, notably around Rangoon. This led the Japanese commanders to believe at one stage that an Allied seaborne landing was imminent in that area.

Operation 'Thursday' was launched from airfields around Lalaghat in Assam, where Colonel Cochran had concentrated his transport and glider force. To maximise the initial lift it was decided to see if two WACO gliders could be towed behind a single C-47 Dakota. In great secrecy and at night, trials were carried out; it was found to be possible, providing the Dakota tug was stripped of all superfluous internal fittings and carried the bare minimum of fuel. The operation was to make extreme demands on the skill and courage of No 1 Air Commando's glider pilots; flying at night over some of the most inhospitable terrain in the world in their overloaded WACOs, they were to land deep inside enemy country, in clearings which could be ambushed or strewn with obstacles. The Dakota tug crews were no less brave, as they were required to come back again and again in the following weeks, day and night, often in the face of heavy Japanese fire, to deliver men, mules and equipment and evacuate ever growing numbers of casualties. As the Allied air offensive intensified, photographic sorties were flown to check the state of the glider landing zones, or LZs, in the selected Indaw area. All had been visited during the 1943 expedition when one, now code-named 'Piccadilly', had been used several times by Dakotas for re-supply and casualty evacuation missions. Wingate planned to land five of his six brigades on three LZs: Piccadilly, Broadway and Chowringhee. The initial landings would take place on the nights of 5 and 6 March. As soon as glider-borne engineers had cleared airstrips, the main force would land in Dakotas.

One Chindit brigade, Fergusson's, was to be inserted on foot. In October 1943, Stilwell, tired of waiting for a British offensive which would divert Japanese attention from the Myitkyina area, had set out with Chinese troops down the Hukawng Valley from northern Burma. The Japanese resisted and progress was slow, but at the end of February the US 5307th Provisional Regiment had joined the march, commanded by Brig. General Merrill. The American equivalent of the Chindits, they had undergone similar training. Known as 'Merrill's Marauders' their presence, augmented by a detachment of tanks, invigorated Stilwell's advance against the redoubtable Japanese 18th Division. Stilwell now used Merrill's men for flanking attacks in the Japanese manner; the Chinese pinned down the Japanese as the Marauders worked their way round to the rear. Behind Stilwell's advance, US Army engineers built a road which, once Myitkyina was taken, would re-establish the land link with China. On 5 February, Fergusson's 16th LRP Brigade set out from Ledo on a line of march to the west of and parallel to that of Stilwell and Merrill, aiming to reach the Indaw area at the same time as Wingate's airlifted main body.

On the afternoon of 5 March, Wingate held his final briefing for Operation 'Thursday' on the airfield at Hailakandi, near Lalaghat. A number of senior commanders were present, including Slim, Baldwin, Cochran, and Maj General Stratemeyer, USAAF, commanding the Allied Eastern Air Command. During the briefing an officer arrived bearing a series of air photos taken earlier that day, showing the surface of the LZ at Piccadilly covered with great logs. Wingate's immediate reaction was that the Japanese had somehow got wind of the operation, possibly betrayed to them by the Chinese. Someone recalled that in 1943, press photographers had taken pictures of C-47s on the ground at Piccadilly, which had subsequently appeared in 'Life' magazine. Tense and exhausted by the immense strain of planning and mounting this great operation, Wingate all but broke down, calling for its cancellation on the spot. Slim took him quietly aside and pointed out that the other LZs, Broadway and Chowringhee, were both clear of obstructions. He was also anxious to avoid a public scene such as that on the banks of the Chindwin in the previous year when Wingate, finding that all the boats had been removed to the far bank, had flung himself down on the sand in a paroxysm of rage. Wingate replied that the LZs could well be surrounded by concealed Japanese troops lying in ambush, and that any attempt to land would result in slaughter. Then he calmed down and, after telling Slim that the responsibility was his, agreed to proceed. Slim was content: he had borne other responsibilities during the past two years and knew that cancellation at this stage, with the men keyed to fighting pitch, would be calamitous. Calvert, commanding the Chindit brigade destined for Piccadilly, stated his readiness to go ahead with a landing on one of the other LZs. It was agreed that if the initial landings were successful, he would send back the signal 'Pork Sausage' so that the main airlift could go ahead at first light. If things went drastically wrong he would halt the operation with the code-word 'Soya Link', a wry reference to the most detested item in 14th Army's rations.

While this drama was taking place the troops were getting to know their glider pilots, one of whom turned out to be the former juvenile film star Jackie Coogan, at that time married to the celebrated pin-up and film star Betty Grable. Private Worrall of the 1st Battalion King's Liverpool Regiment found himself in the next glider, jammed in with nineteen others, all festooned like him with equipment, weapons, ammunition and rations. Cochran was faced with re-briefing his pilots when the Piccadilly landing was cancelled; they had been rehearsing it for weeks day and night with models and air photos, and were confident that they knew the position of every tree and obstacle in the area. Now they would be towed up into the night sky, to be released, after a dangerous 2½-hour flight over mountainous jungle, for a blind landing on an unknown LZ. Cochran was a master of man-management; standing on the bonnet of a jeep, he told the pilots that he had found a much better LZ for them. It was called Broadway.

As dusk fell the gliders began to take off at five-minute intervals behind their straining tugs. Soon they were labouring over mountains reaching 7,000 feet and more into the sky. In turbulent air, tow ropes snapped and gliders vanished into the dark below, to land as best they could in mountainous jungle. Out of 67 which left Hailakandi only 32 arrived over Broadway, which lay in darkness; the pathfinders sent ahead with lamps to mark the LZ had come down some 50 miles away (surviving this, they set out on foot, arriving three days later). Private Worrall's glider cast off from its tug over the LZ, seen dimly far below as an open area of country punctuated by clumps of dense woodland and forest. The actual strip was in open grassland flanked by dried paddy fields. The pilot did little for his passengers' morale by yelling out, 'Hell, it's going to be murder, no lights on the ground', and giving a pessimistic running commentary all the way down.

Seconds before landing, he shouted for some of the passengers to go aft, as the glider was nose-heavy. Worrall did so, crawled up a narrow plank in the tail and promptly put a foot through the glider's bottom. He was struggling to regain the cabin when the pilot shouted a final warning that the strip ahead was blocked with wrecked gliders. Then there was a terrific crash. The tail broke off and Worrall was thrown out. He got to his feet and walked over to the twisted wreckage, from which only four men emerged unhurt. The rest were lying dead and dying in the tangled, twisted remains, a mass of metal tubing, wood, canvas, equipment and bodies. Worrall looked in disbelief at the mangled remains of friends with whom he had been enjoying a last cup of tea and a sing-song in the charwallah's hut at Hailakandi only a few hours before. He tried to drag one of them out, but the man's arm came off in his hands and he passed out, to be revived by a medical sergeant slapping him in the face.

Similar scenes were being enacted all over the LZ as the gliders continued to come in, many to hit the wrecks of those already down, some to miss the cleared ground altogether and crash into the surrounding trees. Most of the light bulldozers had been lost, but as soon as there was enough light, Calvert toured the area and put all hands to work to clear the strip with their bare hands. In the worst hour of the night, when it seemed that the landing had gone disastrously wrong, he had decided to stop further landings until the LZ could be sorted out, and signalled 'Soya Link' back to Chindit HQ, provoking a bitter outburst from Wingate against Slim. A few hours after sunrise, however, with the strip cleared of wreckage and marked out, he sent 'Pork Sausage', and the mercurial Wingate regained his spirits. By dark, the first C-47s were arriving with reinforcements, and evacuating the night's casualties. During that night, gliders started landing at 'Chowringhee', followed by C-47s with the rest of the force. Within four days, 9,000 troops, 1,360 mules and 250 tons of equipment had been landed without a single further casualty.

The arrival of Fergusson's brigade on foot brought the force's strength to 12,000. Four out of Wingate's six brigades had now been inserted; a fifth, Brigadier Perowne's 23rd, had been deployed for operations on the northern flank of 4 Corps. So far the Japanese had not reacted, but it was obvious that they soon would. It was time to abandon 'Chowringhee', which was impossible to defend, and set up the first Stronghold. Code-named 'Aberdeen', it was nearly 40 miles north of Indaw and within easy striking distance of the Indaw-Mogaung railway. Only two hours after

'Chowringhee' had been evacuated it was heavily attacked by Japanese aircraft, but all they hit were crashed gliders; serviceable gliders had been recovered with the new 'snatch' technique developed by the Air Commando: a tug aircraft trailing a hook on an elasticated rope flew over a glider equipped with a special harness enabling it to be caught up and towed straight into the air. Take-off was spectacular, but it resulted in the salvage of dozens of gliders and the safe evacuation of hundreds of sick and wounded from places where transport aircraft could not land.

Fergusson's column was also making for 'Aberdeen'. It included the 2nd Battalion of the Queen's Regiment. There was a good spirit in this close-knit and efficient unit. All ranks counted themselves lucky in their Anglican padre, the Revd G. Pritt of the Royal Army Chaplains' Department. Church of England clergymen often pursue unusual hobbies, and Pritt's was codes and ciphers; he was accordingly always welcomed by the signals platoon, where he gladly helped out. On 19 March, after their 300-mile march, the Queen's arrived at Aberdeen. 'It lay in a smiling fertile valley,' wrote an officer, 'commanded by the Kalet Taung mountains, and dotted with well-built houses and neat gardens.' By the end of the month an airstrip had been completed and Brigadier Tom Brodie's 14th LRP Brigade had flown in. The Force was now almost complete and the campaign could start. Columns began to move out in all directions to attack Japanese outposts, harass lines of communication and block roads and railways. At Wingate's request, more units, including the West African brigade, were flown in to act as Stronghold garrisons, freeing Chindits for mobile operations. Calvert blocked the railway near Henu and set up a Stronghold nearby, named 'White City' because of the hundreds of supply-drop parachutes which were soon draped over the surrounding trees.

The Japanese, sensing the presence of a hostile foreign body, began to react. 'Aberdeen' came under heavy attack, and other columns reported that resistance was stiffening throughout the 'Thursday' area. Wingate now asked Slim for reinforcements. He could not have timed the request at a worse moment. The main Japanese attack had burst on 4 Corps, and all priorities were being given to the Imphal and Kohima battles. Transport aircraft were at a premium, and the airlift of 14 LRP brigade into 'Aberdeen' had been at the cost of moving 5 Division from the Arakan to Imphal. Furthermore, Slim had been nettled by the way in which Wingate had procured the 14th Brigade airlift, by-passing him with a personal signal to Mountbatten. Slim, notwithstanding, continued to give Wingate all the support he could spare.

Meanwhile, the Japanese were closing in on the remaining LZs. For some days 'Broadway' was surrounded at close quarters and the airlift had to be suspended while the enemy were thrown out. Earlier, some Spitfires had been flown in to provide much-needed cover against attacks by Japanese fighters operating from bases in Siam. A number of these were shot down, boosting morale on the ground, but shortage of early-warning radars enabled the Japanese to put in a surprise low-level airstrike which caught and destroyed most of the Spitfires on the ground. Reluctantly, the RAF withdrew the survivors to safer airfields in Assam. Lack of fighter cover did not deter the RAF and USAAF transport crews from continuing the Broadway airlift despite the risk of interception, and many seriously wounded or critically-ill soldiers owed their lives to the airmens' devotion and courage.

By the end of March 'White City', under Calvert's energetic command, was a strongly-defended base for many successful operations against the Japanese lines of communication. Elswhere, Wingate had ordered Fergusson to attack Indaw, a key railway centre with an important airfield. Its Japanese garrison, some 2,000 strong, was well-placed, controlling the principal supply of good drinking water, whilst Fergusson's men were beginning to suffer from acute dehydration. The 2nd Leicesters went into the attack on 26 March, but the element of surprise had been lost and they were repulsed with heavy casualties. Three days earlier, the Queen's battalion had been ambushed south of the town, losing their mortars and most of their mules. His mission foiled, Fergusson withdrew, ordering his columns to concentrate back at 'Aberdeen'. Far worse news now reached the Chindits: on 24 March Wingate had been killed while flying from Imphal back to his headquarters at Sylhet.

Battle for Survival

"for a brief moment in our lives he made us bigger than ourselves."

A S SOON AS it had been confirmed that there were no survivors in the burnt-out wreck of the B-25 bomber in which Wingate had been flying, Slim appointed Brigadier W. D. A. Lentaigne, commander of 111th LRP brigade, to take command of Special Force. Lentaigne put his Brigade Major, Major J. H. Masters in command, oddly, without promoting him, and told him to concentrate the brigade's five columns for an attack on the important Pinbon-Pinlebu track, along which large numbers of Japanese reinforcements constantly marched.

Wingate's death came at a crucial moment. The Japanese offensive into Assam was charging ahead as the forward divisions of 4 Corps strove to get back onto the Plain of Imphal. Operation 'Thursday' was in full swing, with up to 30 columns marching and counter-marching deep in Japanese-held territory. Wingate's theories of Deep Penetration were facing their supreme test. If correct, the presence of these columns in the enemy's rear would have a significant effect on the battle for Imphal and on the conduct of operations in northern Burma. Events were to show that there was little effect on 'U-Go', the Japanese having launched it without over-dependence on the vulnerable L of C, sustaining themselves on captured British stocks where they could lay hands on them. In the north, however, the Chindits were to be of considerable use to Stilwell, as will be seen.

Lentaigne was a Gurkha officer with a fine fighting record. Observing his somewhat donnish appearance and old-fashioned metal-rimmed spectacles, who would have supposed that he had already killed a Japanese officer in single combat with his own sword? However, he certainly did not possess the extraordinary presence – indeed, charisma – of his incredible predecessor, with whom it was well known he disagreed on many issues. Lentaigne was a professionally competent, conventionally-minded officer of the type Wingate detested, and he was certainly not Wingate's personal choice as his successor, had he been given the chance to nominate one. In a letter to Slim, years later, Bernard Fergusson mentioned this matter: . . .

> . . . I was amused and not a bit surprised at your saying [in *Defeat into Victory*, which had just been published] that no less than three officers told you that Wingate had told them that they were to be his successor . . . he told me, on the

Ledo road – it must have been the end of January 1944 – that Mike (Calvert) was his nominated successor, and that he knew I was senior to Mike, but he didn't care a damn. This was a month after I had sought to resign . . . I told him that I thought Mike was absolutely the right chap to take on from him, and that I wouldn't have felt up to it even if he'd considered me; and that in any case he would remember that I wanted to go back to the [Black] Watch after that year's fighting. He smiled his sinister smile and said: 'Nonsense; you are going to be one of my marshals!'

The gathering strength of the opposition, coupled with a reduction in friendly air support due to the higher priorities of 4 Corps, and the loss of the Broadway Spitfires, brought Lentaigne under increasing pressure. His men were now visibly tiring under a well co-ordinated Japanese counter-offensive. The importance of Indaw as a likely British objective had been recognised quickly by the enemy, who launched a series of attacks on the Strongholds.

The first to receive attention was 'White City' on 17 March. Calvert's men defended themselves stoutly, inflicting heavy casualties with well-sited field artillery and Bofors anti-aircraft guns firing over open sights. It was here that the 1st South Staffordshires and 3/6th Gurkha Rifles fought shoulder to shoulder in a desperate hand-to-hand battle. When the two battalions charged a Japanese position, the defenders rose from their foxholes to meet them in the open. In this bloody head-on encounter, Lt Cairns of the South Staffords had his left arm hacked off by a Japanese officer's sword, but he killed his opponent and fought on with the sword until he collapsed. Calvert ran over to try and help, but there was nothing he could do. Cairns looked up at him; 'Have we won, Sir? Was it all right? Did we do our stuff? Don't worry about me.' He was awarded a posthumous Victoria Cross.

The pitched battles now being forced onto the Chindits were what Wingate had always tried to avoid, knowing that his lightly-equipped troops could not match the Japanese in a stand-up fight, well provided as they were with motor transport, artillery and mortars (in particular the six-inch variety whose huge bomb had a flight time of 90 seconds and was devastating when it exploded). He had preached the doctrine of the Stronghold believing that if hotly pursued, a column would be able to take cover in well-protected positions, relying on air supply and casualty evacuation as it fended off the attackers. He had written some months before his death:

The ideal situation for a Stronghold is the centre of a circle of thirty miles' radius consisting of closely wooded and very broken country, only passable to pack transport . . . (it) should ideally consist of a level upland with a cleared strip for Dakotas, a separate supply dropping area, taxi-ways to the stronghold, a neighbouring friendly village or two, an inexhaustible and uncontaminatable supply of water within the Stronghold. The motto of the Stronghold is NO SURRENDER.

More and more reliance now had to be placed on the Strongholds, and Special Force, from being the agile strike force envisaged by its inspired creator, was forced onto the defensive, a role for which it was not fully equipped.

At the end of the first week in April, with the Imphal battle resting on a knife-edge, the Japanese made a fatal mistake. Instead of pressing on to Dimapur, where huge pickings awaited them, they closed on Kohima and became bogged down when its garrison there resolutely held out. The 23rd LRP Brigade, kept aside for contingencies, was ordered by Slim to deploy on the northern flank of the Japanese thrust towards Dimapur, where it successfully harassed Japanese supply columns. Two more of Lentaigne's brigades, Brodie's 14th and Masters' 111th, were ordered to leave the Indaw area and march west to augment 23rd Brigade's operations, but were recalled when Stilwell, whose advance on Myitkyina had again been halted, angrily accused his allies of not pulling their weight.

At bay in their Strongholds or on the march, the Chindits were totally dependent on air supply, whether landed or air-dropped. It was fairly safe to ask for an air-drop when the column was on the march in forested country where the chance of enemy interference on the ground was slight. In open country it could be perilous and was nearly always carried out by night. A long 'L' of blazing petrol cans was set out as drop-zone marker, and the troops then took cover to a flank as the supplies cascaded down, some on parachutes, some free-dropped. The parachute supply had caused problems in the earlier expedition and a substitute for the costly silk canopies had to be found. It was jute, which was readily available in India. Maj General Snelling, Slim's chief adminstrative staff officer, ensured that 11th Army Group and HQ India set up the industrial operation needed to produce these 'Parajutes' by the thousand. They constituted one of the logistic triumphs which helped to beat the Japanese, together with the 'Bithess' road and, above all else, the harnessing of air power to the supply of the army in the field.

For the RAF and USAAF pilots and their crews of cargo despatchers it was a matter of honour to complete their hazardous missions, fraught with increasing peril as the monsoon approached and broke. The airfields in Assam were shrouded in cloud and mist, and it was necessary to take off blind and climb thousands of feet into clear air in order to cross the mountains with safety before cautiously letting down through the murk onto the central plain where, fortunately, visibility was better. There were no weather radars on aircraft of that era, and Dakota crews had to hope for the best when flying blind on instruments; inadvertent entry into a cumulonimbus thunder-cloud spelt disaster as the aircraft would be gripped by phenomenal air currents and turbulence, capable of tearing the wings off a plane and hurling it to destruction far below.

One can only speculate as to the fate of dozens of aircraft posted 'missing' during supply missions, but many must have spent their last terrifying minutes thrown around like toys as lightning flashed and huge hailstones struck them; the spectral blue glow of St Elmo's Fire, caused by static build-up, would have lit the interior of the plane where the RASC and RIASC despatchers fought the effects of gravity, alternatively weightless, then jammed helplessly to floor or roof. Freight would break loose from its lashings as the plane, thrown on its back and completely out of control, plunged wildly in the black core of the storm. Finally the dreaded sound of airframe failure under stresses unimagined by designer or builder, and the last terrible seconds as the contorted mass of disintegrating metal took its brave crew to their deaths.

It was frequently necessary for column commanders to put their men on half rations and this, coupled with water shortage, began to sap mens' energy and endurance. To boost morale under these trying conditions, every effort was made to include mail and newspapers in the airdrops. To allay the anxiety of families at home, Wingate had thoughtfully devised a standard letter which was sent periodically to Chindits' next-of-kin:

It is probable that you will not receive any letters from your husband, No . . Rank . . Name . . . for some time to come. This does not mean he is unwell. For the present, however, the type of operations in which he is taking part make it impossible for him to write to you but he will do so as soon as he can. Please, however, go on writing to him as your letters will greatly cheer him up and please ask his relations and friends to write to him too . . .

'White City' remained under continual attack and as the defenders were now suffering heavy casualties it was decided to abandon it in May. A new Stronghold code-named 'Blackpool' was set up 30 miles south-west of Mogaung and manned by Masters' 111th LRP Brigade. Masters, later famous as the author of 'Bhowani Junction' and other novels and autobiographical works vividly capturing the spirit of British India, was a 4th Gurkha officer like Lentaigne and, also like his commander, had no great love for Wingate, preferring highly mobile operations and distrusting the Stronghold theory. He knew that one reason for the prolonged survival of 'White City' had been its distance from any large Japanese concentrations. 'Blackpool', on the other hand, was only five miles from a considerable Japanese garrison which, in view of the threat now posed to its communications, reacted swiftly and effectively to the latest British incursion.

Masters likened 'Blackpool', laid out on a series of thickly forested ridges and re-entrants, to ' . . . a sharp-spined animal, lying head down, outstretched, the airstrip on its right side.' In the cover provided by the re-entrants he sited the medical sections and dumps of supplies and ammunition. Most of the brigade's mules were sent to a safer place well clear of the Stronghold, but Masters retained a number for local use, including 'Maggy', his personal baggage-carrier.

On 8 May, the 1st Cameronians and 2nd King's Own Royal Regiment began to dig and wire their positions as the engineers got to work on a glider strip. Within hours there were signs of Japanese activity as patrols probed and observed the Chindits. By dusk on the first evening five WACO gliders were released overhead. They carried light bulldozers so that a Dakota strip could be built as quickly as possible. One crashed, but the rest got down safely, and work began at once. During the night the first Dakotas arrived. Two, hit by Japanese fire, crashed in front of the horrified garrison. Then the first ranging rounds of enemy artillery fire began to come down, and it was clear that 'Blackpool' was going to be under attack from the start. On the second night, as Japanese infantry edged their way in towards the partly completed defences, more Dakotas gallantly landed under fire with urgently-needed supplies of ammunition. They were unloaded, engines running, under heavy small arms, artillery and mortar fire, as the Cameronians and King's Own, already down to half-strength, fought to hold the enemy at bay and dig in at the same time. As more aircraft came in with landing lights ablaze, furious hand-to-hand fighting was going on barely 300 yards from the edge of the strip. Fortunately the Japanese persisted in attacking the strongest part of the perimeter, held by the King's Own. Already the garrison, denied sleep for four days, was on the verge of exhaustion.

Brodie's 14th LRP Brigade was ordered to set up another Stonghold to the west in order to take the heat off 'Blackpool', but it was some distance away and moved very slowly, its men almost as exhausted as Masters', whose 111th Brigade was soon fighting for its very survival. There was no question of its being able to conduct offensive operations for it was closely beleaguered. Masters appealed furiously to Lentaigne for help but could only obtain permission to abandon 'Blackpool' '. . . if it seemed his brigade was about to be obliterated.' Every day more Japanese artillery pounded the perimeter and searched the re-entrants where growing lines of stretcher cases awaited treatment or burial. Two more battalions slipped in to join the garrison, the 1st King's Liverpool from Calvert's brigade and the 3/9th Gurkha Rifles, part of the 'floating reserve' attached to Special Force, as were the artillery within the perimeter. The monsoon now broke in earnest. Slit trenches, each with its complement of two hollow-eyed men, filled with water, and 'Blackpool's' defenders fought on in conditions reminiscent of the Ypres Salient in World War I. They now inhabited a landscape of shattered trees hung with tattered parachutes, bloodied clothing, human limbs protruding from shallow graves, thousands of brass cartridge cases, ration boxes, entrails, unburied Japanese corpses, dead mules – all putrefying in the humid heat. The Cameronians relieved the King's Own in their ruined sector, to be promptly attacked by the best part of the Japanese 53rd Division. Fighting was at close quarters, to and fro amongst the shattered perimeter wire and flooded foxholes dug by the King's Own; at one stage, as the monsoon rain bucketed down, the Cameronians were forced back, fighting as they went, onto the airstrip perimeter; one of their officers, totally exhausted, tripped and fell headfirst into a flooded crater. Struggling to get out he saw what he was being watched by a Japanese soldier, equally exhausted and propped against a tree-trunk. Neither was capable of further fighting; they just roared with laughter and went their ways into the murk.

The padre of the King's Own at 'Blackpool' was the Revd W. H. Miller of the Royal Army Chaplains' Department. He was in the unenviable position of a non-combatant caught up in a bloody battle where frightening demands were constantly made on his services and faith. He had volunteered in response to a call by Wingate for more Chindit chaplains, undergone jungle training in India and flown to 'Broadway' with a load of mules. After two days he marched off with the brigade to endure the lot of the infantry. One day on the march, each man carrying his sixty pounds, was much like another: reveille at 3 am followed by 'stand-to', in total silence. Breakfast was eaten out of mess tins at 5.45 and at 6.30 came the order to saddle up. The mules would be loaded and the day's march begun. Every hour the column stopped for ten minutes. At midday there was a longer break for a brew-up and snack. Then back on the march until 6.30 pm when the column halted for the night. The column was vulnerable by night, with the mules unloaded and tethered in their lines. Sentry duties were taken very seriously and to be found asleep when on duty called for extreme measures. In 111th LRP Brigade it was not uncommon for men to be flogged or subjected to humiliating punishments, such as being tied to trees. As the days went by, the incidence of such cases increased. The air-drop, normally every fifth or sixth day, was a major event as it brought luxuries such as a rum ration, cigarettes (even if they were the vile 'Victory Vs' made in India) and tinned items from the British ration scales to relieve the monotony of the rich, but insubstantial, American 'K' ration, which was the Chindits' staple diet. Sometimes there was fresh bread, newspapers, and mail.

After a few weeks of this, Miller noted, fatigue and sickness began to dull performance and the incidence of self-inflicted injuries went up. The only hope of escape was by air, and some men went to extremes to ensure that they got out that way. When out of contact with the enemy, the padre's duties were those of welfare officer as much as priest, for the troops appeared to have little need for formal acts of worship. Back in India, one soldier had poured out a tale of woe about the conduct of his wife, from whom he had been separated for five years. Miller had carried out the usual procedures of discreet enquiry through welfare organisations back in England, but with little success. On the day following a mail drop at 'Blackpool' the soldier walked off into the trees and shot himself. He had received a letter from his wife which read: ' . . . Darling, You are now the proud father of a son . . .' There were thousands of such cases in all theatres of war, but for Chindits, far from home and deep in enemy territory, personal crises took on a new dimension.

As the siege intensified, the meagre defences began to succumb to the bombardment. For the last three days and nights at 'Blackpool' it seemed to Miller that ' . . . all Hell and its angels was let loose – the inferno, the racket, the bloody deaths, the stern looks on mens' faces, the stench, the mud. Who can ever forget these things?' His priestly duties were now grim, prompt burial of the dead being imperative to avoid pestilence. Even so, shellfire continually threw the remains of corpses, friend and foe alike, around the shrinking perimeter. Bloated bodies of mules lay everywhere. Aircraft had long stopped landing, as the strip was now in Japanese hands. The pilots still brought their Dakotas over at night to drop supplies; a final daylight drop had resulted in four out of eight aircraft falling to Japanese fire and only half a load of ammunition was recovered. Consequently, the ever-increasing numbers of wounded faced an unpleasant future.

Padre Miller spent as much of his time as possible at the Main Dressing Station where doctors, surgeons and medical orderlies worked non-stop under fire to deal with the stream of casualties. On one occasion, finding signs of life in what he thought to be a corpse awaiting burial, he was told sadly by a doctor that the man had no chance and had been put there to die quietly. Miller had been about to bury him alive.

On 14 May Masters knew that the end was near; the Japanese were on the point of breaking in. Calvert's Brigade's attempt to raise the siege had been frustrated by flooded rivers and lack of boats. Masters ordered a break-out to the west, and prepared his men for the final effort. As he looked around in the incessant bombardment, he saw his mule 'Maggy', quietly feeding on bamboo shoots; her entrails hung out of a great gash in her belly, made by a shell splinter. 'She seemed in no pain,' he wrote afterwards, 'and I hugged her neck. Then Briggs shot her for me.'

The plight of the seriously wounded was dreadful. They could not be moved, neither could they be left to the Japanese. Wingate had laid down that only the bare minimum of medical staff would march with the columns; serious casualties were always to go out by air, but at 'Blackpool' this was now out of the question. In the last hours of the Stronghold, a large number of sick and wounded lay helpless on the ground. A medical officer drew Masters aside and showed him a row of stretchers lying in the path, the hopeless cases, still alive but only just. In Masters' own words:

Maj Gen D. T. ('Punch') Cowan commanded 17 Indian Division, from shortly after the Sittang bridge disaster of 1942 until the final stages of the 1945 campaign. Here he holds a meeting with his senior staff officers at the back of the truck in which he lived. *(IWM)*

Punjabi troops lead mules to a forward position. *(IWM)*

Throughout the fighting around Kohima the Naga hillmen rallied loyally
to the help of the 14th Army. Their only complaint was that they were
issued with shotguns for self-defence, instead of the rifles they wanted
to kill the Japanese. Here, Major Sewell of the Royal Artillery examines
one such weapon at the request of his cheerful Naga companion. (*IWM*)

Chindits brewing up on the
line of march during their
first deep penetration attack,
Operation 'Longcloth' in 1943. (*IWM*)

The Lushai Brigade was probably the most consistently effective deep penetration force in the 14th Army. Consisting of Chin Levies operating in their favourite hill country, and other carefully selected units, it harassed the Japanese line of communication and provided much valuable intelligence. Here its commander, Brig Marindin, walks in the Chin Hills with his bodyguard of Assam riflemen and levies. He estimated that in 1944-5 he covered over 1,200 miles in this way. *(IWM)*

Officers of the Devons after their ferocious fight on Nippon Hill. *(l to r)* Maj Wallser MC, Capt Mile RAMC, Lt Mann, Capt Moult, Capt Pope. *(IWM)*

Lt Gen G. A. P. Scoones, commanding 4th Corps at Imphal. Tired, drawn and looking much older than his 51 years, he is seen here talking with the commanding officer of an Indian battalion at the height of the battle (*IWM*)

Burman hill tribes also rendered great service to the 14th Army, using their local knowledge and matchless jungle craft for patrolling. Havildar Raldon, of the Chin Levies, served in the celebrated Lushai Brigade, which showed no mercy to those Japanese unlucky enough to fall into their hands. (*IMW*)

High in the Naga hills, on the Jessami track, jeep drivers pause for a break. The state of the road in this picture represented 'good' going: there are some signs of recent repair work on the side of the hill. In the monsoon, roads like this would frequently be washed out. (*IWM*)

For the Chindits, survival depended to a great extent on the RAF's ground parties, one of which accompanied each column. During 'Operation Thursday' in 1944 Flight Sergeant Stainthorpe and Sergeant Brown of the RAF operate their high-powered transmitter in the jungle. Contact with base airfields in India enabled the RAF and USAAF to provide prompt air support. *(IWM)*

The building of a fleet of cargo boats on the Chindwin required quantities of hardwood from the forests. Elephant power was used to bring the logs, cut by Forestry companies of the Indian Army, to boatyards at the water's edge. *(IWM)*

Temporary graves and parachute canopies in the trees tell their own grim story on Garrison Hill after the battle of Kohima. Maj Gen Grover, commanding 2nd Division, said that for destruction and horror, conditions here exceeded anything he had seen on the Somme in 1916. *(IWM)*

On patrol in Arakan, 1944, men of the Royal Garwhal Rifles move cautiously in dense bamboo jungle. Progress could be agonisingly slow under such conditions – often not more than a mile a day – and the undergrowth harboured ticks carrying the lethal scrub typhus, as well as innumerable leeches. *(IWM)*

Admiral Lord Louis Mountbatten believed that as Supremo he should be seen by as many of the men of his command as possible. His charismatic personality did much to sustain morale throughout SEAC. Here he is seen talking to an officer of the King's Own Scottish Borderers. *(IWM)*

. . . the first man was quite naked and a shell had removed the entire contents of his stomach. Between his chest and pelvis was a bloody hollow, behind it his spine. Another had no legs and no hips, his trunk ending just below the waist . . . another had no face, and whitish liquid was trickling out of his head and onto the ground . . .

The doctor had filled these men with morphine and on Masters' orders another dose was administered to all whose eyes were still open. Then they too were shot.

As the nightmare march got under way in torrential rain, Padre Miller watched, appalled, as Japanese artillery ranged onto the column, killing men and mules and blowing away the paths along which the men were struggling. He was greatly moved by the conduct of the Nigerian soldiers who had been sent from the west to help 111th Brigade in its agony:

When a mule slipped over the khudside [hillside] it was a giant of a West African who picked it up and set it on its feet again. When there were steps to be hewn out of the steep and slippery mountainside, the West African was there. When the sick and wounded were so exhausted that they could only sink down on the track, it was the West African who bore them to safety on his wide strong shoulders. When men were dying from hunger, a West African would be the first to share his own ration . . . their unwearied, unselfish and Christ-like service will not be forgotten by the men who came to rely on them.

The brigade now reached Lake Indawgi where two Sunderland flying boats of the RAF, affectionately known as 'Gert' and 'Daisy', were able to land and pick up the sick and wounded. Many owed their lives to the pilots who took their cumbersome aircraft so deep into enemy territory. Two thousand men of 111th Brigade remained on their feet, exhausted and angry with other LRP brigades in the area who, though nowhere as hard-pressed, had failed to come to their rescue. Masters, on being told to march his brigade to join Calvert's and attack Mogaung, signalled Lentaigne that his brigade should be medically examined, and every man found unfit for combat service evacuated at once. When the request was refused, he asked to be relieved of his command; his men had been marching and fighting for 110 days on an inadequate diet of 'K' rations, a calorific deficiency of 800 a day against that which the medical authorities had recommended to Wingate. All had lost around three stones in weight. Lentaigne granted Masters' request to be relieved, and signalled Mountbatten that Special Force was physically and mentally worn out, '. . . and to keep them in contact with the enemy until a particular objective is made good is really not practical politics'. The political objective was continued support of Stilwell's drive for Myitkyina, and it was an issue which at one stage threatened Anglo-American relations.

Masters stayed long enough to watch the medical examination of his brigade, whose 4½ battalions now mustered 2,200 men between them. Of these, 118 were pronounced fit to continue: seven British officers, 21 British soldiers, and 90 Gurkhas.

Mogaung was a key Japanese base and communications centre and it was certain that they would defend it to the last man. Lentaigne was under heavy pressure to maintain Special Force in the area despite the fact that it had been on operations for weeks longer than the maximum laid down by Wingate. Stilwell had complained bitterly that the British had been 'shadow-boxing', whilst his Chinese troops were bled white on the march to Myitkyina. Merrill's force was also temporarily out of steam, having marched and fought non-stop for two months in order to keep the Chinese going. The strain gave Merrill a heart attack and he was evacuated, returning later to his post. The Marauders had been up against the Japanese 18th Division, a crack formation which had severely punished the Chinese as they moved down from Ledo, and had it not been for this American presence Stilwell would have been humiliated by the patchy showing of his Chinese troops.

The 18th Division was commanded by one of Japan's best soldiers, Lt General Tanaka Nobuo. Tanaka's striking appearance owed much to his forked beard – a rarity in Japan – and his ability had been proved in China as well as in the capture of Singapore. He now braced his men for the defence of Myitkyina. He had already cost the Allies dear, for had they been able to take the town early in 1944 it would have been possible to re-open the land link with China and return Stilwell's Chinese – probably Chiang's best troops, trained and equipped in India – to their homeland. As it was, the Marauders, despite exhaustion, brought off a notable coup on 17 May by rushing Myitkyina airfield. Reinforcements, including British anti-aircraft batteries, were quickly flown in, and it seemed that the campaign on the northern front was about to be won; but the onset of the monsoon and the run-down state of Stilwell's troops put an end to that. Myitkyina town was not to fall until 4 August.

Meanwhile, Calvert was moving to the attack of Mogaung, held by another formidable Japanese division, Lt General Takeda's 53rd. Calvert initially attacked from the east with the 1st Lancashire Fusiliers, who suffered heavily. The town was riddled with well-concealed bunkers and, as usual, the Japanese used many snipers, one of whom shot Major Wavell, the Viceroy's son, in the left wrist; he insisted on taking his place in the queue at the dressing station but his hand could not be saved.

'Lifebuoy' flame-throwers, used to kill the snipers in their hides, were so named because of the round tank of fuel carried on the operator's back. They proved highly effective at Mogaung against defenders dug in under houses. On Waterloo Day, 18 June, Calvert called for a last effort from his dwindling units. The King's, already depleted after going to Master's help at 'Blackpool', were now down to less than 100 all ranks; the South Staffords had only one subaltern, and he had already been wounded four times since landing at 'Broadway' three and a half months earlier. Later that day, the long-awaited Chinese began to arrive; they turned out to be first-class troops and Calvert, who spoke some of their dialect, was able to establish excellent relations with them.

The attack which finally took Mogaung went in on 24 June. More good Chinese troops had now arrived; they watched in amazement as the 3/6th Gurkhas stormed the railway bridge over the river. Heedless of intense Japanese fire, Capt Allmand, crippled by trench foot as the result of weeks in the monsoon, charged the main Japanese machine gun position at the head of his men, throwing grenades as he struggled through the deep mud. He destroyed the position at the cost of his own life and gained a posthumous VC. The attack now went straight on into the town centre, using artillery, close air support, flame-throwers and anti-tank projectors to blast the defenders out of existence. From among the flames, as Calvert gave his orders during the street fighting, could be heard the screams of incinerating Japanese. By sunset on 27 June nearly all the defenders were dead: very few men of the four battalions comprising the garrison escaped alive.

The enemy were still fighting as fanatically as ever, as the Lancashire Fusiliers discovered. One of their officers, in a bayonet charge, spared and passed a wounded enemy soldier who immediately shot him dead, to be killed by the officer's batman, himself killed by yet another apparently helpless Japanese casualty. 'Never pass a wounded Jap' became the battalion's watchword after this expensive lesson. Outside Mogaung one of the Fusiliers' patrols came across a well-camouflaged Japanese field hospital. The first soldier to enter the wards was shot dead by one of the patients. In another ward, five Japanese crawled out of bed, put their heads against a grenade and pulled the pin. The only prisoners taken were too ill to hold a weapon; they refused food or treatment and starved themselves to death.

Calvert was greatly displeased to hear on the BBC that 'Stilwell's troops had taken Mogaung'. It had been an Anglo-Chinese victory, but the Chinese commander was the first to apologise handsomely to Calvert, telling him that it was the Chindits who had taken the town, to the great admiration of the Chinese troops. Typically, Calvert signalled Special Force Headquarters: 'Chinese reported taken Mogaung. My Brigade now taking umbrage.'

It was the Chindits' greatest triumph, the first town of any size in Burma to be retaken, to the fury of Stilwell who had earlier claimed this honour when it seemed (and had been widely proclaimed in the American Press) that Myitkyina had fallen. He now redoubled his efforts to capture it, demanding that Calvert go to his support. Calvert refused point-blank; he felt that his men had done far more than had been asked of them and that they deserved a rest. Stilwell ordered him, through Lentaigne, to report to him in person. After an icy reception from the old General's staff he confronted 'Vinegar Joe'. It was soon clear that Stilwell's notably obsequious staff, who were terrified of him, had failed to keep their master informed of the progress and condition of the Chindits or of their epic fight at Mogaung. For once, Stilwell recognised that he had come up against someone impervious to his bullying. The two men parted on good terms, and Calvert returned to his brigade.

Operation 'Thursday' was at an end. Within days the survivors were being flown out to India, apart from some small detachments left to support Merrill which, despite Stilwell's voluble protests, were taken out in August. They had long exceeded the period calculated as the limit of endurance for deep penetration units and had fought some of the bloodiest battles of the campaign.

The medical condition of 'Thursday's' survivors was appalling. Mountbatten was aghast when shown the official medical reports on the post-operation examinations of all Special Force personnel. They confirmed what Calvert, Masters and other brigade commanders had been saying for weeks. From the official medical history of the war in Burma it is evident that Wingate, with his belief in the power of mind over matter, placed a low value on preventive medicine; the statistics for avoidable sickness on Operation 'Thursday' make this clear. Dysentery and chronic diarrhoea accounted for nearly 10 per cent of those evacuated by air. Water discipline was slack in many of the columns, and it seems that there had never been a rigid insistence on the use of water purifying tablets or of boiling water taken from streams and stagnant pools. One column commander actually forbade the use of toilet paper, as it would betray the presence of his unit if left lying on the surface. The normal procedure of digging individual holes and burying excreta does not seem to have occurred to him. When another column passed along the track used by his, the ground was well fouled and dysentery spread like wildfire. Even in the static Strongholds, latrines were carelessly dug and left uncovered.

Malaria claimed nearly 60 per cent of those evacuated, and this figure includes only those who were so ill that they could not stand up and march. Almost every man in Special Force was found to be suffering from benign tertian malaria at one time or other. The killer was cerebral malaria, which could have been kept at bay by regular self-dosage with Mepacrine. One of its symptoms was the total apathy of its victims as they sank towards coma and death; at this point there was a slight chance of survival if they could be kept conscious and their interest stimulated. In the 2nd Black Watch, serving with Brodie's 14th LRP Brigade, this was attempted by the use of the bagpipes. All ranks were supposed to hold a personal supply of Mepacrine, but the nature of Chindit operations made close supervision by officers and NCOs difficult. It seems that the health education given to Chindits in India failed to inculcate the vital self-disciplines; doctors continually reported finding untouched supplies of the drug on the corpses of cerebral malaria victims.

The Chindits, and particularly their strangely inspiring leader, will continue to fascinate for years to come. Wingate's complex personality set him apart from other men. He never made the slightest attempt to court popularity, neither did he seem to mind what he said to his superiors. If he was convinced of the truth or correctness of anything, he said so. In the private correspondence of 1956 between Brigadier Bernard Fergusson and Field Marshal Sir William Slim, already quoted, Fergusson confessed to being 'still baffled by Wingate' ten years and more after his death:

> I have thought a great deal about Wingate, and I am still greatly puzzled by him. Archie Wavell . . . concluded that he was that rare thing, a genius. He applied the word to him quite deliberately after years of cogitation. We all know that geniuses are supposed to be on the borderline of lunacy; and I think he crossed it once, or twice. . . . I can't say that I liked him, but my admiration for him was intense and genuine. He made me and a lot of other people pull out stops of endurance, imagination, boldness, which we never imagined ourselves to possess in our make-up . . . I think the biggest contribution he made to the winning of the war in Burma was his demonstration of the uses of air supply . . .

Fergusson was reluctant to go back into Burma on the second Chindit expedition, wishing to rejoin his regiment, the Black Watch. He had told Wingate that after his experiences on operation 'Longcloth' in 1943 he would not command troops under him again unless two conditions were fulfilled: (a) that the men must have adequate food, and (b) that the locals must never again be deluded into helping the Chindits on the untrue supposition that the British were back to stay. Shortly before 'Thursday' was launched, Fergusson accused Wingate of reneging on these:

> He flew into a rage, said I was trying to bargain with him and altogether it was a most painful interview. He shoved a blank sheet of foolscap at me, and said I must accept his decision or resign; so I resigned. He then forbade me to tell anybody, or to seek advice from anybody, 'and that goes for your friend Wavell!' Two days later in Delhi he told me of various things which met my point, and with my agreement tore up my resignation. Among them was a statement that you [Slim] had promised to fly two divisions into Indaw when I captured it, and that there would be no withdrawal from there. I never knew that this was false until you yourself told me in London after the war . . . he was quite certainly a megalomaniac; but my goodness he was a great fighting man, and I am so deep in his debt that even now I feel disloyal in being impartial about him.

In his reply to Fergusson, Slim dealt with the points raised on Wingate:

I doubt if he was a genius except for short intervals, even if he had what most people consider a qualification for the role in that he crossed the borderline of lunacy, as you say, more than once. All the same, I do agree with you that he was a great leader and, however he did it, got the most extraordinary efforts out of people.

Not everyone will agree with Fergusson's thesis on the relationship between genius and mental instability. In his study of the Chindits, Brigadier Shelford Bidwell concluded that Wingate was a hysteric, paranoid, and a manic depressive or cyclothyme. But none of these comes near insanity. Despite this, Bidwell points out that Wingate had an extraordinary ability to persuade highly intelligent people of the feasibility of his plans. As highly articulate on paper as in speech, he exercised a mesmeric effect on his audiences, who realised that they were in the presence of a very special man.

Many years after his death, when it seemed to many of his old followers that his reputation was being eroded by the official historians as well as by a new generation of academics who had grown up since the war, the Chindit Old Comrades assembled a collection of memoirs, mostly very short, privately printed so that they would have a copy for their children and children's children, as a reminder of the man under whom they had served. Brigadier Peter Mead, who as a young staff officer had been responsible for much of the air support for 'Thursday' wrote that

> In his lifetime he inspired in others extremes both of admiration and dislike but, at his death and for years afterwards there seemed to be little doubt as to his high merit as a military commander . . .

On one occasion Wingate ordered the 7th Nigeria Regiment to parade for General Auchinleck, C-in-C India, in exactly the state in which they had finished their final test exercise before going into Burma. One of the battalion's officers wrote:

> As a 'civilian' soldier I counted myself lucky that there were very few regulars in my unit. General Wingate's visit astounded and delighted me. Here was a completely IRREGULAR soldier proposing to do all sorts of things that were highly unorthodox which would infuriate and stun the regular attitude of mind . . .

Another officer arrived at HQ Special Force to assume a staff appointment:

> I was met by an officer in a pith helmet, no rank badges. 'Can you swim?' 'Yes.' 'Well, swim that river.' 'As I am?' (he was in full kit, with rifle). 'Of course.' On completion of this: 'Well done. Go and get changed.'

Wingate's influence over non-European troops was extraordinary. During training in India, Sergeant Abiodun of the 6th Nigeria Regiment told Wingate that the native porters brought from West Africa were a menace because of the noise they made at night. Wingate at once called for a repeat of the exercise and accompanied Abiodun to hear for himself. As a result he got rid of the porters and replaced them with mules. In Abiodun's own words:

> This made me realise that General Wingate was a 'Good General' who believed in seeing things for himself – in moving with his soldiers and studying their problems . . . May his great soul rest in peace.

Perhaps the last word on Wingate and the Chindits can be left with a former Gurkha officer, Robert Rhodes James, who served with 3/4th Gurkha Rifles in Masters' brigade. After the Chindit reunion of 1979 at the Royal Hospital, Chelsea, he wrote:

> The evening wore on. Important men made speeches and others listened and dreamt. It is wholly fanciful, but comforting, to think that above the drone of speakers and the gruff bonhomie of ageing men we could make out faint traces of other sounds: the clank of mule harness, the sucking of boots out of mud, the swish and thud of a parachute, and rain in the trees. These were the sounds that came with the man we were especially remembering that evening; the strange man we followed because he had ideas and because, for a brief moment in our lives, made us bigger than ourselves.

The March on India

". . . a perpetual flux; a vortex of combining and disintegrating units."

BY 1944 THE WAR was going badly for Japan. Since the battle of Midway in June 1942 the United States Navy had gained naval superiority in the Pacific. It was becoming increasingly difficult for the Japanese to sustain their war effort, as most of the strategic supplies from the South-East Asia Co-Prosperity Sphere had to go by sea. American submarines were sinking scores of irreplaceable cargo ships as they made their way to Japan, and war production was faltering. As the Imperial Navy had been flung onto the defensive, the planners in Tokyo looked to their army for a spectacular victory, whose propaganda value would match its political and economic advantages. Above all, it was essential to think of something that would draw Allied attention away from the western Pacific theatre, if only for a short time.

The logical choice seemed to be an advance outside the original bounds set for the Co-Prosperity Sphere. There was little to be gained from an offensive in China; the best answer was undoubtedly to invade Assam, seize the British stockpiles there, and advance as far as possible into India in the hope of igniting a popular rising against British rule. The overall plan was finally signed in Tokyo in January 1944. Phase I was the attack in the Arakan. Phase II was 'U-Go', the offensive against Assam.

The invasion in India had long been the aim of Lt General Mutaguchi Renya, commanding the Japanese 15th Army from his Headquarters in Maymyo, where in a more leisurely age, only three years past yet gone for ever, the King's Own Yorkshire Light Infantry had staged impeccable ceremonial parades and mounted guard at Flagstaff House. Mutaguchi persuaded the C-in-C of Burma Area Army, Lt General Kawabe Masakazu, of the virtue of his plan; in turn, Kawabe convinced the Imperial General Staff in Tokyo. On receiving news that 'U-Go' had been approved, Mutaguchi wasted no time in assembling his forces and moving them up to the Chindwin.

At HQ 14th Army in Comilla, Slim was aware that a Japanese offensive was in the wind. For many months, unknown to all but a carefully vetted handful of his Intelligence staff who had been cleared to handle this 'Ultra' material, he had been privy to highly secret information obtained from intercepted Japanese signals. These indicated that the Japanese Burma Area

Army was already in difficulties with its supplies and that if it attacked, it would be with the aim of securing large quantities of 14th Army's supplies as quickly as possible. To do this it would be necessary to capture the administrative installations on the Plain of Imphal. With these in their possession the Japanese could invade Assam and even Bengal with confidence.

An important element in Mutaguchi's plan was the use of the Indian National Army and its Commander-in-Chief, Subhas Chandra Bose. Bose was a curious figure. Born in 1897 into a prosperous and respected Bengal family, he had followed a brilliant career at Cambridge by passing with distinction into the Indian Civil Service. He decided, however, to devote his life's work to the cause of Indian nationalism and joined the Congress party, where he had advocated open rebellion rather than the non-violence preached by Mahatma Gandhi.

After a spell as chief executive of the city of Calcutta, where he wielded enormous political influence, he was exiled by the British authorities to Mandalay. By 1938 he had become President of the Congress Party and was soon at odds with almost all its other leaders, especially Pandit Nehru. The year 1941 found him once more in detention, but he escaped to Afghanistan and made his way to Germany, where he married an Austrian lady. He started to recruit Indian prisoners of war for an 'Indian National Army' but this was not a success, probably because he had no knowledge of soldiering. Rommel hastily declined his offer of two INA battalions for the North African campaign, and they were consigned to garrison duty in Holland where, after a mutiny, they were disarmed and disbanded.

Finding Bose an increasing embarrassment, the Germans shipped him off on a hazardous voyage to Singapore by submarine in 1943, and here he renewed his efforts to raise an army of liberation for India. This time he was much more successful. Some 60,000 Indian army personnel had been captured by the Japanese in Malaya and Singapore. Many of them had been little more than raw recruits when sent to fight in Malaya in 1941. They had not been fully assimilated into their regiments and many of them had served under inexperienced young British officers who had been given little time to absorb the culture of the men under their command. As a result, once separated in captivity from their British and Indian officers, the young Indian jawans were easy meat for propaganda of the sort now addressed to them by the highly articulate Bose. There was already a cadre to build on, for before Bose's arrival in Singapore one Captain Mohan Singh had started an Indian National Army, but had disbanded it following a disagreement with the Japanese. Very soon, Bose's eloquence had persuaded some 20,000 former Indian Army soldiers and others to join the INA. He cleverly absolved them of any guilt they might have over breaking their oath of allegiance to the King-Emperor by telling them that they were to be the

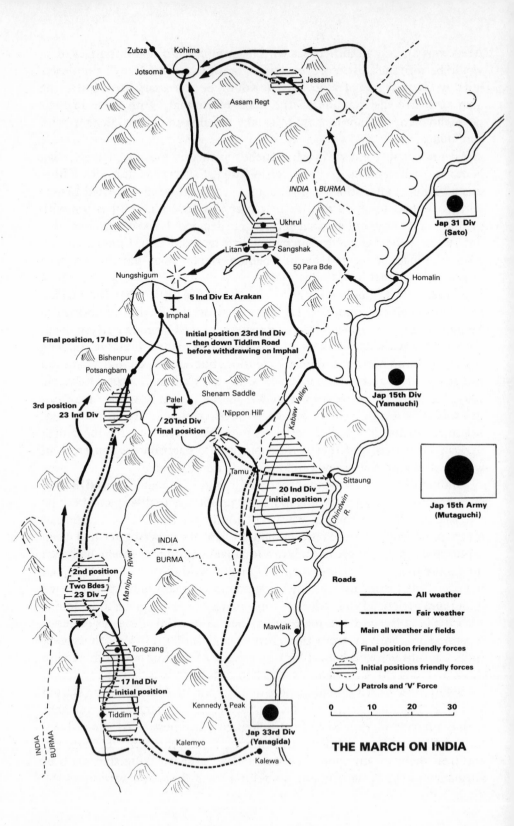

THE MARCH ON INDIA

liberator-heroes of the new India, hailed and venerated by all on their triumphant return home. The capital offence under Indian Army Law of 'Bearing arms against the King-Emperor', was, he assured them, no longer valid.

From Singapore Bose went to Tokyo where he met, among others, General Mutaguchi, who immediately welcomed the idea of an INA contingent at the head of his drive on India. Bose, like the Burmese politicians then resident in Tokyo, declared an Indian Government-in-Exile, which was immediately recognised by the Japanese, German and Italian governments; also, rather curiously, by Prime Minister de Valera of the Irish Republic.

The INA first saw action in Burma in the Arakan at the end of 1943, where it performed indifferently. To their surprise, the INA soldiers found that there was no mass movement on the part of their brethren in 15 Corps to join them. On the contrary, when they advanced with cries of 'Jai Hind' (Victory to India) they were shot at by Indian soldiers who regarded them as traitors. It is noteworthy that there were very few cases of mutiny in the Indian Army after the appearance of the INA. When one Sikh INA officer made the mistake of approaching a Sikh infantry unit in the Arakan, he was killed in single combat by another Sikh officer, to thunderous applause from the latter's unit.

At Mutaguchi's request an INA 'division', was assigned to 'U-Go' as well as various lines-of-communication troops in the rear areas, where they were encountered by Chindit columns during Operation 'Thursday'. The Japanese army had serious misgivings about the INA, and their commanders were reluctant to employ them in front-line operations. Perhaps they thought that troops who had already changed sides once might be tempted to do so again – a suspicion to be justified before long by the Burma National Army. Behind the lines, the INA gained an unsavoury reputation for brutality as security troops and prison guards. They were increasingly used as porters and for other menial duties. As a result, the morale of the INA started to slide, and went on sliding until the end of the war. Its men soon realised that, instead of being greeted as heroes by Indian units of 14th Army, they would be shown little mercy if captured alive. Before long, Slim had to issue an Army Order to ensure that INA prisoners (or 'Jifs' – Japanese Indian Forces – as they were widely known in 14th Army) were given a more kindly welcome when taken.

★ ★ ★

At the beginning of 1944, Lt General Scoone's 4 Corps was deployed behind the Chindwin along 200 miles of frontage, most of which was covered by no more than observation posts and patrols. There was a huge void between the two forward divisions, as 17 Indian Division was deployed around Tiddim and 20 Indian Division around Tamu, almost 100 miles to the north, while 23 Indian Division was held around Imphal as Corps reserve. All these formations contained a proportion of British units, but the only all-British formation to take part in the forthcoming battles in Assam was 2 Division, which at the beginning of 1944 was still training for amphibious operations in India. Intelligence sources predicted a three-pronged Japanese attack; in the south against 17 Division, then up the 120 miles of all-weather road to Imphal. Further north, there would be an attack, first against 20 Division, then up the good road from Tamu to Imphal. It was also forecast that the equivalent of a brigade – the infantry group of a Japanese division – would strike across country via Ukhrul to cut the vital road link between Imphal and the railhead at Dimapur, capturing Kohima en route.

The lie of the land put 4 Corps in a vulnerable position. The Dimapur-Imphal-Tiddim road runs more or less parallel to the Chindwin and Manipur rivers, and 17 Division stood at risk of being cut off from its line of retreat if hard pressed in the Tiddim area. There was also a grave risk, which duly materialised, of Imphal being cut off from Dimapur. In terms of 18th century warfare, 4 Corps was effectively 'formed to a flank', a fact abundantly clear to the Japanese planners.

There were several courses open to Slim at the beginning of 1944. He could advance across the Chindwin and bring the Japanese to battle between that river and the Irrawaddy; he could sit tight and receive the expected Japanese attack well forward of Imphal on the line of the Chindwin; or he could retire in good order on Imphal once he was sure that the Japanese were fully committed to an offensive, and fight the decisive battle there, on ground of his own choice. This last was his preferred option, and Giffard supported it for a very good reason. Both men were privy to highly classified and sensitive signals Intelligence made available through 'Ultra', which indicated that the Japanese logistic system was in delicate health. It might, however, be up to sustaining Mutaguchi's troops in a defensive battle fought between the Chindwin and the Irrawaddy, when Slim's land lines of communication would be stretched, becoming impossible if 14th Army was still locked in battle on the wrong side of the Chindwin as the monsoon broke. Slim, who knew his enemy, considered that this was a distinct possibility. If, however, the Japanese pinned everything on a drive for Imphal, he believed that it would be the decisive battleground. The enemy would be fighting at the extremity of a vulnerable and uncertain line of communication and 4 Corps would be sitting on its own reserves of food, fuel and ammunition. If the monsoon then broke, the Japanese would have to cope with quagmires, washed-out roads, broken bridges and disease; and they had no air supply capability.

For months, active patrolling had harvested a mass of Japanese maps and documents which gave Slim a good idea of likely Japanese thrust lines. He did not, however, know the date of Mutaguchi's offensive and made the assumption, wrongly, as events turned out, that it would come in mid-March. In February, steps were taken to evacuate the 'useless mouths' from Imphal and thousands of civilians, coolies, and base troops began to leave by road and air. Orders were also given to the commanders of the forward divisions to be ready to move back into Imphal as soon as the strength and direction of the Japanese thrusts had been confirmed. This was not welcomed by the commanders concerned. They had been deployed in their present area for some months and had spent much effort in making and improving roads and tracks, building bridges, setting up dumps of stores, fuel and ammunition, and generally preparing to advance across the Chindwin as the opening move of the 1944 campaigning season. As none of them was allowed into the charmed 'Ultra' circle, they could not be taken fully into Slim's confidence; all the same, they trusted him implicitly and stood ready for whatever was to come.

The 9th Battalion, The Border Regiment, was typical of the British units serving at that time in 17 Indian Division, where, with two Gurkha battalions, it was part of 48th Indian Infantry Brigade. It had been raised in 1939 in County Durham from men of the 24/25 year old call-up and stiffened by regulars on leave from the Regiment's 2nd Battalion then stationed in India. Its soldiers were therefore mature and responsible. Most of the 9th's men came from the Border's own recruiting area, the counties of Westmorland and Cumberland, giving the unit a strongly regional character. After training in England, the battalion sailed for India, where it underwent intensive jungle warfare training.

Very soon, the battalion had accustomed themselves to life without lavish scales of motor transport. Instead, they mastered the mule. A strong bond developed between handlers and mules. The tough feet of these animals required no shoeing and, unlike horses, mules were happy with a mixed diet including young bamboo. They proved steady under fire and seldom bolted, standing quietly in their harness as their handlers comforted them. In close combat they were certain targets, for the Japanese realised their value and shot them whenever they could. Training of muleteers was supervised by the Indian Army Veterinary Department and later by the Royal Army Veterinary Corps, whose official historian was to write that:

> . . . students returned to their units with a tremendous respect for the pack animal, which they had previously regarded as a vehicle.

In fact, the Lakelanders who formed a large part of the 9th Borders were quick to realise that the mule is a stout-hearted and willing friend who gives of his best in return for a little kindness and the application of some simple rules of management, feeding and attention. The men of the 14th Army cared for their animals and paid attention to their health. When an Indian mountain battery was visited by the Corps Commander, Lt General Messervy, he was amazed to find that the battery's only tent was pitched over a carefully-dug stable housing a solitary, magnificently-groomed mule. A notice board proclamed her name to be 'Memsahib'. When asked why so much trouble had been taken to house this animal when the rest of the battery were surviving in lean-to shelters and bashas, the Havildar proudly patted 'Memsahib' and replied, 'There will be horse shows, General Sahib!' On the Japanese side, equally reliant on animal transport, disease wrought havoc amongst their pack animals, especially the killer disease Surra, against which they had little or no defence.

The 9th Borders bore their share of General Cowan's intensive patrolling programme. The aim was to dominate the area and obtain hard information on the Japanese build-up. A rifle company would be sent out for days on end, setting up bases from which platoons would operate, setting up their own bases in turn. A typical platoon on the march had two scouts, in sight of the leading section for early warning of any enemy who might be patrolling the same area. Behind the leading section came platoon HQ: a subaltern, warrant officer or sergeant in command, signaller, and the 2-inch mortar detachment. Known as 'the platoon commander's artillery', the mortar fired a useful high explosive bomb up to 500 yards, smoke bombs to mask movement, or parachute flares for illumination by night. Two or three riflemen completed the HQ party. Then came the mules carrying the platoon's rations, extra ammunition, wireless batteries, and spare clothing. Two more rifle sections brought up the rear, with a rearguard of two or three riflemen. In open country, extra scouts marched out on the flanks, but in the jungle this was not practicable.

Every four hours or so, the platoon commander selected an emergency rendezvous to which all ranks would make their way if scattered by an ambush. All communication was by hand signal and in total silence. The Japanese, on the other hand, frequently betrayed their position by chattering noisily on the march. They also tended to bunch and follow fixed daily movement patterns, making them relatively easy to ambush. Once in their defensive positions, however, they were absolutely silent by day, especially at dawn and last light, when British troops tended to be noisy.

A platoon base would be carefully selected to provide good fields of fire and adequate warning of an enemy's approach. The base would be ringed, if time permitted, with barbed wire, booby traps and trip-flares. When on patrol from the base, all ranks wore woollen 'caps, comforter', jungle green uniform and jungle boots. Camouflage cream was applied to the face. The platoon commander carried a rifle and bayonet, dagger, binoculars, torch, compass and map case. NCOs were armed with Tommy guns or the British

Sten sub-machine carbine and a kukri. The Gurkha knife was popular, as a lethal close-combat weapon and for chopping brushwood. Each man carried his personal weapon and at least 50 rounds of spare ammunition. All carried a blanket, spare socks, and cardigan – for the nights were cold – and three days' rations: three tins of sardines, a tin of cheese, three packets of hard tack biscuit, tea, sugar, tinned milk, and a 'Tommy Cooker' for the ritual 'brew-up'. All carried several extra water bottles, purifying tablets, a supply of Mepacrine, and insect repellant for use after dark.

The area to the front of 17 Division's forward positions was contested by patrols of both sides, and it was not unusual for opposing patrol bases to be sited within a mile of each other. Pitched battles were rare, but at night both sides sought to 'Jitter' the opposition; and soon, the 9th Borders were as good at this as the Japanese.

Back in the company base, daily life followed well-practised routine. 'Stand-to' was an hour before dawn, when weapon slits were manned, equipment and weapons checked, and a sharp lookout maintained. Cooking fires were then lit, underground so as not to betray the position by smoke. The three company cooks now prepared breakfast. Water was strictly rationed and for all practical purposes such as ablutions, each man got one pint a day, the rest being held at the company cookhouse. Some of the day's personal ration would be used for shaving; this simple daily discipline did much for self-esteem and morale. Breakfast often began with a porridge of pounded hard tack known as 'burgoo', described by one officer as '. . . a mixture which looked like porridge but which did not taste like it – apparently made of old leaves and chewing gum.' This was washed down with tea, followed by tinned bacon or the inevitable soya sausage and baked beans. The midday meal or 'tiffin' consisted of bully beef or sardines, jam and biscuit. Imaginative cooks did their best to inject variety into this monotonous diet by adding curry powder to the bully stew. Occasionally there was mule meat. As a special treat there might be tinned fruit pudding. There were no fresh vegetables in these patrol bases, and the vitamin deficiency was made good with pills. Before dark there would be a lighter meal before the evening 'stand-to'.

Little sympathy could be expected by anyone who went sick with malaria in a well-disciplined battalion such as the 9th Borders. If it was found that a malaria case had failed to take his dose of Mepacrine, neglected to roll down his sleeves and anoint himself with insect repellant at sunset, or not used his mosquito net when in the base, he could be assured of disciplinary action. Health discipline was now strictly enforced throughout 14th Army, and after a number of commanding officers had been sacked when their unit's sickness statistics indicated slack discipline, the rest took the hint.

It is impossible to describe the fighting on the Imphal Plain, the defence of the 'gate of India', the siege of Kohima and the hundreds of other miniature battles which took place between March and June 1944 in the Naga Hills, as one would a set-piece 'conventional' battle such as El Alamein. At Imphal the battle swirled around for several weeks in an apparently random manner before the Japanese recoiled in defeat. The hundreds of chance encounters, ambushes, frontal attacks, and stern defences simply cannot be charted and never will be. In the end, decisions rested with lance-corporals commanding hard-pressed sections, out of touch with even their platoon commander. Once battle was joined, senior commanders – and this means from Company level upwards – could do little but hope that they had properly trained and equipped their men for their ordeal by fire. In the last resort, victory depended on the morale and skill-at-arms of individual soldiers in their lonely weapon slits. These qualities and virtues had to be sustained at a high level for longer than any other of the British or Indian Army's battles in modern times. Perhaps Imphal and Kohima are best described in the words of Evelyn Waugh: '. . . perpetual flux; a vortex of combining and disintegrating units; like the confluence of traffic at some spot where many roads meet, streams of mechanism come together, mingle, and separate again . . .'

Waugh was describing a motor race, in 'Vile Bodies', but any veteran of these battles will acknowledge the striking similarity of image.

In addition to the sources of intelligence already mentioned, Slim and his commanders had the services of 'V' and 'Z' Forces. As the retreat of 1942 got under way, volunteers were recruited for special duties behind enemy lines; many of those who came forward were residents of Burma whose knowledge of the country and its peoples were invaluable. They were formed into small units for independent operations, allotted to various parts of Burma, and allowed to recruit locals so that best use could be made of their skills. As most of the hill tribes remained loyal to the British Government it was from among these that the most useful scouts and intelligence-gatherers were found.

Equipped with a high frequency radio powered by a bicycle-type pedal generator, a 'V' Force officer would establish himself in a safe hide, far up in the hills above the Chindwin, often deep inside Burma, from which he could observe Japanese movements and report them back to HQ 14th Army. In the hills around Imphal a particularly effective team of Naga hillmen was run by an Englishwoman, Ursula Graham-Bower, long a resident in the district.

Deeper inside Japanese-held Burma, another Intelligence agency was at work. This was Force 136, a branch of Special Operations Executive, or SOE. One of its officers was Hugh Seagrim of the Burma Rifles, whose heroism became a byword. In 1943 he lived as a Karen and kept the Rangoon-Mandalay railway under constant observation, passing details of military traffic back to India. When the Japanese, aware of his presence, started to terrorise the Karen tribesmen, Seagrim voluntarily gave himself up to save them, to be tried by court-martial as a spy, having been captured wearing tribal dress. He impressed his captors, not only by his height (he stood six feet four inches) but by his frankness and courage under trial. He accepted the legality of the proceedings and pleaded in vain for the lives of the Karens on trial with him. He had no complaints at his own death sentence, he told the court, but they had done no more than carry out his orders. He was shot, with seven of his Karens, on 2 September 1944 and posthumously awarded the George Cross. He was not the only hero in his family, for one of his three brothers, sons of a Norfolk country parson, had already gained a posthumous VC commanding a battalion of the Green Howards in North Africa in 1943.

Although plenty of good intelligence was available to 14th Army, the Japanese attack, when it came, nearly threw the defence off balance. There are several reasons for this. As already mentioned, the commanders of 17 and 20 Divisions were aware of the plan to retire onto the Imphal Plain and to destroy the enemy there, but were unhappy at the idea of retreating without giving the Japanese a bloody nose as they crossed the Chindwin. Slim had decided that the decision to withdraw would be made when Cowan and Gracey, the two forward divisional commanders, were satisfied as to the strength and direction of the Japanese attack. He later admitted that this was an error on his part, and that the decision to start the rearwards movement should have been his. As things turned out, the retirement was started almost too late.

On 7 March 1944, Japanese patrols of their 33rd Division began to feel their way forward in the Tiddim area, testing the reaction of their old enemy, 17 Indian Division. At the same time, reports, from 'V' Force began to pour in; the enemy was approaching in great strength. That day, having sent Wingate and Special Force off on Operation 'Thursday', Slim paid a visit to HQ 4 Corps in Imphal. He approved Scoones' plans for the withdrawal onto the Plain, but emphasised that permission to retire was only to be given when he, Scoones, and his divisional commanders were all certain that the main enemy offensive had actually begun. At this point General Giffard allotted the two uncommitted LRP brigades to Slim, to be used as a counter-penetration force should one be required. Slim also decided to switch one of the Arakan divisions, 5 Indian, to Imphal by air, and ordered Christison to carry this move out between 13 March and 14 April, indicating his relaxed view of the situation at that point. Events were soon to call for far greater urgency.

Scoones now set up his administrative plan for the withdrawal of Imphal. Supplies of all sorts were placed in dumps along the Tiddim-Imphal road and work was intensified on the Plain, where defensive 'boxes' were laid out for occupation by 17 and 20 Divisions on their arrival.

Although Scoones and his subordinates knew that a hard fight was at hand, a sense of crisis was slow to develop. Early on the morning of 9 March, a two-man Gurkha patrol overlooking the Manipur River reported seeing a large force of Japanese infantry, with mules and pack artillery, fording the river and marching off fast in a westerly direction at last light the previous evening. As aerial reconnaissance failed to confirm this sighting, it was discounted by the Operations Staff at 4 Corps. It was, however, completely accurate; the Japanese, masters of concealment, had evaded detection and were even then pressing on over the hills to cut 17 Division's escape route. Similar Japanese columns were on the march everywhere. Some set up road blocks, others made a beeline for the supply dumps known to have been set up on 17 Division's withdrawal route. Information about them had been passed to the Japanese by one particular hill tribe, the Kuki, who had decided to throw in their lot with the enemy. They had already betrayed a number of 'V' force posts in the hills but despite warnings from many sources, their treachery had not been publicised.

By 13 March Scoones knew that the Japanese had stolen a march and ordered Maj General 'Punch' Cowan to get 17 Division on the road to Imphal. At the same time he sent two brigades from his only reserve, 23 Division, down the Tiddim road from Imphal with orders to keep it open at all costs. Suddenly the situation had become critical; the enemy was coming on much faster and in greater strength than anticipated. He was also at least two weeks earlier than Slim expected. Although the thrust over the hills towards Kohima and Dimapur had been correctly foreseen, its speed and weight had not. Slim and Scoones had estimated that the most the enemy would be able to sustain in that hilly and heavily-forested country would be a brigade-equivalent. It was now clear that a full Japanese division was aimed at the most vulnerable objective of all – the huge railhead at Dimapur, ten miles long and a mile wide, stretching along the railway and defended only by lines-of-communication troops. In the path of this thrust was the hill town and Nagaland administrative centre of Kohima, with a decidedly scratch garrison; and in the area of Ukhrul, part of the untried 50th Indian Parachute Brigade, which happened to be there only because its commander had asked for permission to carry out collective training near the front under operational conditions. 'Tim' Hope Thomson, a Royal Scots Fusilier, was at 32 the youngest brigade commander in the Indian Army despite never having served with Indian troops. He had been selected for this command because, as a very early volunteer for airborne duties in 1940, he had acquired great experience in airborne operations. His brigade had been formed two years earlier with one British, one Gurkha and one Indian battalion. The British battalion had since gone to the Middle East and in March 1944, 50th Brigade's strength was made up by the temporary attachment of an infantry battalion, the 4/5th Mahratta Light Infantry.

Unaware of the impending Japanese attack, Hope Thomson carried on with the brigade's training programme, and at this point the battalions were exercising separately. One, the 153rd Gurkha, was more than a hundred miles away near Kohima when the real situation became apparent.

On the Tiddim road, Lt General Yanagida's 33rd Division, spoiling for the fight, started off well in its three-pronged advance. One column raced up the road from Fort White; the left-hand column made for Milestone 100 to set up the first of a series of blocks; the right-hand column aimed for Milestone 109 where, close to the village of Tongzang, there was a large divisional supply depot, whose capture would be a great prize. By 13 March Scoones had a good idea of Japanese dispositions, having received reports from 'V' Force posts in the hills confirming everything that the earlier (and discounted) Gurkha patrol had seen. A large Japanese force was now positioned only a mile from the dump at MS 109 and the bridge over the Manipur River. Most of 17 Division, however, was still in its original positions to the south. On the evening of the 13th, Scoones ordered Cowan to start his retirement up a road which, unknown to Scoones, was already cut in several places. Whether because he was worried about the fate of several outlying detachments, or simply because he was unaware of the gravity of the situation, Cowan waited until midday on the 14th before issuing orders for the division to get on the road that evening.

As darkness fell, 17 Division formed up for its march back to Imphal; 16,000 men, 2,500 vehicles and 3,500 mules were spread for several miles up the road. To the south, the sky glared redly as Tiddim burned. Engineers laid mines in the road and verges as the tail of the column passed, then blew up all the culverts and bridges so carefully constructed in the last few months. The first road block was encountered at MS 132, beginning the first of many well-practised but time-consuming engagements. There were now Japanese between the Division and the Manipur River bridge; in the ranks of the 33rd Division there was an air of impending victory over an old foe. Cowan now needed to break through the blocks, and extricate his Division. On the night of the 16th, he had to signal one of his brigade commanders, who was having a spirited fight up in the surrounding hills; 'Forget those bloody Japs and keep your eye on the ball!'

By day the RAF delivered a series of highly accurate airstrikes, while the Division's artillery, often firing over open sights, blasted the Japanese off their positions. Not surprisingly, 17 Division was highly motivated and aggressively confident. Brigadier Cameron, commanding 48th Brigade, was a veteran Gurkha officer who had cause to remember the Sittang River disaster and had a score to settle. Then, commanding a battalion of his regiment, he had been forced to abandon riflemen with whom he had soldiered happily in absolute mutual trust for 20 years, since they had joined as young recruits. The experience of that night had turned his hair white.

The ferocity with which 17 Division turned on its pursuers surprised the Japanese. Once there had been a time when they only had to outflank their enemy and throw roadblocks across his line of retreat to cause total collapse. Things had changed and in one counter-attack the Japanese lost all six of their leading tanks. The commander of their 215th Infantry regiment, believed that his formation was about to be destroyed, called his staff around him to bid them a ceremonial farewell before burning the cipher books and regimental flag (although this was a revered symbol, it was the flagstaff itself which actually held the 'spirit' of the regiment; in this case it survived). Rallying, the Japanese broke into the supply depot at MS 109 on 18 March, a rich haul containing two months' fuel, food and ammunition for 17 Division, as well as lines of reserve vehicles of every type. An orgy of looting followed, watched with interest by Gurkha patrols on the surrounding hills. Crazed with British-issue rum and other liquor from canteen stores, Japanese soldiers careered around the valley bottom in captured jeeps or wallowed amidst stacks of unfamiliar foodstuffs. Large quantities of uniform and weapons were taken and a few days later the 9th Borders found themselves fighting Japanese clad in jungle green and using captured British weapons. A week later, the depot changed hands briefly and some of its contents were recovered. There was a grim reminder of the perils of capture by the Japanese army; the mutilated and tortured bodies of two Indian soldiers were found amidst the heaps of looted stores.

The diversion provided by the loss of the dump at MS 109 enabled 17 Division to break away and get back across the Manipur River, blowing the bridge on 26 March. Less than ten days later, having fought a further series of well-conducted actions, the Division was safely back on the Plain, ready to take its place in the next stage of the battle. It owed its survival partly to the quality of its troops and their supporting artillery, partly to the support given by the RAF, which had now achieved air superiority by driving the Japanese out of the sky. Apart from tactical close support air-strikes controlled by air contact teams of RAF officers travelling in their radio trucks with the ground troops, the certainty of the air supply system kept morale high. Whenever the Japanese put in one of their familiar flanking movements to block the road, there was no panic. For the Japanese, on the other hand, life was getting more difficult every day as their communications steadily stretched out behind them. Slim's old Chinese general had been right. The Japanese 33rd Division had taken to the field on strictly limited scales of supplies, and unless it could get its hands on the Imphal stockpiles it faced catastrophe within days.

Further north, the central prong of the Japanese drive had set out some time after 33rd Division pushed off up the Imphal road. Part of this Division, under the command of its infantry group commander, Maj General Yamamoto, had turned right to head off on a more direct route towards Imphal via the road junction at Witok which, if taken quickly, would set Yamamoto's troops firmly in the rear of Gracey's 20 Indian Division. The aim of this thrust was for the Yamamoto Group to reach the Imphal Plain as quickly as possible, capturing on its way the forward airfield at Palel, where RAF fighter and supply-drop squadrons were based. If these could be forced back to safer bases in Assam and Bengal, much of the sting would have been taken out of the RAF's support for 4 Corps.

While readying itself for an advance in the Spring, 20 Indian Division had been deployed well forward along the west bank of the Chindwin, patrolling energetically across the river. Much preparatory work had therefore been done to improve roads in the divisional area, as well as the establishment of substantial stockpiles. Gracey, like Cowan, was reluctant to throw all this up and abandon it to the enemy. Nevertheless, he began to thin out his forward brigades. On 15 March the enemy were seen to be crossing the Chindwin in great numbers, 25 miles to the north of 20 Division's left flank. A patrol of the Frontier Force Rifles watched them building rafts and launching assault boats, followed at night by a pontoon bridge, which was carefully dismantled during the hours of daylight and hidden from the eyes of the RAF under cover of the river bank. These were units from Lt General Yamauchi's 15th Division, with orders to hook round to the north of Imphal '. . . in spite of all hardships' to complete the encirclement begun by 33rd Division. Gracey had no intention of yielding ground at Palel; he knew the importance of its airfield to the RAF. His Division fell back slowly, fighting confidently all the way, and took up a strong defensive position on the Shenam Saddle, ten miles south-east of Palel, from which the Japanese failed to eject it.

When the Japanese attack was launched against 20 Division, the Devons bore the brunt. The enemy took a prominent feature called Nippon Hill and beat off a counter-attack by the Borders and Gurkhas. On 11 April 1944 the Devons went in, preceded by artillery fire and Hurribombers, then a mortar concentration on suspected Jap positions. In the words of the regimental history:

> The operation was like a rat-hunt. The bunker positions were honeycombed with holes and tunnels. The Jap soldiers would pop out of one hole, throw a salvo of grenades, and vanish down another hole . . .

The attack cost the Devons 19 dead and 68 wounded but they got onto the top and wired in to await the inevitable Jap attack:

> It hadn't been dark long before there came the first unmistakable signs of attack, followed by explosions along the wire, the chatter of machine guns on fixed lines, and the cries of the Japs. The Devons beat off the first wave and waited for the next. The second assault was held on the wire but left the company dangerously short of ammunition . . . then they came a third time and actually penetrated

into the two forward bunkers. The only hope was help from the gunners. This arrived, bursting with splendid accuracy along the line of the wire, while the men of 'A' Company fought the Japs out of the bunkers with grenades and the bayonet.'

At dawn, 68 dead Japanese were counted on or near the wire and many others had been dragged away.

Soon after, a Japanese called out in good English for 'B' Company to surrender, promising fair treatment for all who did. '. . . If this was the officer subsequently seen lying wounded near the outer wire, it was additional proof, if any was needed, of the extreme tenaciousness of the enemy, who generally had to be stamped to death like a snake.' When two NCOs approached this man, '. . . intent on a valuable prisoner, he behaved entirely to form. Sgt Leech tried to pick him up and was rewarded with a bite on the hand. Cpl Venner hit the Jap on the head with his steel helmet, which only made him bite deeper and refuse to let go. The patrol was in an exposed position and delay was dangerous. Cpl Venner had to draw the officer's ceremonial sword and kill him with it, before Sgt Leech could get his hand back.'

(The Devons handed over the hill to a battalion of the Frontier Force Rifles, who lost it that night.)

The northern prong of the Japanese attack was perhaps the most dangerous of all. Scoones reacted by scraping up a garrison for Kohima and ordering it to hold on. A collection of battalions of variable quality began to dig and wire along the straggling ridge on which Kohima stands: Assam Rifles, Burma Regiment, some Gurkhas and Nepalese troops. There was no brigade headquarters of coordinate the defence and a large number of administrative personnel, including 1,500 hospital cases, threatened to be more hindrance than help as the better part of a Japanese infantry division bore down on them. Astride the enemy's approach, however, and by sheer chance, lay 50th Indian Parachute Brigade, still unaware of the impending avalanche as it exercised around Ukhrul.

As the crisis developed, Mountbatten had been visiting Stilwell. During his visit he had sustained a painful and potentially dangerous eye injury when a thorn branch hit him in the face. When he heard of the Japanese thrust he was in hospital with both eyes bandaged, but left his bed and flew down to see Slim at Comilla, where he ordered the immediate reinforcement of 4 Corps by air. The leisurely airlift of 5 Indian Division from the Arakan now went into overdrive and further reinforcements were sent for: 7 Division to follow by air, and the British 2 Division, training for amphibious operations in South India was gathered together and deployed around Dimapur. Mountbatten later claimed that if he had been told of the Japanese attack sooner, he would have ordered the move of 5 and 7 Divisions to begin a week earlier. He was certainly displeased with what he considered

Giffard's apparent lack of urgency in responding to the crisis and immediately used his enormous influence to obtain more transport aircraft from the Americans, signalling the Chiefs of Staff in Washington that on his own initiative he had diverted 30 Dakotas from the China Airlift and intended to keep them for a month. This enabled Slim to get 5 Division up to Imphal in time to play a vital part in the battle there.

There was just time to put part of Brigadier Warren's 161st Indian Infantry Brigade, newly arrived from 5 Division, into Kohima before the roads on either side of it were cut. The British battalion in this experienced formation was the 4th Royal West Kents, and it arrived as the Japanese, who were now well across the Indian border, believed that victory was in their grasp. Radio Tokyo was already proclaiming that the 'March on India' had begun and that 17 Division had been destroyed . . .

★　★　★

For 50th Parachute Brigade the moment had come. On 19 March, Hope Thomson was interrupted in the middle of a routine training conference by alarming news; a strong Japanese force was only two miles away and coming on fast. To meet it, he had his weakened brigade of one infantry and one parachute battalion, two mountain artillery batteries and a field ambulance, all still 30 miles to the rear at Litan, down a road negotiable only by four-wheel-drive vehicles. By dawn the next morning the forward company of 152nd Para Battalion had been virtually wiped out, although the Japanese had been shaken by its furious opposition. When the surviving paratroops made their last desperate charge in mid-morning, Japanese observers saw a British officer, the last of the company still on his feet, shoot himself, an act which greatly stirred them.

Hope Thomson managed to retrieve half his detached Gurkha battalion from the Kohima area, and withdrew the rest of the brigade into a tight perimeter around the hill village of Sangshak. He had asked for an urgent issue of defence stores, especially mines and wire, with which to prepare a reasonably secure perimeter, but none was forthcoming from either 23 Division or 4 Corps, who both seemed too immersed in their own problems to worry about him, other than to order 50th Brigade to hold to the last man in order to buy time for the defence of Kohima. Without wire, and short of even picks and shovels needed to dig weapon slits in the rocky ground, the soldiers of 50th Parachute Brigade prepared their positions as best they could. Back at Litan, HQ 23 Division, with half a parachute battalion and a collection of stragglers, formed a defensive 'box' and hoped for the best. The staff officer in charge was found to be helplessly drunk, and removed, and the second-in-command of 153rd Gurkha Parachute Battalion took over. Litan was totally indefensible, being overlooked from all directions; but HQ 4 Corps, apparently unaware of the true situation, insisted that it be held.

By first light on 22 March, the makeshift Sangshak position was as ready as it ever would be. The garrison was isolated, the Japanese having cut the road to Litan. There ensued five nightmare days and nights for nearly 2,000 men, packed into a perimeter never longer than 600 yards from east to west and 300 yards deep. An air-drop called for on 23 March was a failure, most of the loads going to the besiegers. At night the defenders were kept awake by continuous 'jitter' patrols, interspersed with suicidal charges. After one of these, a map found on a dead officer revealed the entire Japanese plan for the Imphal offensive as well as the projected deployment of their 15 and 33 Divisions. Realising the value of this, the brigade Intelligence Officer made a copy. Accompanied by one of his men he took it through the Japanese lines and across the hills to Imphal. In the next three days he repeated this 36-mile trip no less than three times. Although he had risked his life to get the priceless information to 4 Corps, no attempt was made to make use of it and he received no recognition of his gallantry despite Hope Thomson's immediate citation.

Three days into the battle, the 50th Brigade was still holding off four times its own number of Japanese – two infantry regiments, each of three battalions and their reinforcements. A message of goodwill was received from 23 Division, with the promise of close air support which failed to materialise. Conditions within the perimeter were appalling, with unburied men and mules putrefying in the sun, millions of flies feeding on living and dead alike, and a severe water shortage. The medical staff of the 80th Indian Field Ambulance worked miracles, none more so than Captain Rangaraj of the Indian Army Medical Corps, the first Indian Army doctor to qualify as a parachutist. Six years later he made a great name for himself in Korea as commander of another Indian Field Ambulance with the Commonwealth Division, winning a DSO for outstanding services. Now, however, his main concern was to save the wounded from further injuries as he worked under constant heavy fire.

By the final day at Sangshak, 18 out of 152nd Parachute Battalion's 25 British officers had been killed and only two remained unscathed. Among them were some outstanding young men, volunteers for a type of soldiering they knew involved unusual risk. Some were former Oxford undergraduates, contemporaries of Richard Hillary the author of *The Last Enemy*, and had been part of a set known as 'the long-haired boys' at Oxford in the 1930s. Scholars, sportsmen, lovers of the good life, they volunteered for active service in 1939 in the most adventurous units to be found; few survived the war. They were typified by Lt Robin de la Haye of the 152nd, who fought like a lion at Sangshak. On the last morning he was seen checking his equipment and languidly combing his hair; when asked what he was doing, he replied, 'Oh – I do believe it's another counter-attack.' Five minutes later he was killed at the head of his platoon.

The Indian mountain gunners, firing point-blank as each Japanese attack came in, maintained the highest standards of their regiment. Both battery commanders were killed trying to recover lost guns as the perimeter steadily grew smaller. Even the Japanese were generous in their subsequent praise of the defenders. They also recognised that their all-important schedule had been seriously affected by this unexpected hold-up, giving further time for the defence of Kohima to be made ready.

Towards last light on 26 March, 4 Corps ordered 50th Brigade to fight its way out, giving specific instructions for the route to be followed and ending somewhat incongruously with 'Good luck. Our thoughts are with you'. As this was transmitted in clear speech, Hope Thomson suspected a Japanese ruse, but the correct verification was given to his challenge, and despite his misgivings following such a crass breach of radio security, he issued orders for the destruction of all classified documents and non-portable equipment and told the crew of the surviving guns, mortars and medium machine guns to fire off the rest of their ammunition before destroying them. The brigade had been ordered to march south to begin with, then west towards Imphal in order to avoid Japanese positions.

Masked by the noise of the final mortar and artillery barrage and as the machine guns fired belt after belt of ammunition into the gloom, all able-bodied men were formed up. There were now 500 inside the perimeter, of whom 300 were able to stand up and march. All but the most extreme stretcher cases were carried out to safety by their comrades. The commander of the Field Ambulance, Lt Colonel Davis, wanted to stay with those left behind, fearing the consequences if they were left without protection, but Hope Thomson ordered him to leave. They were dosed with morphine and left to the mercy of the Japanese (who, it must be said, on this occasion treated them remarkably well). Shortly before midnight the survivors, carrying those who could not walk, moved off down the hill.

The Japanese did not interfere; as they were preparing their final assault, timed for midnight, they were struck by a hail of fire as the garrison loosed off its ammunition. When they cautiously entered the abandoned perimeter it was deserted apart from the dead and seriously wounded. One of these, Lieutenant Seaton, had been left behind under heavy sedation, having sustained a terrible facial wound; a bullet had hit him in the mouth, removing all his teeth and most of his jaw. He regained consciousness to find a Japanese soldier searching his belongings, and killed him with his fighting knife. Then, without food or water (for his grievous wounds prevented him from even sipping liquids) and without map or compass, he marched west across three ranges of hills to rejoin the battalion at Imphal. After several months in hospital he rejoined his company and survived the war. Captain Robin Shand, also left behind unconscious, was captured, interrogated, then stripped to his underclothes and led by a rope, hands tied behind his back, as the Japanese continued their advance. On the first night, his captor let go of the rope and Shand rolled several hundred feet down a steep hillside amid a hail of fire. After lying low for a day, and with hands still tied firmly behind his back, he carried on. Eventually he persuaded a friendly old Naga tribesman to cut him free and found his way to Imphal.

Survivors of the brigade continued arriving in friendly lines for many days. They were given a welcome similar to that accorded to Slim when he came out of Burma in 1942. Nobody in 4 Corps wanted to know about their fight at Sangshak. Hope Thomson, who was exhausted, hallucinating and under the impression that his tube of tootpaste was a gun, was hospitalised, deprived of his brigade, demoted and invalided home before he could give a full report on the destruction of his splendid brigade. In an Order of the Day some months later, Slim generously acknowledged its contribution, clearly giving Hope Thomson and his men due credit for holding up the Japanese advance; but Scoones, whose apparent inertia in the face of the Japanese threat had so nearly lost him the 17 Division, never conceded how much he owed to 50th Brigade's great stand. It was over 40 years before a full account of this hitherto neglected battle revealed what actually took place.

Kohima

". . . the place looked like Blackpool on a summer's night, plus a fireworks display."

T HE SHORTEST route from the banks of the Chindwin to Dimapur lay via Kohima, along the tracks over the Naga Hills. On the night of 15/16 March, Lt General Sato Kotokui's 31st Division crossed the river in three places. From each crossing point regimental groups set off in a north-westerly direction. The southerly group made for Ukhrul, where it was drawn into the fight with 50th Parachute Brigade; the middle group made for Jessami; and the northern column, consisting of the 138th Regiment, made straight for Kohima, passing to the north of Jessami. The area was only lightly held by small detachments of levies and there were no concentrations of defending troops nearer than Jessami, garrisoned by the Assam Regiment. The sudden appearance of Sato's regiments, moving on parallel tracks some 30 miles apart, gave rise to a flood of reports from 'V' Force posts and from loyal Naga tribesmen. As the advance proceeded, resistance gradually stiffened, forcing the Japanese to deploy off the line of march to deal with resolute little rearguard parties which, after imposing delay, fell back once more.

It was clear that serious resistance to the Japanese drive on Dimapur would have to be offered around Kohima, and orders were therefore issued to all outlying detachments to fall back there. This was difficult, as many of the telephone lines in Naga country had been cut by the Japanese and radio conditions were bad. One important detachment, the two battalions of the Assam regiment deployed around Jessami, could not be contacted. Efforts were made to drop messages from aircraft to the garrison, now coming under attack from the vanguard of Yamauchi's 15th Division. One message fell into the enemy lines, another landed on the wire defences, from where it was taken by Japanese infantry. Volunteers from nearby units tried unsuccessfully to get through to Jessami, and it seemed that the battalions were doomed. In a final, desperate attempt, a subaltern of the regiment marched alone for 20 miles across the hills. Crawling through the Japanese positions at night, he made his way through the wire to find that the defenders had shifted position and were now dug in some distance away. Hiding in the middle of the Japanese position, he chose his moment and dashed across no-man's land under heavy fire from both sides, to deliver his message. That night the Assam Regiment got clear, and marched back to the main force. The Japanese followed, closing in on Kohima.

The 31st Division was one of the strongest in the Imperial Army. Its commander, General Sato, was known to be a courageous and effective officer prone to furious outbursts of rage if his subordinates, who held him in awe, failed in their duty. The Division's 'bayonet strength' as it went into battle at Kohima was almost 20,000. Of these, less than 3,000 would survive to re-cross the Chindwin three months later. The all-important Infantry Group was under command of Maj General Myazaki, an experienced and respected officer, noted for his humane treatment of prisoners and wounded. The Division was recruited in the northern islands of Japan, where feudal tradition was still strong and the people were mainly subsistence farmers and fisherfolk, inured to a hard life. Sato's men were thus able to cope with the extreme weather of the Naga Hills, where snow fell on the upper slopes during the Kohima battle, reminding them of their homeland. Their physique was impressive. Many were well over six feet tall, and compared to the town-bred Japanese their features were, to European eyes, finer. Six years of hard soldiering in China had built the 31st Division into a formidable fighting formation which would need some stopping. Honoured to be the spearhead of the March on India, its men were highly motivated and aggressive.

The Japanese advance took them across dreadful country; thickly forested, riven by deep gorges, and steeply mountainous. There were few tracks other than those linking Naga villages perched on steep ridges. Despite this, the 31st brought along their guns, some on pack animals, others dragged by their crews and hauled with ropes up precipitous slopes. They also brought their meat ration in the form of herds of oxen. A route had, however, been reconnoitred for them some months earlier by an enterprising Japanese intelligence officer, Captain Nishida. In October 1943, helped by Kuki tribesmen, he evaded detection by the pro-British Nagas and pinpointed a number of 'V' Force posts from which any information about Japanese movements would certainly be passed back to India. Nishida's party, which included members of the INA, carefully noted any tracks used regularly by the British and those upgraded for wheeled traffic by their engineers.

On 14 March, as the main body of 31st Division prepared to cross the Chindwin, Nishida set out on a second patrol. This time his mission was to eliminate 'V' Force's key radio stations. Of these, the most important was the one from which Major Murray, commanding 'V' Force in the Naga hills, transmitted cipher messages back to India. Nishida's men attacked it, destroyed the radio and wounded Murray, who managed to escape to a safer post with the code-books after sending out an alarm signal. As it happened, Murray's alert went unheeded at 4 Corps amidst a torrent of signals traffic.

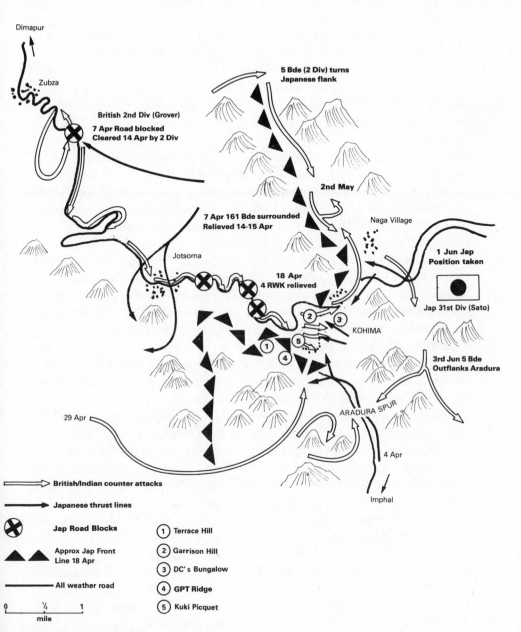

Dimapur

Zubza

**5 Bde (2 Div) turns
Japanese flank**

British 2nd Div (Grover)

**7 Apr Road blocked
Cleared 14 Apr by 2 Div**

2nd May

**7 Apr 161 Bde surrounded
Relieved 14-15 Apr**

Naga Village

Jotsoma

**1 Jun Jap
Position taken**

**18 Apr
4 RWK relieved**

Jap 31st Div (Sato)

② ③

① ⑤

KOHIMA

④

**3rd Jun 5 Bde
Outflanks Aradura**

29 Apr

ARADURA SPUR

4 Apr

Imphal

➡ British/Indian counter attacks

➡ Japanese thrust lines

✪ Jap Road Blocks

◤◤ Approx Jap Front
Line 18 Apr

── All weather road

0   ½   1
       mile

① Terrace Hill

② Garrison Hill

③ DC's Bungalow

④ GPT Ridge

⑤ Kuki Picquet

THE FIGHT FOR KOHIMA

163

Enough information was now reaching Slim from other sources, however, to give him the strengths and directions of the Japanese as they converged on Kohima.

In addition to the divisions airlifted from the Arakan, Slim called for further reinforcements, and within two days of receiving the order to move, 33 Corps Headquarters, under Lt General Montague Stopford, had set itself up alongside Slim's Army HQ at Comilla. The Corps included the all-British 2 Division, commanded by Maj General Grover, summoned from South India. Having been trained for amphibious operations, 2 Division was relatively inexperienced in jungle or mountain fighting, although one of its brigades, 6th Infantry, had suffered heavy casualties in the first Arakan campaign a year earlier. Arriving overland by rail and road, the Division began to form up around Dimapur, much to the relief of its ad hoc garrison of administrative units. Stopford was now given his orders: he was to keep the Japanese off the Dimapur-Kohima road and relieve Imphal, now under pressure from all sides, as soon as possible.

At Kohima the position became critical on 4 April, when forward elements of 31st Division occupied the northern parts of the town. This is situated at a point where the road from Dimapur to the rice plain of Imphal crosses a north-south ridge line at an altitude of almost 5,000 feet before heading south to Imphal, some 50 miles distant as the crow flies. Sato set up his command post on the high ground to the east, from where he had a panoramic view of the battlefield. Some days earlier, on 29 March, 161st Indian Infantry Brigade had been sent up from Dimapur to hold Kohima, then withdrawn when the threat to Dimapur seemed to be greater. As 2 Division began to arrive there, it was decided to send 161st Brigade back and on 5 April, led by the 4th Battalion Royal West Kents under Lt Col Laverty, they headed up the road to find the Japanese already in partial occupation, with reinforcements pouring in from Sato's marching columns as they arrived over the hills. The Royal West Kents managed to get into Kohima before the road was cut, and Brigadier Warren concentrated the rest of the brigade around the village of Jotsoma, three miles short of the now-beleaguered West Kents.

A strong Japanese road block was set up at Zubza, eight miles further back towards Dimapur, and 161st Brigade was also cut off. In Kohima the West Kents were a welcome addition to the garrison, commanded by Colonel Richards. Already in residence were the Assam Rifles, some Nepalese troops, and two companies of the Burma Regiment, created in 1942, after the retreat, from survivors of various Burma Rifles battalions. Many of these were Burmese-born Gurkhas, descendants of soldiers who, having given good service in the Burmese wars of the previous century, had been awarded grants of land. Apart from these and the West Kents, there were about 1,500 non-combatants, including hospital patients and convalescents. On 7 April a company of 5/7th Rajputs from the main body of 161st Brigade at Jotsoma got through to Kohima and were added to the garrison, which was also able to get rid of 200 non-combatants by sending them back safely down the road.

At first, the defenders held a series of small hillocks along the ridge, but from the start the Japanese held all the dominant ground. As the battle continued, the dwindling garrison was forced into an ever-shrinking perimeter. This was finally less than 400 yards across and completely overlooked by the enemy, whose snipers were active around the clock, making daylight movement virtually impossible. (But not for the Deputy Commissioner, Mr Pawsey, whose administrative offices and pleasant bungalow were on the ridge, and who toured the area whenever possible, wearing an elegant Panama hat, thereby raising the morale of all who saw him. It was due to his extraordinary influence over the Naga people that their loyalty was guaranteed throughout the campaign.)

As the numbers of wounded steadily mounted, the work of the doctors and their medical orderlies became extremely difficult. The senior medical officer, Lt Colonel Young, had made his way through Japanese positions to enter Kohima and in the next two weeks he operated on over 400 cases, using a knife which, he reported, eventually looked more like a hacksaw. Two direct hits on the dressing station on 13 April produced horrible scenes of carnage, and the medical staff, of whom three-quarters were Indian, worked on in a welter of severed limbs, blood, excrement and scattered entrails. Lt Colonel Young and a few volunteers raided the civil hospital, now in Japanese hands, to purloin medical supplies from under their enemies' noses.

Before the battle, Kohima had been a pleasant hill station, the centre of administration for a large area of Nagaland. There were barracks for the Depot of the Assam Rifles, a jail, a small hospital, District Commissioner's residence with tennis court, and a club house. At the north end of the ridge was a straggling Naga village. Battle damage soon ruined this pleasing scene as the perimeter gradually shrank. Water was a particular problem and in very short supply once the Japanese, after capturing the main storage tanks, cut the distribution pipes. It then had to be taken from a small spring under continual sniper fire, and rationed to half a pint a day per man. Attempts to air drop water in the inner tubes of motor tyres were not entirely successful, and thirst remained a besetting problem. The plight of the wounded was desperate, as they had to lie unprotected in the open, where mortar and artillery fire inflicted further injuries and killed many.

A mountain battery of the Indian Artillery had managed to get into Kohima with the Royal West Kents, but the closeness of the enemy made it impossible for them to bring their guns into action. The sole 25-pounder gun already there was knocked out within 24 hours. Instead, the Indian gunners fought as infantry, often hand-to-hand. Three miles down the Dimapur road, jammed in with 161st Brigade, there was priceless artillery support in the form of three mountain batteries: the 2nd (Derajat), 11th (Dehra Dun), and 12th (Poonch). The observation and command posts of the 2nd Battery had gone into Kohima with the Royal West Kents before the road was cut, together with several Forward Observation officers, who were parcelled out to the infantry in their trenches around the perimeter. From these, they immediately registered targets for defensive fire, which now broke up a succession of Japanese attacks.

The weapons of these mountain batteries were 3.7-inch pack howitzers or 'screw guns', designed to be broken down into mule or pack-horse loads. The Indian Mountain Artillery were considered an élite body (not least by themselves) and had absolute priority on the line of march; the warning shouts of their men were enough to drive any marching unit off the track as the guns went through at a sharp trot, gun crews running briskly alongside, officers mounted. The sights and sounds of a screw gun battery on the move were unforgettable. During the siege at Kohima, their average range of engagement was 3,700 yards, and such was the proficiency of the gunners that when fighting was raging across the Commissioner's tennis court at a range of ten yards, shells were being placed with great precision onto the Japanese positions without risk to the West Kents on their side of the net.

Every day, undeterred by Japanese ground fire, Dakotas wheeled around overhead, lined up and dropped ammunition by the ton to the mountain batteries at Jotsoma, most of it landing within yards of the guns. Similar missions kept the Kohima garrison supplied. At the end of the siege the entire area was festooned with parachutes, draped on the branches of shattered trees or on the roofs of wrecked buildings.

It was essential to raise the seige, and 2 Division moved up from Dimapur. On 14 April a set-piece attack by tanks and infantry on the Zubza block enabled 5th Brigade to break through to 161st Brigade at Jotsoma. It was now possible to bring the divisional artillery to bear on the besiegers; to ensure pinpoint accuracy before the attack on the Zubza road-block, every field gun in 2 Division had been individually registered, a lengthy process taking five hours, which was to pay dividends as the battle moved on.

In the attack by the 1st Cameron Highlanders which broke the block, the infantry were supported by devastating gunfire, rushing the Japanese position with few casualties to themselves. The attack involved a hard climb up a steep hill, slippery with mud, but this did not prevent tanks getting to the top. Japanese soldiers could be seen running for their lives during the preliminary bombardment but many stayed to fight it out with the Highlanders, one of whose company sergeant majors captured the sword of a Japanese officer when he slew him in single combat, cheered on by the rest of his company. Having cleared the Zubza block, General Grover had every

The height of the monsoon, near Bishenpur, in July 1944. The scene is typical of the conditions under which the RIASC had to work to get supplies to the forward troops. *(IWM)*

Madras Sappers and Miners at work on a 'corduroy' road east of Kohima, on the Jessami track, in August 1944. *(IWM)*

Men of the 10th Gurkha Rifles consolidate after the capture of the hill feature known as 'Scraggy'. The steepness and bareness of the terrain, and the constant monsoon cloud cover, can be clearly seen. (*IWM*)

A low-level attack by the RAF on the Burma-Siam railway, east of the Sittang, in 1944. The picture gives a good idea of the open terrain that covers most of central Burma. By repeated attacks on the railway bridges, Allied airpower was able to throttle the Japanese lines of communication at will. (*IWM*)

Supplies go forward to Tamu in an assault craft across the swift-flowing Lokchau river in August 1944. Such scenes were to be found everywhere across the front during the monsoon season. (*IWM*)

During intensive fighting on the Aradura
Spur in June 1944, the CO's Orders Group of
the 2nd Bn Durham Light Infantry assembles.
(l to r) RSM Hogbin, Lt Col Robinson
(in rear), Maj 'Conky' Greenwell, Lt Miles,
Maj 'Tank' Waterhouse. Greenwell and
Waterhouse had earlier played leading
roles in the fighting on Kohima Ridge.
(Durham Light Infantry Museum)

The River Chindwin was one of the 14th Army's lifelines during the final months of the campaign, DUKW amphibious load-carriers of 387 Company, RASC, here seen on the Upper Chindwin, were widely used for the resupply of forward troops. *(IWM)*

The beach-head at Kangaw, showing the narrow channel along which the landing craft had to make their way for some ten miles, before reaching the landing. *(IWM)*

At an airstrip on the Plain of Imphal in March 1944 newly-arrived reinforcements from 15 Corps in the Arakan await the move to their battle positions. The C-47 Dakota nearer the camera is from the USAAF, the other is an RAF plane. The red centres were removed from roundels to avoid confusion with the red sun markings on Japanese aircraft.

(Robert Hunt Library)

In July 1944 the 11th East African Division began its march down the unhealthy Kabaw valley to meet the 5th Indian Division at Kalewa. Here, Askari approach the end of their long journey.
(Robert Hunt Library)

Men of the RIASC clear a drop zone and
sort out vital supplies after an
accurate airdrop along the Tiddim road.
(IWM)

Lt Gen Sir Oliver Leese, C-in-C ALFSEA,
visits 36 Division, driven by the
Divisional commander, Maj Gen Frank
Festing. But why an army jeep carries
an AA badge remains a mystery. *(IWM)*

reason to be proud of his Division, most of which was in combat for the first time. Very early that morning, he recorded in his diary, a Japanese 'jitter' patrol had made its way into one of his forward brigade areas and attacked the night harbour position of 'C' Squadron, 150th Regiment Royal Armoured Corps, whose troopers, caught in their bivouacs, barely had time to mount their tanks and close down. The Japanese, now under fire from the tanks' machine guns, were chased to the top of a steep hill from where they shouted 'Come up to us', a challenge enthusiastically accepted by the 7th Worcesters, who mounted a 'pheasant drive' with three rifle companies. The enemy were forced into a dip and wiped out. Japanese casualties, Grover noted, included two carrier pigeons, shot down by the Worcesters.

Passing on through the traffic jam at Jotsoma, 6th Brigade now made contact with the West Kents, who were relieved in their shattered positions by the 1st Royal Berkshires. The exhausted garrison, undefeated after 12 unremitting days of continuous close-quarter fighting, looked like ghosts. Lt Colonel Frank Owen, editor of 'SEAC' described the West Kents as they emerged from their positions:

> . . . the dead lay unburied. Little squads of grimy and bearded riflemen stared blankly at the relieving troops; many were too dazed to realise that they were saved, and too tired to believe their sleep-starved eyes . . .

Since the start of the siege on 5 April the Battalion had fought off virtually an entire Japanese division, regiment by regiment. Thirteen of its officers and 201 of its men had been killed or died of their wounds and it had endured no fewer than 25 full-scale infantry attacks, all supported by artillery and mortars. Over 400 casualties had been sustained by other units of the garrison. If proof were needed that good free men could take on and throw back the best of the Japanese Army, it lay with the officers and men of what they themselves would be the first to describe as a very ordinary Territorial battalion, whose name will nonetheless go down in the annals of the British Army.

The fighting spirit of the 4th Royal West Kents is typified by the actions which gained a posthumous VC for Lance Corporal John Harman. When his section was pinned down by extremely heavy fire from a Japanese machine gun only 50 yards away, Harman sprinted forward and lobbed a hand grenade which wiped out the gun crew. He returned to his men with the captured weapon on his shoulders. Shortly after this he again charged forward alone and killed the entire crew of a second machine gun post with rifle and bayonet. As he walked calmly back he was raked by a third gun. Mortally wounded, he got back to his men, said 'I got the lot; it was worth it' and died.

The firepower of 2 Division's 72 25-pounders was now added to the battle for the ridge. It was the turn of the Japanese infantry to feel the destructive and maddening effects of continual bombardment and this, coupled with their lack of medical cover, must have made life more unendurable for them than for the West Kents and the battalions who now took over their positions. For the siege went on despite the breakthrough of 6th Brigade and the growing strength of 2 Division as it moved up to the battle. The 1st Royal Berkshires, who had been the first relieving unit, were joined on 21 April by two companies of the 2nd Durham Light Infantry, who had to fend off a series of Japanese attacks as they tried to dig in amidst the shambles of the earlier battle. The place was now like a charnel-house, with hundreds of dead, British and Japanese, lying around in advanced stages of decomposition, together with dozens of bloated mule carcasses. The Durhams and the Royal Berkshires were on the slopes of what became known as Summerhouse Hill, the rest of Kohima still firmly in Japanese hands. Summerhouse Hill was overlooked by a closely adjacent feature known as Kuki Picquet from which enemy snipers operated at less than a hundred yards' range. Between the two was No-man's land, a short stretch of saddleback ridge copiously planted with panji stakes and swept by enemy fire.

On 22 April a concerted attack was made on Kuki Picquet, as additional units of 6th Brigade had managed to join the Berkshires and Durhams. The attacks, carried out with great gallantry by the 1st Royal Welch Fusiliers and the 1st Royal Berkshires, were driven back with heavy loss, and the Durhams were ordered to follow up.

Before they could start the assault, the Japanese counter-attacked. In the small hours of 23 April, after a short bombardment with artillery and grenade launchers, the enemy charged. A report in the Durhams' Regimental Newsletter by Major 'Tank' Waterhouse, commanding 'C' Company, gives a vivid impression of what it was like in the front line at Kohima. Japanese artillery had ignited some of the parachutes hanging in the shattered pine trees, which then in turn caught fire. An ammunition dump exploded:

> . . . the place looked like Blackpool on a summer's night, plus a firework display. The Japanese now charged 'C' Company . . . shoulder to shoulder, the leading wave wearing respirators and throwing phosphorus grenades. They were knocked down, but as one man fell another took his place. The inevitable happened and the Jap broke through in the centre . . . I managed to get my company to form a line about 'C' Company HQ, and we held the Japs there . . . we were now lying shoulder to shoulder and suffering very badly from spring grenades. Captain Martin Wilson, the second-in-command, was badly hit but refused to be moved until the others had been evacuated . . . [he died of his wounds later that night] . . . all the telephone lines had gone and most of the wireless sets. Our gunner OP officer had been killed and it took us nearly three hours to get any defensive fire. About 0400 hrs we started to counter-attack. Bill

Watson of 'D' Company was killed leading one of them . . . last seen clubbing Japs with the butt-end of a Bren gun. The Japs were taking a pretty good beating and we could hear them shouting and screaming just below us. They seemed to have had just about enough and some officer was trying to organise them to attack again.

When 'A' Company tried to retake ground lost during the night they too were thrown back with heavy casualties by the enemy still dug in on Kuki Picquet.

Another officer, Lt Pat Rome, had good cause to remember that dreadful night as he recovered, a few days later, from wounds received on Summerhouse Hill. He commanded a platoon of 'D' Company which had moved up from Jotsoma on the backs of tanks. He and his men marvelled at the sight of the Royal West Kents as they came out of battle:

> . . . haggard from lack of sleep, filthy and bearded . . . Garrison Hill struck me as being a most unpleasant place. The 'bag' of Japs accumulated by the West Kents . . . lay all over the place in varying stages of decomposition . . .

Getting 'D' Company's kit off the road and up into the front line was hard and dangerous work.

> What a climb! Ammo, water, food, packs, everything had to be carried up from the road – about 400 feet and pretty steep . . . in full view of the Japs the whole time . . . the Japs evidently living up to their reputation of doing nothing by day, you couldn't see a sign of life from their trenches – some 50 yards away in places – you never can . . . ·

Lt Rome shared a hole with his platoon sergeant, Sgt Brannigan, and his batman, Private Joe Wilson. On the evening of their arrival:

> . . . we pulled a groundsheet over the entrance . . . lit up cigarettes and chatted . . . it wasn't a bad war, really; we had a good hole and a prospect of a good night's sleep . . . everything was quiet; at about 8 o'clock we settled down. The shell and mortar bombs woke me up at about 2 o'clock. They were coming pretty thick and fast . . . I stuck my head out of the hole and found the area thick with smoke, smelling of cordite and lit by fires. An ammo dump on the hill was blazing away merrily, a dump of food and stores was also burning. Some of the trees had caught fire . . . the dull thud of bully beef cans exploding! . . . suddenly we heard them yelling and a high pitched scream: 'Charge!' . . . Brens opened up on my perimeter and all hell was let loose . . . The rapid stuttering crackle of the Japanese light machine guns, the heavier thudding of the Brens; grenades, Stens, mortars, the Banzai-yelling Japs – and above all the area illuminated by fires and heavy with smoke, with figures dashing hither and thither . . .

Lt Rome and Sergeant Brannigan got out of their hole. The sergeant was killed almost at once, as was Private Wilson:

> It was a question of grenades and still more grenades and shooting when you saw

something . . . the remainder of the night was a confused memory, set against a background of fire, smoke and noise . . .

Men were falling all around him. Rome vividly recalls a wounded soldier begging him to fetch him, crying, 'I'm blind, I'm blind . . .'

Standing up, lying down, walking and crawling, throwing grenades, more grenades, keep the bastards at a distance. Watching their grenades coming over – a little blue light sailing through the air, then down and BANG! . . . I stood up and SMACK I was knocked round and found my arm hanging limp and useless and numb . . . I thought it was broken but it didn't hurt which was fortunate . . .

He crawled around the position, found a rifle sling which he looped around his neck, and put his arm through it. The survivors were now sitting in their holes, backs to the wall resolved to sell their lives dearly. The screaming died away. Expecting another Japanese charge, the Durhams cocked their weapons and waited; there were shouts of 'Hold it' from hole to hole. They took stock;

. . . a little Jap was found in the middle of us lying on the ground, saying, 'Tojo . . . Tojo'. He was despatched . . . I can't remember daylight coming. I remember talking to Roger and hearing five minutes later that he was dead.

At first light, the Japanese on Kuki Picquet resumed their sniping. The Durhams were partly on the forward slope, pinned down and obliged to use Japanese corpses for cover. 'A' Company launched their forlorn counter attack, led by Major Peter Stockton, brandishing a kukri. When they were driven back they carried their wounded with them as snipers took their toll of the walking wounded. The Durhams' stretcher-bearers went again and again into the open to retrieve casualties and were continually sniped. Two of them were recommended for immediate VCs for this display of sublime courage. They failed to get even a 'mention'.

Lt Rome stayed in the Company position, making himself as useful as his wounds permitted by carrying Bren gun magazines from hole to hole. As he was doing this,

. . . a Jap jumped up off a forward trench and ran towards us screaming and waving his arms. He bought it in a big way. He was unarmed. Perhaps he'd had too much.

Towards last light Rome was able to get back down to the Regimental Aid Post where his wounds were dressed and from where he was evacuated, to rejoin the battalion five months later. His actions that night gained him the Military Cross.

Two days of relative calm followed; the Durhams amalgamated the survivors of 'C' and 'D' Companies and tidied up the area as much as they could. At midnight on 27 April, as Major Waterhouse recalled,

. . . the fun started again, if you can call it that. The Japs attacked with about two companies. The leading men carried bags full of grenades but no weapons. They again broke through owing to sheer weight of numbers got on the plateau, running round and shouting 'Tojo! Tojo!' before digging in. The Durhams counter-attacked at first light, led by Captain 'Conky' Greenwell, blowing a hunting horn. . . . A great sound, and they caught the Japs with their pants down . . . they packed up and ran and found cover in our own smoke, which was blanketing Kuki Picquet. Fire support was first class, . . . 3.7s, 25 pounders, our own mortars fired 1,300 rounds and caused the Japs heavy casualties.

On 30 April the Durhams were relieved for 48 hours' rest out of the line, then went back into the fight. They continued at Kohima for several more weeks, taking part in the bloody fighting for the recapture of Aradura Spur, the southwards continuation of Kohima ridge. Here they suffered yet more casualties. In a letter home, an officer of the battalion wrote of his grudging admiration for the Japanese in even reaching Kohima:

The country he had come across . . . it was a pretty good marvel that he ever got as far as he did. [After describing the battle on the ridge he continues:] We were ringed by snipers and had to be supplied from the air. No shaving of course, and we grew pretty good beards . . . and then we took part in the early stage of Kohima Ridge attack and had a pretty bad time again. The CO got killed this time and we got the second-in-command of the Royal Berkshires to command us. [After ten days out of the line they were back] . . . in the awful grind up the Aradura Spur.

The monsoon had now broken and the Durhams, as were all the other units in 33 Corps, fighting the Japanese, the weather and the hills.

The Kohima Ridge was finally cleared by a combination of infantry, tanks, artillery and accurate air-strikes. Each small Japanese position had to be winkled out individually and the enemy fought to the death. The casualties in 2 Division included three brigade commanders killed in action and many battalion commanders, so intense was the fighting. General Grover considered it to have been worse than anything he had seen on the Somme in the 1914-18 war.

Victory at Kohima would have been even more difficult to achieve without the services of the Naga tribesmen, who cheerfully offered to do anything that would rid them of the Japanese. As intelligence-gatherers they were matchless, moving freely and fearlessly in enemy-held territory. Most of them showed great skill in map-reading and in the interpretation of air photos. Their greatest value, however, was as porters. Men and women alike, bearing enormous loads of ration boxes and ammunition, they supplied the forward units, moving quickly up forty-degree slopes where the British floundered. They had to be compelled to accept payment, and only objected when, for their self-defence, they were issued with shotguns when they wished to carry rifles like their allies the British. 'All the troops', wrote Grover in his diary, 'are filled with admiration for these stout-hearted, cheery little hillmen'.

Japanese resistance continued, now desperately, at Kohima, where they still held much of the higher ground, until the end of May, when the tattered and emaciated remnant of the once-proud 31st Division began to fall back towards the Chindwin. Sato had made a terrible mistake by laying siege to Kohima at the beginning of April. As soon as he realised that it was being held by a determined garrison, he should have left a holding force and marched straight for Dimapur, where frantic efforts were still being made to assemble a credible defence. Had he got there at this stage, the result could have been catastrophic for 14th Army. Sato fell victim to that identifiable trait in the Japanese military mind – a mulish habit of proceeding woodenly according to plan and failing to use initiative to exploit what could have been a Japanese triumph.

Imphal

"Now is the time to capture Imphal."

KOHIMA HAD HELD, and Dimapur was no longer threatened. Slim could now give his attention to the situation at Imphal, which came under siege on 5 April, a day after Kohima, when the Japanese succeeded in cutting the Kohima-Imphal road. For two years Imphal had been the forward administrative base of 4 Corps and during this period a large network of depots, airfields, hospitals, dumps and maintenance installations had mushroomed on the Plain. When it was clear that 'U-Go' had started in earnest, there was a mass exodus of non-combatants by road and air, and those left began to prepare themselves for battle, not without misgivings in many of the administrative units.

Scoones had laid out his defences so that he could react to threats from all points of the compass. The small town of Imphal, the capital and administrative centre of the princely state of Manipur, lay in the middle of a natural bowl measuring 20 to 30 miles, surrounded by high forested hills providing excellent viewpoints for enemy observers, who could see any movement on the open plain below.

The northern sector of the perimeter was held by 5 Indian Division, (less 161st Brigade which had been detached to go to the aid of Kohima). This Division, following its successful campaign in the Arakan, from where it had been airlifted at very short notice, was confident and ready for another brush with the enemy. It was in a position to receive the first Japanese attack at Imphal, which came in the north with their seizure of the commanding heights of Nungshigum. Here several peaks dominated the area, the highest of which lay 1,500 feet above the plain. The only approach to the steep ridge at the summit, where the Japanese had dug in by last light on 12 April after repelling an earlier counter-attack, was up the razor-back itself. Early on 13 April a heavy artillery barrage and attacks by dive-bombers were laid down on the Japanese positions atop Nungshigum while Lee-Grant tanks of 'B' Squadron, The Carabiniers (3rd Dragoon Guards) moved slowly up the ridge in support of a battalion of Dogras. As the barrage lifted, the Japanese, apparently unscathed, emerged from their trenches full of fight. It was an extremely difficult operation because of the narrowness of the front – one tank's width – along the ridge, and the determination of the enemy to hold on at all costs. Whoever held the summit of Nungshigum held the key to Imphal, for it was only five miles to Scoones' HQ in a village clearly visible to observers on the top. Here, in the largest and most comfortable house, the Corps Commander stayed calmly at his post, spending what spare time he had in the cultivation of orchids. Even closer lay the main all-weather airfield on the plain which, if captured or rendered useless by observed artillery fire, would gravely affect the vital air supply of 4 Corps and deprive the wounded of their chance of rapid evacuation to hospitals in India.

The Carabiniers did not fail, although they paid a terrible price for their victory. As the tanks cautiously edged their way up the ridge they came under increasingly heavy fire from resolute Japanese infantry who at first would not believe that tanks could be driven up this extremely steep hill. It was necessary for the tank commanders to stand up with open hatches in order to guide their drivers as they edged upwards. Japanese carrying explosives flung themselves repeatedly at the tanks, climbing onto the engine decks to kill the crews. Well before the Carabiniers got near the summit nearly all the commanders had been killed, but without hesitation other crew members replaced them and the attack went ahead.

Squadron Sergeant Major Craddock took command when all the officers had been killed. He was closely backed up by Subedar Ranbir Singh of the Dogras; although neither had a word of the other's language they conversed effectively in eloquent sign language as they swept onto Nungshigum and killed its defenders. Ever since, 13 April has been celebrated as Nungshigum Day by the Carabiniers' successors, when 'B' Squadron parades without officers, under command of the Squadron Sergeant-Major, to commemorate Craddock's fine action.

With Nungshigum secure, 5 Indian Division turned to the clearance of the Mapao Spur, running north from Scoones' HQ. Like Nungshigum, it offered excellent panoramic views of all that took place on the plain, and it was imperative to drive off the Japanese. It took several attacks to push the enemy back to where he could not overlook Imphal. Twenty-five miles to the south-east, Gracey's 20 Indian Division was fighting its own isolated battle. It will be remembered that as the Japanese advanced forward from the Chindwin, 20 Division, which had previously been deployed astride the Sittaung-Tamu road, had fallen back as far as the Shenam Saddle, a prominent hill feature covering the important RAF airfield at Palel on the fringe of the plain. Here it took up a defensive position which held out against every Japanese attack.

Imphal was a great test for the Indian Army, the culmination of two years' steady rebuilding for which much credit is due to General Auchinleck who, as C-in-C India, was responsible for turning an over-stretched and inadequately-trained army into a great 'orchestra of war' by 1944. In 1942 the policy of 'milking' battalions in India, Burma and Malaya of their most

IMMPHAL

Approx perimeter 4 April 1944

Corps HQ

Div HQ

Major Medical Units (Hospitals)

Airfields

Airstrips

All weather road

Other Roads

Track

Kohima
80 miles

Kanglatongbi

Mung Ching 4997'

6993'

Sengmai

Mapao Ridge

Nungshigum 3833'

17

7340'

Ukhrul 30 miles

HQ 4 Corps   4

5

Imphal Plain

Imphal 2569'

Nungmai Ching 5135'

Loiching 6606'

Tungmai Ching
3695'

Buri Bazar 3094'

Bishenpur

Silchar track

HQ 23 Ind Div

Suspension
Bridge

Potsangbam

HQ 20 Ind Div   20

Tiddim 125 miles

Tamu 36 miles
'Crete'

Palel

'Scraggy'

Shenam Saddle

'Nippon Hill'

183

experienced personnel for service in the Middle East had resulted in units with a dangerously high recruit content and a shortage of long-service Indian NCOs and British officers. Urgent steps had since been taken to sort this out. By 1944 hundreds of young British officers were being sent to India to complete their training for service with the Indian Army. One of these, Lt Gadsden, can be taken as a typical 'wartime' Indian Army officer. Arriving to finish his officer training at Bangalore, he was almost overwhelmed by the strangeness and sheer size of the Indian sub-continent. His first task was to learn Urdu, the Indian Army's language, taught by a munshi (tutor) in an accent incomprehensible to many Indian soldiers from other areas. Bangalore Garrison was not a friendly place for young officers. The senior Indian Army officers who ran the training establishment were absorbed in their own family circles, based on bungalow and club, and cold-shouldered the 'temporary gentlemen' passing through.

On joining his battalion of the 14th Punjab Regiment, Gadsden found himself in a different world. First, he had to meet the Indian senior ranks. His Subedar was a Punjabi Mussulman, and from him he learned to respect the religious customs of his men. The Viceroy's Commissioned officers – the VCOs – were all long-service men, respected fathers of the regimental family whose word was law. The Subedar encouraged the young British officers to mix socially with their soldiers in a way unknown in the British Army. Gadsden drank tea and ate sweetmeats in the soldiers' lines several times a week. The young jawans responded, gathering round to sing songs and perform their folk dances at camp fires as the battalion trained in the Himalayan foothills. It was a happy and healthy life, and the wartime officers soon fell under the spell which India could weave. After a few months up in the hills the transformation was complete. As Gadsden writes:

> It took but a month or two for all of us to become dedicated Punjabis and the officers who took the battalion to war the following year had built up the morale to a high point in the intervening training period.

There were plenty of similar units in Gracey's division as it faced the problem of defending 25 miles of frontage in difficult terrain which would have taxed a division of three brigades. As it was, 20 Division had only two, spread over several hundred square miles of broken, hilly country criss-crossed by deep nullahs [watercourses]. It was ideal for the bold patrolling favoured by the Japanese. Gracey deployed his brigades so that they held the higher points for good observation, and patrolled vigorously to deter Japanese penetration. At times the enemy threatened to break through. Maj General Yamamoto, commanding 33rd Division's Infantry group, well supported by artillery, pushed up the main Palel road and between 4 and 10 April the battle was in the balance. Until the Japanese finally withdrew, 20 Division yielded only two more miles of ground and successfully held another series of hilltops, known as Crete West and Scraggy, against every attack.

The fighting around Palel involved units of the Indian National Army in the shape of the Gandhi Brigade, somewhat curiously named after the main protagonist of non-violence. Its men, known as 'Jifs' – Japanese-Indian Forces – were held in contempt by Indian Army soldiers and Japanese alike. Initially they had been used by the Japanese as guides and interpreters, but at their own insistence were committed to front-line duty. On the night of 2/3 May, the Gandhi Brigade launched an attack which went disastrously wrong for them. The 'Jifs' ran straight into an ambush gleefully prepared by Indian and Gurkha units, who despite Slim's earlier orders, took few prisoners. In the aftermath of this performance many Jifs were found wandering unhappily around in the jungle, looking for a British unit to which they could surrender. Those INA personnel who elected to soldier on for the Japanese found themselves treated with ever-greater scorn, and were frequently assigned to menial duties.

Japanese units still fought on in the Palel area and for several weeks, well into June, this sector gave Slim cause for anxiety. The enemy were finally seen off by 23 Indian Division, which took over the sector in May. The final Japanese gesture, which drew grudging admiration from their opponents, was a daring raid by an officer and a small party of volunteers who penetrated the defences of Palel airfield by night, destroying a number of aircraft on the ground with explosive charges before escaping.

Some of the most ferocious fighting at Imphal took place in the south-west corner, where Lt General Yanagida's 33rd Division had followed its drive up the Tiddim road by hooking round to cut the Imphal-Silchar track. From Imphal town a reasonably motorable road led south-west to Bishenpur, some 15 miles distant, where the Silchar track branched off to the west, first going over the hills to Tairenpokpi, then across an important suspension bridge which, if destroyed, would cut Imphal's remaining overland supply route. The Japanese accordingly made a determined drive for Bishenpur on the night of 14/15 April; at the same time a desperate mission set out to destroy the 300-foot long suspension bridge. Three members of this party got onto the bridge with a powerful demolition charge. When challenged, one jumped over the side to his death far below, and the other two blew themselves up with the bridge.

To meet the threat to Bishenpur, 17 Division, rested and eager to re-enter the fight, confronted the old enemy, 33rd Division, around the village of Ningthoukdong, where the Japanese established themselves in a strongly defended position and clearly meant to stay. Several attempts to shift them failed with heavy loss. Meanwhile the battle for the Silchar track continued unabated. Casualties to the British officers of Indian units, readily identifiable in this close-quarter fighting, were extremely heavy. Slim paid tribute to one of them in *Defeat into Victory*:

> One young Lieutenant Colonel, commanding a battalion that had already lost three-quarters of its officers and who had already been severely wounded in the stomach by grenade fragments, was again hit while leading his men. When asked why, at this second wound, he had not gone back at least as far as the Field Ambulance to have his wounds properly dressed, he admitted that the grenade wound in his stomach was a nuisance as it made getting around rather difficult, but he could still keep up with his men, so there was no need to go back. As to the second wound, 'The bullet,' he explained, 'has passed straight through my shoulder so it causes me no inconvenience'. No wonder the Japanese never broke through. When, a little time afterwards, I wished to promote this very gallant officer, I found to my grief that he had been killed later in the battle.

Slim's character is poignantly revealed in this passage. The humanity of his leadership was now apparent to his entire command, who knew that he would never commit them to battle unless he was quite certain they were trained, equipped and mentally prepared. In an earlier war, he had witnessed scenes, at Gallipoli in particular, which made him absolutely determined never to throw mens' lives away. He also had the gift of honest self-appraisal and, when things did go wrong, always examined his own performance first, before looking for fault in others. His was not the showman's approach – he could seem almost gruff on first acquaintance – but long service with Gurkhas enabled him to identify closely with them and soldiers of all races in this most multinational of armies. He never tired of seeing his beloved Gurkhas in and out of action. Years later, at a Burma Star Association Reunion in the Royal Albert Hall, he regaled a hugely appreciative audience with the story of the Gurkhas who were clearing Japanese corpses away after a bloody encounter at Potsambam near Bishenpur (like so many other Burmese place names, anglicised to 'Pots-and-Pans'). The bodies were being bulldozed by the score into pits for mass burial, when one 'corpse' was found to be very much alive. A Gurkha immediately drew his kukri to finish him off, to be stopped by a passing British officer. The Gurkha looked up, baffled. 'But, Sahib – we can't bury him *alive!*'

The battle at Potsambam took place during yet another particularly desperate attempt by the Japanese 33rd Division to destroy 17 Division around Bishenpur, at one time penetrating to within half a mile of General Cowan's headquarters. A scratch force under command of HQ 50th Parachute Brigade, now recovered from Sangshak and hungry for revenge, fought non-stop for five days, mostly hand-to-hand. At one point the battle raged amidst the mule lines of 63rd Brigade which had been temporarily over-run. Few Japanese survived; as usual they fought to the death, their gunners staying at their posts until put to the bayonet or kukri. The 33rd Japanese Division had gone into action uplifted by an Order of the Day signed by Maj General Tanaka, its infantry group commander, couched in terms indicating the type of motivation which drove Japanese soldiers to death in battle:

> Now is the time to capture Imphal. Our death-defying infantry group expects certain victory . . . You men have got to be fully in the picture . . . regarding death as something lighter than a feather, you must tackle the task of capturing Imphal. For that purpose it must be expected that the division will be almost annihilated. I have confidence in your firm courage and devotion and believe that you will do your duty; but should any delinquencies occur you have got to understand that I shall take the necessary action. In the front line, rewards and punishments must be given on the spot without delay . . . Further, in order to keep the honour of his unit bright, a commander may have to use his sword as a weapon of punishment, exceedingly shameful though it is to shed the blood of one's own soldiers on the battlefield . . . The infantry group is in high spirits, afire with valour and dominated by one thought only – the duty laid upon them to annihilate the enemy. On this battle rests the fate of the Empire. All officers and men, fight courageously.

With the failure of 33rd Division's forlorn hope at Bishenpur the tide now turned in 4 Corps' favour. To the north, operations were going ahead to clear the last Japanese from the entire Kohima area. First, the ridge had to be secured; this was a costly operation, for they were well dug in; each bunker had to be attacked in turn and its occupants destroyed like vermin. The Aradura Spur, dominating Kohima from the south, required a long and painstaking operation before it was finally cleared, and 33 Corps pushed down the road towards Imphal. Although the Japanese had long since outrun their original administrative plans, they hung on, and despite shortages of food, medical supplies and ammunition, their stubborn opposition was undiminished. But if evidence was needed of their ultimate failure, it was provided by the arrival of the monsoon. By this time, Mutaguchi had reckoned on being in Dimapur, or at least in undisputed possession of the Imphal Plain. Now his men, utterly miserable, sick, half starved and militarily beaten by a better opponent, had to survive as best they could in one of the most unfavourable operational areas in the world.

Life also became difficult for their opponents. As the rains came down, roads and tracks were washed out, and air operations were seriously curtailed when dense cloud-banks enveloped the hills. Petrol ran short in Imphal, and engines were taken out of trucks, converting them to trailers which were then towed in trains around the muddy roads. At the end of May, 2 Division was still struggling in the rain for possession of the top end of the Aradura Spur, and Scoones was beginning to show signs of impatience at Grover's lack of progress. However, his Division, untrained in jungle warfare, had been flung into the battle two months earlier and had had little respite since. Many of its battalions were showing distinct signs of fatigue, as recorded in his diary after personal visits to the front line, and he knew that they could not be over-stretched. Those of 6th Brigade, including the Durhams, had sombre memories of the Arakan over a year earlier, when units which had been asked once too often to go into the attack had refused to cross their start-lines. More recently, in the Second Arakan battles, battalions had been thrown into the line for difficult attacks against strongly defended hill-top positions when they were patently unable to deliver. Here again, there had been distressing failures on the part of good units who had already given their all, and needed rest.

Slim was fully aware of the strains under which battalion commanders were operating, but he knew that he had to continue attacking at Imphal until the enemy had been defeated. It would not serve his purpose if the Japanese were allowed to slip away and retire unchastened to the far side of the Chindwin. They had to be pinned down and beaten unambiguously on this battlefield, and it did not worry him that the process might yet take several weeks. The lives of his troops were worth far more than the prospect of rapid victory. Mountbatten was similarly inclined, and his operational directive of 8 June set a date for the re-opening of the Kohima-Imphal road as '. . . Not later than mid July'. This left Slim to get on with the business of steady attrition, while the garrison at Imphal fended for itself – which it was now perfectly capable of doing.

Meanwhile, 14th Army enjoyed the services of a small but valuable addition to its order of battle. Some years before the war a small group of progressive officers of the Royal Artillery had formed a flying club at Larkhill on Salisbury Plain. Apart from recreation, they had a second and at first closely-concealed aim. For many years, control of artillery fire from the air had been carried out by the RAF, using techniques evolved during World War I and scarcely changed during the next twenty years. The members of the Royal Artillery Flying Club considered that they had a better idea; this was to base light aircraft in the field alongside artillery units, to be flown by gunner officers who would engage targets and adjust fire using normal voice radio rather than the antediluvian 'clock-code' system of signal panels and one-way Morse still used by the RAF's Army Co-operation squadrons. It was agreed reluctantly by the Air Ministry that the RAF would provide the light aircraft and technical ground crews, and the Royal Artillery the rest, including pilots, for the new Air Observation Post Squadrons which began to see active service from 1942.

In 1944, one such unit, 656 Air OP Squadron Royal Air Force, arrived in Burma, equipped with Auster light aircraft. It first saw action in the Arakan, where its value was immediately apparent. In March 1944 one of its Flights moved up to Imphal, and in April it was joined by Squadron Headquarters and another Flight on the main airfield, close to Scoones' HQ and under the protection of anti-aircraft guns. Each division had its own airstrip, and pilots used these frequently. On one occasion, at the height of the battle when Japanese infiltration was widespread, a pilot landed at one of these strips and, as was normal, taxied over to one of the splinter-proof aircraft pens, where a field telephone was connected to divisional headquarters. There was no answer to the pilot's calls and he now noticed a distinct absence of ground crew on the strip. There was also a considerable amount of firing close at hand, and when a troop of tanks from the Carabiniers appeared on one side of the field and started to fire their machine guns and main armament into the trees at the other side, he realised that he was in the middle of a small but lively battle. Running back to his Auster he switched on the ignition and swung the propeller. At once the engine started and the aircraft began to taxi off down the runway, the pilot running frantically alongside as he tried to regain the controls. He managed this and took off with the Japanese only 100 yards away. Eyewitnesses in the Carabiniers' tanks swore that his legs were still dangling out of the aircraft as it took off and flew away.

Far away to the north, the 'spare' Chindit columns which had not been committed to 'Thursday' were hard at work harrying Japanese lines of communication. The effects of this on enemy morale were considerable; mule trains making their way forward through supposedly 'safe' areas to bring supplies to 31 Division around Kohima found themselves the victims of ambushes, and much Japanese material was thus intercepted. This, rather than the static defence of 'Strongholds', was much nearer the sort of activity which Wingate had envisaged when he created Special Force. The Japanese supply system was now in terminal collapse, as all the loot captured in the first heady days of the advance from the Chindwin had long since been consumed.

On 22 June, well before Mountbatten's deadline, light tanks from 33 Corps coming down from Kohima linked hands with elements of 5 Indian Division. The great siege was over and, as the monsoon poured down from above, the relentless pursuit of Mutaguchi's Army began.

Maintenance of Morale

"The troops . . . appeared to be bored, forgotten and serving in appalling conditions . . ."

F ROM THE moment in 1942 when Bill Slim took over command of Burma Corps, he knew that the Japanese army was not his only enemy. He had also to fight the demoralisation of his own troops; he had to restore their will to fight on when everything was going wrong; and he had to revive their morale when they were baffled and frustrated by the apparent ease with which the Japanese had defeated them.

In 1939 the military organisation of India was based on the British and Indian armies, each with differing welfare requirements stemming from totally dissimilar cultures. During nearly two centuries of soldiering in India – the old 'Shiny' of Kipling's day – the British in their cantonments had evolved an acceptable way of life. For officers this was based on the mess, the club, and a carefully regulated social and sporting life governed by the seasons which annually drove Europeans off to hill stations. For British soldiers, there was plenty of sport and, in the evenings, the wet canteen. There was no NAAFI, for in India its functions were fulfilled by the well-tried unit contractor system. Many battalions had been served for generations by the same family business, which followed the unit wherever it went. In the retreat from Burma in 1942, most contractors, who always had a shrewd idea of what was going on, correctly judged that the army would soon be back in India. Accordingly they left Burma in good time to set up business in Assam or East Bengal, to await the arrival of their retreating customers.

At the beginning of World War II, all British troops in India served on regular engagements in cantonments hundreds of miles from each other, having all the characteristics of independent communities. As the contractors catered in their canteens solely for the needs of the flesh, a number of philanthropic organisations offered services with moralistic undertones. The YMCA, Salvation Army, and Miss Sandes' Soldiers' Homes fell into this category. The last-named was a remarkable example of gritty private enterprise tempered with evangelical fervour. Back in the 1870s, a Miss Sandes, daughter of a British Army officer stationed at Tralee in Ireland, had been appalled at the level of drunkenness in her father's unit.

The soldiers had no social outlet other than the wet canteen, where they drank their pay away every week. She acquired the use of a house and established a haven of peace where, in a regime of strict abstinence, young soldiers could relax in comfortable surroundings, eat cheap but wholesome food, and read improving tracts. The success of Miss Sandes' enterprise led her to establish her Homes wherever the army served, and thousands of young men would be grateful to her for a century to come.

As the war progressed there was a radical change in the composition of the British Army in India. No longer an all-regular force, it had become a citizen army, its men accustomed to urban diversions and less able to make their own entertainment (the old army excelled at this, whether in the form of unit 'smokers', revues, or even serious drama; the Royal Signals had a particularly strong dramatic tradition). The strangeness of the country, its oppressive climate, and the lack of female company constituted a culture shock which affected the morale of these new soldiers very quickly. They had little chance of settling down in cantonments for any length of time because of the need to train for battle, and a degree of rootlessness permeated the ranks.

As late as August 1942, there were only three military welfare officers for the whole of India Command, and they were already grossly over-worked because of the flood of 'compassionate' cases brought by the growing numbers of wartime soldiers from the UK. Supplies of welfare goods were sent to Welfare Depots in Calcutta and Bombay for redistribution to units, and much depended on voluntary workers. There was a fund, set up by the Viceroy, which dealt out money to units for the purchase of amenities, but the system was haphazard. Many units began to feel that they had been completely forgotten as they waited for sports kit, radios, books and such items as stationery, toilet requisites and confectionery. None of these could be sent from Britain at this stage. Everything had to be found locally in India.

Action was taken in August 1942 to set up a proper Directorate of Welfare at GHQ India, with Brigadier G. M. B. Portman in charge, a post he held with great success until the end of the war. He could expect little help from the War Office in London until after the end of the war in Europe, and his work was hampered because officers appointed to posts in his organisation were either those found unsuitable to serve in the field with troops, or were elderly 're-treads' lacking the interest and energy so essential for this sort of work. Welfare received a considerable boost, however, in the Autumn of 1944 when Maj General Grover, who had recently commanded 2 Division in Burma, was appointed Director of Welfare at the War Office.

For Welfare officers, conscription produced a huge increase in the number of marital and other family problems to be dealt with, and a Legal Aid system had to be adopted in India in July 1943. To help with compassionate cases, which were made even more difficult by the problems of communication with home, a branch of the Sailors', Soldiers' and Airmens' Families Association (SSAFA) was established at GHQ Delhi, with branch offices at Calcutta, Bangalore and Lahore, three of the great pre-war cantonments.

Apart from poor reception of short-wave transmissions by the BBC in London, good broadcasting was not available at the start of the campaign, a deficiency quickly picked up by the Japanese, whose Radio Tokyo English-speaking programmes were of high quality and widely listened to. Radio Tokyo also broadcast in Hindi and Urdu to soldiers of the Indian Army in an effort to seduce them across to the INA. Sometimes this backfired; during the second Arakan campaign, Radio Tokyo announced in its Hindi news that in ten days the Japanese Army would be in Calcutta. 'Not if they travel by Indian Railways!', shouted a havildar just back from leave. From July 1943 there were two hours of 'light entertainment' in English each day on All-India Radio. Apart from this, the British had nothing except Radio Tokyo or endless programmes of 'Hindi Film Hits', a diversion which quickly palled.

With Mountbatten's arrival, things began to improve. He understood the needs of the citizen-servicemen, and used his influence with show business to obtain good live entertainment for his Command. But even with his energetic support it was painfully clear by mid-1944 that South-East Asia Command lacked facilities of every sort. The only supplies of welfare stores were those obtained through the efforts of commanding officers or the generosity of private benefactors, amongst whom the tea-planters of Assam deserve to be mentioned, both for their energetic collection of goods but also for their warm hospitality to British soldiers on short leave.

By September 1944 matters came to a head. An increasing number of MPs received letters from their constituents that contained bitter complaints about poor welfare facilities in the Command. The troops, they informed ministers, appeared to be bored, forgotten, and serving in appalling conditions of hardship, fighting an enemy who was still being portrayed in the British Press as ridiculous and contemptible. The troops obviously knew better and wanted their MPs to get this across somehow. In the face of growing back-bench complaints, Churchill sent Lord Munster, Under Secretary of State at the Home Office, on a fact-finding mission to the Far East. On his return he made a statement to the House of Commons and at last things began to happen. Churchill directed that more aircraft be made available to fly casualties and compassionate cases home from India. Leave facilities were improved. More mobile cinema units were sent out, and by the end of the campaign the troops could hope to see a recent release in the forward areas once or twice a month.

Conditions of service in India and the Far East had long been a vexed question. As early as March 1942 there had been complaints from officers and men in regular battalions that they had long outrun their six-year tour, and many of these began to display reluctance when sent back into the line. The so-called 'Python' scheme was now introduced with the aim of reducing the length of service in the Far East to a minimum. Priority for return to the UK would henceforth go to those who had served longest in the theatre, and the target maximum time in the Far East was laid down as four years. Some personnel, who had been on particularly arduous operations but were not yet eligible for Python, could now be granted 28 days' home leave on their GOC's recommendation. British officers serving in the Indian Army were not eligible for either of these schemes but now qualified, after five years' service in India, for two months' home leave. The advent of four-engined transport aircraft made these schemes feasible, and a steady stream of men began to return home.

The impact of the improvement in welfare services in SEAC during the last year of the war is evident from the following comparisons.

In September 1944 the beer ration in Burma was three bottles a month per head. Other than those brewed in India, all beers were subject to Import Duty, making them very expensive. A year later, the ration was five bottles a month, and duty had been lifted from imported brands. The cigarette ration was always a bone of contention; in 1944 a tin of 50 foul 'Victory Vs' was issued each week, but there was no free issue in India. In 1945, 50 a week were issued free in India, and in SEAC the ration was now 100, still labelled 'Victory V', but with a higher content of Virginia tobacco.

Broadcasting improved; in 1944 there was a 'General Forces Programme', sent out on feeble transmitters which could not be picked up in many areas of the theatre on the small welfare issue radios. All-India Radio had stepped up its English entertainment to 30 hours a week. Things had barely improved in 1945. 'Radio SEAC' had been established in Ceylon but its broadcasts were hard to pick up in the remoter parts of the theatre on unit welfare sets, of which there was a great shortage. Although 7,500 sets were sent from the UK in 1945, many arrived unserviceable, and most of those that still worked were incapable of picking up the programmes.

Live entertainment in 1944 had been confined to base and rear areas, but a year later there were numerous small concert parties of professional artistes recruited by ENSA (Entertainments National Service Association) and these were worth their weight in gold. Larger concert parties were less of a success. Apart from the difficulty of accommodating them adequately in the forward areas, the artists themselves tended to fall out with each other and their managers. Amateur concert parties had always existed at unit and formation level, and these did much to keep spirits up. Indian units had their own dance troupes and the Gurkhas, as ever, produced hilarious

'Nautches' in which the younger riflemen dressed up as very convincing dancing girls, and the opportunity was taken to lampoon their officers mercilessly. Perhaps it was the West and East Africans who did least well, although by 1945 quite sophisticated African concert parties were performing in Burma.

Books, probably the simplest, cheapest and most satisfying form of welfare, had been neglected in the first years of the war and supplies consisted entirely of what could be collected in India. In 1945 a consignment of 650,000 books was sent from England, but as it took six months to reach Burma it was of limited use. Apart from *SEAC* there was no supply of up-to-date newspapers until a reliable and frequent air route had been set up late in 1944. After that, consignments of the London Sunday papers were flown out, and the ever-enterprising *News of the World* set up a press in Bombay to satisfy the Army's thirst for current and other affairs.

Local leave facilities steadily improved, although the time taken to travel from a unit in Burma to a hill station in the Himalayan foothills could effectively halve the actual time spent at a leave hostel. By mid-1944 the entitlement for local leave was four weeks in a calendar year. Leave hostels were to be found in every major city and hill station; from Ranchi via Delhi to Dalhousie, 7,700 feet up in the Himalayan foothills, was a three-day journey. All who served in Burma shared three wishes: to escape from the heat; to sleep eight hours a night without interruption; and to use a flushing lavatory. Many soldiers opted to go no further than Calcutta, described by one gunner as 'a Dreadful city . . .' where they stared aghast at a depth of squalid poverty beyond their imaginations, but nevertheless contrived to enjoy the fleshpots. Others elected to make the long journey to Darjeeling, where the last stage was a breathtaking climb on an ancient steam train to 7,000 feet at an average gradient of 1 in 25; it was, and still is, one of the unforgettable great railway journeys in the world.

Food became an obsession with most who served in Burma and senior commanders found that the morale of their men was closely bound up with what they had to eat. This was well before the age of deep freezers, and facilities for the handling of refrigerated and chilled food were minimal in Burma. Slim's army included many religious groups with particular dietary requirements, and this added to the many problems of Maj General Snelling, his Principal Adminstrative Officer.

The supply of fresh food was complicated by the length of the lines of communication. If troops in the Arakan wondered why their diet was so monotonous, it was because their food came down the brick road from Chittagong to Cox's Bazar, then by pack pony to the mouth of the Naf River where it was transferred to country boats which took their loads down the coast to Maungdaw, from where it might go on by jeep track or pack mule. No fresh food could survive this, and everything was tinned or dried. Even the adoption of air supply hardly improved things, for rations frequently had to be stacked at airfields for some days before they were airlifted. Neither in the Arakan or Assam were there any sources of fresh meat and vegetables, but in Bengal some 18,000 acres of land were used for vegetable growing to supply the lines of communication. Efforts to set up poultry and pig farms, and to rear chickens on a large scale, met with mixed success. When operations were static, things were easier for the supply officers. An attempt to bring 'European' fresh vegetables forward of Chittagong or Dimapur ended disastrously with trainloads of rotting vegetables in railway sidings. From December to April it was possible to introduce fresh oranges, and from July to August, pineapples. Otherwise it was plantains (green, banana-like fruit) unpopular with British troops. For eight months of the year, forward units were obliged to subsist on a diet of pumpkins, Indian vegetables (also unpopular) bully beef, and soya link sausage (universally loathed). Indian troops were fed on dehydrated goat meat and minced dried mutton from Australia. The West and East Africans were accustomed to a simpler diet consisting mainly of ground mealie ('posho' to East Africans) and meat.

Naturally, much depended on presentation if so monotonous a diet was to remain palatable, and a major cooks' training programme got under way in India in 1942. At that time the Army Catering Corps was still in its formative stage and could only send small teams of instructors and advisers out to India. The Indian Army meanwhile set up a scheme for training regimental cooks. Between them the ACC and the Indian Army turned out over 22,000 Indian and some 3,000 British cooks by the end of the war. Early catering advisers' reports from Burma show that whilst the ration was theoretically adequate and provided the required amount of nutrition for active service, it was actually sub-standard. Cooking equipment was poor and there was nothing in India's ordnance depots with which to replace unserviceable stoves or other kitchen items. Training was therefore given in the construction and use of improvised ovens at 4 Corps' own catering school at Imphal (whose staff in due course found themselves fighting as infantry). A useful item on the syllabus was the use of local resources in the field, particularly the many uses of bamboo; as container, stove, kitchen tool and eating utensil.

By mid-1944, fresh meat was still in very short supply, although some 40 tons were sent up from Dimapur by road each day. Experiments in sending trainloads of 'meat on the hoof' forward to Dimapur and Chittagong had to be abandoned because of the high mortality rate. In that climate, unchilled meat began to smell within hours, and it was difficult to keep flies at bay.

As more and more unit cooks passed through the training schools, messing standards improved. It was noticeable that British troops serving in Indian formations fared better than those in all-British ones like 2 Division because they became used to the Indian ration scales, developing a taste for the spices and richness of a wide variety of cuisines from all over India, from the fiery vindaloos of the south to the less ferocious dishes of northern India. Many would carry this appreciation of Asian food with them to the end of their lives.

Back to the Chindwin

"The Japs are getting more than they bargained for."

EARLY IN June 1944, Giffard was confident that the Japanese had been decisively beaten at Imphal, and that he could now give Slim a directive for the next phases of the campaign. His eyes were on the reconquest of Burma from the north, for the fleets and landing ships promised, and needed, for a seaborne invasion had still not materialised. Burma would therefore have to be taken the hard way. Slim was already resigned to this and had started to think deeply about it. Giffard's directive now told him what to do. First, he was to re-open the Dimapur-Imphal road. Then he had to clear the enemy from the Imphal and Kohima areas. Finally, he was to get ready to move forward across the Chindwin and exploit his bridgeheads on a frontage of about 120 miles.

First, however, the Japanese had to be driven off Indian soil and pursued relentlessly all the way back to the Chindwin at the height of the monsoon. Slim knew he was asking a great deal of his troops, but he also knew that they would back him all the way. Before starting on the reorganisations needed for a very different type of campaign on the central plains after the monsoon, he had to finish off the enemy in Assam.

Around Ukhrul the remnants of the Japanese 15th and 31st Divisions had rallied and were regrouping, either for another attack or as a preliminary to withdrawal to the Chindwin. Whatever their aim, they had to be dealt with quickly before they gained second wind.

Three months earlier, the Japanese had assumed that Imphal and its contents would be in their hands within three weeks of crossing the Chindwin. The appalling consequences of an administrative plan based on that assumption were now clear. General Kawabe, commanding the Burma Area Army, had visited the front in June where he met Mutaguchi for a serious discussion on the way forward. Kawabe quickly saw for himself that the situation was already hopeless; 14th Army's strength was growing daily whilst Mutaguchi's men were beginning to falter. Nevertheless, he had ordered them to fight it out to the end. But in the first week of July, Mutaguchi ordered 33rd Division to give up its attempts to break through on the Silchar track and start a withdrawal; 'Ha-Go' was indeed over.

On 1 July Slim had completed the encirclement of Ukhrul, where a dour battle ensued in heavy rain, ending with the retreat of the badly-mauled survivors of the two Japanese divisions. The weather was now appalling, and it was barely possible to keep the momentum going. One major problem was the evacuation of casualties. The historian of the 1st Devons records that elephants were being used at this stage to get wounded men to the rear. When the MO sent out parties of men to help the overtaxed stretcher bearers they were told to carry shovels so that casualties who died during the dreadful journey would at least get a decent burial. Even with elephants, three miles could take 16 hours and at one point the bearers had to make crude rafts and float the stretchers across flooded streams. Terrible sights greeted the pursuing troops as they struggled to keep up with the enemy. Sickness had now entered the field against the Japanese and their dead lay in hundreds at the side of the road. Many had clearly felt death coming upon them, and had constructed little 'death houses' where they now lay. The Border Regiment came across many of these:

> . . . Japanese graves, marked with wooden uprights inscribed with coloured hieroglyphics, were much in evidence . . . burned out trucks, some with the charred remains of their drivers at the wheel, littered the tracks . . . Near our bivouac area was what remained of a Jap field hospital – nothing but a huddle of leaf-boughed shelters under which lay some four hundred skeletons.

Lt Colonel Harvest of the Devons was out wildfowling to vary the monotony of the officers' diet, when he stumbled on a Japanese medical post, a series of small bashas full of dead men.

> . . . several had collapsed, burying their inmates. Arms and legs protruded from the ruined roofs and in most cases the bones had been cleaned by red ants . . .

One estimate is that of 100,000 men who marched on India, 50,000 now lay dead in battle at Kohima and Imphal, and 20,000 died of sickness on the retreat back to the Chindwin. Lt General Yamauchi, commander of 15 Division, was dying. He had always been something of a man apart from his colleagues, having spent much of his life in the West, adopting many European habits. Wherever he went, his luckless servant was responsible for pitching the general's European-style 'thunderbox', for Yamauchi disdained the Asian-style latrine. For weeks he had been a sick man, keeping to his quarters and writing gloomy poems. He was dismissed by Mutaguchi at the end of June, and died shortly afterwards. The next Japanese general to go was Sato, sacked on 7 July, three days after Kawabe had decided to call a halt and pull back from the Imphal area.

The monsoon also took its toll of 33 Corps as it followed the Japanese. Its normal strength was 88,500, of whom about 45,000 were actually pursuing the Japanese. Between July and December 1944 the corps suffered over 50,000 casualties, of whom only 49 were killed in action; 20,000 were so ill from the effects of soldiering in the Kabaw Valley that they had to be evacuated to India, and despite rigorous enforcement of anti-malarial precautions and daily dosage of Mepacrine, there were 20,000 malaria cases of various degrees of severity.

After the enemy's expulsion from Ukhrul, 23 Division led the pursuit as far as Tamu at the head of the Kabaw Valley, then handed over to the newly-arrived 11 East African Division. Slim now pulled most of his divisions back to India; the Indian soldiers were reluctant to go as they lost their overseas allowance and were consequently out of pocket. However, 17 Indian Division had been officially a 'Light' Division for many months, and it needed to re-equip and re-train for the battles of the central plains, for which it had to be mechanised.

The East Africans were ready to move off at the end of July. Many of their officers had been the guests of Ouvrey Roberts' 23 Indian Division as it cleared the first 50 miles of road down from Ukhrul and had learned a lot from its professionalism. The 11 EA Division consisted of battalions of the King's African Rifles. Like the Royal West African Frontier Force, it was a type of gendarmerie, trained and equipped for peacekeeping between the tribes of East Africa; its battalions were recruited in Kenya, Uganda, Tanganyika and Nyasaland and, like the RWAFF, there was a large complement of British officers and senior NCOs. The KAR had served creditably in East Africa during World War I and had seen more recent service in Somalia and Eritrea against the Italians. It had expanded considerably since the outbreak of war and the 11th Battalion was a typical wartime creation. Its commanding officer was Lt Colonel Birkbeck of the Border Regiment. Sent to Nyasaland in 1940 with a recruiting team, he soon found that he was up against strong competition from organisations like the Witwatersrand Native Labour Organisation, which regarded Nyasaland as a prime recruiting ground for mineworkers in the South African gold and diamond mines. Birkbeck's battalion, unlike regular KAR units whose men were volunteers on long service engagements, was to be made up of any men he could dissuade from going down the mines.

The 11th KAR were shaped into a good battalion through patience, good humour and the example of good officers. Slim's dictum, that there were no such things as good or bad units, only good and bad officers, would have applied here. Their officers soon discovered that the East African tribesman, like those of the RWAFF, displayed an uncanny sixth sense in the bush. He could 'point' a concealed enemy like a well-trained gun dog, and there were numerous cases where an African soldier insisted that the enemy was close at hand but was disbelieved by his British officer, often with tragic results. The Askari rapidly gained confidence and excelled at 'killer' patrols, when they silently stalked Japanese sentries as though they were on the plains of East Africa. The effect on Japanese morale was profound. The enemy knew that Africans were in the field against them and had already heard that many of them filed their teeth down to sharp points.

This made it easy to believe that they ate their enemies, an idea which appalled the Japanese, who could not conceivably go to join their ancestors through the bowels of black men. On one occasion a Japanese soldier was sitting quietly in the jungle when he became aware that he was under observation by a silent African soldier at five yards' range. He threw down his rifle and fled, screaming hysterically.

In August the Japanese High Command in Burma changed with the sacking of General Kawabe. His successor was General Kimura Hyotaru. A highly intelligent officer whose mild bespectacled appearance concealed a quick brain, he was known by Slim and his staff to be a formidable opponent. He was given his briefing in September by the Commander-in-Chief of the South-East Asian Theatre, Field Marshal Count Terauchi. Whilst Kawabe had been given instructions to stand and fight on the west bank of the Chindwin, the remnants of 15th Army were clearly in no state for this. They had been decisively beaten and Terauchi now directed Kimura to regard southern Burma as the northern boundary of the Greater East Asia Defence Zone. Furthermore, he was told not to expect any further reinforcements from Japan, nor could he expect to be supplied with food from outside Burma. From now on, Burma Area Army had to forage for itself. Kimura therefore decided that he would retire behind the Irrawaddy and deploy his troops to fight what he knew would be the clinching battle on the plains to the south of Mandalay. At the same time he decided to hold a line in the north for as long as possible in order to deny the Burma road to the Allies, thus impeding the Chinese war effort.

As 1944 drew to its eventful end the Japanese were busily trying to reconstitute their forces in Burma; that they made a remarkably good job of it will be seen from their performance in the battles around Meiktila and Mandalay in the early part of 1945. Their job was made more difficult by the Allied air forces, which now had a combined strength of 1,200 combat aircraft against the Japanese total of 64 for the defence of Burma. Amongst the newer types being used by the RAF with devastating effect against ground targets was the Bristol Beaufighter. Originally designed as a night fighter, its armament of cannon and machine guns and robust airframe strength made it ideal for ground attack. It was also fast, and its silent approach earned it the nickname of 'whispering death' from the Japanese. Mosquito light bombers, considerably faster than the Beaufighter, were also operating in the theatre, together with the later marks of Spitfire and American-built P-47 Thunderbolt fighters.

Meanwhile, 11 East African Division continued to move down the Kabaw Valley towards its rendezvous with 5 Indian Division, which was coming down the Imphal-Tiddim road, where 17 Division had such a narrow escape earlier in the year. The monsoon had eased off but the going was still almost impossible. An Indian light tank unit in support of the East

Africans took three weeks to cover 50 miles along the glutinous track, and the situation was no better at the end of September, as 5 Division struggled on down from Imphal at an average speed of two miles a day. Between these two somewhat sluggish prongs, operating in the wild hills above the Kabaw valley, was the Lushai Brigade, commanded by Brigadier Marindin. This force excelled at guerilla warfare and its soldiers wore a variety of dress which reflected the piratical character of its commander. A mix of Indian Army and other units, it probably made a greater contribution in terms of nuisance value than many larger formations. It would have found favour with Wingate, combining as it did the professionalism to be expected from regiments of the Frontier Force – Jats and Punjabis – with the freer approach of the Assam Rifles.

As the East Africans toiled down the Kabaw, they came across scenes similar to those found earlier by the Border Regiment. One officer wrote:

> Every few yards we came upon either a skeleton, or a hut with a dead body in it. Apparently Jap troops who could go no further built a small hut of branches, and in it, lay down to die.

Others, perhaps more fortunate, had managed to get their hands on a grenade, held it to their head, and pulled the pin. The same KAR officer noted that his Africans saw little in the way of welfare goods, unlike the British units whose 'vociferous clamour' obtained for them supplies of cigarettes, writing paper, toiletries, and reading matter. In December, he summed up the division's operations:

> Since July we have not seen a house – or a woman – or slept in anything except our ordinary clothes – had a bath in anything except a bucket – been to bed later than 8 pm – seen an egg – or eaten (except on the rarest occasions) anything that hadn't come out of a tin.

In November 1944 a number of changes also took place in the structure of SEAC. In order to give Slim a clear run at Mandalay without the distraction of operations in the Arakan, Christison's 15 Corps was placed under the command of a new headquarters, Allied Land Forces, South-East Asia (ALFSEA), replacing the old 11th Army Group, which also took over command of Slim's sprawling lines-of-communicaions areas. In the same month, Giffard was replaced. For some time he had been crossing Mountbatten; although the two men respected each other, they were fundamentally different. Giffard, lacking the glamour and sparkle of a Mountbatten, or Montgomery's obsession with publicity, never became a household name because the very idea would have appalled him. But in many ways Giffard was as much the architect of victory in Burma as Slim was its builder. The two generals had worked closely together and trusted each other implicitly. In *Defeat into Victory* Slim pays a moving tribute to his old friend: '. . . He had seen us through our efforts to become an army and through our first and most desperate battles. Fourteenth Army owed much to his integrity, his judgement, his sound administration, his support in our darkest hours, and to the universal confidence inspired amongst us. We saw him go with grief . . .'

Giffard's replacement was Lt General Sir Oliver Leese, who inherited what had become a huge command embracing 14th Army, Christison's 15 Corps in the Arakan, the Lines of Communication, the Indian Queen Garrisons and the Northern Combat Area Command, now under Lt General Dan Sultan, following the departure of Stilwell, removed by the President of the United States at Chiang's request. Stilwell's relations with the Chinese Generalissimo had deteriorated to the point where he openly referred to Chiang as 'the Peanut', and welcomed the chance to escape from his insupportable master. President Roosevelt promoted him to the rank of full General, and he returned to the USA, where he died two years later. Stilwell had been a difficult but honest ally, and although Mountbatten, Slim and others felt the lash of his tongue, feeling that his nickname of 'Vinegar Joe' was well earned, he had succeeded in keeping Chinese forces in the field against all odds.

Leese, a former Coldstreamer, came to ALFSEA with a glowing reputation from the 8th Army in Italy where, as Montgomery's successor, he had breathed life into a campaign which had stalled. He brought with him a large entourage of officers from his 8th Army staff, all with proven track records in the North African and Italian campaigns. The idea of carrying such a 'circus' around had always been repellent to Slim, who invariably arrived alone to take over a new appointment. There certainly could be no greater contrast of styles between the predominantly 'Indian' 14th Army and the 8th, justly proud of its victorious record in North Africa, but whose staff clearly regarded 14th Army as something of an anachronism and its commanders as 'sepoy generals'. A hint of this is allowed to creep into *Defeat into Victory*, where Slim writes: 'His (Leese's) staff, which he brought with him, and which replaced most of our old friends at General Giffard's headquarters, had a good deal of desert sand in its shoes and was rather inclined to thrust Eighth Army down our throats. No doubt we provoked them, for not only were my people a bit sore at losing General Giffard but, while we had the greatest admiration for the Eighth Army, we also thought the Fourteenth Army was now quite something . . .' Neither was there much in common between Leese and Slim, the products of widely differing backgrounds. Leese, from Eton and the Household Brigade; Slim, an uncomplicated meritocrat who had made his profession of arms in the tightly-knit family of a Gurkha regiment.

Although Slim quickly established a good working relationship with Leese he privately mourned Giffard's departure. Some of Slim's staff, perhaps unfairly, disliked Leese from the start. Few of them had ever been in professional contact with a senior officer of the Guards Brigade, of which Leese was an outstanding example, as attested by a fine fighting record in World War I and an unbroken series of successful appointments in command and staff since the beginning of World War II. His friendly, bluff manner was held by some in 14th Army to be no more than false bonhomie; unlike Slim's 'sepoy generals' he had difficulty in communicating and identifying with Indian troops, whilst they spoke the languages of their men. As his headquarters was far away in Ceylon (although he succeeded in moving it forward to Bengal) he was inevitably absent for much of the time from what Slim's staff regarded as the 'front'.

Leese also found it difficult to adjust to the hot-house atmosphere of Mountbatten's glittering SEAC headquarters at Kandy, which bore no resemblance to anything that he (or for that matter, any other regular soldier of his vintage) had ever encountered. By late 1944, it was swollen to a strength approaching 7,000 all ranks, and abounded with elegant and apparently under-employed staff officers whose qualifications for serving there appeared to Leese to be mainly social. HQ SEAC had long been the subject of derision in 14th Army, where it was known as 'Wimbledon – all balls and rackets'. On the night of his arrival at Kandy, Leese was summoned to a full-dress ball in honour of Mountbatten's birthday. Hurriedly changing into a borrowed dinner jacket, he went to the ball in Supremo's party and was astonished when the Admiral was greeted passionately on arrival by an extremely beautiful Wren officer in an elegant ball gown. It was certainly a very different headquarters to that of 8th Army and light years from that of the 14th. Some compared it to the court of a Renaissance prince, and Mountbatten would have enjoyed the simile.

By October 1944, as 14th Army toiled forward onto the line of the Chindwin, the strategy for 1945 had been agreed by Mountbatten and his allies. Before Stilwell's departure, he had been invited to study two plans. The first, code-named 'Capital', required Stilwell to advance south from Myitkyina as 14th Army pushed forward across the Chindwin and Irrawaddy to capture Mandalay and Pakokku, consolidating on a line joining these two places and extending to Lashio. This would secure the northerly overland route to China and enable the airlift to avoid the worst of the 'Hump', and thus carry greater payloads per aircraft.

The second plan, 'Dracula', envisaged an amphibious operation to capture Rangoon from the south, followed by a rapid advance up the Irrawaddy valley to join hands with 'Capital' in the area of Myitkyina after driving the Japanese out of central Burma. Any Japanese forces left behind in the Arakan-Akyab-Ramree area were to be cordoned off and starved into submission or extinction. Successful completion of 'Dracula' would produce an additional bonus, as the 'old' Burma road would once more be opened, giving access direct to China from Rangoon.

Stilwell's first reaction to 'Dracula' was favourable, providing it involved no reduction of British commitment to 'Capital'. American strategy in the Burma theatre had a long-term aim: economic domination of a post-war China ruled by Chiang Kai-shek. For the British, 'Dracula' was the more important, as it was essential, in Slim's view, to have control of Rangoon port by the next monsoon in May 1945, in order to maintain 14th Army in central Burma. He had seen the state of the Imphal-Tiddim road in the recent rains and knew that even with massive improvements, it could not on its own sustain two large corps in major operations if persistent bad weather grounded the air transport force.

Unaware that the Japanese High Command had already decided to pull back behind the Irrawaddy, Slim's initial plan was to establish bridgeheads over the Chindwin for 4 Corps at Sittaung in the north, and 33 Corps at Kalewa in the south. They would then destroy the enemy on the Shwebo Plain, between the Chindwin and Irrawaddy, before advancing on Pakokku and Mandalay to link with Stilwell's forces, now augmented by the British 36 Division, as they advanced from the northern front. Intelligence reports from the Arakan indicated that Kimura was thinning out and redeploying troops from there in order to defend the line of the Irrawaddy south of the great bend where it sweeps west after passing through Mandalay before turning south again past Yenangyaung, Magwe and Prome. Kimura knew that the approach to the Irrawaddy along this stretch of the great river would involve Christison in crossing the Arakan Yomas, the heavily-forested range of hills with few passes, running parallel with and to the west of the Irrawaddy. On discovering that the Japanese were reducing their Arakan force, Slim asked Leese to authorise an 'offensive-defensive' campaign in the Arakan rather than the more passive role allotted to 15 Corps for the rest of 1944.

It was not until December 1944 that Slim was convinced that the Japanese had withdrawn behind the Irrawaddy. He also realised that 'Capital' and 'Dracula' would have to be modified; 'Dracula' because of the continuing shortage of assault shipping, and 'Capital' because he could no longer rely on having possession of the port of Rangoon in the next rains; this affected his planning for operations forward of the Irrawaddy; it might even be necessary, on logistic grounds, to prune the forces allocated to what he knew would be a hard-fought battle. When Chiang Kai-shek heard that both plans were, as he saw it, being watered down, he reacted by calling for the return to China of his two best divisions – those which Stilwell had marched into India in 1942 and had trained and equipped to a far higher standard than any other Kuomintang formation. Two months before Stilwell's precipitate departure, Slim had agreed to detach Maj General Festing's 36 Division to Mogaung, from where it set off down the line of the railway towards Indaw. On arrival at Stilwell's forward headquarters, Festing had entered the command post to find the American at his map board, his back to the entrance. Festing introduced himself with the words: 'Festing reporting for duty. Any orders?', to which Stilwell, without turning round, replied: 'Take Taungyi!'. Festing did so, and after a further five months of marching and fighting in support of Northern Combat Area Command, 36 Division made contact with patrols of 5 Indian Division who had crossed the Chindwin and were feeling their way towards the Irrawaddy.

For the first time since 1942, a British division was operating astride a railway line, and although Allied air attacks had destroyed most of the rolling stock and locomotives on the Burmese rail network, the Royal Electrical and Mechanical Engineers (REME) adapted jeeps to run on rails and were able to improvise 'trains' which hauled the division's requirements down the line as it advanced towards Indaw, the scene of Bernard Fergusson's reverse earlier in the year. Also heading for Indaw was 19 Indian Division, from a bridgehead across the Chindwin. Mountbatten's staff had calculated that it would take five weeks for them to reach Indaw and had decreed that they be airlifted. In fact, they made it in only eight days, to link up with the delighted General Sultan on 16 December. Northern Burma had been restored to the Allies; the destruction of the Japanese in central and lower Burma could now begin. Slim advised HQ ALFSEA that he planned to fight his major engagement on the plains to the south of Mandalay. As the plans were being drawn up, a major administrative overhaul was in progress.

It was the Japanese who now enjoyed the use of better lines of communication, for their road, rail and river routes ran with the 'grain' of the country. They had already set up numerous large depots and communication centres behind the southern and central sectors of the front, and were busily regrouping and re-equipping their combat troops to face what they also recognised was going to be a crucial test.

Slim, on the other hand, had to get all his supplies and men across two major mountain ranges on very limited tracks, and over the Chindwin, which had never been bridged. By early 1945, the administrative staff calculated, there would be a requirement to shift 10,500 tons of supplies, fuel and ammunition forward every day along a road and track-based line of communication stretching back 400 miles to Assam and East Bengal. Even when the Chindwin had been bridged there would be a requirement for hundreds of small load-carrying craft for transport up and down the river, and later on the Irrawaddy. The Japanese had removed or destroyed all river craft as they withdrew, so orders were now placed in India for prefabricated boat sections for assembly on the banks of the Chindwin. At Kalewa, one of the main launching sites, a boatyard was set up after the Japanese had been ejected.

Once across the Irrawaddy, and until airfields abandoned by the Japanese had been brought back into service, Slim's corps would be out of economic range of transport aircraft based in Bengal, and many important administrative installations were now moved forward to Imphal. Their re-establishment alongside all-weather airfields was a stupendous achievement, carried out in a few weeks by American, British and Indian engineers. No account of this campaign can omit the work of the United States Army Engineer and Transportation Corps, whose lavish provision of heavy plant, road-building and railway engineering skills was a decisive contribution to victory.

Slim had already acknowledged that he would have to reduce the fighting strength of 14th Army once it was across the Irrawaddy because of its uncertain road links with administrative depots to the rear. The monsoon started in May, so he would be making this reduction just as his men were still embroiled with the equivalent of ten divisions of tough and determined Japanese, backed by good communications to their rear and supported once more by tactical aircraft operating from bases in Siam, which lay out of range of Allied fighter-bombers based in Assam. He therefore decided to inject a considerable amount of deception into his battle plan in the hope of forcing an early decision.

The appalling weather of the 1944 monsoon, turning the rudimentary roads and tracks of the Chin Hills into quagmires, had not stopped 14th Army from reaching and crossing the Chindwin on schedule. The Chindwin was now bridged for the first time in its history by a prefabricated structure brought down by road from Imphal and assembled on the river bank. Now came the preparation for the battle on the far side of the Irrawaddy. An opposed river crossing has always been one of the most difficult of military operations, and the Irrawaddy was the greatest river barrier faced by any Allied army in World War II. Flexibility and deception were the two principles of war used by Slim in his plan, later to be described admiringly by the Japanese as the 'Master Stroke' of the Burma campaign. Now known as 'Extended Capital' it involved a feint in the north as the entire 4 Corps (now commanded by the dashing Lt General Messervy) was passed in total secrecy around the rear of 33rd Corps. This move had to be completely undetected by the Japanese, who had deployed to meet a direct threat to Mandalay. Instead of this, Slim's main crossing was to be made by 4 Corps far to the south, its objective the key Japanese base and communications centre at Meiktila. Stopford's 33 Corps was given one of Messervy's divisions, 19 Indian, and ordered to concentrate around Shwebo, where it would clearly pose a threat to Mandalay. On 15 January 1945, 4 Corps began its secret move, down past Tamu and Kalemyo. At its head was 28th East African Brigade, flaunting divisional signs and thoroughly entering into the spirit of the game. Then came 7 and 17 Indian Divisions, re-equipped, reorganised and re-trained for the open warfare ahead. Messervy took with him his entire corps artillery, a tank brigade, and many additional supporting units. While his Corps moved in total radio silence, 19 Indian Division was generating a torrent of bogus radio traffic to convince the enemy that 4 Corps was about to join 33 Corps in a drive for Mandalay. The march discipline and traffic control of 4 Corps were superb, and because the Japanese could not get a reconnaissance aircraft within 50 miles of the Irrawaddy, the great march was undetected.

Invaluable assistance to the engineer roadbuilding programme was given by elephants. These were under the control of Lt Colonel J. H. Williams, known as 'Elephant Bill', who had spent his working life in the Burma teak forests. The elephants were used as pack animals, carrying up to 600 lbs; but their great value lay in their intelligence when used as bridge builders. An 'Elephant Bridge' was made with tree trunks dragged by the animals to the bridging site and laid in the river, parallel to the stream, ten to fifteen feet apart. They were then spanned with other tree trunks. Each elephant had its own driver, or 'Oozie' who controlled it with a stick; but after doing any job once, the elephants knew how to do it again without prompting.

As soon as 4 Corps had redeployed in the south, 33 Corps could start, with the aim of compounding the enemy's confusion. Its divisions had emerged from bridgeheads across the Chindwin on 24 December 1944: 20 Indian Division moved down the east bank of the river, and the British 2 Division made a beeline for Shwebo, arriving there on 5 January, then turning south along the Mandalay road to strike out for the point on the Irrawaddy bank where it was to make its crossings. On 19 February Private Lockwood of the 2nd Durham Light Infantry – last heard of as they battled their way up the Aradura Spur – was able to write home: '. . . We are back in action again. It has been easy up to now except for the marching – we have done close on 200 miles . . . The Japs are getting more than they bargained for, he is having to take the knock where he feels it most, he hasn't got half the stuff we have . . .' The battalion had been in good form ever since the last days of the Imphal battle, when they had spear-headed 2 Division's drive to link up with 4 Corps. The exhilaration of those days can be recaptured in another letter, this time from an officer:

We would be the leading battalion, capture and hold the ground where the Jap was holding on, then in an hour or so the whole war would roar past us and we would be left miles behind until it was our turn to lead again . . . On the last day when we linked up with 4 Corps we were leading . . . It really was great fun, just like walking up partridges . . . the company got four prisoners the other day – a thing we never got in the early days – an officer and 3 men, all in a pretty bad state of repair. The officer was very browned off and uncommunicative but the troops were very cheerful indeed, rather like dogs who expected a good hiding and got a good meal instead . . . I lived in a captured Jap position for several days – a regular eye-opener. I used to think the Geordie was the best digger of all – but the Jap has him cold in this respect . . .

This was to be the shape of operations from now on, as the Japanese, still fighting grimly, pulled back in the face of 14th Army's irresistible advance.

As the advance moved towards and across the Chindwin, the gunners of 136th Field Regiment settled into a daily routine suited to a more mobile form of warfare. At first light each troop stood to. If the unit was on the move, the night's defence slits and gun pits were now filled in. After breakfast the guns were limbered up and the battery got on the road. On arrival at the new position it was essential to get the guns into action immediately, as the battery command post staff got the zero lines recorded. The towing 'quad' was unloaded; each gun's crew took off the ammunition, stores, camouflage nets, and crews' kit. The quad was then driven off to the waggon lines, close at hand in case of an emergency move.

It was now time for some domestic administration. Some gunners were detailed off to help the cooks, others dug latrine pits, weapon slits and the gun pits. Each gun had to be manned during this time, so the No 1 and two gunners did this. The weapon slits were initially dug to two feet for immediate protection, then when time permitted to 5ft×6ft×2ft. The gun pit had to be dug to permit 360 degree traverse. All this took the whole day with a midday break for tea and bully beef. A hot meal was served at 1700 hrs.

At last light, it was compulsory to put on long trousers and roll sleeves down, and stand-to took place with all weapon slits and gun pits manned. After stand-down, guard posts were double manned. All ranks took their share, two hours on, two off. At night in the jungle there was a lot of wild life to be heard, if not seen. 136th Regiment recorded sightings of elephant, bears, wild pig and panther. During their time in the Arakan, Japanese 'Jitter' patrols prowled around all night. On one occasion, shortly after their arrival in the forward area, a subaltern went round the battery's defence posts to check them and was caught by a Japanese patrol. The gunners listened in the dark to his death cries, unable to help him. It was a chastening experience which brought home the dangers of leaving the unit area after dark.

The Amphibious War

"Use an Army map. Everything that's blue is yours. All else is mine."

AFTER THE defeat of the Japanese in Arakan in April 1944, Slim obtained Giffard's permission to pull Christison's 15 Corps back to sit out the monsoon. There was no longer a significant threat to Chittagong, and two of 15 Corps' experienced divisions, 5 and 7 Indian, had been airlifted up to Assam to join the battle at Imphal. The town of Buthidaung had little military significance, was hard to defend and extremely unhealthy. Christison therefore redeployed his corps west of the Mayu Range, from which it continued to patrol vigorously forward and dominate the area. The West Africans in the Kalapanzin and Kaladan valleys were withdrawn to the headwaters of these rivers, taking up positions covering the Indian frontier, ready if required to deal with any surprise Japanese raid towards Chittagong and East Bengal.

The Japanese, however, were now incapable of serious offensive action. Their forces in south-west Burma consisted of Lt General Sakurai's weakened 28th Army and an independent mobile brigade, but there was still plenty of fight left in them, and Sakurai was no mean opponent. Like Christison, he saw the monsoon as a time for regaining strength before the next season's campaigning.

The 1944 monsoon was severe in the Arakan. Roads became glutinous and impassable, bridges were washed out, and certain areas became so malarious that even Mepacrine failed to keep the more virulent strains of the disease at bay. Patrolling was limited to a depth of only a few miles forward of the main defensive positions, and the main preoccupation of all ranks was keeping dry. The Japanese were in a parlous state, short of every type of medicine and increasingly reliant for food on what they could forage for themselves. Their ranks were steadily reduced by sickness. Morale plummeted, as· indicated by letters found on dead soldiers, revealing growing disillusionment, acceptance of the fact that they will never see their wives and children again, that the Allied air forces are now supreme, and that starvation is as dreaded an enemy as the British and Indian armies.

During the rainy season, Christison's staff had been planning for the 'offensive-defensive' phase which lay ahead. Hundreds of small wooden boats, built on the coast at Maungdaw, were laboriously transported in sections over the hills to the upper Kalapanzin valley where they were assembled and carefully hidden from chance aerial observation. There was a brief crisis when a sudden Japanese probe up the Kaladan surprised a force of African and Indian troops, driving them back in some confusion to the Indian border at Daletme, but the secret hoard of boats remained undetected, and a visit by the corps commander was enough to restore confidence in the units involved. As usual, Christison travelled widely around his Corps area, a shrewd but genial and relaxed figure whose pastime of bird-watching resulted in a book, *The Birds of Arakan*, which he somehow found time to compile.

81 West African Division spent the monsoon high up in the hills above the sources of the Kaladan River in country so wild that an entire British regiment was said to have disappeared there without trace during the war of 1824. Despite hard conditions the African soldiers did well. One of their officers wrote of them at this time that '. . . they lived at their firing positions in a state of perpetual discomfort and watchfulness, and yet they never failed to greet me with a joke and a laugh. Without a murmur of complaint they defended a country they despised, in a quarrel whose implications they did not understand. They had volunteered to fight for Britain and if the British brought them to a wilderness that was sufficient reason. They squatted down in their trenches, polished the leather charms they wore next to their skin, prayed to Allah for his protection, and good-humouredly got on with the job'.

The rains started to die away in October and the ground began to dry out. It was time to finish off the Japanese in the Arakan. In November 15 Corps left 14th Army, and came under the direct command of General Leese at Headquarters ALFSEA. This move relieved Slim of the burden of fighting separate battles just as he was planning the destruction of Burma Area army on the central plains.

General Christison kept the feast of St Andrew on 30 November with a special dinner for his staff, regaling them with 'Haggis' (made from porcupine), 'Roast Beef' (breast of adjutant stork) and fresh pineapple. Christison deemed it prudent not to divulge the secret of the banquet, which was much enjoyed by his guests. He had another cause for celebration; shortly before, he had been knighted. On 14 December 1944, at an impressive investiture held on the Plain of Imphal at the King's command and with his special permission, Field Marshal Earl Wavell, Viceroy of India, conferred the accolade on Slim and his three corps commanders, Christison, Scoones and Stopford, in recognition of their part in the year's decisive victories over the Japanese.

The advance of 15 Corps had begun three days earlier, and when Christison knelt for his accolade before the Viceroy he knew that Buthidaung had passed back into his hands, taken by 81 West African

Division in a rapid descent of the Kalapanzin Valley. Donbaik fell to the 8th Oxford and Buckinghamshire Light Infantry on 23 December, and on Boxing Day troops of 25 Indian Division stood at Foul Point, last seen by British units at the beginning of the ill-fated campaign of 1942-43. The Japanese had melted away in accordance with General Sakurai's careful plans. His main preoccupation was no longer Akyab, from which he was planning to withdraw in great secrecy. His 28th Army now intended to hang on to the key passes over the Arakan Yomas, the natural barrier protecting the flank of all Japanese forces in the lower Irrawaddy valley. If these passes could not be held, the Japanese army still lined up against Slim opposite Mandalay would be in mortal danger.

Christison now had a different team from the one with which he had won his battles nine months earlier. In the Mayu peninsula he had 25 and 26 Indian Divisions, with only four British battalions between them, and inland, the 81 and 82 West African Divisions. Also under the command of corps headquarters were an Independent East African Brigade, a Commando Brigade, a Tank Brigade and a mass of engineers and artillery. The 3rd Commando Brigade was to be the spearhead of amphibious operations which lay ahead. It consisted of two Royal Marines and two Army commandos, units of battalion-size specially trained and equipped for seaborne assault. The Army commandos were all-volunteer units drawn from over 60 regiments and corps. Raised in 1940-41 in response to Churchill's call for airborne and raiding forces as a means of carrying the war to the enemy, their men were billeted in the United Kingdom on the civilian population instead of being housed in barracks. For food and maintenance they were entitled to a subsistence allowance (13/4d a day for officers, 8/6d for soldiers) which was paid to their landlady, who welcomed the additions to her household as they brought double ration books. The 3rd Commando Brigade was part of the welcome reinforcement of naval forces in the Far East, a belated response to Churchill's and the Chiefs of Staffs' promises of 1943. A considerable fleet was now at sea in the Bay of Bengal, strong enough to deal if required with the Japanese fleet based at Singapore.

As this force bore down on Akyab at the turn of the year, a signal was received in the command ship from Mountbatten, whose meteorologists in Ceylon had predicted a cyclone in the area. He advised cancellation. Christison was determined to go ahead, as was the naval commander, Rear Admiral Martin, who had risen from the lower deck and whose fighting spirit would have gladdened Nelson. Christison signalled Leese for his support and immediately got it in the reply he had hoped for: 'Do what you feel you must to achieve your object with least delay and casualties. Whatever your decision I will back you and protect you from Supremo's wrath. You are the man on the spot. Good luck.'

As the fleet arrived off Akyab early on New Year's Day 1945, an Auster aircraft of 656 Air OP squadron, flown by a Royal Artillery officer, Captain Jarrett, passed over the island, to find no sign of the enemy. Instead, islanders were out in the open, waving white sheets and home-made Allied flags. Jarrett put his plane down on a cleared stretch of the island's main airfield, which had been cleared of obstacles by locals, who told him that apart from a handful of Japanese, the island had been evacuated. Leaving Gunner Carter, his observer, as temporary military governor, Jarrett flew back to Corps HQ with the local headman as passenger. A heavy naval and aerial bombardment of the island was about to begin but Jarrett was able to convince Christison that the Japanese had gone.. The bombardment was called off at the last minute, to the obvious disappointment of the assembled press corps, embarked with the fleet and agog to report on the event from a safe viewpoint. Christison, accompanied by Air Vice-Marshal the Earl of Bandon, commanding 224 Group RAF, flew ashore next morning in an L-5 light aircraft as the assault went in unopposed, and Gunner Carter handed Akyab over to his corps commander. The few remaining Japanese were herded into a corner of the island and dealt with by the York and Lancaster Regiment.

The strain of campaigning under extreme conditions in the Burma monsoon was not limited to front line soldiers and affected senior commanders too. After a visit to the 82 West African Division in December 1944, accompanied by his new Chief of Staff, Lt General 'Boy' Browning, Mountbatten privately mentioned the eccentric behaviour of the divisional commander to Christison. Mountbatten's party had been driven around the divisional area by their host, Maj General Bruce, who flaunted a pair of pearl-handled revolvers, appeared to have been over-imbibing, and rapidly became lost, driving his guests well forward of the Africans' forward positions. Christison decided to see for himself and made his visit shortly after, accompanied by an American general who had expressed a wish to see around the forward areas. On arrival at the headquarters of 82 Division, Bruce, whose behaviour seemed strange to Christison, insisted that his guests went forward with him in a jeep which he drove, followed by an armed escort. Very soon he was obviously lost, and this was confirmed within minutes when the little convoy came under small arms fire. Christison ordered everyone out and a distinguished party of generals and ADCs took cover as the escort trotted off into the bush to tackle the ambush party. The shock was too much for the American general who, suffering a fatal heart attack there and then, was borne to the rear by an extremely senior stretcher party.

Christison removed Bruce from his post and he was confined to a military hospital in Chittagong. As he had clearly lost the confidence of his brigade commanders, there was no alternative to giving him an adverse report on grounds of medical unsuitability to continue. When a staff officer took the report to hospital for Bruce to initial, the patient produced a revolver from under the sheets and pointed it at him with the words: 'Tear it up or you're a dead man!' Command of 82 Division now passed to Brigadier Hugh Stockwell, who led it until the end of the war.

With Akyab secure, Christison's next objective was to cut the Japanese supply routes along the coast, then seize Ramree Island. This would compel the Japanese to withdraw from their fastnesses in the Kaladan Valley, where 81 West African Division was once more pushing steadily forward. The assault on Ramree was clearly a task for the 3rd Commando Brigade.

Each of the four Commandos in the brigade consisted of about 540 officers and men of whom virtually all could be counted as 'bayonet strength'. A small headquarters controlled the Commando in battle. The basic sub-unit was the troop of two sections, or one load of an assault landing craft. One troop was equipped with Vickers medium machine guns or 3-inch mortars. For heavier support the Commando had the services of a field artillery battery, a troop of 19th Lancers (Indian Army) with Sherman tanks, and a field company of Indian Engineers. Being designed for maximum impact in the assault, a Commando was not geared for sustained operations. No 1 Army Commando had seen active service in North Africa, where casualties had reduced it to a strength of 120. Before leaving that theatre its commanding officer had re-equipped it with the American Garand semi-automatic rifle which gave the unit far greater firepower at close quarters than the bolt-operated Lee-Enfield. These Garands, and a large number of Thompson sub-machine guns firing a heavy .45-inch bullet, added considerably to the unit's close range hitting power.

The only common features in an Army Commando drawn from so many regiments was the green beret worn by all ranks in combat, and a shoulder-flash bearing the emblem of a salamander, whose legendary ability to emerge unscathed from the fire appealed to the unit. The Royal Marines Commandos were also volunteers, heirs to a tradition of amphibious warfare going back to the 18th century.

The first step in the series of landings which now took place was a descent on the Myebon peninsula down the coast from Akyab. The approaches to the beaches there were through extremely complicated tidal channels which meandered through mangrove swamps. These had to be carefully surveyed beforehand. The commandos landed at Myebon on 12 January 1945. As they came ashore the Marines, followed by an Indian infantry brigade, had to struggle through deep mud, but managed to secure their objectives. After ten days of consolidation, the next phase went ahead. This was the capture of Kangaw, a small town lying astride the main Japanese escape route, where strong opposition could be expected. Kangaw village was dominated by Hill 170, a scrubby feature with several crests from which all roads passing through the village could be observed. This was the primary Commando objective.

In order to get as far as possible inshore, Admiral Martin took enormous risks. When he mentioned that he had no up-to-date charts of the innumerable creeks and inlets and no tide tables, Christison, who knew his man, replied '. . . Yours is the only close fire support I can get. If your charts are out of date, chuck them overboard. Use an Army map. Everything that's blue is yours. All else is mine.'

As the landing craft made their way up the maze of creeks, Hurribombers flew low overhead, laying a dense smoke screen to shield the boats from the eyes of Japanese observers. The approach involved a journey up some ten miles of winding narrow waterway, where a Japanese ambush would have brought disaster. The landing craft were already well past their expected lives and were kept operational only be the ingenuity and devotion of their naval and Royal Marines crews. There was no opposition, much to the relief of Lt Colonel Ken Trevor of No 1 Army Commando; his own regiment was the Cheshires, and he described this approach to battle as being like a pleasure trip up the Dee. In order to achieve complete surprise there was no preliminary air or naval bombardment and the attack came from an unexpected direction. It did not take long, however, for the Japanese to react to this thrust at their vitals. For the first 24 hours success was in the balance as resistance built up and fanatical attacks were launched by the Japanese to force the Commandos back into the sea. Their defensive positions were carefully concealed and skilfully sited, and enjoyed a surprising amount of accurate artillery support. Christison put ashore an additional infantry brigade supported by Sherman tanks of the 19th Lancers, carrried ashore on flat-bottomed lighters whose trim was delicately adjusted by rotating the tanks' turrets.

After a week of Japanese counter-attacks the Commandos moved forward to take Kangaw village, finally cutting the Japanese escape route. There was now a desperate attempt to dislodge them, the enemy throwing in a succession of suicidal attacks against Hill 170. For 36 hours the issue was in the balance. One of Trevor's men, 'Tag' Barnes, recalled the tension as a Japanese night attack came in. The Commandos crouched in their hurriedly-dug slits on the hill, grenades ready to throw. Section commanders gave whispered orders – 'prepare to throw' – as the rustling in the undergrowth grew louder and louder and closer. Suddenly, the Japanese were among them, screaming and throwing grenades. The noise was overwhelming; then, just as suddenly, the enemy were gone, leaving their dead, many of them actually in the defenders' trenches. Two hours later, the tin cans on the wire could be heard, being gently rattled. A quiet voice came from the darkness, asking in perfectly accented English, 'Commandos, are you still there?' This was repeated, over and over; always closer. Suddenly the Japanese opened up at ten yards' range. Barnes' Bren gunner was mortally wounded, dying in his arms. The wooden stock of his Garand rifle was shattered, but it still fired. The final attack was at 3 am. As daylight came it revealed a frightful sight: Japanese in their hundreds lay in front of, and inside, the Commandos' position.

After this battle was over, Christison flew over the scene in an L-5. There below lay the Japanese dead, quite literally piled high only yards in front of the Commandos' slit trenches. During the attack the tanks of the 19th Lancers were singled out for destruction, and one suicide squad managed to destroy a Sherman with its crew before being blasted away. One commando troop counted 340 Japanese dead in one corner of its defences; nearly all were victims of grenade or bayonet, so closely had the battle been fought. The living were mixed in with the dead and had to be killed off individually. By 3 February it was possible to count over 700 Japanese dead on the slopes of Hill 170 and a total of 2,500 were killed in an area no larger than that of Wembley Stadium. The Commandos and the 51st Indian Infantry Brigade had both performed superbly and gained two VCs in the process. One of them went posthumously to Lt Knowland of the Norfolks, serving in No 1 Commando. He had recklessly exposed himself to enemy fire throughout the battle, at times firing a 2-inch mortar at close range, covering the gallant stretcher bearers with a Tommy gun, passing ammunition around his troop's position and cheering his men on until he was killed.

Two Indian officers were promoted in the field to command their units after their British COs became casualties, the first in the Indian army to be accorded this honour. One of them, Major Thimmaya, finished the war as a brigadier and went on to be Commander-in-Chief of the post-Independence Indian Army.

Christison and his staff had been aboard the cruiser HMS *Phoebe* during the battle, acquiring much practical experience in the command of amphibious operations. They had enjoyed matchless support from the fleet and well-coordinated air support from the RAF, Indian Air Force, Fleet Air Arm and the light aircraft pilots of the Air OP, flying their Austers off the Royal Navy's light carriers to provide close observation and fire adjustment for naval gunfire support.

As attention turned to the capture of Ramree Island and its important airfield, good news arrived from the Arakan, where 81 West African Division captured the important town of Myohaung, one of the last main Japanese garrisons in the area and the ancient provincial capital. Under their new commander, Maj General Loftus-Tottenham, a carefully-chosen former Gurkha, the 81st had justified all the hopes placed in it, and had certainly expunged the unhappier memories of its setbacks in the 1944 campaign, when it had been called on to perform tasks beyond its capacity at that time.

The Master Stroke

". . . he always fights a battle going in where he took a beating going out."

ON 13 FEBRUARY 1945, Slim wrote to his daughter Una at her school in India:

> We have started a very big battle and there will be a lot of heavy fighting for some time now. However, we got our first lot of troops over the Irrawaddy last night so that's a good beginning. I shall be so busy for the next few weeks I won't be able to write a lot but I WOULD like to hear from you . . .

There was much that the commander of 14th Army would have wished to add. On the point of fighting the culminating battles of his career, he was under enormous strain. He had been continuously on active service, with only the shortest breaks, for almost five years, far longer than any other senior British commander in World War II. He had experienced the bitterness of defeat but had seen a revived army – one which owed its confidence and skill to him as much as anyone – fight the Japanese to a halt in the Arakan, at Kohima and Imphal, then chase the enemy back to the Chindwin. Now it was crossing the mighty Irrawaddy and going for the enemy's throat. He was dog tired and at times it showed in bouts of irritability. His constitution had been weakened more than he would admit by a severe bout of malaria at the height of the battles in Assam. Even under this dreadful burden of responsibility, he could still find time to write cheerful letters to his family.

Whatever his private fears, Slim never showed them in public. Accounts written by those who saw him in those days identify the qualities which made him such a great leader. His approach was not histrionic. As a speaker he used no tricks of oratory; but throughout his life, those whom he had addressed would carry his message with them to the end of their days. He never 'flannelled', as he knew how quickly soldiers notice falsehood and insincerity. Talking to one infantry unit before an attack, he simply told them about the operation in which they had a part, and took them into his confidence by explaining how their battalion fitted into the greater plan. He spoke informally, in a conversational voice, making no attempt to dismiss the dangers the troops were about to face. At the end, an enthusiastic voice shouted from the back of the crowd, 'We'll be right behind you, general!' to which Slim replied with a gruff chuckle, 'Not on your life. You'll be a very long way ahead of me!' The troops loved it all the more because they knew that he had frequently been at the 'sharp end' (and would nearly become a battle casualty himself at Meiktila a few weeks hence). His own staff would gladly work all hours for him without coercion. There was an aura about him, some said, which set him apart from them and stamped him as an incomparable leader.

The battle for the Irrawaddy crossings started on 11 January when 19 Indian Division, after its rapid march down from Indaw, got across at Thabeikkyin. Forming a strongly defended bridgehead, it triggered the expected reaction from the Japanese, who saw it as the prelude to a series of crossings aimed at Mandalay. When Slim was satisfied that Kimura's eyes were firmly fixed on 19 Division's bridgehead, two more of 33 Corps' Divisions, 2 British and 20 Indian, were put across the river at Ngazun, opposite Myinmu and only 35 miles due west of Mandalay. Kimura, now absolutely convinced that these were the main crossings, attacked the new bridgeheads with everything at his disposal.

Slim's tactical headquarters was now well forward at Monywa on the lower Chindwin. On his way there, he had passd close to the spot where Burcorps had started the last leg of its painful retreat in 1942. The melancholy relics were still there; burnt-out tanks, hundreds of vehicles, military kit of all sorts, looted and then discarded. One night, Slim paid an unheralded visit to the War Room, installed in a ruined house. Two staff officers were sitting in front of the maps and the elder was briefing the younger, a new arrival on the staff. 'Uncle Bill,' he said, 'will fight a battle HERE.' When the younger officer enquired why, he was told 'Because he always fights a battle going in where he took a beating going out.' Smiling to himself, Slim left them to it.

With the main Japanese force still deployed to fend off a direct threat to Mandalay, Slim now ordered a series of pre-planned diversionary crossings with the object of diluting Kimura's forces. The Japanese commander was now receiving disturbing intelligence reports from as far south as Nyaungu, 150 miles downstream. As these began to multiply, uneasy thoughts entered his mind. He had been tricked, and the evidence now lay before him: 4 Corps was poised to cross the Irrawaddy at a point where it could rush to Meiktila, the main Japanese administrative centre for their 15th Army. This was the moment for 19 Indian Division to capitalise on the enemy's confusion and it renewed its advance on Mandalay from the north, sending a brigade off to the east to take Maymyo.

On 19 February, 4 Corps began to cross the Irrawaddy around Nyaungu against only light opposition – proof indeed of the complete success of Slim's deception plan. Three days later 7 and 17 Indian Divisions, with 255th Indian Tank Brigade, burst out of the bridgehead to drive hard for Meiktila, 80 miles distant. The tank brigade, advancing astride the main road with two mechanised infantry brigades, was under orders to disregard its flanks and rear, leaving them to follow-on formations. On the night of 28 February patrols of 17 Division were entering the outskirts of Meiktila, which the Japanese, once they had recovered from their surprise, proceeded grimly to defend. The town had been prepared for this with dozens of bunkers, which had to be eliminated one by one. Virtually no prisoners were taken, and many Japanese were found dead in their trenches with aerial bombs clutched between their knees, stones in their hands to strike the detonator as a tank passed overhead. The climax came on 1 March when the garrison was finally overwhelmed. Of an estimated 2,000 Japanese in the town, only a handful got away. The last 50, trapped with their backs to the lake, finally jumped into the water in full fighting order and were drowned. Meiktila and its valuable airfield were firmly in 4 Corps hands on 3 March. In the wake of the spearhead, other brigades mopped up behind and captured further airfields at Thabuktong, where two more brigades were flown in on light scales.

By 7 March, Mandalay was being approached from all directions by jubilant British and Indian troops. Maj General Rees of 19 Division ordered an attack on Mandalay Hill, which dominates the ancient City of Kings, whose hundreds of beautiful buildings gleamed white and gold in the sunshine. He gave strict instructions that the holy places were to be spared. Rees was a devout Welsh chapel man, given to community singing with any of his men who cared to join him in the fiery revivalist hymns he loved. He was also totally devoid of fear, striking terror into his staff by his habit of commanding from the front, prominent in general's uniform and vivid red scarf. During the fighting at Mandalay his orderly was killed by a sniper's bullet while talking to him. Instead of blanketing the city indiscriminately with artillery fire or carpet bombing, Rees called for precision airstrikes by fighter-bombers which took on target after target as the troops followed confidently, close behind the bomb bursts.

The main Japanese stronghold was in Fort Dufferin, an ancient fortress with sides a mile long and immensely strong earthen ramparts reinforced with brick. Medium artillery was hauled up to within a few hundred yards of these walls, to batter away at them over open sights in 18th century style. When adequate breaches had been made, several attempts to storm the fort failed, and it was some days before it fell, when the survivors of its garrison stole away by night.

The Japanese had no intention of letting Meiktila go and launched desperate counter-attacks with two divisions of Lt General Honda's 33rd Army. From 5 to 29 March, they surrounded the town. Here, Maj General 'Punch' Cowan had his headquarters, from where he conducted a masterly battle; although in a sense besieged, his brigades were continually striking out at their enemy. All hung on his ability to hold on to the main airfield,

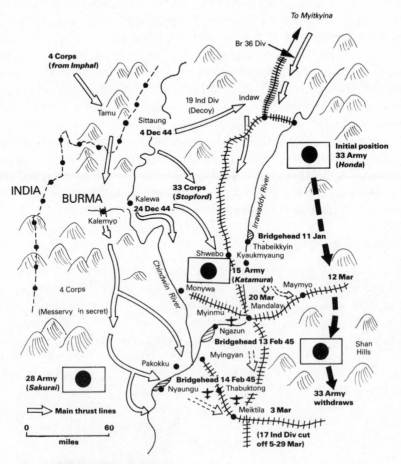

4 Corps
(*from Imphal*)

To Myitkyina

Br 36 Div

Tamu

Sittaung
4 Dec 44

19 Ind Div
(Decoy)

Indaw

**Initial position
33 Army
(*Honda*)**

INDIA

BURMA

Kalewa
24 Dec 44

Kalemyo

**33 Corps
(*Stopford*)**

Irrawaddy River

Bridgehead 11 Jan
Thabeikkyin
Kyaukmyaung

Shwebo

**15 Army
(*Katamura*)**

Maymyo

12 Mar

Chindwin River

Monywa

20 Mar
Mandalay

4 Corps

(*Messervy* in secret)

Myinmu

Ngazun

Shan
Hills

Bridgehead 13 Feb 45
Myingyan

Pakokku

**28 Army
(*Sakurai*)**

Bridgehead 14 Feb 45
Nyaungu

Thabuktong

**33 Army
withdraws**

⇨ **Main thrust lines**

Meiktila **3 Mar**

0   60

miles

(17 Ind Div cut
off 5-29 Mar)

THE MOVE TO THE IRRAWADDY
OPERATION 'EXTENDED CAPITAL'
– THE 'MASTER STROKE'

Dec 44-Feb 45

219

which for some time was in no-man's-land, with patrols from both sides fighting it out by night, and unarmed transport planes running the gauntlet to bring in supplies and reinforcements by day. Cowan's performance was all the more praiseworthy because, at the height of the battle, he was told of the death of his son in action at the capture of Mandalay. By unhappy chance, several British generals lost their sons during the Burma campaign; Christison's son was killed in the retreat from Rangoon in 1942; Smyth's son was killed in Italy, and Loftus-Tottenham lost one son in Burma and another in Italy.

As the battle raged at Meiktila, the Japanese were counter-attacking elsewhere. Sakurai's 28th Army, still on the west bank of the Irrawaddy and further downstream, moved troops up to attack the ferry points at Nyaungu, and Maj General Yamamoto's infantry group attacked them on the east bank. All these attacks were driven off, and Kimura had played all his cards. Slim now prepared for the drive on Rangoon.

Ramree to Rangoon

Meanwhile, the campaign continued along the Arakan coast. Following the capture of Akyab and the landings at Myebon and Kangaw, Christison looked towards Ramree Island. Possession of its airfield was essential if Slim was to be sustained in central Burma after the breaking of the monsoon, and although it was hoped that 14th Army would arrive at Rangoon before then, it was wise to plan for the worst case. The Japanese gave every sign of their determination to hold onto Ramree for as long as possible, realising the problems which would beset Slim if they could keep him out of Rangoon, dependent on a dubious overland line of communication.

On 21 January the 15-inch guns of the battleship HMS *Queen Elizabeth*, which had taken part in the bombardment of the Turkish forts in the Dardanelles 30 years before, opened fire on the Japanese defences at Ramree. The *Queen Elizabeth* was supported by several British and Australian cruisers and many smaller warships. The seaward defences had been reconnoitred by the Beach Pilotage Sections, which went close inshore by night to examine beaches and check the whereabouts of any obstacles. These were found to include underwater mines, remotely detonated from the shore, and the landing craft carrying the beach master was sunk by one of them. Sensing confusion even before the first wave of craft got ashore, Christison boarded a landing craft and personally led the assault through a gap in the minefield and onto the beach, gaining the unusual distinction of the immediate award of the DSO, a rarity for a senior officer. Like Rees of 19 Indian Division, Christison was of the school which believed that leadership can only be applied from the front. Ramree had been held by 1,000 men, and although they were well dug in, their position was cleverly outflanked and they were forced into one corner of the island where, amongst crocodile-infested swamps, most of them died from drowning, disease or starvation. Only 20 ever surrendered.

The Ramree landing called for special efforts from units and personnel with little experience of amphibious operations. The 3rd Commando Brigade had now been withdrawn to reorganise after its astonishing feats at Kangaw, as had many of the naval and Royal Marines landing craft crews. Jawans of the Indian Army had therefore been given instruction in boat handling and formed the majority of the crews on subsequent operations. They took readily to this unusual trade and performed with distinction. Christison had always taught his men that they should be versatile and ready to adapt. In the Arakan the previous year, when Japanese infiltrators were active in 15 Corps rear areas, at one time threatening to attack his headquarters, he had encountered a transport unit of the Royal Indian Army Service Corps whose Madrassi drivers, unexpectedly in the forward area and standing-to at dawn for the first time, terrorised neighbouring units with a fusillade of rapid fire from every weapon. When it was over, their platoon commander, a jemadar, was called on to explain his troops' conduct:

> General Sahib, my men very new, very frightened. They are saying only drive lorries, not fighting. So, I am saying to them, Japans over there. Fall in; load; five rounds rapid fire. Now they think they are killing some Japans as they are not firing back. Not frightened any more, sahib.

While greatly amused by this, Christison had already issued instructions which became the letter of the law in 15 Corps. They covered what he called the 'Three Vs for Victory': Fire, Military and Health Disciplines. Fire discipline was simple; it simply meant 'one round, one Jap.' By applying the other disciplines, the men of 15 Corps were acknowledged as the smartest in the theatre, with exceptionally high standards of turn-out and saluting. The Corps' medical record was equally good, even though its operational area was in one of the most unhealthy regions of Burma. The official historian of operations in the Arakan over a century earlier had written of its health problems and they had not changed:

> The season also brought with it, its usual pestiferous influence, in the midst of a low country over-run with jungle, and intersected with numerous and muddy rivers . . . within the first eleven months after landing at Rangoon nearly one-half the Europeans died . . . in like manner, in Arakan at least three-fourths of the European force perished, and of those who survived, few were again fit for service . . .

The operational efficiency of 15 Corps was now being adversely affected by increased demands of 4 and 33 Corps in the Mandalay area for air transport support. Christison had to start thinning out as his own logistic resources began to diminish, and 81 West African Division was withdrawn, together with most of the tank brigade which had given such sterling service at Kangaw. Other formations followed, but there was still work for 15 Corps to do. Leese now directed that major air maintenance bases were to be established at Akyab and Ramree and any remaining enemy pockets in the Arakan eliminated. The Corps was also ordered to advance further down the coast to Taungup, 100 miles past Kangaw, and to press on beyond there to open the road to Prome on the Lower Irrawaddy as a means of reducing pressure against 14th Army's advance towards Rangoon.

The first requirement was to capture the vital pass over the Arakan Yomas at An, through which the remnants of Sakurai's 28th Army had to march in order to rejoin the main body of Burma Area Army in the Irrawaddy basin. The pass was strongly held for that reason by elements of the Japanese 55th Division centred on Taungup and An itself. Christison's plan was for Stockwell's 82 West African Division to attack An from the north-west as a brigade of 26 Indian Division landed at Ruywa, some 20 miles to the west. This landing took place on 16 February but a fierce Japanese counter-attack announced the enemy's intention of holding on, and reinforcements had to be sent ashore. When visiting Stockwell's divisional headquarters in the field, Christison had a narrow escape when two Japanese riflemen emerged from the undergrowth and charged his jeep, to be killed only yards away by his African escort.

Just when it seemed that the Japanese at An were about to be encircled and dislodged, Slim's demands for yet more transport aircraft compelled Leese to order the withdrawal of most of those supporting 15 Corps, and Christison, now totally reliant on air supply, was forced to pull his troops back to the coast just when success was in his grasp. Undeterred, and relying now on supply from the sea, he landed another brigade north of Taungup. It got to within five miles of the town and was then halted by an exceptionally strong road block. This, with the Japanese retention of the An pas, meant that the enemy was still able to move up and down the coast and also switch troops to and from the interior. One reason for the staunch resistance of 28th Japanese Army was the devotion of all ranks to Sakurai, for whose personal safety they were ready to make great sacrifices, as will be seen.

Rangoon recaptured

On 11 April it was time to strike for Rangoon. Messervy's 4 Corps set out from Meiktila down the Sittang Valley, and Stopford's 33rd down the road to Prome. As the two Corps crossed their start lines, John Masters, former Chindit now on the staff of 19 Indian Division, stood with many others, including 14th Army's senior commanders, as the formations thundered by. Tanks carrying infantry, guns, lorries, sped past in dense clouds of dust: '. . . British, Sikhs, Gurkhas, Madrassis, Pathans. This was the old Indian Army, going down to the attack for the last time in history, exactly two hundred years after the Honourable East India Company had enlisted its first ten sepoys . . .' They had nearly 300 miles to go and were in a hurry, brushing aside any opposition in their path. As Messervy's men roared down the Sittang valley, they could see despondent columns of beaten enemy troops trudging south on the hills at the side of the road. Elsewhere, Japanese military policemen, unsuspecting as the leading tanks bore down on them, supposed them to be friendly until run down at their posts. One team of Japanese engineers, having prepared the demolition charges for a key bridge, were resting when the first 33 Corps unit arrived, and never woke up. The sole concern of the Japanese now appeared to be that of getting out of the way, to regroup if possible further south.

Other movements were afoot, including the switch of the Burmese National Army's allegiance. Early in 1945, there had been hints that Aung San was highly disillusioned with the Japanese; in April he asked for, and was granted, a safe conduct to visit Slim at Meiktila. This was the culmination of a carefully conducted Intelligence operation following reports that Aung San was shifting position. In November 1944 a former BNA man, who had been 'turned' by British Intelligence agents as the result of kindly treatment, was parachuted into the Pegu area where he contacted his former chief. Aung San was already uncertain as to the outcome of the war, and when the BNA was ordered to the front by the Japanese in March 1945 he decided that the time had come. On 16 May he came to Slim at Meiktila, dressed as a Japanese major general, complete with sword. From the start he impressed Slim, who described him as '. . . neat and soldierly in appearance, with regular Burmese features in a face that could be an impassive mask or light up with intelligence and humour.'

At first Aung San claimed to represent what he called 'The Provisional Government of Burma, set up by the Anti-Fascist Peoples' Freedom League'; he also considered himself to be a fully accredited Allied commander. Slim quickly disabused him of this, but handled him with firmness, tact and good humour. When he said to him 'Go on, Aung San, you've only come to me because we're winning', he replied: 'It wouldn't have been much good coming to you if you weren't.' Slim took to him; he liked his honesty and, as he wrote later, '. . . In fact I was beginning to like Aung San!' It was agreed that the BNA would henceforth be fed, clothed and paid by the British and pass unconditionally under command of 14th Army. Aung San was as good as his word. At once, disciplined bodies of BNA soldiers began to give themselves up. Renamed the 'Patriot Burmese Forces' they proved invaluable, rounding up Japanese stragglers and dacoits, and they were to play a useful role in the final battles of 1945 as the remains of the Japanese army in Burma made their last desperate efforts to escape.

On 3 May, 33 Corps reached Prome and 4 Corps were at Pegu on the Sittang. Both were almost at their last gasp, having made huge demands on their respective administrative systems. They were now temporarily at a halt due to a combination of administrative difficulties, worn-out equipment and hardening Japanese resistance.

Kimura, seeing the main threat to Rangoon as coming down from Prome, had stripped the city of its troops and sent them north, holding 33 Corps well up-country. It was time for SEAC to revive 'Dracula', the plan for an attack on Rangoon from the sea. Parachute landings would be made on the Japanese coastal batteries at Elephant Point, guarding the seaward approach to Rangoon. Then, after the river channel had been swept clear of mines, 26 Indian Division would pass upriver to Rangoon in assault craft for a direct attack on the city. This involved a thiry-mile passage upstream against unknown levels of opposition. Rear Admiral Martin, who was given to making rousing signals, did so now to all ships: 'Guts and good seamanship'. The Navy then got on with the dangerous task of clearing the mines laid by both sides since the beginning of the war. The weather forecast was gloomy, with the threat of a cyclone in the Bay of Bengal; tides and currents were problematical, and the charts were hopelessly out of date.

Early in April 50th Indian Parachute Brigade assembled at Chaklala in East Bengal. It was not currently at operational pitch. Half of one of its Gurkha battalions was on long leave in Nepal and another half-battalion on its way to join a newly-formed Indian parachute brigade, hundreds of miles away. The 152nd Parachute Battalion, veterans of Sangshak, had been split to form two other battalions. It was therefore necessary to form an ad hoc battalion group for 'Dracula'. At Chaklala it was augmented by the arrival of the brigade field ambulance (in which a number of Sangshak survivors, including Rangaraj, were still serving), some pathfinders, engineers, signallers and an Intelligence section.

After three quick exercises to shake down, the battalion group moved to Akyab on 20 April, where it was augmented by 200 extra men from other parachute battalions. Here it was discovered that 40 of the American transport crews 'borrowed' from 4 Corps had never dropped paratroops before and that their aircraft were not fitted with the rails and other equipment needed for dropping personnel. These were hurriedly fitted, and the crew chiefs trained as jumpmasters. Some Royal Canadian Air Force transport aircraft were produced, and cargo racks fitted to them for container dropping.

There would have to be two lifts, as there were insufficient aircraft to put all the troops down in a single drop. The drop-zone was some five miles west of Elephant Point. Among the first to jump were pathfinders, signallers and the intelligence section, followed by representatives of the press, members of Force 136, whose job was to contact the local patriot forces, and the battalion HQ Defence platoon. On the morning of 1 May the first aircraft took off from Akyab before dawn on the four-hour flight. At the same time the seaborne force was starting its long run-in; the sea was extremely rough and most of the troops were soon prostrate with seasickness despite heavy sedation, and certainly in no condition to fight when disembarked. It was just as well that the landings were unopposed. The Japanese had already abandoned Rangoon and were heading east.

P-Hour for the first parachute drop was 0710 hrs. There was no anti-aircraft fire and virtually no opposition on the ground. The DZs were quickly laid out by the pathfinders to await the second wave, which came in during the afternoon. There was one mishap; part of the fire-plan included a strike by heavy bombers on the coastal batteries. Although these were already abandoned, the strike went ahead; the bombers' aim was inaccurate and many bombs landed amidst the paratroops, causing a number of casualties. A supply drop came in later in the day and it then rained non-stop for three days. The monsoon was imminent and within hours the entire area was flooded to a depth of three feet. On the morning of 2 May the great armada passed upriver. Apart from a single Royal Marine, each assault craft was crewed entirely by soldiers of the Indian Army, many of whom had not even seen the sea until a few weeks earlier.

Within 24 hours the docks were in British hands. Rangoon had been liberated. The city, although much neglected by its recent occupants, impressed its new conquerors, reminding them of Colombo '. . . except it's obviously a far wealthier place . . . magnificent bungalows and more official-looking buildings. All the gardens overgrown, and some bungalows damaged . . . here in the town the bomb damage is more apparent – also lack of drains and non-working of same . . .'

Rangoon Jail out at Mingaladon, the pre-war home of the Glosters, had been used by the Japanese to house Allied prisoners of war. When the Japanese pulled out, the prisoners got onto the roof where they painted 'Japs Gone' in large letters. Several British aircraft flew low overhead, but appeared to take no notice. The prisoners therefore decided to authenticate their message in a way which would tell the pilots aloft that no Japanese had painted it. They simply added the words 'Extract Digit'.

HMS *Una*

Slim was still a long way from Rangoon at the beginning of April and although the battle of the plains was over, there was another campaign to be won. If the monsoon arrived earlier than usual, he would be left floundering in the middle of Burma with an army dependent on motor transport for its mobility, unlike his army in 1944, which could move on foot with the help of plentiful animal transport. It was essential to secure a good river port on the Irrawaddy, as Kalewa had been left far behind. Myingyan was chosen, but its Japanese garrison held out for some time after the fall of Mandalay and Meiktila, and a major operation had to be mounted to clear them out.

Within days, piers were being constructed, slipways repaired and wharves made ready to handle huge amounts of stores. Up-country, the rivers were now busy once more with country boats and military craft, including the invaluable amphibious DUKWs, plying up and down. Not all these waterways were entirely safe, however, for parties of Japanese stragglers and stay-behind groups continued to operate against the lines of communication. At Mountbatten's suggestion two armed river boats were constructed and commissioned into the Royal Navy, which manned them. Armed with light automatic cannon and machine guns they gave useful service as escorts and saw action on several occasions. On 15 April, Slim wrote another letter to his daughter:

> Last Monday I launched a small ship for the Royal Navy Flotilla which will fight on the big Irrawaddy river. It is a small ship but it is a real warship with guns and a crew of Royal Navy sailors and it will fly the White Ensign, the naval flag. And I named it after you! The first warship launched to help Fourteenth army against the Japs is called HMS *UNA*. I doubt if any young woman of your age (except perhaps some little princess) has ever had a warship (even a little one) named after her.

With the arrival of 26 Indian Division at Rangoon, it seemed that 14th Army had been cheated of their rightful prize. However, a far worse bombshell was now to shake every man in Slim's command. At the very moment of his triumph, it was rumoured that 'Uncle Bill' had been sacked.

The 'Sacking' of Slim

"I have only one ambition, and that is to go on commanding 14th Army until the Jap is finally beaten flat."

WITH THE FALL of Rangoon Slim's career had been crowned with victory. He could now proceed with the final stages of his great campaign to destroy the Japanese on Burmese soil. A situation arose, however, which threatened to turn his triumph to ashes. Even after nearly half a century, the so-called 'sacking' incident raises passions among those who were involved, particularly those who served in 14th Army. First, it is essential to put the matter in perspective.

At that time, Slim was still virtually unknown in Britain. Mountbatten and Stilwell were household names, and Alexander was credited with having saved Burma Army in 1942 when it was actually Slim's calmness, resolution and leadership which salvaged something from that unholy mess. Winston Churchill had never set eyes on him and, as he preferred to appoint to high command those generals he knew personally, he had reservations about this Indian Army Officer whose track record prior to 1944 had included no sensational victories. Indeed, Slim's first taste of command at brigade level in East Africa had been marred when his British battalion broke and ran under air attack at the Battle of Gallabat, and many (not least himself, as is clear from his own writings) thought he was lucky to have been given a second chance, this time commanding 10 Indian Division in Iraq. Here he was conspicuously successful. Earlier he had been resigned to spending the rest of the war in some military backwater. Now through lobbying by the two divisional commanders in Burma, both former colleagues of his in the 1/6th Gurkha Rifles, he found himself in the unenviable post of Burma Corps Commander just as the 1942 retreat got under way.

As a Corps and Army commander in the subsequent campaign, Slim was stoutly backed by General Giffard. But after Imphal, Giffard was removed from his post by Mountbatten, who considered that his reaction to the Japanese threat against Assam had been too slow. He had also disputed Mountbatten's assertion that the 1944 campaign should be fought through the monsoon. Mountbatten did not deal kindly with dissenters. Giffard's successor, Lt General Sir Oliver Leese, came from a radically different background to any of the senior officers who had served in Burma since the early days, and this was to be one cause of the problems which now arose.

Leese's appointment as C-in-C 11th Army Group and Allied Land Forces South-East Asia was announced in London on 28 September 1944. To date his performance had been outstanding; under his command 8th Army had fought its way up Italy to the area of Florence and he had coped most diplomatically with the egocentric General Mark Clark, commander of the American 5th Army. His entire career had an almost textbook correctness. Eton, the Coldstream Guards, distinguished service in World War I, and a happy tour of duty in the twenties as adjutant of the Officers' Training Corps at his old school (where one cadet, Quintin Hogg the future Lord Chancellor, recalled his 'earthy language' on parade). He was at the Staff College in the late twenties, together with Philip Christison. Both were taught there by Montgomery. A hearty extrovert and star of the traditional Staff College pantomime, he was highly regarded as Army Commander in Italy by all ranks; brave, careful of his soldiers' lives, a meticulous planner, approachable and friendly, and not given to flights of windy oratory. He is remembered by those who served with him as a thoroughly straight professional soldier, honest and entirely without guile.

Leese's appointment was welcomed by Mountbatten, who wrote personally to him saying that it was . . . 'my great ambition to get the finest fighting soldier in the British Army to take charge of the major British effort against Japan as soon as the war with Germany had reached a point at which such an officer could be spared . . .' The actual selection had been made at the instigation of General Pownall, Mountbatten's Chief of Staff, on a visit to London. General Sir Alan Brooke, Chief of the Imperial General Staff, endorsed it and Churchill gave his unqualified approval. Leese therefore started out for Ceylon to report to Mountbatten's HQ at Kandy confident that he enjoyed powerful patronage. On the day his appointment was announced, he wrote to a friend expressing his pleasure and excitement at the new job. In that letter lie the seeds of the misfortune which would attend him in Burma. It lists the names of the 8th Army staff officers he intended to take to India with him. More were to join the party until Leese's entourage numbered some 30, each of whom would displace some long-serving member of Giffard's well-tried team.

Leese and his staff boarded a Dakota which set out for the Far East on 1 November 1944, stopping en route at Brussels. Paris, Malta, and Cairo, where General Paget openly criticised the size of what he termed 'Leese's circus'. On 7 November the aircraft arrived at Delhi, and a few days later Leese reported for duty at Kandy, where he was carefully briefed by Pownall on 'how to deal with Mountbatten'. As already related, Leese found the atmosphere at Kandy exotic after the breezy and down-to-earth character of his HQ in Italy. 'A pity, somehow,' he wrote home, 'as it gives the playboy atmosphere, in terrible contrast to those from the battle.' He immediately decided to spend as little time as possible at Kandy and to conduct affairs from HQ ALFSEA at Barrackpore, outside Calcutta, where he arrived on 14 November to meet Slim and Christison.

The commander of 15 Corps was no stranger, but he had never come across Slim and was wary of him from the start, for the two had followed widely different paths, shared no common circles of interests or friends, and operated in totally different ways. For a start, Slim never took a 'circus' with him to a new appointment, preferring to draw on the experience of those who were already immersed in the situation. For him, Leese was the product of another world, with fundamentally differing ideas on all basic matters of soldiering. There could not be a greater contrast, for example, between the methods of man management, lifestyle and discipline in a regiment of Foot Guards and those of a Gurkha Rifles battalion. Both were elitist, but otherwise they shared little common ground.

Leese's new command was probably the most widely dispersed of all. From his HQ at Barrackpore he had to attend frequent meetings at five separate locations and even by air the time taken to reach them was daunting; HQ India (Delhi), 8 hours; HQ SEAC (Kandy), 10 hours; HQ NCAC in North Burma, 6 hours; HQ 14th Army (Comilla), 5 hours; and Christison's 15 Corps in the Arakan was 6 hours away.

It was at Akyab on 7 May 1945 that the commander of 15 Corps received the first inkling of a row that was to divide staffs across the whole command. Leese had called for a meeting which involved Christison in what he remembered as . . . 'a ghastly overnight journey by destroyer' up the coast. After breakfast, Leese took him aside and told him that

. . Dickie (Mountbatten) has felt for some time that Slim has become a very tired man and I must say I agree. Now, Dickie has suggested that I send Slim on indefinite leave, and I have done so. He has already left 14th Army. A new Army is to be formed for the invasion of Malaya and the recapture of Singapore. For prestige reasons it is to be known as 14th Army and the present 14th is to be called the 12th Army and it will clear up in Burma. Stopford is to command it. You, with your combined operation experience, are to take over 14th Army. You are to take five days' leave, then go to GHQ Delhi and start planning for Malaya and Singapore. When you are ready, Dickie and I will come and approve the plan.

Christison was stunned, as well as gratified, by this totally unexpected turn of events. He asked Leese if Slim had been sacked. Leese replied that he had not:

. . It was all very tricky. You know all this guff about Dickie being jealous of Slim, and I don't like the idea. I wanted *him* to do it [i.e. formally sack Slim] but he said no, I was the immediate superior. So I sent George Walsh [one of his staff officers] to Bill to see what his reactions would be. Bill flew into a rage and demanded to see me, and I had to tell him that both Dickie and I felt that he needed a rest. He demanded to be flown to the UK there and then. So that's the position.

Privately Christison thought that Walsh, who was renowned for his tactlessness, was an unwise choice to handle this delicate affair. He was also disturbed by the way in which sudden advancement had come to him, but having informed his equally surprised staff, he accepted their congratulations and was suitably 'dined out' before flying to Delhi. After three weeks' intensive planning with his new staff, he presented the draft plans for the invasion of Malaya to General Auchinleck, who was understandably low-spirited, his wife having just left him for Air Chief Marshal Sir Richard Peirse. On 5 July, Christison was summoned to Leese's HQ at Barrackpore, where he found the Commander-in-Chief in his bath, drinking a large whisky. His first words were,

> Christie, I've been sacked. You are to take my place at once. I'm for home. Brookie [Sir Alan Brooke, CIGS] went to Churchill and told him the Indian Army wouldn't fight without Slim. When Churchill asked 'Who sacked Slim?', Brooke had answered 'Leese', to which Churchill had replied 'Well, sack Leese'. I gather I'm carrying the can for Dickie over this.

So much for Christison's view of the situation. He had been profoundly embarrassed by events to date, for although he had not been under Slim's direct command since the previous November, he greatly liked and admired him. He was also devoted to his old friend Leese, who had backed him to the hilt over his decision to go ahead and attack at Akyab, and had given him free rein in the tactical handling of 15 Corps. Now, he was to take over from this honest and capable Guardsman, whose reward for years of outstanding service was to be military oblivion. Christison braced himself for yet another change of appointment; for the next six weeks he presided over the far-flung fortunes of two British/Indian and two Chinese armies, an American brigade group and various French and Dutch formations now being assembled for the re-occupation of Indo-China and the Netherlands East Indies. He moved his HQ to Rangoon and made plans for the destruction of the remaining Japanese units on Burmese soil.

Much signalling and letter-writing had been going on at high level, unknown to either Slim or Christison. On 5 May, two days after his meeting with Mountbatten, when the matter of Slim's replacement had first come up, Leese had sent a long signal to Sir Alan Brooke, copying it to Mountbatten. It can be paraphrased as follows:

> 1. Now that the present phase of operations is finished, I consider that it is time for certain changes in command.
> 2. I propose forming HQ Burma Army, based on 33rd Corps, and wish to give the command to Slim who, having reconquered Burma, is now tired, and would like him to command and administer the country he has won.
> 3. I wish to put Christison in to 14th Army. He has immense experience of amphibious warfare and 14th Army's next operation will be predominantly

amphibious. He did well in DRACULA and I am confident that he can command an Army. I would like to carry out the Malayan operations with my old team of generals reshuffled.

4. I have not spoken to Slim or Christison and seek approval in principle before approaching them. Am visiting them 6 and 7 May. If you can give approval will get their reactions, then ask formal approval. Supremo agrees, having discussed.

When the news broke at Slim's HQ following Leese's visit there was consternation, followed by furious reaction. One of Slim's Liaison Officers remembers being called for by the Army Chief of Staff, Maj General 'Tubby' Lethbridge

. . . who straightway blurted out through a mixure of emotion, anger and Scotch, 'Uncle Bill has been sacked; he wants to see all of us senior staff at 10 am tomorrow' . . . I stood there speechless, wondering if Tubby had gonè round the bend . . .

Next morning, Slim assembled his immediate staff, and

. . . with a voice that never wavered and with words I shall never forget, said, 'I have a very painful announcement to make to you, gentlemen. Two days ago the C-in-C visited our HQ as you know and told me that I was unsuitable for the coming operations and could not command 14th Army further. I can't tell you what a painful announcement this is for me to make when, as you all will guess, I only have one ambition and that is to go on commanding 14th Army, of which I am extremely proud, until the Jap is finally beaten flat. But that is not to be. I have been offered command of 12th Army, the static army to be left behind to mop up the mess we have left the Japs in. I have refused. I have been asked to reconsider my decision and I am doing so to the extent that I am going off, now, to talk things over with my wife. I am not a rich man. I am telling you chaps now, who have helped me through so many tough spots before.

I want no mention of this outside these four walls; and I want no adverse criticism of it and no action on anyone's part in sympathy for me. There are higher loyalties you owe than just to me your immediate commander; you have your loyalty to your C-in-C and to your King and Country. That is all, gentlemen'. He turned and left us. Minutes later, it seemed, still in silence, we filed out with averted eyes; I knew that tears were falling down other cheeks as well as mine.

When Slim's staff had come to their senses after this bombshell they gave vent to their views: '. . . Sacked on the very day he'd achieved victory' . . . 'Oliver Twist and Mountbatten must be out of their minds . . . stark, raving mad' . . . 'I never trusted that affected, silk-handkerchief-waving Guardsman . . .' Morale sank to a low ebb. For many days there were no signs of further moves. An officer working closely with Slim at this time on the official despatch for the campaign noted, . . . 'Only once or twice did he mention his position and then only to repeat, ". . . and I'm sure I've done no wrong"'. There was to be no news for another three weeks. Meanwhile, Slim could be heard at night, endlessly pacing up and down his room.

His official biographer put a different interpretation on Leese's actions, which in his view stemmed from his increasingly uneasy relationship with the Supreme Commander. Before he left London for India, Leese had been advised by Montgomery, his former mentor, that Mountbatten was . . . 'a most delightful person but I fear his knowledge of how to make war is not very great. You ought to go out there as his Army C-in-C and keep him on the rails'.

On his arrival, however, Leese was to find that 14th Army was very firmly in Slim's hands and that he was increasingly serving Mountbatten as a senior courtier, spending much of his time travelling around the far-flung theatre. He soon crossed Mountbatten's bows on a relatively minor matter, rejecting one of Supremo's suggestions in a widely distributed signal; he had no appreciation that whilst Mountbatten was always open to advice, he was hypersensitive to public criticism or opposition. On this occasion Mountbatten was deeply hurt as well as extremely angry, privately telling his wife, Lady Edwina, that Leese was . . . 'A stupid, vain and dangerous man, and like all bullies, collapses when really stood up to'. This was as wrong-headed a judgement on Leese as it was unfair, but it coloured the relationship between the two men from then on, and it is reasonable to think that when the confrontation over Slim's position came up, it provided a reason for dispensing with the luckless Leese.

All accounts agree that it was on 3 May that Leese visited Kandy. Mountbatten later stated that he was surprised to be told that Slim was tired and that Christison should command Operation 'Zipper', the landings in Malaya. This does not entirely tie up with Christison's account of the meeting at Akyab a few days later, when Leese attributed the remarks about Slim's tiredness to Mountbatten, though adding himself, . . . 'and I must say I agree'. But it seemed to Christison that the idea of moving Slim had actually come from Mountbatten. From Akyab, Leese went up to Meiktila, where he saw Slim privately and asked for his views. At the end of this interview, which Slim reported to his staff as described above, Leese got the impression that Slim was '. . . at heart, happy'. He was wrong. Slim, was anything but happy.

Meanwhile, alarm bells were ringing in Whitehall. Brooke, as CIGS, was supposed to be consulted on all top military appointments in order that they could receive Churchill's approval. It now seemed that the selection and appointment of crucially important posts in the Far East had been taken out of his hands. Brooke was probably the most experienced operator in politico-military circles who has ever been the professional head of the British Army. He was outraged by what he regarded as Leese's gross breach of protocol. After careful thought he sent two signals on 18 May, one to

Mountbatten and one to Leese, making his views abundantly clear. The signal to Leese was in the following vein:

1. I wish to make it quite plain that I consider the manner in which you have attempted to carry out changes in highest appointments under your command has been most unsatisfactory and highly irregular.

2. You are serving under a Supreme Allied Commander to whom you should make proposals . . . no definite action could even then be taken without my approval or that of Secretary of State and possibly even PM . . .

3. No recommendations have been received from Supremo and now you repeat that you have discussed these proposed changes with Slim without anyone's approval.

4. I find it hard to understand how you can spare the service of General Slim at this juncture (he having been so successful in Burma) I . . . have discussed with Auchinleck (C-in-C India) and there is NO repeat NO employment for Slim in India. You seem to fail to understand officers cannot be returned to UK or India in this manner . . .

5. Under the circumstances I cannot approve the appointment of Christison for HQ 14th Army and consider Slim should remain in command unless you can produce very much better reasons for a change than you have done to date.

It is impossible not to sympathise with Leese at this point. He had been acting, as he thought, in the best interests of all and in conformity with what he saw as Mountbatten's wishes. Now he had received this broadside from the very man on whom his own professional future depended. There is no doubt that Brooke sensed this as well, from the tone of the signal which he sent on the same day to the Supreme Commander:

1. Leese has told me of suggestion that Slim should go from 14th Army to 'Burma Army' and Christison go to 14th Army.

2. He has put this tentatively to Slim who prefers India or the War Office.

3. Have told (Leese) that he should make any proposals to you, and await your recommendations.

4. Have expressed surprise and displeasures that he approached Slim, whose record is outstandingly successful . . . have told him I will not agree to his supersession by Christison.

5. There is NO repeat NO prospect of job for Slim in India, or elsewhere.

Signals now began to fly around as a major damage limitation exercise was mounted. Leese was summoned to see Mountbatten, and on 22 May he sent a personal signal to Slim. It confirmed that Lt General Stopford was to be given command of 12th Army and would sort out the rest of the campaign in Burma. Slim was to be entrusted with 14th Army and the forthcoming operations in Malaya. He was to report to HQ ALFSEA at Barrackpore on 24 May to discuss planning for these operations and some leave for himself. The signal ends: '. . . Supremo hopes you will return Rangoon for Victory parade.'

On the same day Mountbatten signalled Brooke to confirm that there were to be no changes in Army or Corps commanders, apart from the move of Stopford, as senior Corps commander, to command 12th Army. Brooke was glad to agree to this.

It seemed that all was settled and there was great joy at HQ 14th Army, where for three weeks there had been unrelieved gloom. Slim kept to himself, seeing few of his staff except those involved in drafting the official despatch on the campaign. Then, just as the HQ was about to close at Meiktila and move down to Rangoon, and the staff officers were waiting to get aboard the transport, the Assistant Military Secretary (the officer responsible for personnel matters affecting senior appointments) arrived, grinning, with a personal signal for Slim, who read it slowly in the privacy of his office. The listening staff then heard . . . 'At long last, an enormous deep chuckle or two . . . "Ha Ha Ha!" . . . and we were up the stairs . . . one look at Bill Slim's face, creased with smiles, was enough; things had come right, thank God.'

Slim had not only been spared the indignity wished upon him from above; he had been chosen to succeed Leese as C-in-C ALFSEA. In *Defeat into Victory* he dismisses the incident in a few words, but went as far as to draft an account which he decided to leave out of his book, mainly because those involved were still very much alive in the mid-fifties, and because he fought shy of provoking acrimonious debate which in his estimate would serve no useful purpose at the time.

In the unpublished account Slim mentions the visit of Leese to Meiktila on 7 May 1945. 'He abruptly said he had decided to make a change in its (14th Army's) command. This came as a complete shock to me.' It will be recalled, however, that a senior staff officer, Walsh, had already been sent to Slim to sound him out on the possibility of such changes, and one is driven to the conclusion that he failed entirely to get his message across. Slim continues:

> I asked who would replace me and was told it would be Christison. I enquired when, and (Leese) replied 'As soon as possible'. I agreed . . . General Leese then said I would remain in command in Burma and I demurred . . . it would reduce me to the status of a Corps commander . . . much better that I should go altogether. His answer was that it would mean the end of my military career.

Slim noted that Leese seemed disturbed by his subdued response to the proposals. Here he was absolutely correct, for Leese had not come prepared for a muted reaction, especially when Slim emphasised that he would make no public protest, would not even ask to see Mountbatten, and would go directly to India and ask to retire altogether. Slim did not even tell his senior officers – in the words already reported – until the morning of 9 May, and the Corps Commanders were in the dark until the 12th. The staffs of Army and

Corps HQs were now extremely restless and on 17 May Leese again sent Walsh to Meiktila where he assured Slim that he, Leese, had not lost any confidence in him, that there was no question of his being relegated to command of a Corps and that he would command their new 12th Army in Burma. As Slim made very clear, he did not consider this to be a worthwhile exchange for the Army he had led to victory, and Walsh returned, chastened no doubt, to his master.

On 23 May, after further flurries of letters and signals, Leese confirmed to Slim that he would after all remain in command of 14th Army. On the following day Slim flew to Calcutta and saw both Leese and Mountbatten at Barrackpore, where he confirmed his willingness to continue serving under Leese (although, privately, he felt that it would be 'without much confidence'). He then joined his wife and daughter for the happiest of reunions and flew home with them to England for some leave.

It might be thought that his arrival in the UK would have been the cause for considerable publicity of the type accorded to Montgomery following his victory at El Alamein, but this was not to be. Mountbatten's Chief of Staff, Browning, had informed him by signal that Slim and Leese 'had settled' and that the Slims should be flown home; but he recommended that for 'security purposes' there should be no public announcement. The reasoning behind this is obscure. The war in Europe was over and its skies were clear. Alexander's flight to Burma in 1942, much of it over enemy-held territory, had necessarily been a top secret undertaking, but there was now no excuse for denying Slim a measure of well-earned if belated public recognition. He met Churchill for the first time and in his own direct manner told the Prime Minister to his face that the troops of 14th Army would not be voting for him in the impending general election. He knew his men; they had loyally and stoically served their time in an extremely unpleasant campaign which they could all see had no valid cause. Burma was clearly on its way out of the Empire, and India on the verge of Independence and Partition. They had fought on because they wanted to destroy the Japanese army in Burma, and having done that they wanted to go home and get out of uniform.

The prospects held out by Attlee's Labour Party in the summer of 1945 appeared far more inviting than a return to the old ways of the 1930s, which is what the Conservatives seemed to be offering. With the undoubted help of the armed forces' vote, Churchill's wartime government fell to a sensational Labour landslide. Slim also met Clement Attlee, shortly to be Prime Minister in the postwar Labour administration. The two men immediately took to each other. They had much in common, both having seen action in Gallipoli in 1915, and each possessed qualities of compassion and humanity which characterised their respective public lives. It was Attlee who, in 1948, recalled Slim from retirement – he had joined the Board of British Railways in April that year – and appointed him Chief of the Imperial General Staff, promoting him Field Marshal in 1949.

As the Slims flew back to England, Mountbatten set about making his peace with Whitehall, and particularly with Brooke, to whom he wrote a long, almost ingratiating, letter on 7 June 1945. He began by saying that he had told Leese that the whole of 14th Army was seething with rumours . . . 'that their beloved Bill Slim had been sacked'. In order to put the PR record straight, and after consulting Lt Colonel Frank Owen the editor of 'SEAC', a photo call had been arranged before Slim emplaned for England, showing Supremo, Leese and Slim posing amicably together. This graced the pages of 'SEAC' on 3 June.

Mountbatten went on to describe the reactions of the senior Generals (Slim, Christison and Stopford) in the theatre, having had individual private talks with all of them in Delhi. Christison had reported on his startling meeting with Leese when, according to him, Leese opened with 'Congratulations. I have decided to give you 14th Army'. Christison had gone in good faith to tell his staff and duly celebrated with them. Later, Mountbatten wrote, 'Christison remarked very sadly that his position had been made very difficult . . .' Stopford, on the other hand, had clearly been given the impression by Leese that he was about to be removed from command of his Corps and he was surprised when, on 7 May, Leese asked him if he was prepared to serve with Slim in future. Leese, according to Mountbatten, had been putting it around that Slim and Stopford would not serve together, but this was not so; Slim had carpeted Stopford for some lapse or other, but it was taken in a proper spirit and they remained good friends. (When Stopford expressed his amazement at being given 12th Army, Mountbatten assured him that it was on his personal recommendation.)

Slim's private talk with Mountbatten is described in much the same way, reflecting adversely on Leese. Slim is reported as saying that after his first talk with Leese at Meiktila, he felt 'a great shock' and that he felt . . . 'he hadn't done too badly in the last 18 months . . . anyway as to be sacked in such ungracious terms . . .' Later, according to Mountbatten, Slim had told him that whilst he would continue to serve under Leese . . . 'I do not see how any of the Army or senior Commanders can have much faith in their C-in-C'. There is no corroboration of this in any of Slim's papers.

It is clear that in his lengthy letter to Brooke, Mountbatten is distancing himself from an immediate subordinate, Leese, who has compromised him by mishandling the removal of a specific officer, in this case Slim. Leese is blamed for virtually everything that has gone wrong. He is loathed, Mountbatten tells CIGS, by all in GHQ India because he had attempted to sack Slim, the Indian Army's most outstanding officer. At the same time, Mountbatten acknowledges that this will be the second C-in-C he has been obliged to sack (the first having been Giffard) and that it might be thought in London that it was he, not Giffard and Leese, who was at fault.

Mountbatten's letter ends rather lamely by stressing how well he and Leese had got on, that Leese was now . . . 'most apologetic and chastised (sic), and doing his best to sort things out, but that the confidence of the staffs was badly undermined.' There is a very strong hint that Mountbatten would not entirely mind if Leese were to be removed, for he ends:

It is extremely difficult to do the right thing in a straightforward and honourable way, when so much distrust and suspicion has already been sown by *actions which took place outside my control* [author's italics]
Yours very Sincerely
Dickie Mountbatten

Brooke responded by personal signal on 19 June, making the following comments on Leese, in what must be seen as a deliberate move to get Mountbatten off the horns of a largely self-induced dilemma:

1. He (Leese) had now lost the confidence of most of his senior commanders (but not, as it happened, of Christison, who despite the embarrassment caused to him personally, was able to understand Leese's position).
2. He had put himself in a position where Slim would find it difficult to serve under him.
3. He had lost the confidence of the staff at GHQ India, where feelings towards him had never been other than cool.
4. He had quarrelled with Naval, Air and American commanders.
5. He had acted . . . 'against your instructions . . . as you say, "he has certainly started off on the wrong foot"' . . .
6. 'All things considered . . . can only assume that you too have lost confidence in Leese.'
7. 'You ask for advice; this is what I would do. There is no alternative to replacing Leese as soon as possible . . . I fear that (Leese) has found himself unsuited to his present employment.'
8. Brooke goes on to express his appreciation of Mountbatten's concern over the sacking of two Land Force commanders in succession . . .' there is no comparison with the effects of keeping him on.'
9. 'If considering change would you consider Slim as possible replacement for Leese . . . should you decide that Oliver Leese should go you can reply on my full support.'

This was the end for the unfortunate Leese. He was the first to admit to his mistakes and never, to the end of his life, indulged in recriminations. He had tried to do his duty in an honourable manner but freely conceded that by taking out his 'circus' of 8th Army staff officers in the first place he had committed a cardinal error. Far too many of them had angered the predominantly 'Indian' staff at ALFSEA, HQ India and 14th Army with their confident assertions that the only way to win the war was by adopting 8th Army's procedures and methods. On 2 July, Mountbatten wrote to Brooke, having sacked Leese. He had eagerly seized the lifebelt thrown from Whitehall. After expressing his gratitude for the CIGS's advice and support he concludes:

> I thought it would interest you to know that Auchinleck, Power (the naval C-in-C), Park (Air Officer in Chief), Wheeler (Senior US Officer) and Browning (Chief of Staff SEAC, who had succeeded the sacked Pownall) have all gone out of their way to express their great satisfaction that Slim should be relieving Leese.

Despite Mountbatten's earlier wish that Slim would be sent back in Rangoon for the victory parade, he did not return to the theatre until 14 August 1945. The atomic bombs had already been dropped on Hiroshima and Nagasaki, and the war against Japan was over. The Rangoon parade had come and gone back in June, very soon after Slim's departure on leave. Mountbatten stood on the saluting base, clad in immaculate naval white uniform, as torrential rain poured down on the soggy ranks of those marching and driving past, watched by crowds of distinctly apathetic Burmans.

At Kandy, amidst the unfamiliar panoply of that strange headquarters with its myriad staff officers, advisers, hangers-on and servants, Slim quickly mastered the work required of his new post. He got on well with Mountbatten, who later wrote of him that:

> I had picked him out on first meeting him at Barrackpore in October 1943 as the man whom I wished to fight the Burman campaign . . .

But Slim was not to remain at Kandy for long. The huge headquarters began to wind down, and he left in November 1945 to take up the post of Commandant at the Imperial Defence College in London.

SOVIET T
ON DN

MOSCOW, Sunday: The trial centre of the Ukraine work. spells the beginning Dnieper bend.

The Soviet break-throu yesterday serious threatens the Krivoi Rog-Nikopol sector they will be cut off.

Stalin, in his Order of the I says: "Our troops penetrated the line to a depth of 23 miles an 80-mile front.

"Three German tank divisi one mechanised division and f infantry divisions were route

"In commemoration of the tory, the units which took par the capture of Kirovograd henceforward assume the n of the city."

Laid Down Their Arms

Describing the capture, Soviet communiqué said: "tanks broke into the south-w and south-east outskirts while fantry came out on the no West suburbs and engaged Germans in street fighting.

"In fighting at the approac to Kirovograd and in its sim the Germans suffered enorm losses Many German units occ resistance, and laid down th arms."

In the Vinnitsa region troop the First Ukrainian Army h

SEAC

DAILY NEWSPAPER OF SOUTH EAST ASIA COMMAND

No. 1   MONDAY, 10 JANUARY, 1944   ONE ANNA

Printed by courtesy of THE STATESMAN in Calcutta.

Good Morning!

First light is breaking over this awakening city as the birthday issue of SEAC (pronounce it See-ack) comes flying off the presses. The baby weighs totally 312 lbs and is expected to grow up to be the Greatest Little Giant in the World.

SEAC is produced in the head offices of The Statesman, Calcutta for the men of the South East Asia Command in the forwardmost areas. The printing and publishing are done free of cost to us, & generous war gift by The Statesman, enabling us to sell for one anna only. The policies and editorial staffs of SEAC and The Statesman are separate. Neither one of them is in any way responsible

BIRTH

So SEAC is born and Admiral Lord Louis Mountbatten writes our birth notice here, directs our aims and gives us fatherly advice.

✻

TODAY the Naval, Military and Air Forces of the South East Asia Command have their own daily newspaper. It has always seemed to me essential that there should be a daily newspaper for all ranks and ratings in any command.

Fortunately, the task of producing such a paper for us has been undertaken by Frank Owen, who left the editorship of the "Evening Standard" in Lon-

239

A Lee/Grant tank fords a stream north
of Imphal. Note the 75mm gun, and the
37mm gun with all-round traverse in
the commander's turret. Lee/Grants
were obsolete at this stage of the
war, and had been largely replaced by
Shermans. But they served well enough
as infantry support tanks in Burma, and
were dreaded by the Japanese. (*IWM*)

HMS *Una*, launched by Slim on 9 April 1945, and named after his daughter. With a sister ship, HMS *Pamela*, she was commissioned for armed escort duty on the Chindwin and the Irrawaddy. Armed with a Bofors gun, twin Vickers guns and an Oerlikon cannon, she was powered by three Ford V-8 engines and had a maximum speed of 10 knots. Living conditions on board were appalling, but the crews stuck to their job and both ships saw combat. *(The Hon Mrs Una Rowcliffe)*

In the absence of arrester wires and hooks, members of the crew of the escort carrier HMS *Khedive* rush forward to bring safely under control an Auster light aircraft of 656 Air OP Squadron RAF, flown by an officer of the Royal Artillery. *(IWM/Museum of Army Flying)*

A hero's return.
A garlanded Naik Nand Singh VC
comes home to his village in
Patiala and receives his proud
mother's blessing. *(IWM)*

Despite their antiquated
appearance, Japanese artillery
pieces were remarkably
effective, and invariably well-
served by crews who stayed with
their guns until killed. *(IWM)*

A Japanese 'tankette', which clearly owes
its design to the Vickers light tanks of
the early 1930s, is towed away for close
inspection near Tamu in August 1944. *(IWM)*

Maj Gen 'Pete' Rees, the energetic
commander of 19 Indian Division, cracks
jokes with his men as they make their
way forward. *(IWM)*

Men of the 9th Royal Sussex Regiment, in 36 Division, take up their positions while Maj Gen Frank Festing, inseparable from his pipe, chats to a mortarman at the side of the track. *(IWM)*

During the drive for Meiktila in March 1945, Indian troops lie in wait for a group of Japanese infantrymen about to break cover from a blazing house in the village of Seywa. *(IWM)*

Commandos go ashore at Myebon from landing
craft of the Royal Indian Navy, in March 1945.
This landing was soon followed by the fighting
for Kangaw, held to be one of the bloodiest
engagements of the entire Burma war. *(IWM)*

The victors. Slim with Chambers of 26
Division and Air Vice-Marshal Vincent in
Rangoon, soon after its recapture. *(IWM)*

Twelve months after their epic fight at Kohima, men of the 4th Royal
West Kents pay a final visit to the battlefield before returning home.
In the foreground is the temporary grave of Lance Corporal Harman, VC.
After the war all 2nd Division's dead were re-interred in the
beautiful cemetery adjacent to the house of the former District
Commissioner at the top of the ridge.   (*IWM*)

The Last Act

"Play what you like as long as it's not the 'Charge'!"

THE FALL OF Rangoon, the culminating point of 14th Army's campaign, passed almost unnoticed in a Europe whose people were either deliriously celebrating the end of the war against Germany or, if on the losing side, emerging from their shelters to look around in shock and disbelief at all the many sights of defeat and destruction. It was however, essential that pressure against the Japanese armies be maintained, particularly in Burma where they had to be given no chance of regrouping for a stand on the line of the Sittang River, the only logical line of defence left to them.

General Kimura's Burma Area Army was in disarray. Two of its components, 15th and 33rd Armies, had suffered heavy casualties at Imphal, then at Mandalay and Meiktila. Sakurai's 28th Army, formerly in the Arakan, had regrouped in the hills north of Pegu. A sizeable mixture of formations which had survived the Meiktila battle were trapped for the time being in the area between Meiktila and the Yenanyaung oilfield, preparing to break out east towards the Sittang. Another, larger group had already redeployed east of the Rangoon-Toungoo road in the Sittang valley. The surviving elements of 15th and 33rd Armies had been ordered to exert themselves to the limit and hold open an escape route for 28th Army. All the time, small parties of Japanese were filtering across Lower Burma, making their way east, succumbing to ambushes laid across their path, some by British and Indian units, others by Aung San's Patriots whose ranks included many former Burma Rifles soldiers, well-equipped and trained. Even more dispiriting for the Japanese, especially those travelling in small parties burdened with their sick and the pathetic 'comfort girls' from the military brothels, were the activities of Burmese villagers. Infuriated by the systematic looting carried out by the Japanese, they turned on the recent occupation force: Japanese falling into their hands could not expect mercy or even a quick death. British troops who came across the scenes of native ambushes were sickened by what they found: gold teeth hacked from the jaws of their owners while the victims were still alive and disembowelling of the sick and wounded were among the least of the atrocities committed.

To prepare for the invasion of Malaya, planned for August and September, a rapid reorganisation of ALFSEA now took place under the temporary command of Lt General Sir Philip Christison, who took up his headquarters in Rangoon. His former Corps HQ moved back to India to form part of the new 14th Army, and for intensive amphibious warfare training prior to the Malayan operation. The remaining British and Indian formations in Burma, 4 and 33 Corps, were regrouped as 12th Army, commanded by Lt General Sir Montague Stopford, whose orders were to complete the destruction of the remaining Japanese forces on Burmese soil.

The exceptionally heavy rains of the monsoon added to the misery of Kimura's troops as they struggled to retain a semblance of order. They were short of rations, fuel and ammunition; disease claimed thousands of victims. Despite the weather, the RAF attacked anything that moved on the roads and the Japanese were forced to move only by night.

The 12th Army now enjoyed the benefits of total air supremacy as all signs of the Japanese army's air support had long since vanished. Forward units were accompanied by Visual Air Support Teams in which fighter pilots travelling in radio jeeps could call on the services of 'cabranks' – flights of fighter-bombers wheeling overhead – to strike any target with great precision. Once Magwe airfield had been made serviceable, the fighter-bombers operated from only 50 miles behind the forward troops, giving remarkable speed of response to calls from the Air Support Teams. This, in conjunction with artillery support (which, unlike the fighter-bombers, could operate day and night and in any weather) kept the Japanese on the run. Their radio communications were now only fitful and it became hard for them to maintain contact between their scattered units except through couriers; and these, as they found to their cost, could be intercepted.

Food became a grave problem for the Japanese once the villages had been stripped of supplies. Rice and bamboo shoots were staple fare, eked out with snakes, rats, birds and whatever fish could be caught in streams and lakes. Although water was no problem at that time of year, lack of salt was. Troops engaged on strenuous operations sweat out a litre of fluid an hour, and with it about two grammes of salt, which has to be replaced in one form or another. It now became a very rare commodity in the battered Burma Area Army as it tried to find trouble-free routes to the east. Even in its hour of travail, however, the Japanese army remained dangerous; most of its soldiers still fought to the death, but individuals were now beginning to surrender rather than take the usual way out with a grenade. One Japanese officer caused great amusement, not least to 12th Army's gunners, by surrendering with the words, 'Don't shoot. I am non-combatant. I am artillery officer'.

West of the Sittang the low-lying ground had flooded, and the only means of surface movement were by country boat or on causeways. The going became impossible for 12th Army's tanks and the campaign's pace slowed to that of the marching infantry. Across central and lower Burma small but fierce engagements flared as retreating Japanese were brought to battle. It reflects great credit on 12th Army that pressure was maintained at this difficult time; many British units were well below strength, as personnel who had served more than three years and eight months overseas were now sent home. In July, for instance, two battalions, the 2nd King's Own Scottish Borderers and 2nd South Lancashire, had to be taken out of action as their strength had fallen below 50 per cent. However 4 Corps, operating in the Sittang valley, had closed up to the river line and was in continual contact with the fleeing enemy.

A large Japanese force was still trapped west of the Sittang and another force of 2,000 was located east of the river. All signs pointed to its use in a desperate thrust across the Sittang to divert attention as Lt General Sakurai's 28th Army made its bid for freedom. Further Japanese forces were identified to the north near Toungoo. Messervy, commanding 4 Corps, strengthened the protective cordon with which he intended to block any break-out to the east.

At the beginning of June, Sakurai's army, numbering some 30,000 men, was deployed around the Pegu Yomas, ready for the break-out. This could not be postponed much longer because of mounting sickness and shortage of supplies. Failure of radio communications meant that Sakurai had only the haziest notion of the whereabouts of other surviving Japanese formations. He knew, however, that remnants of the other two armies were waiting for him on the far side of the Sittang, ready to retreat south towards Tenasserim, where it was intended to regroup and make a stand. His problem was to find a way through the cordon and get across the river, still in full spate and likely to be so for several weeks. He knew this would involve very heavy casualties, but the only alternatives were death by disease and starvation, or surrender. He carefully reviewed the situation in his HQ at Pinmenzali, 100 miles north of Rangoon and some 50 miles west of the Sittang, and decided to make the attempt on 20 July, despite the protests of some of his subordinates who considered that this gave insufficient time to prepare ad hoc river-crossing equipment. Each man in 28th Army was to carry three 4-metre lengths of rope made from rattan, and pairs of men were to carry between them a 5-metre bamboo pole, 34 of which made a primitive raft to support ten swimming men and their equipment. Given the swift flow of the Sittang this was a desperate expedient.

The chosen crossing sites were south of Toungoo and 28th Army was split into four main groups, each with its own crossing site. Preparations went ahead and Sakurai's troops braced themselves for the final effort. Meanwhile, on 2 July a chance encounter between a patrol of 1/7th Gurkha Rifles and a Japanese column on the fringes of the Pegu Yomas had resulted in an outstanding Intelligence coup. A number of maps and documents found on the bodies of dead Japanese officers were taken to HQ 17 Division.

Here there was an Intelligence section in which was serving Lt Levy, a former university languages tutor who, because of his ability to learn almost any language quickly, had been sent on an intensive Japanese course in 1944 and posted to the Burma theatre. He immediately recognised the significance of the maps and papers; they were nothing less than the complete break-out plan for Sakurai's 28th Army. Working day and night, Levy and his small section translated and interpreted the mass of documentation and sent copies to all formations in 4 Corps by 7 July. A copy was on Mountbatten's desk in Delhi by 16 July. All was spelt out in minute detail, right down to the number of spare shoes and nails to be carried for each packhorse on the line of march.

Messervy ordered reinforcements of artillery, tanks and infantry to the crossing areas shown on the Japanese plans, between Pyu and Nyaunglebin. Further south, in the area around the Sittang bridge of unhappy memory, the Japanese 33rd Army began a diversionary attack on 3 July to draw Messervy away from the main 28th Army crossing sites. Soon, three Japanese divisions, albeit down to a strength of about 3,000 apiece, had moved against one brigade of 7 Indian Division, whose most vulnerable outpost was at Nyaungkashe, about three miles from the west end of the Sittang Bridge. Here, the 4/8th Gurkha Rifles held positions only a few inches above flood water level. No digging was possible and movement was restricted to causeways and dykes. The Japanese, on higher ground across the river, were able to overlook the whole of the flood plain. The Gurkhas' position soon became untenable, and on the night of 7 July they marched out across the flooded plain to the west in a hollow square, their wounded in the middle. Three of 136th Field Regiment's 25-pounder guns, breech blocks removed and dial sights smashed, had to be left behind; they were the only guns lost to the enemy by 7 Division in the entire campaign, and it hurt to abandon them, if only temporarily, in the closing rounds of the battle.

For the stocky Gurkhas it was a difficult march; the flood waters were at least four feet deep and few of the riflemen could swim. However, the Japanese were too exhausted to pursue. With daylight came the realisation that the enemy had also retired. During the following days, there were some bitterly fought engagements in the bridge area, notably on 27 July when a patrol of the 1st Queen's clashed head-on with a Japanese force, killing over 30 Japanese in hand-to-hand fighting, but sustaining almost as many casualties themselves.

Gunners and Gurkhas

For the last six months of the campaign, 136th Field Regiment had been with 89th Indian Infantry Brigade, providing fire support for the 2nd King's Own Scottish Borderers, 1/11th Sikh Regiment and 4/8th Gurkha Rifles, who paid them a handsome compliment after the battle of Sittang bend, where the gunners had been forced to leave three guns which could not be moved because of floods:

Nearby we found the Battery from 136 Field Regiment . . . who had given us such excellent support during all our troubles in the front line; a finer bunch of people you could not find. They admired the Gurkhas and the Gurkhas liked them, and their officers and ours might well have belonged to the same unit, so intimate and friendly was the give and take . . .

The breakout of 28th Army was the climactic disaster for the Japanese, and has been likened to a gigantic, well-organised pheasant shoot. All 4 Corps' formations had copies of Sakurai's marked maps and as the Japanese, in dozens of small parties, closed on the river from the west they were killed in hundreds. For almost three weeks they continued to arrive; few even reached the river without heavy casualties sustained in ambushes. Sakurai was still moving on horseback with his devoted staff. He reached the Sittang very early on the morning of 28 July, and gazed on the river with mixed feelings. This had been the scene of his greatest triumph; now he watched as the strong current bore hundreds of his men downstream to their deaths, powerless to help them as they cried out in their extremity. His staff found a small boat and forced him to board it, one of the last to go over, at 2 am on 28 July. Looking back, he could still see the dark figures of drowned and drowning men passing down the river. Sakurai's horse also drowned and he now found himself riding again on an ox, as he had been forced to do at one point during the flight from the Arakan.

For two more weeks the Headquarters group of 28th Army trekked south through the dense forest, heading towards Moulmein in Tenasserim, where it was hoped to rally the remnants of Burma Army and turn on that relentless pursuit. On 15 August, however, the Emperor decided that Japan had suffered enough and signed an Imperial Rescript telling his people they must 'endure the unendurable' and surrender. Sakurai heard the news but pressed on south, until on the evening of 18 August he crossed the Salween estuary and arrived at Moulmein, to be greeted by the commander of Burma Area Army – or what was left of it.

Earlier that day General Kimura had signed the instruction commanding all Japanese troops in Burma to lay down their arms and sent it out, together with the Emperor's Rescript, to all known unit locations. So great was the chaos into which the Japanese had fallen that it was many days before isolated stragglers heard the news; even then many did not believe it, thinking it was a British ruse. Stopford had ordered his men to stop fighting on 15 August, but it was not until the 22nd that the first formal surrenders began to occur. Some, like the surrender overtures of Honda's 33rd Army, contained a measure of farce; a delegation from 4 Corps made contact with Honda's staff, represented by several officers, an NCO carrying a white flag, and a bugler who was most anxious to know what he should play on meeting the British delegates. Obviously there was no 'surrender' call in the Japanese military music manual and none of the distracted officers in the party seemed to know what to do. When the British team came in sight, the bugler looked back over his shoulder in agonised indecision, to be told 'Play what you like as long as it's not the "Charge!"'

On the day that Kimura signed the cease-fire order at Moulmein, Slim returned to the Far East as C-in-C ALFSEA, and Christison took over 14th Army in India. It now consisted of 15 and 34 Corps and was training hard for the re-occupation of Malaya. Known as Operation 'Zipper' it would take place over the beaches of the west coast of Malaya at Port Dickson. It was fortunate that this was not an opposed landing as the beaches had been inadequately surveyed, and many of the heavily laden landing craft ran aground on offshore sandbanks; they would have provided Japanese gunners with juicy targets, and the loss of life would have been appalling.

Postlude

"An Army passes, but its loves remain,
Freedom – and a way home through jungle rain."

ONCE OPERATION 'Zipper' had been launched, a sense of anti-climax began to pervade the Allied forces in the Far East. Thousands of men were now driven solely by the urge to get home and out of uniform as quickly as possible to resume normal life, in what they trusted would be as agreeable a world as that painted in the recently-victorious Labour Party's election manifesto. The majority of Far East servicemen and women had, after all, voted Attlee into power and were looking forward to a share in the better life he had promised.

As the British re-established their rule over Burma, Malaya, Borneo, Sarawak and Hong Kong – at times fully aware that the locals were not universally overjoyed to see them back – the French and Dutch were also attempting to regain the *status quo* lost so dramatically, and easily, to the Japanese onrush of 1941. Problems immediately arose in the Dutch East Indies, where the Japanese surrender left a vacuum which both the Dutch and the strong Indonesian Nationalist movement tried to fill. The latter were at once seen to be the stronger, for the Dutch, weakened by five years of German occupation, were in no condition to re-assert their presence militarily, and the British and Indian armies were obliged to go in to keep order. Allied Forces Netherlands East Indies, or AFNEI, was therefore established under the command of Lt General Sir Philip Christison, whose thankless task it was to maintain law and order and save human life.

The situation had been complicated by the Japanese, who had set up a Fatherland Defence Force during their occupation. Its 69 battalions of locally-recruited troops, officered by Indonesians and trained on Japanese lines, existed as an auxiliary defence force and had not been intended by the Japanese to be the cadre of a national liberation army; but this is what they became. In addition, the Japanese had trained a large guerilla force which formed the hard core of resistance to the Anglo-Dutch forces when they returned in August 1945, the month in which the Republic of Indonesia was proclaimed by Achmed Sukarno. After five years of bitter fighting, the Dutch acknowledged Indonesian Independence in 1950. In 1945, however, the Allies had to deal with several other locally-raised military organisations, including 26,000 members of the Hei-Ho, a sort of Indonesian Home Guard officered by Japanese. The British managed to rescue thousands of civilian internees from Japanese prison camps, but failed to keep the peace between Indonesians and Dutch, and it was with great relief that the British and Indian formations left in 1946.

Mountbatten continued as Supreme Commander until 1946, when the headquarters at Kandy was finally closed down. His performance since 1943 had earned him great prestige in South-East Asia and he was a natural choice as the last Viceroy of India, succeeding Wavell in February 1947, with a remit from Attlee's government to preside over the transfer of power to an independent united India. He had not long been in New Delhi when it became clear that irreconcilable differences between Hindu and Muslim would make it impossible to create a single state out of British India, and Mountbatten had to work towards a practicable partitioning between the two major religious groupings and their respective political leaders, Jawaharlal Nehru and Mohamed Ali Jinnah. The creation of India and Pakistan took place amidst scenes of nation-wide carnage, during which the Indian Army, to the grief of those who had served it for so long, was broken up and divided between the two new states, retaining its discipline to the end.

The bloody shambles marking the emergence of India and Pakistan as two sovereign states was a source of great sadness to Mountbatten and to all who had served India and its peoples for generations in the Indian Army. So great was the young Viceroy's prestige that he was invited to become India's first Governor-General as she took her place among the members of the Commonwealth. But in 1948 he returned to Britain to resume his naval career, for there was another ambition to be realised. To his infinite satisfaction he was appointed First Sea Lord in 1955 and felt that he had obtained due reparation for the wrong done to his father in 1914. Mountbatten still had further to go, for in 1959 he became the first holder of the new post of Chief of the Defence Staff. He was now an Admiral of the Fleet and had been created Earl Mountbatten of Burma.

Laden with honours, he continued to lead a full life until murdered by the IRA in 1979. As Supreme Commander South-East Asia he had been one of Churchill's inspired choices, for although – as Montgomery had said to Leese – he had initially little or no idea how to wage war at the highest level, he had all the attributes needed to captivate the Allies and motivate the vast multi-national array of sailors, soldiers and airmen under his command. He was also quick to learn. With the backing of the energetic and purposeful Edwina, he put a special stamp on SEAC which marked it out as something different from anything else on the Allied side. He knew how to use his considerable influence to get what he wanted for his Command. He knew, for example, that when he hijacked a considerable portion of the USAAF's transport fleet in 1944, nobody would dare to gainsay him, not even Stilwell. His weak point lay in his overweening personal vanity; he could not abide criticism or the disagreement of subordinates. His relationship with Slim was ambiguous, and his handling of Leese, whilst not as contemptible as Montgomery's treatment of his Chief of Staff, de Guingand, effectively killed Leese's career.

At the end of the war problems arose over the disposal of the returning Indian National Army Soldiers. There were some 25,000 'Jifs' at the time of the Japanese surrender, most of them former members of the Indian Army. Although there was pressure in some quarters to treat them all as liable to court-martial on charges of 'bearing arms against the King-Emperor' (a capital offence) sheer numbers rendered this impossible. Wiser counsels prevailed, notably those of Field Marshal Auchinleck, who as an old Indian Army hand fully understood – indeed sympathised with – the predicament in which so many young jawans had found themselves early in their captivity. The returned soldiers were therefore categorised as 'White' – men who had not behaved in a notably disloyal way, of whom there were 3880, 'Grey', those who had been moderately active in the INA and held posts of responsibility (13,211) and 'Black', those who had been prominent and were known to have taken part in atrocities or other extreme activities (6177). The 'Whites' were offered reinstatement in the army with no loss of seniority, and the 'Greys' dismissed the service with 40 days' paid leave. Many of the 'Blacks' were brought to trial, but public uproar leading to serious riots persuaded the authorities to drop proceedings. Instead, many prominent INA men became national heroes in the new India.

Subhas Chandra Bose would certainly have faced trial on charges of treason had he survived, national hero or not; but he was killed in a plane crash, probably while trying to escape to the Soviet Union after the Japanese surrender. For many years the Indian Government's attitude towards his memory was ambivalent, but in 1992 it was decided to bestow on him, posthumously, the nation's highest award, the Bharat Ratna or Jewel of India. This had already been awarded to members of the Nehru family – Jawaharlal (Pandit) Nehru, his daughter Indira and her son Rajiv. It had also been accepted by distinguished foreigners such as Mother Teresa and Nelson Mandela. Bose's family, however, turned down the award indignantly. It will be recalled that when he was in Germany at the beginning of World War 2, Bose married a Austrian lady, who subsequently gave birth to his daughter, now Anita Bose-Pfaff, a fifty-year-old professor of economics at Augsburg University. Professor Bose-Pfaff and Bose's nephew both claimed that as 'Netaji' – the name by which Bose was generally known by his supporters – was ignored for years by the Nehrus, the belated recognition was irrelevant. A somewhat chastened spokesman for the ruling Congress Party accepted this, but added that '. . . the Nation is grateful to Netaji and proud of him being a son of India.'

Aung San and his Burmese Patriot Forces were well placed at the end of the war. The former BNA was legitimised and, with the rapid departure of British forces on demobilisation, formed the cadre of the reconstituted Burma Rifles. The fine service of the hill tribes during the war was acknowledged by the re-raising of Karen, Chin and Kachin battalions, but the 1st, 3rd, 4th, 5th and 6th battalions were now exclusively Burmese units, as were a number of Military Police battalions. All these were predominantly ex-BNA men, giving Aung San a strong military power base. Yet more ex-BNA soldiers were enlisted into Aung San's personal army, known as the Peoples' Volunteer Organisation (PVO), effectively the military wing of the Anti-Fascist Peoples' Freedom League or AFPFL. This strong political organisation soon came into direct opposition with the newly restored but toothless colonial government. Faced with the sight of the PVO drilling with weapons in the streets, the Governor conceded Aung San's demands for immediate independence, inviting him to form a government, which he did in 1947, having extracted a promise of full independence within twelve months. However, Aung San had not, as the Governor seemed to think, convinced the hill tribes that he was the legitimate leader of his nation, and the Communists also entered the lists against him. They bore him a grudge because he had earlier purged them from the AFPFL. He also had a number of determined political rivals, notably U Saw, the pre-war Prime Minister, exiled by the British but now returned. The nation was in political turmoil, but if there were numerous Burmese parties and sects struggling for power, virtually all of them agreed on one issue; they wanted the British out as quickly as possible, and for an independent Burma to leave the British Commonwealth.

In April 1947, Aung San gained a spectacular victory in the General Elections for the new Constituent Assembly, but his triumph was short-lived. Only three months later, U Saw's gunmen burst into a cabinet meeting and slaughtered Aung San and all but one of his cabinet, the survivor having been party to the plot. U Saw and Aung San's assassins died soon after in a revenge killing, but the damage had been done. Aung San showed great promise as a young and charismatic leader who had moderated his former extreme policies and was on the way to uniting the peoples of Burma. Within 18 months of Independence, civil war was raging. Burma has reverted to its ancient name of Myanmar; it is still a beautiful land populated by charming and handsome people but stability is still far off. Aung San's daughter, Aung San Suu Kyi who won hands down in the first more or less democratically-run elections in years, has been unable to take post as prime minister and lies under house arrest in Rangoon. As in so many other former colonial possessions around the world, Independence did not bring bliss in its wake. Recent visitors, although severely restricted to areas where their safety can be assured, have found abundant evidence of the war in the hundreds of ancient military vehicles still serving as tractors in the teak forests.

Mountbatten decided that the surrender of the Japanese in the Far East would be conducted ceremonially and with maximum publicity. He was determined that the Japanese officer class, which he blamed for the militaristic development of their country, should be publicly humiliated by parades at which they would surrender their swords. A Japanese officer's sword was his most treasured possession. Many were exquisite examples of the swordsmith's art, dating back to the Middle Ages. A series of surrender parades and ceremonies was ordered, the culmination being the one held in Singapore, where all the stops were pulled out in an effort to exorcise the memory of Britain's abject surrender there in 1942. The sword he had earmarked for himself was that of Field Marshal Count Terauchi, Commander-in-Chief of Japan's forces in South-East Asia and thus his opposite number.

Terauchi, distinguished member of an ancient noble family, had met Mountbatten 20 years before in Tokyo, when the latter had accompanied the Prince of Wales on a world tour aboard the battle-cruiser HMS *Renown* which included a visit to Japan. The two aristocrats had got on well then, and Mountbatten was anxious to treat Terauchi honourably even as he deprived him of the ancient sword. Unfortunately, by August 1945 Terauchi, afflicted by a stroke, was a very sick man, unable to attend the Singapore ceremony. Mountbatten accepted the medical report and had Terauchi installed in a comfortable house on the Malayan mainland in Johore, where the old soldier died shortly after. His sword, however, went to the conqueror, and hangs to this day at Broadlands, the Hampshire home of the Mountbatten family. In holding these surrender ceremonies Mountbatten and Slim ignored the arrogant order given by Gen Douglas MacArthur (C-in-C Pacific Theatre) that senior Japanese officers were not to be publicly humiliated by having to give up their swords. MacArthur had no business to attempt to impose such an edict and it was disregarded in South-East Asia Command.

General Yamomoto's sword was handed over by its owner to Lt General Sir Philip Christison. For over 40 years it hung in his home at Melrose in the Borders, to which he returned on his retirement from the Army in 1949. He dedicated the following years to public activities, most of which were voluntary, and farmed his orchards. As a boy he had been a chorister of Edinburgh Cathedral and music vied with history and the study of wildlife amongst his many interests and relaxations. Well into his nineties he sang in his parish choir and at one time was a member of the BBC's Scottish Committee on Music, Piping and Gaelic Language. In the mid-eighties he decided that it was time Yamamoto's sword went home, and had it returned to the family of the long-dead Japanese General, an act questioned in some quarters but which did not surprise anyone who ever met this upright and generous-hearted soldier. A delighted letter was received in due course from the Yamamoto family, together with a photograph showing the sword hanging at the family shrine above the urn containing General Yamomoto's ashes. When questioned about this gesture, Christison would reply that, as a Christian, he had always been taught to forgive one's enemies. 'But' – with a grin – 'that doesn't mean you must *forget* . . .!'

Leese's fall from grace after the 'sacking' of Slim deprived the Army of a fine leader. He never complained, and on his return to England reported, as required, to Brooke at the War Office. The CIGS was saddened by the whole incident, and by Leese's demeanour, which was contrite and apologetic. He held one more post, as GOC Eastern Command, but his heart was no longer in it and he retired, still a Lieutenant General. His latter years – he died in 1978 – were dogged by ill health which involved the loss of a leg; but he derived much pleasure from his Presidency of the MCC in 1965 and the affection of his many friends. Described by all who knew him as being as straight as a die, he had plenty of professional ability and showed it as Commander of 8th Army; but he lacked the guile needed for the sort of position in which he found himself at ALFSEA. His error of taking with him the staff who had done well in Italy but had no experience whatever 'East of Suez' left him without the advice which would have been given gladly by Giffard's staff, had they not been displaced by the 'circus'.

Wavell, whose lot it was to preside over the loss of Singapore and Burma as well as so much else in the face of the Japanese onslaught, was perhaps one of the most attractive leaders the British Army ever had. Scholarly, ill at ease when talking informally to soldiers, but a great trainer of men and an imaginative commander, he had the misfortune to be near the top of his profession at the very beginning of a major war, notoriously the time when the heads of Britain's armed forces pay the penalty for the neglect and parsimony of politicians. It is inconceivable that, given the resources available to Wavell on his assumption of the post at ABDA, he could have saved the day. The damage had been done years before, in Whitehall and New Delhi, by Treasury officials bent on balancing their budgets and political placemen intent on holding on to office, heedless of the long-term effects. These were the men who, from their cool offices hundreds and thousands of miles away, sent the Glosters to war a shadow of what a regular infantry battalion should be, and condemned the retreating Burma Army to the unopposed attentions of the enemy's air power.

Wavell did, however, make one fundamental mistake and that was persistently to under-estimate the enemy, despite everything he was told by men who had actually fought the Japanese. After handing over his Viceregal duties to Mountbatten in February 1947, Wavell became an Earl and was appointed Constable of the Tower of London and Lord Lieutenant of the County of London, but he did not enjoy these honours for long. He died in May 1950 and, at his own request, was buried in the cloisters of Winchester College, his old school and a place he loved. Three years later his son, the Second Earl, followed him. He had survived the second Chindit expedition, losing a hand in the process, but fell to a stray bullet during a skirmish with Mau Mau terrorists in Kenya.

Slim had greatly impressed Attlee when the two met during the summer of 1945, and it is not surprising that the Labour Prime Minister called him out of retirement in 1948 after he had served barely a year as Deputy Chairman of British Railways. He was appointed as Chief of the Imperial General Staff by Attlee in succession to Montgomery, a conspicuous failure in the job, who instigated an ineffectual and petty-minded campaign to have Slim excluded. Slim brought to his task all his qualities of humanity at a time when the Army was without direction or a sense of purpose, run down and existing on wartime stocks of equipment which were rapidly becoming obsolete.

From whatever aspect, here was a great man. No courtier, and virtually unknown in Whitehall's corridors of power, his physical and moral courage were unquestioned. The latter, as he explained in a talk to the Police College in 1948, shortly before his appointment as CIGS, is

> . . . to do what you believe is right, no matter what may be the consequences to yourself. Often it means doing something which is unpopular . . . in Burma, as you may have heard, one of the things I used to insist on was discipline, and this included men saluting officers, and officers *returning* their salute. Sometimes when a man failed to salute, the young officer would fail to check him – partly because he was shy, partly because he did not want trouble and partly because he thought if he did he might become unpopular. It was really a lack of moral courage.

Slim knew the value of will-power, because it is essential for a commander to impose his will on his own people as much as on the enemy. He was particular about the training and selection of his staff, for he knew the effect a cheerful and efficient headquarters can have on the troops it is supposed to serve. He always 'looked after the little men' – his mess waiters, orderlies, sweepers, signallers, drivers, cooks, clerks, and never took them for granted. He could talk to them without condescension or affectation. At a Burma Star reunion, late in his life, he stressed the importance of the Team:

> You licked not only the toughest of all human enemies, but also jungle, mountain, climate, disease, distance and separation. You turned defeat into victory. And we did it because we were all of one team – not out for which service or which arm or which formation got the credit or who got the cushy jobs . . .

As Sir Frank Messervy said: 'The troops loved him – they knew that they could trust him. I never saw him cross – never. I never saw him edgy.'

There were occasions, however, when Slim had to sack senior officers who were also old friends, a matter which caused him much grief. Amongst these was Major General Grover, the Commander of 2 Division, which had suffered very heavy casualties in the fighting around Kohima. Grover had trained his fine division to a high pitch of efficiency for amphibious operations and it was unfortunate that its bloody baptism had to be in a type of warfare and in terrain which differed utterly from its experience to date. It says much for both men that they remained good friends to the ends of their lives; and Grover's subsequent appointment in 1944 as Director of Army Welfare at the War Office ensured that 14th Army received, during the last six months of the war, the long overdue attention it merited.

In 1949 came promotion to Field Marshal, and on his retirement from Whitehall, Slim became Governor-General of Australia. It was a politically-sensitive appointment, for the Australians were beginning to think in terms of an Australian-born Governor; they had loyally accepted the post-war appointment of the Duke of Gloucester, but that of another Briton could have raised problems. Slim, however, was warmly welcomed and his days at Yarralumla – the Governor-General's Canberra residence – were amongst the happiest of his life. He now had enough time to write his masterwork, *Defeat into Victory*, which as a study of high command will probably never be rivalled, and is also a revealing glimpse into the mind and spirit of a really great soldier.

The final years of 14th Army's commander were spent amongst those he loved best and in that most historic of places, Windsor Castle, where he was Constable and Governor – a rare combination of two great honorific posts in the gift of the Monarch. In 1960 he received what many regarded as a belated peerage. He could not, as so many would have wished, choose the title 'Slim of Burma', for none deserved it better. It had already been appropriated by Mountbatten, so Slim, typically, chose 'Yarralumla' to the huge delight of the Australian people. Just before he died, he was visited by his old chief, Mountbatten. They reminisced quietly together until the nurse asked Mountbatten to go, as Slim was very tired. He just had the strength for a few words as his guest turned to leave him for the very last time: 'We did it – together'.

The ranks of those who wear the Burma Star are thinning now. Most of the leaders are gone, but General Christison attained his one hundredth year in November 1992 and, when interviewed for this book in 1991 was still active and with unimpaired memory for the hectic events of half a century ago. Hope Thomson of 50 Para Brigade died in 1989, his reputation cleared at long last. Like many whose careers were blighted by unsympathetic senior officers – in his case Scoones, the otherwise admirable Commander of

4 Corps at Imphal – Hope Thomson never complained and got on with his army life. In the mid-fifties he achieved the wish of all good infantrymen and was given the command of the 1st Battalion of his regiment, the Royal Scots Fusiliers in Malaya, where it rendered good service against Chin Peng's Communist Terrorists on the Malaya-Thailand border.

John Masters, Gurkha officer and the defeated commander of 111 Brigade at 'Blackpool', marched out in despair although he could hardly be blamed for the reverse. His men had already been near exhaustion when ordered into their vulnerable and illusory 'Stronghold' and had never stood a chance of holding off a Japanese force of such strength. When his dreadful march towards the safety of Indawgi Lake had ended, and the dazed survivors were taking stock of themselves, he was approached by the chaplains of the brigade, who asked permission to hold a church parade service. Masters refused angrily at first, but agreed when the padres told him that it was not a celebration of victory but of thanksgiving and recollection. As the men gathered in the open, Masters noted that the Cameronians had posted the sentries traditionally prescribed in that regiment for nearly 300 years whenever the unit went to prayer. Standing at the four corners of the field, in curiously ritualised poses, were the riflemen detailed off to watch out, not for Japanese, but for enemies of the stern covenanting faith which had fired the old 26th Cameronians back in the 17th century.

Masters left the Army when his old regiment of Gurkhas was absorbed into the new Indian Army, preferring not to transfer, as he could have done, into one or other of the Gurkha regiments that remained in the British service. Instead, he immortalised the 200 years of the Raj in a series of outstanding books such as *Bhowani Junction* and *Night Runners of Bengal*, some based on the historical experiences of his own family.

Matron Agnes ('Make it clean') McGearey continued to serve in the QA's, soon renamed the Queen Alexandra's Royal Army Nursing Corps. In the early 1950s she was the respected matron of the British Military Hospital at Taiping in North Malaya, renowned for the efficient yet cheerful manner in which she directed her nursing staff. She still plied her patients with champagne when she felt it would benefit them, and one light aircraft pilot who had survived a sensational crash into the jungle found himself, once in her charge, at the centre of a succession of parties held in the officers' ward by Matron and her most attractive QAs. There came a time when all could see she was losing weight, and after a while the medical consultant told her what she already knew: that she had terminal cancer and had but a few weeks to live. Before she flew home to spend her last days with relatives, she was the calm yet radiant centre of a farewell party in the divisional headquarters mess. Elegantly dressed, sipping her favourite champagne and smoking a cigarette through a long holder, there was no sign of despair or foreboding. Her faith was strong, she accepted what was in store, and left the party in high spirits, never to return.

Wingate must remain for ever the great enigma. There can be no doubt that his first expedition, Operation 'Longcloth', however small its military value and the dreadful state in which the survivors regained safety, was a turning point in the whole campaign. Here, at long last, was someone who had hit back at the previously all-victorious enemy. His appeal to Churchill was that of a man who answered a desperate need for a national hero and who could deliver success in battle at that stage of the war; a very scarce commodity needed urgently by Churchill as a bargaining counter with his increasingly powerful American Allies.

Bernard Fergusson rightly assessed Wingate as a great fighting man; he also had the high intelligence and military professionalism required for promotion to the highest ranks. His personality, however, was flawed. There are many witnesses of his irrational behaviour at times of stress. Fergusson, in his postwar correspondence with Slim, recalls one young Chindit officer, Lt David Hastings, son of the eminent barrister Patrick Hastings KC, who was present when Wingate, irked by the slowness with which a column was getting across the Irrawaddy in 1943, threw himself on the ground, tearing at it with hands and teeth in his fury. On seeing this, Hastings had turned to a fellow officers and remarked . . . 'that if I get out, I'm not going to serve under a loony ever again'. He did not have to, for two days later he was killed in action.

Although many disliked him or thought him mad, Wingate was *admired* and men would follow him anywhere, once under the spell. He magnetised highly intelligent officers such as Fergusson, Masters and Calvert, even when they disagreed fundamentally with his theories of irregular warfare. His soldiers were proud to serve under such a leader. Slim, who supported him when things were not going well for Special Force, nevertheless had reservations, probably because he did not approve of 'special' forces, considering them not cost-effective. Wingate's Special Force, using the infantry resources of a Corps and a disproportionately large slice of the available air transport force, accounted for some five 'division months' out of 14th Army's total of about 250 for the entire campaign. For example, 17 Division alone was committed operationally for 40 'division months'. Special Force played no decisive role in the 1944 battles at the gate of India, and had only a subsidiary effect on operations in Stilwell's sector. No man, however, who wore the Chindit flash on his uniform, will ever forget the extraordinary privilege of serving in that company.

Major Pat Rome, whose experiences as a subaltern in the 2nd Durham Light Infantry are recounted in this book, now lives in a beautiful village on Salisbury Plain; with others, he has made the long pilgrimage back to Kohima to look once more on Kuki Picquet, the District Commissioner's garden, and the great sweep of hills which embrace that long ridge, a thousand feet higher than the summit of Ben Nevis, where British, Indian,

Burmese and Gurhka soldiers tamed and beat down the best that the Japanese army could throw at them. It is also a place where many young men rest, watched over by a stone bearing the text of 2 Division's memorial:

> *When you go home*
> *Tell them of us and say*
> *For your tomorrow*
> *We gave our today.*

The campaign produced much verse, some tragic, some thoughtful, some incredibly bad. It was also an excuse for the humour, never far below the surface in the British Army, which singles it out above all others, and which could be found in the pages of regimental news-sheets as well as in *SEAC*;

> *Japs on the hilltops*
> *Japs in the Chaung*
> *Japs on the Ngakyedauk*
> *Japs in the Taung*
> *Japs with their L of C far too long*
> *As they revel in the joys of infiltration . . .*

The gap between the 'sharp end' and the rear areas was never as marked in Burma as in the France of World War I, perhaps because there was no true 'front line' and always a strong threat of Japanese infiltration to well behind corps headquarters and even beyond. It did not however prevent some wag from contributing these lines to *SEAC*:

> *Sticking it out in Tiddim,*
> *Living on biscuits and beef*
> *But how are the boys down in Delhi?*
> *Still living up to their beliefs?*

> *Sticking it out in Kennedy*
> *Eight thousand feet up on the Peak*
> *But what of the boys down at Poona?*
> *It is said that their bath tubs now leak.*

> *Waging a war up in Tuitim*
> *Pushing the Japs off the road,*
> *But what of the chaps at Simla?*
> *My God, those boys have a load!*

> *Think of the stink at the river*
> *Surrounded by vermin and flies,*
> *But Oh! The poor chappies in Lucknow*
> *They're in it right up to their eyes!*

Perhaps the last word can be left with Lockhart Howell's poem '14th Army':

> They have gone past, men of the Shield and Sword,
> Last of our fame, and half the world away
> From all familiar things. So let them rest
> Now that the battle's done. The jungle way,
> From Naga Hill and over Chindwin's banks,
> Will hear no more their green-limbed stealthy tread
> Or watch with fevered eyes where tanks have gone,
> And little boats, and where a man lies dead.
> Across their air-lines blow the purple clouds,
> Water, and grass, and nameless twilight things
> Press after them and cover close their tracks.
> And where their voices whispered, Silence clings.
>   An Army passes but its loves remain,
>   Freedom – and a way home through jungle rain.

Appendices

Appendix I

Victoria Crosses awarded during the Campaign in Burma 1942-45

Havildar PARKASH SINGH, 5/8th Punjab Regiment (Jat Sikh)

In January 1943, during an attack on heavily entrenched Japanese positions at Donbaik in the Arakan, several Bren Gun carriers were pinned down under heavy mortar and machine gun fire. Two were knocked out and as their crews ran out of ammunition they were rushed by Japanese infantry. Havildar Parkash Singh drove forward in his own carrier and, acting on his own initiative, rescued the crews of the disabled carriers, together with their weapons. Two weeks later, in the same area, three carriers were put out of action on a stretch of open beach covered by enemy guns. Havildar Parkash Singh again drove forward, rescued the crews of two of the carriers, then went forward again under heavy fire, attached a tow to the third carrier and brought this back, with its wounded crew, to safety.

Havildar GAJE GHALE, 2/5th Royal Gurkha Rifles (Gurkha)

In May 1943, in the Chin Hills, Havildar Gaje Ghale commanded a platoon of young and inexperienced soldiers ordered to assault a strongly defended Japanese position on a hill-top. The approach was along a knife-edge ridge, devoid of cover and with near-vertical slopes to each side. While forming up, the platoon came under heavy fire but the havildar steadied his men before leading them forward. He was wounded in the arm, chest and leg by grenade splinters but closed with the enemy. Bitter hand-to-hand fighting ensued. Covered with blood from many wounds, the Havildar charged repeatedly, shouting the Gurkha battle-cry of 'Ayo Gurkhali'. His men were inspired by him to carry the Japanese position. Gaje Ghale refused to have his wounds attended to until ordered to the rear by an officer.

Lieutenant ALEC GEORGE HORWOOD DCM,
**1/6th Queen's Royal Regiment (West Surrey) attd 1st Battalion
The Northamptonshire Regiment**

At Kyauchaw in January 1944, Lt Horwood was in action with his forward mortar observation post, supporting a company's attack on a Japanese position. He was under heavy fire all day but at night he managed to get back with vital information about the enemy. Next day he established another observation post further forward and supported two attacks with accurate mortar fire. While carrying out reconnaissance he deliberately drew enemy fire to himself so that their exact position could be noted. The following day he volunteered to lead a fresh attack during which he was mortally wounded. *[Posthumous award]*

T/Major CHARLES FERGUSON HOEY, MC,
1st Lincolnshire Regiment

In February 1944, near the Ngakyedauk Pass, Major Hoey's company came under very heavy machine gun fire from an enemy strongpoint. Although wounded severely in the head and in one leg, Hoey struggled forward alone, destroyed the enemy position and killed its occupants single-handed, without further loss to his own men. He died shortly afterwards from the effects of his wounds. *[Posthumous award]*

Naik NAND SINGH, 1/11th Sikh Regiment (Sikh)

During the second Arakan campaign in March 1944, Nand Singh was wounded six times in an assault when leading his men against Japanese entrenched on a steep hillside overlooking the Kalapanzin Valley. In the words of an eyewitness, 'He literally carried the position single-handed', killing seven Japanese and capturing three sets of trenches. He led his men up a very steep knife-edge ridge to take the first trench with the bayonet; although severely wounded he then crawled forward under fire. He was again wounded, by a grenade, but despite severe facial wounds pushed on and took the second trench. Shortly after, he charged the third trench and killed its occupants with the bayonet.

Lieutenant GEORGE ALBERT CAIRNS, Somerset Light Infantry, attd South Staffordshire Regiment

On 13 March 1944, at Henu during the second Chindit expedition, Cairns's unit made an attack on a hill-top strongly held by determined Japanese. At the top of the hill the enemy emerged from their trenches and ferocious hand-to-hand fighting took place. In single combat with a Japanese officer, Cairns had his left arm severed by his opponent's sword but killed the Japanese officer, took up his sword, led a successful charge and killed a number of the enemy with it before collapsing through loss of blood. His example inspired all who saw it, enabling them to overwhelm the opposition. *[Posthumous award]*

Lance Corporal JOHN HARMAN,
4th Queens Royal West Kent Regiment

On 8 and 9 April 1944, during the siege of Kohima, L/Cpl Harman's section was under very heavy fire from a Japanese machine gun at a range of under fifty yards. He broke cover and, advancing alone, attacked the Japanese position with rifle and bayonet, destroying the machine gun and killing its crew. He then used grenades to clear a bake-house where Japanese soldiers were hiding in the ovens. On the second day he again went forward alone to destroy a machine gun post, killing the crew; as he was returning to his section's position, the Japanese gun on his shoulder, he was fatally wounded. *[Posthumous award]*

Jemadar ABDUL HAFIZ, 3/9th Jat Regiment (Mussulman Rajput)

Jemadar Abdul Hafiz was ordered to recapture a position taken by the Japanese near Imphal in April 1944. Before leading his two sections into the attack he told them that no Japanese could stop them; shouting the Rajput battle cry, he raced up the bare hillside at the head of his men. The Japanese opened fire at point-blank range, wounding the Jemadar in the leg; but he went on, seizing a machine gun by its barrel while one of his men killed the gunner. He then took a Bren gun from a dying man and charged the enemy, killing many of them. Such was the ferocity of his attack that the enemy fled. Abdul Hafiz then died from his wounds; his last words were 're-organise! I will give you covering fire!'. But he was too weak to pull the trigger. *[Posthumous award]*

T/Captain JOHN NEIL RANDLE, 2 Battalion Royal Norfolk Regiment

Capt Randle took over command when his company commander was severely wounded during an attack on a Japanese-held ridge at Kohima in May 1944. Though wounded himself, he inspired his men to press on and capture the enemy position. Next day, ignoring his painful wound and under heavy fire, he led a further attack which was held up by a well-sited enemy bunker. With total disregard for his own safety, Randle charged the bunker single-handed, silenced the enemy with a hand grenade, and then flung himself across the slit so that his body sealed the aperture. His sacrifice saved many lives and enabled his battalion to gain its objective. *[Posthumous award]*

A/Sergeant HANSON VICTOR TURNER,
1st Battalion, West Yorkshire Regiment

On 6 June 1944, at Ninthoukhong, Sgt Turner's platoon was pinned down by very heavy fire from a well dug-in Japanese position. He calmly reorganised the platoon, which had been caught in the open, and withdrew it to better fire positions less than 50 yards to the rear, where it withstood a succession of desperate enemy attacks, inflicting heavy casualties. At first light the next morning, Sgt Turner decided to take the battle to the Japanese and went forward five times on his own, armed with satchels of grenades, killing and wounding many enemy troops. On the sixth attack he was killed in the act of throwing a final grenade. [*Posthumous award*]

Captain MICHAEL ALLMAND,
Indian Armoured Corps, attd 3/6th Gurkha Rifles

On 11 June 1944 Capt Allmand's platoon came under very heavy fire during an attack on the Pin Honi Road Bridge. On this occasion he charged alone at the enemy, killed three Japanese with the kukri, and inspired the rest of his unit to capture the Japanese position. Two days later, he found himself in command of a rifle company when all the other officers had been killed or wounded. He continued to set an outstanding example of courage and leadership although suffering acutely from trench foot, and was killed at the head of his men in the attack on the bridge at Mogaung. [*Posthumous award*]

Rifleman TULBAHADUR PUN, 3/6th Gurkha Rifles

On 11 June 1944, in the same action as that in which Captain Allmand gained his VC, Rfn Tulbahadur Pun was in one of two platoons pinned down by extremely heavy fire near the Mogaung railway bridge. Most of his section had been wiped out, and the section commander led the remaining two men in a desperate charge, but he and the other man were wounded. Tulbahadur Pun seized a Bren gun and firing it from the hip, continued the charge alone, across 30 yards of open ground which was deep in mud, pitted with flooded shell holes and littered with logs and shattered trees. With the light of dawn behind him he was clearly silhouetted and an easy target; but he reached the enemy position, from where he gave accurate covering fire which enabled the survivors of his platoon to gain the objective.

Rifleman GANJU LAMA, MM, 1/7th Gurkha Rifles

In June 1944, at Ningthoukhong on the Plain of Imphal, the perimeter of Rfn Ganju Lama's defensive position was broken and Japanese infantry and tanks poured through, pinning the unit to the ground with heavy close range fire. A counter-attack was ordered but came under heavy fire from the enemy tanks. Ganju Lama crawled forward on his own initiative with a PIAT (an anti-tank launcher). Despite a broken left wrist and a wounded right hand, he closed to 30 yards before opening fire, knocking out two tanks. He then went forward alone and took on the tank crews, killing or wounding them all. Only a few weeks earlier he had been awarded an immediate MM for knocking out another tank with his PIAT.

T/Major FRANK GERALD BLAKER MC, Highland Light Infantry, attd 3/9th Gurkha Rifles

At Taungni, in July 1944, Major Blaker charged single-handed to the summit of a steep hill to attack a Japanese machine gun post overlooking his unit's position. He was wounded first in the arm by a grenade burst, then three times by machine gun bullets from the strongpoint he was attacking. He fell to the ground but sat up and exhorted his men to the attack with the words, 'Well done, 'C' Company; I'm going to die, but you'll go on, I know'. Before he died he watched his men overrun the Japanese position. In an earlier operation, Blaker had led his unit for some time over extremely difficult terrain to carry out a highly successful encircling attack.

[Posthumous award]

Naik AGANSING RAI, 2/5th Gurkha Rifles (Gurkha)

In June 1944, Naik Agansing Rai's company attacked two strongly-held Japanese positions known as 'Water Picquet' and 'Mortar Bluff' overlooking the Bishenpur-Silchar track at the edge of the Imphal Plain. Casualties mounted and the attack began to falter but Agansing Rai led his section forward to attack the Japanese position despite withering fire. His Bren gunner killed one of the enemy and he killed the other three with a machine gun. The rest of the company followed them onto the hill but came under fire from a light gun at close range. Again, Agansing Rai took the initiative and charged the gun; when his Tommy-gun jammed he took up a Bren, ran forward, killed three more Japanese and took the gun. Later, with a Tommy-gun and grenades, he led an advance on another bunker to kill its four occupants.

Subedar NETRABAHADUR THAPA, 2/5th Royal Gurkha Rifles

In June 1944, Subedar Netrabahadur Thapa was in charge of an isolated but vitally important defensive position at 'Water Picquet'. The enemy made repeated attacks but for over eight hours not a man quit his post and not a yard of ground was given up. This was despite heavy artillery and mortar fire and wave after wave of infantry attacks. At one point the Subedar and his runner went forward with grenades and kukri to counter-attack the Japanese on the wire. The ferocity of the enemy attack would have justified a withdrawal by the numerically inferior Gurkhas but this was not considered, and the position held after a night of incessant fighting. The Subedar's body was found next morning, bearing many wounds; but his kukri was still in his hand, and beside him lay a dead Japanese with his skull cloven in two.

[Posthumous award]

A/Subedar RAM SARUP SINGH, 2/1st Punjab Regiment (Rajput)

Before an attack on a hill position near Tiddim in October 1944 Jemadar Ram Sarup Singh said to his company commander, 'Sahib, either the Jap or myself die today.' He led a section which drove the Japanese from their bunkers and then faced ferocious counter-attacks. Wounded twice, he bandaged himself with his puttees and led a bayonet charge in which he was seen to kill four Japanese. Five yards from another Japanese bunker he was hit in the chest with a burst of fire; with his last breath he shouted out to his Havildar, 'I am dying but you carry on and finish these devils.' When volunteers were called for to go out and recover his body, every man in the company stepped forward. *[Posthumous award]*

Sepoy BHANDARI RAM, 16/10th Baluch Regiment (Dogra)

During operations in the Maungdaw-Buthidaung area of the Arakan in November 1944, Sepoy Bhandari Ram's platoon had to advance along the spine of a narrow ridge with almost sheer sides. A few yards from a Japanese bunker, Bhandari Ram was hit; but although one arm hung limp, he crawled to the assistance of two wounded comrades under heavy fire. A grenade actually burst on him but he crawled on. When only a few yards from the Japanese post, he pulled the pin on a grenade with his teeth and threw it into the midst of the enemy with dire effect. Desperately wounded, semi-conscious, and drenched in blood, he now asked if the position had been taken. On being told it had, he said, 'I don't mind dying now – I've done my job'. Carried to the regimental aid post, his life was saved.

Havildar UMRAO SINGH, Indian Artillery

In December 1944, Havildar Umrao Singh's gun position in the Kaladan Valley was attacked by Japanese infantry. He inspired his gun detachment to fight the enemy off four times, when all but two of his men were dead or wounded. He had been hit twice by grenade fragments and was bleeding freely. When the final Japanese attack came in he seized a gun bearing rod (a heavy metal shaft used to adjust the trail of the gun), and used it as a club. He was seen to fell three Japanese before being overwhelmed and left for dead. When a counter-attack recaptured the gun he was found, still alive but with seven grave head wounds, and ten Japanese soldiers dead around him. The gun had been saved, and was in action again the next day.

Lance Naik SHER SHAH, 7/16th Punjab Regiment (Punjabi Mussulman)

In the course of an action at Kyeyebyin in the Kaladan Valley in January

1945, a Japanese platoon charged Naik Sher Shah's post at last light. He crawled around to the rear of the attacking enemy and charged them from behind, breaking up the attack. At midnight another Japanese attack formed up. Again, Sher Shah went forward and dispersed the attackers. Whilst returning, he was hit by a mortar bomb which severed one of his legs. Despite his terrible wounds he again attacked the Japanese in their forming-up point and went on firing at them until he was killed. When he was found at daylight, 23 Japanese dead were lying in front of his body.

[*Posthumous award*]

Lieutenant GEORGE ARTHUR KNOWLAND, Royal Norfolk Regiment, attd No 1 Commando

On 31 January 1945, in the battle at Kangaw, Lt Knowland's platoon of 24 men was attacked by some 300 fanatical Japanese infantry. In spite of intense enemy fire, he stood up, firing a Bren gun from the hip whilst some of his wounded were taken to a safer place; for much of the time he was engaging the charging Japanese at ranges down to ten yards. His inspiring leadership enabled the survivors of the platoon to hold out successfully for 12 hours, until relieved. Throughout this time he was constantly on his feet around the platoon position, exhorting his men, distributing ammunition and firing a two-inch mortar which he rested against a tree, causing further heavy casualties to the enemy. He continued to do this until mortally wounded. [*Posthumous award*]

Jemadar PRAKASH SINGH, 14/13th Frontier Force Rifles (Dogra)

During the advance to Mandalay in February 1945, Jemadar Prakash Singh's position was fiercely attacked. Wounded in both legs, he was ordered back to company HQ but when he heard that his platoon non-commissioned officers had all been wounded he crawled forward and re-assumed command. Propped up by his batman, he fired a 2-inch mortar whose crew had been killed and continued to encourage his men. When all his bombs had been fired off, he crawled around the platoon distributing ammunition taken from dead personnel. Hit again, he took up a Bren gun. A third wound put him out of action but he lay down facing the enemy, shouting encouragement to his men. A fourth wound was fatal and he died after telling his company commander not to worry about him – he could look after himself. [*Posthumous award*]

Naik GIAN SINGH, 4/15th Punjab Regiment (Jat Sikh)

In March 1945, during an attack on Japanese troops dug in astride the

Kamye-Myingyaw road, Naik Gian Singh made two lone charges with Tommy-gun and grenades. When another platoon was pinned down he ordered his Bren gunners to cover him as he rushed at the enemy foxholes. Then, although wounded several times, he came to the rescue of his own section and wiped out the crew of a Japanese anti-tank gun, capturing it single-handed. He then led a platoon to clear the enemy position, where 20 Japanese dead were subsequently counted. He repeatedly refused to obey orders to report to the Regimental Aid Post until the end of the action.

Naik FAZAL DIN, 7/10th Baluch Regiment (Punjabi Mussulman)

Naik Fazal Din led his platoon against an enemy position near Meiktila in March 1945, and silenced it. Suddenly, a group of six Japanese, including two officers, charged at his men. He went to the aid of a Bren gunner who was under attack and received a sword thrust in the chest. As the sword was withdrawn, Fazal Din seized it and killed its owner with it. He then killed two more of the Japanese and continued to cheer on his men, waving the sword until he collapsed at platoon HQ. He died shortly after at the Regimental Aid Post. The official citation reads: 'Such supreme devotion to duty even when fatally wounded, and his presence of mind and outstanding courage has seldom been equalled and reflects the unquenchable spirit of a singularly brave and gallant non-commissioned officer'

[Posthumous award]

Lieutenant WILLIAM BASIL WESTON, Green Howards, attd 1st Battalion West Yorkshire Regiment

On 3 March 1945, during the attack on Meiktila, Lt Weston was the commander of a platoon engaged on clearing Japanese troops out of the town area. In the course of this desperate house-to-house fighting, in which every one of the Japanese resisted to the end, Lt Weston personally led his men from bunker to bunker, destroying them as they advanced. At the last one, he was mortally wounded, but threw himself at the entrance, pulling the pin from a grenade with the last of his strength and blowing himself up with the defenders. *[Posthumous award]*

Rifleman BHANBHAGTA GURUNG, 3/2nd Gurkha Rifles (Gurkha)

In March 1945, during the attack on 'Snowdon East', a hill feature near Tamandu on the mainland north-east of Ramree Island, Rfn Bhanbagta Gurung's section suffered several casualties from a sniper in a tree about 75 yards away. He stood up in the open and shot the sniper; resuming the advance, the platoon was pinned down again by very heavy fire from a nest of foxholes. Without hesitation, Bhanbagta Gurung charged the foxholes and killed all the occupants. He then threw smoke grenades into a bunker and killed the defenders with his kukri as they emerged. Having done that he entered the smoke-filled bunker, sought out the machine gunner and killed him as well, captured the gun and turned it against an incoming Japanese counter-attack, which was thrown back.

Lieutenant KARAMJEET SINGH JUDGE, 4/15th Punjab Regiment (Sikh)

As Lt Karamjeet Singh's battalion, supported by tanks, advanced near Myingyan in central Burma in March 1945, a series of concealed enemy bunkers opened fire, causing heavy casualties. Karamjeet Singh walked calmly around in the open under heavy fire, calling back the tanks to deal with the bunkers, then led a series of charges which wiped out ten Japanese positions after they had been 'softened up' by the tanks. He was mortally wounded after one of these attacks, but his men continued to carry all before them and cleared the area of enemy. His citation says that '. . . he dominated the entire battlefield . . .'   [*Posthumous award*]

Lieutenant CLAUD RAYMOND, Royal Engineers

Lt Raymond was second-in-command of a reconnaissance patrol at Tabaku in March 1945 when they came under heavy fire from a strongly-entrenched enemy detachment. Raymond was wounded in the shoulder and then in the head but continued to lead his men, even when a third hit shattered one of his wrists. He carried on into the enemy defence and was largely responsible for capturing the position. He refused medical aid until all the other wounded had been attended to, and he died the next day.   [*Posthumous award*]

Rifleman LACHHIMAN GURUNG, 4/8th Gurkha Rifles

The 4/8th Gurkhas were surrounded for three days and two nights at Taungdaw in May 1945. Throughout this time Rfn Lachhiman Gurung inspired his comrades as they repelled repeated Japanese attacks during the enemy's determined efforts to break out to the east. Fighting was at extremely close range and conducted with grenade, bayonet and kukri. As wave after wave of Japanese attacks came in, Lachhiman Gurung threw the enemy's grenades back until one exploded in his hand, blowing off all its fingers. He went on firing his rifle with his left hand, killing many Japanese as they attacked in close order. All these attacks were successfully repulsed.

●

George Crosses awarded in the Burma Campaign 1942-45

Private JOSEPH HARVEY SILK, Somerset Light Infantry

On 4 December 1943, Pte Silk was in the jungle on an exercise. His platoon were on a hillside, cleaning their weapons at the end of the day, when a grenade he was handling ignited. He could not throw it away as he was surrounded by his comrades, so he shouted a warning and rolled on the grenade, which exploded, killing him instantly.   *Posthumous award*]

Temp/Major HUGH PAUL SEAGRIM DSO MBE, Burma Rifles

Major Seagrim, an officer serving in Force 136 in the Karen Hills, had been operating behind Japanese lines since the 1942 retreat, when he was one of those left behind to stir up rebellion amongst the hill tribes. Two officers who were parachuted in to join him at the end of 1943 were subsequently ambushed and killed by the Japanese, but Seagrim continued to evade capture, thanks to the loyalty of the Karens. In 1944, however, the Japanese carried out savage reprisals against the tribes and Seagrim gave himsef up in February. He was court-martialled as a spy, together with a number of Karens, of whom eight were sentenced to death with him. He pleaded in vain for them, and they were all shot on 22 September 1944 at Rangoon.

[Posthumous award]

Flight Sergeant STANLEY JAMES WOODBRIDGE, RAF

Flt Sgt Woodbridge was the wireless operator in a Liberator bomber which made a forced landing in upper Burma after sustaining damage on a raid. The six survivors were captured and tortured repeatedly by the Japanese in an attempt to gain information on Allied air plans. Not one of the men divulged any information. Five were then beheaded, but Woodbridge was kept for further questioning under torture, as it was realised that as the signaller, he had access to codes and ciphers. He would not talk and was duly beheaded.   *[Posthumous award]*

Lance Naik ISLAM-UD-DIN, 6/9th Jat Regiment

On 12 April 1945 L/Naik Islam-ud-Din was on a grenade- throwing exercise when a live grenade fell into the middle of a group of soldiers. Without a moment's hesitation, Islam-ud-Din threw himself on the grenade, undoubtedly saving many casualties at the cost of his own life.

[Posthumous award]

Naik KIRPA RAM, 8/13th Frontier Force Rifles

On 12 September 1945, Naik Kirpa Ram was supervising training in the use of the rifle grenade discharger. A 'shortfall' occurred, with the grenade landing only a few feet in front of the class under instruction. Kirpa Ram attempted to throw the grenade away but it detonated in his hands. Although no further casualties were caused, he died of his injuries.

[Posthumous award]

Appendix II

Burma Army Order of Battle – late December 1941

(Source: Official History: The War Against Japan, Vol. II)
Abbreviations: BAF = Burma Auxiliary Force
BFF = Burma Frontier Force
S&M = Sappers and Miners   FF = Field Force

1st Burma Division (Southern Shan States)

Army HQ Rangoon

Divisional Troops

Artillery: 27th Indian Mountain Regt; 2nd & 23rd Indian Mountain Btys; 5th Field Bty RA (BAF).

Engineers: 56th Field Coy, S&M; 50th Field Park Coy, S&M; 1st Burma Field Coy, S&M.

Infantry: 13th & 14th Burma Rifles; FFs 1st, 3rd, 4th, 5th (each of a HQ, two trooops mounted infantry and three coy-sized infantry columns).

1st Burma Brigade: 2nd KOYLI; 1st & 5th Burma Rifles.

2nd Burma Brigade: 12th Indian Mountain Bty; 1st/7th Gurkha Rifles; Tenasserim Bn. BAF; 2nd, 4th, 6th & 8th Burma Rifles; Part of 3rd Burma Rifles; FF2.

13th Indian Infantry Brigade: 5th/1st Punjab; 2nd/7th Rajputs; 1st/18th Royal Garwhal Rifles.

16th Indian Infantry Brigade: 1st/9th Royal Jats; 4th/12th Frontier Force Regt; 7th Burma Rifles.

Rangoon Garrison: 1st Glosters; Part of 3rd Burma Rifles.

Appendix III

Outline Order of Battle, 17 Indian Division, prior to Sittang Bridge Disaster, 23 February 1942

HQ 17 Indian Division

Divisional Troops

Artillery: HQ 28th Indian Mountain Regt.

Engineers: 24th & 60th Field Coys, S&M; Makerkotla Field Coy, S&M (ISF); 6th Indian Pioneer Bn; A Section of 18th Indian Artisan Works Coy; 1st Burma Artisan Works Coy.

Infantry: 7th/10th Baluch Regt; 2nd Burma Rifles; One Coy each of 4th & 8th Burma Rifles; two columns, FF 2.

16th Brigade: 2 KOYLI; 1st/9th Royal Jats; 1st/7th Gurkha Rifles; 5th/17th Dogras; 8th Burma Rifles; 5th, 15th & 28th Mountain Btys; Section, 5th Field Bty BAF.

48th Brigade: 12th Mountain Bty; 1st/3rd Gurkha Rifles; 1st/4th Gurkha Rifles; 2nd/5th Royal Gurkha Rifles.

46th Brigade: 4th/12th Frontier Force Regt; 3rd/7th Gurkha Rifles; 4th Burma Rifles.

Appendix IV

Senior Staff and Command Appointments, Burma Theatre 1943-45

Source: Supreme Allied Commander's Report. HMSO 1951

Note: Many of the officers listed below were already in situ by 1943. Maj Gen Cowan, for example, had taken over 17 Indian Division early in 1942, following the disaster at the Sittang Bridge. The names of senior officers holding key appointments in Burma Army at the beginning of the campaign are mentioned, where appropriate, in the earlier chapters of this book.

Supreme Allied Commander, South-East Asia Command:

Admiral (Hon Gen & Hon Air Marshal) Lord Louis Mountbatten
GCVO KCB DSO ADC   Nov 1943-May 1946

Deputy SACs:
(a) Gen J W Stilwell, US Army   Nov 1943-Oct 1944
(b) Lt Gen R A Wheeler, US Army   Nov 1944-Oct 1945

Chiefs of Staff
(a) Lt Gen Sir Henry Pownall KBE CB DSO MC   Nov 1943-Dec 1944
(b) Lt Gen Sir Frederick Browning KBE CB DSO   Dec 1944-Jul 1946

11 Army Group (from Nov 1944, Allied Land Forces, S-E Asia)

C-in-C:
Gen Sir George Giffard GCB DSO ADC   Nov 1943-Nov 1944

Allied Land Forces, South-East Asia (ALFSEA)

C-in-C:
(a) Lt Gen Sir Oliver Leese Bt, KCB CBE DSO   Nov 1944-Jul 1945
(b) Lt Gen Sir Philip Christison KBE CB DSO MC   Jul-Aug 1945
(c) Gen Sir William Slim GBE KCB DSO MC   Aug-Dec 1945

14th Army (from Dec 1945, Malaya Command)

GOC-in-C:
Lt Gen Sir William Slim KCB CBE DSO MC   Nov 1943-Aug 1945

12th Army (from Oct 1945, Burma Command)

GOC-in-C:
Gen Sir Montague Stopford KBE CB DSO MC   May-Oct 1945

4 Corps

(a) Lt Gen Sir Geoffrey Scoones KBE CSI DSO MC   Nov 1943-Dec 1944
(b) Lt Gen Sir Frank Messervy KBE CB DSO   Dec 1944-Nov 1945

15 Corps

Lt Gen Sir Philip Christison KBE CB DSO MC ·   Nov 1943-Dec 1945

33 Corps

Lt Gen Sir Montagu Stopford KBE CB DSO MC   Nov 1943-May 1945

34 Corps

Lt Gen O L Roberts CBE DSO   Mar-Nov 1945

2 (BR) Division

(a) Maj Gen J M L Grover MC   Nov 1943-Jul 1944
(b) Maj Gen C G G Nicholson CB CBE DSO MC   Jul 1944-Apr 1946

Special Force (3 Indian Division)

(a) Maj Gen O C Wingate DSO   Nov 1943-Mar 1944
(b) Maj Gen W D A Lentaigne CBE DSO   Mar 1944-Mar 1945

14 Inf Brigade:
Brig T Brodie   Nov 1943-Feb 1945

16 Inf Brigade:
Brig B E Fergusson DSO   Nov 1943-Sep 1944

23 Inf Brigade:
Brig L E C M Perowne CBE   Nov 1943-Jul 1945

77 Ind Inf Brigade:
Brig J M Calvert DSO   Nov 1943-Feb 1945

111 Ind Inf Brigade:
(a) Brig W D A Lentaigne CBE DSO   Nov 1943-Mar 1944
(b) (Acting) Maj (A/Brig) J Masters   Mar-Jul 1944
(c) Brig J R Morris DSO   Mar-Oct 1944

3 (WA) Brigade:
Brig A H Gillmore OBE   Feb-Nov 1944

5 Indian Division

(a) Maj Gen H R Briggs DSO   Nov 1943-Jul 1944
(b) Maj Gen D F W Warren CBE DSO   Sep 1944-Feb 1945
(c) Maj Gen E C Mansergh CB CBE MC   Feb 1945-Apr 1946

7 Indian Division

(a) Maj Gen F W Messervy CB DSO   Nov 1943-Dec 1944
(b) Maj Gen G C Evans CB CBE DSO   Dec 1944-Feb 1946

11 East African Division

(a) Maj Gen G C Fowkes CBE DSO MC   Nov 1943-Jan 1945
(b) Maj Gen E C Mansergh OBE MC   Jan-Feb 1945
(c) Maj Gen W A Dimoline CBE DSO MC   Feb 1945-May 1946

17 Indian Division

(a) Maj Gen D J Cowan CB CBE DSO MC   Nov 1943-May 1945
(b) Maj Gen W A Crowther CBE DSO   Jun 1945-May 1946

19 Indian Division

Maj Gen T W Rees CB CIE DSO MC   Nov 1943-Dec 1945

20 Indian Division

Maj Gen D D Gracey CB CBE MC   Nov 1943-Feb 1945

21 Indian Division

Maj Gen C G G Nicholson CBE DSO MC   Apr-Jul 1944

23 Indian Division

(a) Maj Gen O L Roberts CBE DSO   Nov 1943-Mar 1945
(b) Maj Gen D C Hawthorn CB DSO   Mar 1945-May 1946

25 Indian Division

(a) Maj Gen H L Davies CBE DSO MC   Nov 1943-Aug 1944
(b) Maj Gen G N Wood CB CBE DSO MC   Aug 1944-Feb 1946

26 Indian Division

Maj Gen C E N Lomax CB CBE DSO MC	Nov 1943-Mar 1945

36 Indian Division (later, 36 Division)

Maj Gen F W Festing CBE DSO	Nov 1943-Aug 1945

81 (West African) Division

(a) Maj Gen C G Woolner CB MC	Nov 1943-Aug 1944
(b) Maj Gen F J Loftus-Tottenham DSO	Aug 1944-Mar 1946

82 (West African) Division

(a) Maj Gen G McL I S Bruce OBE MC	Nov 1943-Feb 1945
(b) Maj Gen H C Stockwell CBE DSO	Feb-May 1945
(c) Maj Gen C R A Swynnerton DSO	May-Jul 1945
(c) Maj Gen H C Stockwell CBE DSO	Jul 1945-May 1946

Lushai Brigade

Brig P C Marindin DSO MC	Jan 1944-Feb 1946

Appendix V

Simplified Chain of Command, South-East Asia Command, December 1943

Combined Chiefs of Staff (WASHINGTON)

British Chiefs of Staff (LONDON)
(General Sir Alan Brooke, CIGS)

Supreme Allied Commander, South-East Asia (DELHI, then KANDY)
(Admiral Lord Louis Mountbatten)
Deputy Allied Commander, South-East Asia
(Lt Gen J Stilwell)

EASTERN FLEET   11 ARMY GROUP   ALLIED AIR FORCES
(Lt Gen Sir George Giffard)

Ceylon Garrison   14th Army   Indian Ocean
(COMILLA)   Garrisons
(Lt Gen W J Slim)

4 Corps (IMPHAL)   15 Corps (ARAKAN)
(Lt Gen G Scoones)   (Lt Gen P Christison)

Note: Early in 1944, 14th Army was joined by 33 Corps and 3 Indian Division ('Special Force').

Appendix VI

Outline Order of Battle, 15 Corps (ARAKAN) January-July 1944

[Notes: ISF = Indian State Forces   EA = East African   WA = West African
For names of Commanders see Appendix IV]

Corps Troops

Armour: 25th Dragoons; One Troop 401st Fd Sqn IE; One Coy 3/4th Bombay Grenadiers; Det 254th Bridging Tp IE; 81st (WA) Recce Regt; 3rd Gwalior Lancers (ISF)

Artillery: 6th Medium Regt RA; 8th (Belfast) Heavy AA Regt RA; 36th Light AA Regt RA; 5th Mahratta Anti-Tank Regt.

Engineers: 73rd & 483rd Field Coys IE; Malerkotla Field Coy (ISF); 468th Field Park Coy IE; 853rd Bridging Coy IE; 11th Bridging Sect, IE; 23rd & 24th Bns IE.

Signals: 15 Corps Signals.

Infantry: 12th Frontier Force Regt (Machine Guns); 79th Indian Infantry Coy.

Commandos: 3rd Special Service Bde: 5th Commando; 44th Royal Marines Commando.

5 Indian Infantry Division

Artillery: 4th Field Regt RA; 28th Jungle Field Regt RA; 56th Light AA/Anti-Tank Regt RA; 24th Indian Mountain Regt.

Engineers: 2nd, 20th & 74th Field Coys IE; 44th Field Park Coy IE. 1st Bridging Sect IE.

Signals: 5 Indian Divisional Signals.

Divisional HQ Infantry: 3/2nd Punjab Regt.

Infantry:

9th Indian Infantry Brigade: 2nd W Yorkshire Regt; 3/9th Jat Regt; 3/14th Punjab Regt.

123rd Indian Infantry Brigade: 2nd Suffolk Regt; 2/1st Punjab Regt; 1/17th Dogra Regt.

161st Indian Infantry Brigade: 4th Queen's Own Royal West Kent Regt; 1/1st Punjab Regt; 4/7th Rajput Regt.

Medical: 10th, 45th & 75th Indian Field Ambulances.

7 Indian Infantry Division

Divisional Recce: Horsed element, 3rd Gwalior Lancers (ISF).

Artillery: 136th Field Regt RA; 139th Jungle Field Regt RA; 24th Light AA/Anti-Tank Regt RA; 25th Indian Mountain Regt.
Engineers: 62nd, 77th & 421st Field Coys IE; 303rd Field Park Coy IE; 17th Bridging Sect IE.
Signals: 7 Indian Divisional Signals
Divisional HQ Infantry: 1/11th Sikh Regt (later, 7/2nd Punjab Regt)
Infantry:
33rd Indian Infantry Brigade: 1st Queen's Royal Regt (West Surrey); 4/15th Punjab Regt; 4/1st Gurkha Rifles.
89th Indian Infantry Brigade: 2nd King's Own Scottish Borderers; 7/2nd Punjab Regt [repl by 1/11th Sikh Regiment] 4/8th Gurkha Rifles.
114th Indian Infantry Brigade: 1st Somerset Light Infantry; 4/14th Punjab Regt; 4/5th Royal Gurkha Rifles.
Medical: 44th, 54th & 66th Indian Field Ambulances.

25 Indian Infantry Division

Artillery: 8th Field Regt RA; 27th Jungle Field Regt RA; 5th Indian Field Regt; 7th Indian Light AA/Anti-Tank Regt.
Engineers: 63rd, 93rd and 425th Field Coys IE; 16th Bridging Sect IE.
Divisional HQ Infantry: 8/19th Hyderabad Regt
Infantry:
1st Indian Infantry Brigade: 8th York & Lancaster Regt; 17/5th Mahratta Light Infantry; 16/10th Baluch Regt.
53rd Indian Infantry Brigade: 9th York & Lancaster Regt; 2/2nd Punjab Regt; 4/18th Royal Garwhal Rifles.
74th Indian Infantry Brigade: 6th Oxfordshire & Bucks Light Infantry; 14/10th Baluch Regt; 3/2nd Gurkha Rifles.
Medical: 55th, 58th & 61st Indian Field Ambulances.

26 Indian Division

Artillery: 160th Jungle Field Regt RA; 30th Indian Mountain Regt; 7th Indian Field Regt; 1st Indian Light AA/Anti-Tank Regt.
Engineers: 28th, 32nd & 98th Field Coys IE; 7th Bridging Sect IE.
Signals: 26th Indian Divisional Signals.
Divisional HQ Infantry: 5/9th Jat Regt.
Infantry:
4th Indian Infantry Brigade: 1st Wiltshire Regt; 2/13th Frontier Force Rifle; 2/7th Rajput Regt.
36th Indian Infantry Brigade: 8/13th Frontier Force Rifles; 5/16th Punjab Regt; 1/8th Gurkha Rifles.
71st Indian Infantry Brigade: 1st Lincolnshire Regt; 5/1st Punjab Regt; 1/18th Royal Garwhal Rifles.
Medical: 1st, 46th & 48th Indian Field Ambulances.

36 Indian Infantry Division

[Note: this was effectively a British division, with only a few Indian Army units. The prefix 'Indian' was dropped later in the campaign.]

Armour: 'C' Sqn, 149th Regt RAC
Artillery: 130th & 178th Assault Field Regts RA; 122nd Light AA/Anti-Tank Regt RA.
Engineers: 324th Field Park Coy IE; 12th Bridging Sect IE; Two Coys, 15th Battalion IE; One Sect, 99th Field Coy IE.
Signals: 36th Indian Divisional Signals.
Divisional HQ Infantry: One Coy, 2nd Manchester Machine Gun Battalion.
Medical: 22nd Casualty Clearing Station.

29th Infantry Brigade Group:
236th Field Coy RE
29th Infantry Brigade Signals
1st Royal Scots Fusiliers; 2nd Royal Welch Fusiliers;
2nd East Lancashire Regiment; 2nd South Lancashire Regt.
154th Field Ambulance.

72nd Indian Infantry Brigade Group:
30th Field Coy IE
72nd Indian Infantry Brigade Signals
6th South Wales Borderers
10th Gloucestershire Regt
9th Royal Sussex Regt
69th Indian Field Ambulance.

81 West African Division

Artillery: 1st (WA) Light AA/Anti-Tank Regt; 3rd, 4th & 6th Independent (WA) Light Batteries.
Engineers: 5th & 6th (WA) Field Coys; 8th (WA) Field Park Coy.
Signals: 81st (WA) Divisional Signals.
Infantry:
5th West African Infantry Brigade: 5th, 7th & 8th Battalions, Gold Coast Regiment
6th West African Infantry Brigade: 4th Nigeria Regt, 1st Gambia Regt; 1st Sierra Leone Regt.
Auxiliary Porter Groups: 1st, 3rd & 4th (WA) Auxiliary Groups.
Medical: 5th & 6th (WA) Field Ambulances.

Outline Order of Battle, 4 Corps (IMPHAL) January-July 1944

Corps Troops:

Armour: HQ, 254th Indian Tank Brigade: 3rd Carabiniers; 7th Cavalry (IA); 'C' Sqn, 150th Regt RAC; 401st Field Sqn IE, less a troop; 3/4th Bombay Grenadiers (motorised), less a Coy.

Artillery: 8th Medium Regt RA; 67th Heavy AA Regt RA; 78th Light AA Regt RA; 15th Punjab Anti-Tank Regt; One Battery, 2nd Survey Regt RA.

Engineers: 75th & 424th Field Coys IE; 94th (Faridkot) Field Coy (ISF); 305th Field Park Coy IE; 854th Bridging Coy IE; 16th Battalion IE; 336th Forestry Coy IE; 3rd West African Field Coy.

Signals: 4 Corps Signals.

Infantry: 9th Jat Machine Gun Battalions; 15/11th Sikh Regt; Chin Hills Battalion, Burma Army; 3rd & 4th Battalions, Assam Rifles; 78th Indian Infantry Coy; Kalibahadur Regt (Nepalese); One Coy Gwalior Infantry Infantry (ISF).

Outline Order of Battle, 3 Indian Division (Special Force) HQ

14th LRP Brigade (Brig T Brodie)

54th Field Coy RE
1st Bedfordshire & Hertfordshire Regt
7th Leicestershire Regt
2nd Black Watch
2nd York and Lancaster Regt
Medical detachment

16th LRP Brigade (Brig B E Fergusson)

2nd Field Coy RE
51st/69th Field Regt RA (in infantry role)
2nd Queen's Own Royal Regt (W Surrey)
2nd Leicestershire Regt
45th Recce Regt (in infantry role)
Medical detachment

23rd LRP Brigade (Brig L E C M Perowne)

12th Field Coy RE
60th Field Regt RA (in infantry role)

2nd Duke of Wellington's Regt
4th Border Regt
1st Essex Regt
Medical detachment

77th LRP Infantry Brigade (Brig J M Calvert)

Mixed Field Coy, RE/IE
1st King's (Liverpool) Regt
1st Lancashire Fusiliers
1st South Staffordshire Regt
3/6th Gurkha Rifles
Medical & Veterinary detachments

111th LRP Infantry Brigade
(a) Brig W D A Lentaigne (b) A/Brig J Masters

Mixed Field Coy RE/IE
2nd King's Own (Lancaster) Regt
1st Cameronians
3/4th Gurkha Rifles
4/9th Gurkha Rifles
Medical & Veterinary detachments

3rd (West African) LRP Brigade (Brig A H Gillmore)

7th West African Field Coy (WA Engineers)
6th Nigeria Regt
7th Nigeria Regt
12th Nigeria Regt
3rd West African Field Ambulance

Divisional Troops

219th Field Park Coy RE
Detachment, 2nd Burma Rifles
145th Company RASC
61st Air Supply Company RASC
2nd Indian Air Supply Company RIASC

Attached troops

Four Troops of 160th Field Regt RA
Four Troops 69th Light AA Regt RA
3/9th Gurkha Rifles

Outline Order of Battle, 33 Corps, April-July 1944

Corps Troops

Armour: 149th Regt RAC, less a Sqn Detachment, 150th Regt RAC; 11th Cavalry (IA) (Armoured cars); 45th Cavalry (IA) (Light Tanks).
Artillery: 1st Medium Regt RA; 50th Indian Light AA/Anti-Tank Regt; 24th Indian Mountain Regt (from 5 Indian Division).
Engineers: 429th Field Coy IE; 44th Field Park Coy IE; 10th Battalion IE.
Infantry: 1st Burma Regt, Burma Army; 1st Chamar Regt; 1st Assam Regt; Shere Regt (Nepalese); Mahindra Dal Regt (Nepalese).

2 Infantry Division

Artillery: 10th, 16th and 99th Assault Field Regts RA.
Engineers: 5th, 208th and 506th Field Coys RE; 21st Field Park Coy RE.
Signals: 2nd Divisional Signals.
Divisional HQ Infantry: 2nd Recce Regt; 2nd Manchester Machine Gun Battalion, less a Company; 143rd Special Service Coy.
4th Infantry Brigade: 1st Royal Scots; 2nd Royal Norfolk Regt; 1/8th Lancashire Fusiliers; 4th Field Ambulance RAMC.
5th Infantry Brigade: 7th Worcestershire Regt; 2nd Dorsets; 1st QO Cameron Highlanders; 5th Field Ambulance RAMC.
6th Infantry Brigade: 1st Royal Welch Fusiliers; 1st Royal Berkshire Regt; 2nd Durham Light Infantry; 6th Field Ambulance RAMC.

23rd (LRP) Brigade

(See under 3 Indian Division)

268th Brigade

2/4th and 5/4th Bombay Grenadiers; 17/7th Rajput Regt.

3rd Special Service Brigade

(See under 15 Corps)

Lushai Brigade

1st Royal Battalion, Jat Regiment; 8/13th Frontier Force Regt; 7/14th Punjab Regt; 1st Bihar Regt; One Coy, 77th Field Ambulance.

Outline Order of Battle, Land Forces, SEAC
Sept 1944-May 1945

HQ SEAC (Kandy)

Supreme Allied Commander: Admiral Lord Louis Mountbatten

Deputy:
- (a) Lt Gen J W Stilwell, US Army
- (b) Lt Gen R A Wheeler, US Army (from November 1944)

Chief of Staff:
- (a) Lt Gen Sir Henry Pownall
- (b) Lt Gen F A M Browning (from Dec 1944)

Principal Administrative Officer: Lt Gen R A Wheeler, US Army

C-in-C Eastern Fleet: Admiral Sir Bruce Fraser (to Nov 1944)

C-in-C East Indies Fleet: Admiral Sir Arthur Power (from Nov 1944)

Flag Officer Force 'W': Rear Admiral H C S Martin

11th Army Group (ALFSEA from Nov 1944)

C-in-C:
- (a) General Sir George Giffard
- (b) Lt Gen Sir Oliver Leese

Air Command, South-East Asia

Allied Air C-in-C:
- (a) Air Chief Marshal Sir Richard Peirse
- (b) Air Marshal Sir Guy Garrod (Nov 1944-Feb 1945)
- (c) Air Chief Marshal Sir Keith Park

Commander, Eastern Air Command: Maj General G E Stratemeyer, USAAF.

HQ 14th Army

Commander: Lt General Sir William Slim

Deputy Adjutant & Quartermaster General: Maj Gen A H J Snelling

Army Troops

Armour: 8th KGV's Own Light Cavalry; 11th Cavalry (PAVO) (Armoured Cars); 6th AFV Maint Troop; 2nd Indian Tank Delivry Sqn.

Artillery – detached to Corps as needed: 18th (Self-Propelled) Field Regt RA; 134th Medium Regt RA; 52nd Heavy AA Regt RA; 69th Light AA Regt

RA; 2nd Indian Field Regt; 2nd Indian Light AA Regt; 5th Mahratta Anti-Tank Regt; 656 Air OP Sqn RAF.

Engineers: Four Artisan Coys, two Bridging Coys IE; three Bridging Platoons IE; three Engineer Battalions IE; four Field Coys IE; HQ Forward Airfield Engineers IE; one Airfield Engineer Battalion IE; two Field Coys IE, one Mechanical Equipment Platoon IE; three Works Sects IE; one Quarrying Coy IE.

Infantry: 1/3rd Madras Regt; 1st Assam Rifles; 4th Assam Rifles; Chin Hills Battalion; 25th Gurkha Rifles; Western Chin Levies; Lushai Scouts.

RASC/RIASC: 590th Coy RASC (Tank Transporter): Elephant Coy, RIASC; 387th Divisional troops Coy RASC (DUKWs)

127th GPT Coy RIASC: Four Animal Transport Coys RIASC; 5th Indian Field Ambulance.

Divisions of 14th Army

[Note: these could be, and were, shifted from 4 Corps to 33 Corps as the battle situation demanded.]

2 Division

Divisional Recce Regiment: 2nd Recce Regt RAC
Artillery: 10th, 16th & 99th Field Regiments RA
100th Anti-Tank Regt (Gordon Highlanders)
Engineers: 5th 208th & 506th Field Coys RE
21st Field Park Coy RE
Signals: 2nd Divisional Signals
Divisional Machine Gun Battalion: 2nd Manchester
Infantry:
4th Infantry Brigade: 1st Royal Scots; 2nd Royal Norfolk, 1/8th Lancashire Fusiliers
5th Infantry Brigade: 7th Worcestershire; 2nd Dorsetshire; 1st QO Cameron Highlanders
6th Infantry Brigade: 1st Royal Welch Fusiliers; 1st Royal Berkshire; 2nd Durham LI.

5 Indian Division

Artillery: 4th & 28th Field Regts RA; 56th Anti-Tank Regt RA; 24th Indian Mountain Regt
Engineers: 2nd, 20th & 74th Field Coys IE; 44th Field Park Coy IE
Signals: 5 Indian Divisional Signals
Divisional HQ Infantry: 3/9th Jat Regt (recce battalion); 7/14th Punjab (HQ battalion); [replaced Mar 1945 by an Indian States unit, the 4th Jammu & Kashmir]; 17th Dogras (Machine gun battalion)

Infantry:
9th Indian Infantry Brigade: 2nd West Yorks; 3/2nd Punjab; 4th Jammu
& Kashmir [replaced Mar 1945 by 1st Burma]
123rd Indian Infantry Brigade: 2nd Suffolk [repl Mar 1945 by 7th York &
Lancaster]; 2/1st Punjab; 1/17th Dogras
161st Indian Infantry Brigade: 4th Queen's Own Royal West Kent; 1/1st
Punjab; 4/7th Rajput.

7 Indian Division

Artillery: 136th & 139th Field Regts RA; 24th Anti-Tank Regt RA; 25th
Indian Mountain Regt
Engineers: 62nd, 77th & 421st Field Coys IE; 331st Field Park Coy IE.
Signals: 7th Indian Divisional Signals
Divisional HQ Infantry: 7/2nd Punjab (Recce Battalion); 13th Frontier
Force Rifles (machine guns); 2nd Baroda Infantry (ISF) (HQ Battalion).
Infantry:
33rd Indian Infantry Brigade: 4/15th Punjab; 4/1st Gurkha Rifles)
1st Burma (to April 1945)
89th Indian Infantry Brigade: 2nd King's Own Scottish Borderers; 1/11th
Sikhs; 4/6th Gurkha Rifles
114th Indian Infantry Brigade: 2nd S Lancashires; 4/14th Punjab; 4/5th
Royal Gurkha Rifles.

11 East African Division

Artillery: 302nd & 303rd (EA) Field Regts; 304th (EA) AA/Anti-Tank Regt.
Engineers: 54th, 58th & 64th (EA) Field Coys; 62nd (EA) Field Park Coy.
Signals: 11th (EA) Divisional Signals
Divisional HQ Infantry: 5th King's African Rifles (Recce Battalion); 13th
King's African Rifles (HQ Battalion).
Infantry:
21st (EA) Infantry Brigade: 2nd & 4th King's African Rifles; 1st Northern
Rhodesia Regt.
25th (EA) Infantry Brigade: 11th, 26th & 34th King's African Rifles
26th (EA) Infantry Brigade: 22nd, 36th & 44th King's African Rifles.

17 Indian Division

Artillery: 129th Field Regt RA; 1st Indian Field Regt; 21st Indian Mountain
Regt; 2nd Anti-Tank Regt RA.
Engineers: 6th & 70th Field Coys IE; 414th Field Park Coy IE; Tehri
Garwhal Coy (ISF).
Signals: 17th Indian Division Signals

Divisional HQ Infantry: 6/7th Rajputs (HQ Battalion; repl Apr 1945 by 6/15th Punjab); 6/9th Jats (Recce Battalion); repl Apr 1945 by 6/7th Punjab); 9/13th Frontier Force Rifles (Machine Guns).
Infantry:
48th Indian Infantry Brigade: 1st West Yorkshires; 4/12th Frontier Force Regt; 1/7th Gurkha Rifles.
63rd Indian Infantry Brigade: 9th Border; 7/10th Baluch; 1/110th Gurkha Rifles.
99th Indian Infantry Brigade: 6/15th Punjab [repl Apr 1945 by 1 E Yorks]; 1 Sikh LI; 1/3rd Gurkha Rifles.

19 Indian Division

Artillery: 115th Field Regt RA; 33rd Anti-Tank Regt RA; 4th Indian Field Regt; 20th Indian Mountain Regt.
Engineers: 29th, 64th & 65th Field Coys IE; 327th Field Park Coy IE.
Signals: 19th Indian Division Signals
Divisional HQ Infantry: 1/15th Punjab (HQ Battalion); 11th Sikh Machine Gun Battalion; 1st Assam Regt (Recce Battalion).
Infantry:
62nd Indian Infantry Brigade: 2nd Welch; 3/6th Rajputana Rifles; 4/6th Gurkha Rifles.
64th Indian Infantry Brigade: 2nd Worcesters; 5/10th Baluch; 1/6th Girkha Rifles.
98th Indian Infantry Brigade: 2nd Royal Berkshire; 8/12th Frontier Force Regt; 4/4th Gurkha Rifles.

20 Indian Division

Artillery: 9th & 114th Field Regiments RA; 11th Anti-Tank Regiment RA; 23rd Indian Mountain Regiment.
Engineers: 92nd, 422nd & 481st Field Coys IE; 332nd Field Park Coy IE.
Divisional HQ Infantry: 4/2nd Gurkha Rifles (Recce Battalion from Mar 1945); 4/17th Dogras (HQ Battalion); 9th Jat Regt (Machine Guns).
Infantry:
32nd Indian Infantry Brigade: 1st Northamptons; 9/14th Punjab; 3/8th Gurkha Rifles.
80th Indian Infantry Brigade: 1st Devons; 9/12th Frontier Force Regt; 3/1st Gurkha Rifles.
100th Indian Infantry Brigade: 2nd Borders; 14/13th Frontier Force Rifles; 4/10th Gurkha Rifles.

[Note: for a week in April 1945, 20 Indian Division's three British battalions exchanged with 1/1st Gurkha Rifles, 1/19th Hyderabad, and 2/8th Punjab from 36 Division.]

36 Division

[This Division was serving under Northern Combat Area Command until April 1945.]

Artillery: 130th & 178th Field Regts RA; 122nd Anti-Tank Regt RA; 3rd Meteorological Detachment RA; 32nd Indian Mountain Regt.
Engineers: 15th Engineer Battalion IE; 30th, 58th & 236th Field Coys IE; 10th & 12th Bridging Platoons IE; 324th Field Park Coy IE.
Signals: 36th Divisional Signals
Divisional HQ Infantry: 'D' Coy 2nd Manchesters (Machine Guns); 88th Indian Infantry Coy (Divisional HQ Coy).
Infantry:
29th Infantry Brigade: 2nd E Lancashire; 1st Royal Scots Fusiliers; 2nd Royal Welch Fusiliers.
26th Indian Infantry Brigade: 2nd Buffs; 1/19th Hyderabad Regt; 2/8th Punjab [repl Mar 1945 by 1/1st Gurkha Rifles]
72nd Indian Infantry Brigade: 10th Glosters; 9th Royal Sussex; 6th South Wales Borderers.

Independent Infantry Brigades

268th Indian Infantry Brigade: 4/3rd Madras; 1st Chamar; Mahendra Dal (Nepalese)
Lushai Brigade: 1st Royal Jats; 1st Bihar; Chin Hills Battalion [repl Dec 1944 by 7/14 Punjab]; 1st Assam Rifles (minus two companies).
28th East African Brigade: 7th, 46th & 71st King's African Rifles; 63rd (EA) Field Company (Engineers).

15 Corps (Arakan)

Corps Troops

Armour: 50th Indian Tank Brigade: 146th Regt RAC; 19th Lancers; 45th Cavalry; 2/4th Bombay Grenadiers; 37th Field Sqn IE; 1st Independent Bridging troop RAC; 3rd Independent Delivery Sqn IAC.
Artillery: 6th Medium Regt RA; 8th (Belfast) Heavy AA Regt RA; 36th Light AA Regt RA; 2nd Survey Regt RA; 'C' Flight, 656 Air OP Sqn RAF.
Engineers: 16th, 17th & 20th Engineer Battalions IE; 73rd & 483rd Field Coys IE; Malerkotla Field Coy (ISF); 403rd Field Park Coy IE; 855th Bridging Coy IE.
Signals: 15th Indian Corps Signals
Infantry: 79th Indian Infantry Coy
22nd East African Brigade: 1st King's African Rifles; 3rd Northern Rhodesia Regt; 1st Royal African Regt; 59th (EA) Field Coy (Engineers).

Commandos:

3rd Commando Brigade: 1st and 5th Commandos; 42nd & 45th Royal Marines Commandos.

Divisions of 15 Corps

25 Indian Division

Artillery: 8th & 27th Field Regts RA; 33rd Indian Mountain Regt; 7 Indian Anti-Tank Regt.

Engineers: 63rd, 93rd & 425th Field Coys IE; 16th Bridging Section IE.

Signals: 25th Indian Divisional Signals

Divisional HQ Infantry: 9th York & Lancaster Regt (HQ Battalion); 12th Frontier Force Regt (Machine Guns).

Infantry:

51st Indian Infantry Brigade: 16/10th Baluch Regt; 8/19th Hyderabad Regt; 2/2nd Punjab Regt.

53rd Indian Infantry Brigade: 17/5th Mahratta Regt; 7/16th Punjab Regt; 4/18th Royal Garwhal Rifles.

74th Indian Infantry Brigade: 6th Oxford & Bucks LI; 14/10th Baluch Regt; 3/2nd K E O Gurkha Rifles.

26 Indian Division

Artillery: 160th Field Regiment RA; 7th Indian Field Regiment; 30th Indian Mountain Regiment; 1st Indian Anti-Tank Regiment.

Engineers: 28th, 72nd & 98th Field Companies IE; 328th Field Park Company IE, 7th Bridging Platoon IE.

Signals: 26th Indian Divisional Signals

Divisional HQ Infantry: 5/9th Jat Regt

Infantry:

4th Indian Infantry Brigade: 2nd Green Howards; 2/13th Frontier Force Rifles; 2/7th Rajput Regt.

36th Indian Infantry Brigade: 8/13th Frontier Force Rifles; 1/8th Gurkha Rifles; 2nd Ajmer Regt (Indian State Forces).

71st Indian Infantry Brigade: 1st Lincolnshire Regt; 5/1st Punjab Regt; 1/18th Royal Garwhal Rifles.

81 West African Division

Artillery: 21st (WA) Anti-Tank Regt; 41st (WA) Mortar Regt; 101st (WA) Light Regt.

Engineers: 3rd, 5th & 6th (WA) Field Companies; 8th (WA) Field Park Company.

Signals: 81st (WA) Divisional Signals
Divisional Recce Battalion: 81st (WA) Recce Battalion.
Infantry:
5th (WA) Infantry Brigade: 5th, 7th & 8th Battalions, Gold Coast Regt.
6th (WA) Infantry Brigade: 1st Gambia, 4th Nigeria & 1st Sierra Leone Regts.
[For the third brigade of 81 (WA) Division, see under Special Force.]

82 West African Division

Artillery: 22nd (WA) Anti-Tank Regt; 42nd (WA) Mortar Regt; 102nd (WA) Light Regt.
Engineers: 1st, 2nd & 4th (WA) Field Companies; 9th (WA) Field Park Company.
Signals: 82nd (WA) Divisional Signals
Recce: 82nd (WA) Recce Battalion
Infantry:
1st (WA) Brigade: 1st, 2nd & 3rd Battalions, Nigeria Regt.
2nd (WA) Brigade: 1st, 2nd & 3rd Battalions, Gold Coast Regt.
4th (WA) Brigade: 5th, 9th & 10th Battalions, Nigeria Regt.

Northern Combat Area Command (US/Chinese)

Mars Task Force:
612th (US) Field Artillery Pack Battalion
475th (US) Infantry Regt
124th (US) Cavalry Regt
1st Chinese Regt

Chinese 1st Army:
Commander General Sun Li-Jen: 30th & 38th Divisions

Chinese 6th Army:
Commander: General Liao Yueh-shang: 22nd & 50th Divisions.

[Note: In 1949 Gen Sun threw in his lot with Chiang Kai-shek and went to Taipei. Gen Liao joined Mao Tse Tung and became one of his senior generals.]

Appendix VII

Infantry Regiments of the Indian Army, 1939-1945

By 1939 each of the infantry regiments of the Indian Army had up to five or six active battalions and a training battalion in peacetime; in wartime, considerable expansion took place, leading to a proliferation of 'fractional' titles; thus, the 10th battalion of the Sikh Regiment appears as 10/11th Sikhs. The basic regiments are as follows:

1st	The Punjab Regt	11th	The Sikh Regt
2nd	The Punjab Regt	12th	The Frontier Force Regt
3rd	The Madras Regt	13th	The Frontier Force Rifles
4th	The Bombay Grenadiers	14th	The Punjab Regt
5th	The Mahratta Light Infantry	15th	The Punjab Regt
6th	The Rajputana Rifles	16th	The Punjab Regt
7th	The Rajput Regt	17th	The Dogra Regt
8th	The Punjab Regt	18th	The Royal Garwhal Rifles
9th	The Jat Regt	19th	The Hyderabad Regt
10th	The Baluch Regt		

The Gurkha regiments were recruited in Nepal under the terms of a long-standing treaty. Those marked * continued to serve with the British Army after Partition; the remainder went to the new Indian Army.

1st	(King George Vth's Own) Gurkha Rifles	*6th	Gurkha Rifles
*2nd	(King Edward VIIth's Own) Gurkha Rifles	*7th	Gurkha Rifles
3rd	(Queen Alexandra's Own) Gurkha Rifles	8th	Gurkha Rifles
4th	(Prince of Wales's Own) Gurkha Rifles	9th	Gurkha Rifles
5th	Royal Gurkha Rifles	*10th	Gurkha Rifles

Appendix VIII

Battle Casualties

No two sources agree, even approximately, on the precise numbers of killed, wounded, prisoners and missing on either side in the Burma campaign, despite the meticulous documentation of the well-tried British 'casualty procedures' which recorded every incident affecting an officer's or soldier's military career. On the Japanese side it is even more difficult to arrive at a realistic figure; virtually all the Burma Area Army's records (such as they were) vanished amidst the confusion of the final months. The Japanese made a great point of dragging their dead off the battlefield in order to accord them the appropriate rites of passage, ending with cremation and the removal of samples of ashes for return to Japan. Unknown numbers of their troops died unseen in the jungles and hills of Assam and the Arakan, and many more were borne to their deaths in the swollen rivers of Lower Burma during the ill-fated attempts of 28th Army to regain safety.

The figures given below are derived in the main from Louis Allen's 'The Longest War'. As he went to great pains to inspect Japanese Army records after the war, his estimates are worthy of belief; but he would have been the first to admit that it was impossible to give even a rough guess at the number of Japanese whose bodies lie for ever, undiscovered and unmarked, in the remotest corners of the Burma hills.

[Note: KIA = Killed in action. WPM = Wounded, prisoner, missing.]

Phase of campaign	British/Empire		Japanese	
Retreat from Burma 1942	KIA	1499	1999	
	WPM	11964	452	(a)
1st Arakan	KIA	916	400	
Oct '42-May '43	WPM	4141	700	(b)
1st Chindits	KIA	28	68	
('Longcloth')	WPM	1110	137	
Feb-Jun '43				
2nd Arakan	KIA and WPM	7950 (c)	KIA	3106 (d)
Feb-Jul '44			WPM	2229
2nd Chindits	KIA	1034	4716	
('Thursday')	WPM	2752	595	(a)
Mar-Aug '44				
Withdrawal to Imphal,	KIA and WPM	17587	KIA	11376 (e)
Kohima, Ukhrul, advance			WPM	49267
to Chindwin, Mar-Dec '44				

Phase of campaign	British/Empire		Japanese
Irrawaddy crossing	KIA	2307	6513
-Mandalay-Meiktila	WPM	15888	6399
Jan-Mar '45			
Advance to Rangoon	KIA	446	6742
Mar-May '45	WPM	1710	273
Rangoon to the Sittang	KIA	435	9791
May-Aug '45	WPM	1446	1301 (f)
TOTAL ALL TYPES		71213	107345

Notes:
(a) A suspect figure. Probably includes only 'Missing', and a handful of prisoners.
(b) Estimated.
(c) No breakdown available.
(d) Body count only. At leat 2000 lay uncounted in the hills.
(e) Body count only. An estimated 5000 more KIA and up to 6000 died of disease in the retreat to the Chindwin.
(f) A highly suspect figure. The true number of 'missing' is likely to have been nearer 15,000.

Appendix IX

A list, by regiments and corps, of officers and men of The British Army killed in the Burma Campaign, as listed in the Memorial Book in Rangoon Cathedral.

Note: This does not include personnel from a great number of regiments and corps who were serving on attachment with other units. The entire list includes British and Commonwealth personnel representing no fewer than 225 different cap badges, from all three services. The memorial chapel has suffered recently from neglect and the effects of rainwater leakage through the damaged roof of the cathedral and it seems that unless substantial funding is made available to the diocesan authorities this once beautiful chapel, a fitting memorial to those who died in the campaign, will rapidly go beyond repair. [A recent appeal initiated by the Queen's Own Hussars, successors of the 7th Hussars, has raised £7000 towards restoration of the chapel.]

Regiment/Corps	Officers	Warrant officers sergeants and soldiers
Royal Artillery	129	934
Royal Engineers	57	111
Royal Signals	12	140
3rd Carabiniers	3	69
7th Hussars	2	37
25th Dragoons	2	19
Royal Tank Regiment	8	17
Royal Armoured Corps	20	48
Reconnaissance Corps	11	58
The Royal Scots	15	180
The Queen's Regiment	14	190
The Buffs	6	59
The King's Own Regiment	7	50
The King's Regiment (Liverpool)	11	438
The Royal Norfolk Regiment	15	121
(also recorded as	8	120)
The Lincolnshire Regiment	6	188
The Devonshire Regiment	16	148
The Suffolk Regiment	2	121
The Somerset Light Infantry	11	87
The West Yorkshire Regiment	18	367

The East Yorkshire Regiment	3	19
The Bedfordshire & Herts Regiment	8	20
The Royal Leicestershire Regiment	6	54
The Green Howards	7	25
The Lancashire Fusiliers	18	275
The Royal Welch Fusiliers	14	240
The Royal Scots Fusiliers	7	35
The South Wales Borderers	18	101
The King's Own Scottish Borderers	12	186
The Cameronians	11	189
The Royal Inniskilling Fusiliers	14	314
The Gloucestershire Regiment	20	283
The Worcestershire Regiment	9	176
The East Lancashire Regiment	4	42
The Duke of Wellington's Regiment	10	273
The Border Regiment	11	408
The Royal Sussex Regiment	10	67
The South Staffordshire Regiment	20	111
The Dorsetshire Regiment	11	124
The South Lancashire Regiment	8	114
The Welch Regiment	9	108
The Black Watch	8	80
The Oxfordshire & Buckinghamshire Light Infantry	12	48
The Essex Regiment	5	53
The Sherwood Foresters	5	16
The Northamptonshire Regiment	8	211
The Royal Berkshire Regiment	7	303
The Royal West Kent Regiment	4	158
The King's Own Yorkshire Light Infantry	5	172
The Wiltshire Regiment	7	57
The Manchester Regiment	2	27
The York & Lancaster Regiment	14	142
The Durham Light Infantry	9	127
The Seaforth Highlanders	11	118
The Queen's Own Cameron Higlanders	9	129
The Royal Army Service Corps	7	51
The Royal Army Ordnance Corps	2	74
The Royal Electrical & Mechanical Engineers	–	8
The Royal Army Medical Corps	26	101
The Royal Army Dental Corps	1	1
The Royal Army Veterinary Corps	4	–
The Corps of Royal Military Police	–	23
The Army Catering Corps	–	19

Annotated Bibliography

Allen, Louis *Burma: The Longest War* London, J M Dent, 1984
A masterly account of the campaign written by a former intelligence officer and university lecturer who served in Burma as an interpreter and interrogator, and who subsequently interviewed many senior Japanese commanders to get the Japanese version of the campaign. As Lt Levy (he subsequently changed his name by deed poll) Allen was the officer who realised the significance of the maps and documents captured in June 1945, and which turned out to be the full operation orders for 28 Army's break-out towards the Sittang.

Anon *History of 17 Indian Division, July 1941 to December 1945* Official Press, Calcutta, 1946

Bidwell, Shelford *The Chindit War* London, Hodder & Stoughton, 1979

Bowden, Jean *Grey Touched with Scarlet* London, Robert Hale, 1959
The war experiences of the nursing sisters.

Chenevix-Trench, Charles *The Indian Army and the King's Enemies, 1900-1947* London, Thames and Hudson, 1988
An admirable summary of the achievements of the Indian Army and commentary on the factors which made it unique.

Churchill, Rt Hon WSC *The Second World War. Vols III-V*
London, Cassell, 1950-52
The fascination lies in reading Churchill's memoranda, many of which reveal his impatience with what he felt to be the sluggish conduct of the war against Japan and his complete failure to realise what his generals were up against.

Clarke, Maj E B S, and Tillatt, Maj A T *From Kent to Kohima: The 4th Battalion, The Queen's Own Royal West Kent Regiment (TA)*
Aldershot, Gale & Polden, 1951

Cooper, K W *The Little Men: a platoon's epic fight in the Burma Campaign*
London, Robert Hale, 1973
A beautifully written account of life in a platoon of the Border Regiment.

Crew, Prof F A E *History of the Second World War. United Kingdom Medical Services. Campaigns, Vol V Burma* London HMSO, 1966
The official history which gives graphic details of the state of health of British, Indian and African forces during the campaign, and which is of special interest concerning the lack of medical precautions in Special Force.

Hay, Ian *One Hundred Years of Army Nursing* London, Cassell, 1953

Hingston, Lt Col W *Never Give Up. Vol V of the History of The King's Own Yorkshire Light Infantry* Lund Humphries, 1950

Ienaga, Saburo *Japan's Last War* Oxford, Blackwell, 1979
A distinguished academic's analysis of the nationalistic propaganda and education by which the Japanese people were conditioned for war.

Keegan, John, (Ed) *Churchill's Generals*
London, Weidenfeld and Nicolson, 1991
A series of well-written essays on Slim, Auchinleck, Wavell, and Wingate, amongst others.

Lewin, Ronald *Slim, the Standardbearer* London, Leo Cooper, 1976
A masterly biography.

Mason, Philip *A Matter of Honour* London, Jonathan Cape, 1974
An account of the Indian Army, its officers and men. A scholarly and eminently readable overview of 200 years' evolution of a great army.

Mountbatten, Vice Admiral The Lord Louis *Report to the Combined Chiefs of Staff by the Supreme Allied Commander, South-East Asia, 1943-1945* London, HMSO, 1951

Owen, Frank *The Campaign in Burma* London, HMSO 1946
The author was editor of *SEAC* and, as an experienced journalist, writes attractively. However, as the book was intended as a general history of the campaign for those who fought in it, no note of analysis, still less of criticism, is allowed to creep in.

Robertson, G W, MC *The Rose and the Arrow, a life story of 136th (1st West Lancashire) Field Regiment, Royal Artillery, 1939-45.* Published privately by the regiment's Old Comrades' Association, 1986.
A model of what a unit history should – accurate, balanced and humane.

Ryder, Richard *Oliver Leese* London, Hamish Hamilton, 1987

Seaman, Harry *The Battle of Sangshak* London, Leo Cooper, 1989
The first full account of the fight in which 50th Indian Parachute Brigade succeeded in holding up the Japanese drive on Kohima, but at great cost.

Slim, Field Marshal Sir William *Defeat into Victory* London, Cassell, 1956
The classic among military memoirs, by one of the few great British soldiers who could write really well and who had a marvellous tale to tell.

—, *Campaign of the Fourteenth Army* Officially printed 1945.
Classified 'Secret' at the time, this is Slim's official report on his campaign, and is the document on which he was working at Meiktila during the 'sacking' interlude of May 1945.

Smyth, Brig Sir John, VC *Before the Dawn* London, Cassell, 1957
Includes Smyth's version of 17 Indian Division's withdrawal in Tenasserim and its reverse at the Sittang Bridge.

Stewart, Adrian *The Under-rated Enemy* Britain's war with Japan, 1941-42
A sound analysis of the misappreciation of Japanese capabilities leading to the loss of Burma.

Taylor, A J P *The War Lords* London, Hamish Hamilton, 1977
  Scholarly, if quirkish.
Taylor, Jeremy *The Devons* Bristol, The White Swan Press, 1951
United States War Department *War Department Technical Manual TM-E
30-480* Washington DC, US Government Printing Office, 1944
  A detailed guide to the Japanese Army, its organisation, equipment,
  training, and uniforms.
War Office *Maintenance in the Field. Vol I* WO 1952
—, *Service in hot Climates – a Pamphlet for Officers* WO 1943
—, *The Second World War 1939-45: Army. Army Welfare* (Compiled by Brig
M C Morgan) WO 1953
—, *The Second World War 1939-45: Army Special Weapons and types of
Warfare* WO 1952
Woodburn Kirby and others *The War against Japan, Vols II-V* London,
HMSO, 1958-69
  The official history, giving a detailed and copiously documented account.
  Wingate's admirers have strongly criticised its treatment of him, and as it
  was published some years before details of 'Ultra' had been released,
  there are certain omissions. It is, all the same, a magisterial work.

Unpublished Sources
[IWM = Imperial War Museum]

Amies, Col B J *Memoirs* including description of retreat in 1942 (IWM)
Birkbeck, Maj Gen, T H *11th Bn King's African Rifles* (IWM)
Cane, Lt Col PG *94 Column, 2nd Chindits* (IWM)
Carfrae, Lt Col *Nigeria Regiment, 2nd Chindits* (IWM)
Cookson, Capt D M *Operations with 1st Gambia Regt, Arakan* (IWM)
Churchill College, Cambridge *Churchill Archive; Slim Papers, Roberts
Papers, Christison, Gen Sir P* unpubl. autobiography.
  Also, pencilled notes by WSC on copy of Christopher Sykes' *Wingate*.
Durham Light Infantry Miscellaneous papers and newsletters, 1944.
Durham Museum
Field, Brig L F *Memoir* written when Chief Liaison Officer to Chiang
Kai-shek, 1942 (IWM)
Gadsden, Maj P Letters and memoir. Operations with 4/14th Punjab Regt
in Arakan (IWM)
Grover, Maj Gen J G *Divisional Commander's Diary*
Gurkha Museum War Diaries, various (Gurkha Rifles Battalions, Burma)
Kenjiro, Omori *Diary of Japanese Soldier, 1/151 Inf Regt* (IWM)
Miller, Revd W H *Memoir* Padre with 2nd Bn King's Own, 2nd Chindits
(IWM)
Museum of Army Flying Miscellaneous documents: 656 Air OP Sqn RAF

Queen Alexandra's Royal Army Nursing Corps Museum Personal memoirs of nursing sisters. Burma 1943-45

Regiments of Gloucester Museum *Memoirs*: Lt Col C E K Bagot

Royal Corps of Transport Museum Miscellaneous reports on supplies and transport matters, India and Burma

Salisbury (Duke of Edinburgh's Royal Regiment) Museum War Diaries, Royal Berkshire and Wiltshire Regiments; Regimental Journals

Slim, General Sir William Private correspondence with Brig Bernard Fergusson, concerning Wingate, 1956

Worrall, V R *Memoir* Private soldier, King's Regt. Glider flight to Broadway 1944 (IWM)

Index

Jungle Fighter: Infantry Officer, Chindit & SOE Agent in Burma, 1941-1945
By MAJOR JOHN HEDLEY DSO

The gripping war memoirs of a soldier who fought the Japanese in Burma. As Adjutant to the 4th Burma Rifles, he took part in a number of battles during the British retreat before becoming Intelligence Officer to 63 Indian Infantry Brigade and then III Chindit Brigade. Involved in actions behind enemy lines both for the Chindits and Force 136 – the SEAC equivalent of SOE – he was mentioned in despatches and awarded the DSO. £17.95

Japan's Greatest Victory, Britain's Worst Defeat
The Capture and Fall of Singapore 1942
By COLONEL MASANOBU TSUJI

Written by the Director of Planning and Operations Staff, 25th Japanese Army, Malaya, the mastermind behind a feat unparalleled in military history – the Japanese capture of Singapore – he tells the story of its planning and execution in his own words. Colonel Tsuji 'disappeared' in South-East Asia in the 1960's and his account has been edited by H V Howe, Military Secretary to the Australian Minister for the Army, 1940–1946. £18.95

Valour: A History of the Gurkhas
By E D SMITH

A copiously illustrated history of the Gurkha regiments from their beginnings in 1815 through to the current day – including the Indian Mutiny, the Afghan Wars, the North West Frontier, World War I, World War II, the post-war 'emergency' in Malaya, Hong Kong, the Brunei Revolt, and their subsequent service in the UK, on the Sino-Hong Kong border, Cyprus, Belize and the Falklands. £24.95

The Scottish Regiments 1633–1966
By PATRICK MILEHAM

The twelve Scottish Regiments, one cavalry, one guards and ten infantry of the line, have a collective reputation for fighting second to none but each maintains a distinctive style and ethos. Here, lavishly illustrated in colour and black and white, are the personalities and the campaigns that have distinguished their individual histories – from the end of the Civil War, through the rise and fall of the British Empire to the present day. £35.00

Through Fifteen Reigns:
A Complete History of the Household Cavalry
By J N P WATSON

A former Household Cavalryman traces, for the first time, the careers of the three regiments – The Life Guards, Royal Horse Guards (Blues) and Royal Dragoons (the last two were amalgamated as The Blues and Royals in 1969) – and highlights their very special relationship with the Monarch and their astonishing versatility and adaptability. Since the 17th century, they have switched effortlessly from ceremonial to combat, from equestrian proficiency to keeping the peace, from horse to armour and back again. £30.00

44 (RM) Commando
Achnacarry to the Arakan: A Diary of the Commando at War,
August 1943 – March 1947
By TONY MACKENZIE

The history of a Royal Marine Commando unit from its formation in 1943, through the gruelling training regime of the Commando Depot at Achnacarry, to India and active service in the Arakan – the little-known campaign to clear the Japanese from the jungle-covered hills between the centre of Burma and the Bay of Bengal. £15.95

To order any of these titles (please add £2.00 UK or £4.00 overseas surface mail p&p per copy ordered) or to obtain a free catalogue, telephone 01580 893730 or write to Spellmount Publishers, The Old Rectory, Staplehurst, Kent TN12 0AZ. Please make cheques payable to 'Spellmount Ltd'.